BAPTISTS AND GENDER

In this rich and wide-ranging volume, twenty-three authors explore the theme of Baptist and gender. As Melody Maxwell and Laine Scales, the editors, say in their introduction, traditional Baptist historiography largely ignored gender and although there have been more recent studies that have focused on Baptist women this volume is ground-breaking in the way it studies gender more broadly. The authors shed much fresh light on experiences historically and globally—and taken together these essays make a highly significant contribution to an understanding of a crucial area of Baptist life.

—Ian Randall, research associate, Cambridge Centre for
Christianity Worldwide; and senior research fellow,
International Baptist Theological Study Centre, Amsterdam

Traversing centuries as well as geographies, *Baptists and Gender* offers a wide-ranging exploration of the role of women and gender in shaping Baptist identity. As a result, the editors of this compelling volume challenge all of us who think and write about Baptist life not only to re-examine our received narratives but also to accentuate our stunning diversity. While this book tempers the hagiographic tendencies of the past with its searing honesty of Baptists' ongoing sexism, it also offers moments of progress to cherish and celebrate. I've been waiting for such an inclusive history, one that elevates the story of women to that of men, integrates gender and theology, and places Baptists from the majority world alongside those from England and North America, for a very long time.

—Elizabeth Flowers, associate professor of
American Religion, Baylor University

The contributors to *Baptists and Gender* address an important topic that is only beginning to be fully appreciated by scholars of the Baptist tradition. The chapters ably illustrate just a few of the many different ways gender dynamics have influenced Baptist history— a topic all of us should pay increased attention to in the coming years. The conference where these chapters were to be first presented proved unworkable because of the COVID-19 pandemic. Students and scholars are indebted to Melody Maxwell and Laine Scales for their commitment to publish this helpful anthology despite the cancellation of the conference.

—Nathan A. Finn, provost and dean of the University
Faculty, North Greenville University

T0377729

The James N. Griffith Series in Baptist Studies

This series on Baptist life and thought explores and investigates Baptist history, offers analyses of Baptist theologies, provides studies in hymnody, and examines the role of Baptists in societies and cultures around the world. The series also includes classics of Baptist literature, letters, diaries, and other writings. For a complete list of titles in the series, visit www.mupress.org and visit the series page.

—C. Douglas Weaver, Series Editor

BAPTISTS AND GENDER

Papers for the International Conference on

Baptist Studies IX

Edited by Melody Maxwell and T. Laine Scales

Foreword by *David Bebbington*

MERCER UNIVERSITY PRESS

Macon, Georgia

MUP/ P684

© 2023 by Mercer University Press
Published by Mercer University Press
1501 Mercer University Drive
Macon, Georgia 31207
All rights reserved

27 26 25 24 23   5 4 3 2 1

Books published by Mercer University Press are printed on acid-free paper that meets
the requirements of the American National Standard for Information Sciences—
Permanence of Paper for Printed Library Materials.

Printed and bound in the United States.

This book is set in Adobe Garamond Pro.

Cover/jacket design by Burt&Burt.

ISBN   978-0-88146-913-4
Cataloging-in-Publication Data is available from the Library of Congress

CONTENTS

CONTRIBUTORS

DAVID BEBBINGTON, Emeritus Professor of History, University of Stirling, Stirling, United Kingdom

JOÃO CHAVES, Assistant Professor of Evangelism and Mission, Austin Presbyterian Theological Seminary, Austin, Texas, USA, and Associate Director for Programming, Hispanic Theological Initiative, Princeton, New Jersey, USA

MIRIAM DOBSON, Reader, Department of History, University of Sheffield, United Kingdom

SETH DOWLAND, Professor of Interdisciplinary Studies and Director of the International Honors Progam, Pacific Lutheran University, Tacoma, Washington, USA

MALCOLM FOLEY, Special Advisor to the President for Equity and Campus Engagement, Baylor University, and Director, Black Church Studies Program, Truett Seminary, Waco, Texas, USA

ROSALIND GOODEN, former Director of Training with Global Interaction (now Baptist Mission Australia), Adelaide, South Australia, Australia

LON GRAHAM, Executive Director, Matt 25 Hope Center, Clovis, New Mexico, USA, and Research Fellow, International Baptist Theological Study Centre, Amsterdam, Netherlands

MATTHEW JAMES GRAY, Head of Divinity, Tabor College, Adelaide, South Australia, Australia

GEORGE HANCOCK-STEFAN, Thornley B. Wood Professor of Church History and Missions, Palmer Theological Seminary of Eastern University, St. Davids, Pennsylvania, USA

MICHAEL HAYKIN, Chair and Professor of Church History, Southern Baptist Theological Seminary, Louisville, Kentucky, USA

GORDON L. HEATH, Professor of Christian History and Centenary Chair in World Christianity, McMaster Divinity College, Hamilton, Ontario, Canada

KEITH G. JONES, former Rector, International Baptist Theological Seminary, Prague, Czechia

EIKO KANAMARU, Professor of Baptist History and Church History, Department of Theology, Seinan Gakuin University, Fukuoka, Japan

KEN R. MANLEY, former Principal, Whitley College, University of Divinity, Melbourne, Victoria, Australia

MELODY MAXWELL, Associate Professor of Christian History, Acadia Divinity College, Wolfville, Nova Scotia, Canada

PETER J. MORDEN, Team Leader, Cornerstone Baptist Church, Leeds, United Kingdom, and Distinguished Visiting Scholar, Spurgeon's College, London, United Kingdom

TAYLOR MURRAY, Instructor of Christian History and Creative Producer of Distributed Learning, Tyndale University, Toronto, Ontario, Canada

MATTHEWS A. OJO, Professor of Religious Studies, Obafemi Awolowo University, Ile-Ife, Nigeria

MIKEAL C. PARSONS, University Distinguished Professor and Macon Chair in Religion, Baylor University, Waco, Texas, USA

ADAM RUDY, Independent Scholar, Hamilton, Ontario, Canada

FRANCIS JR. S. SAMDAO, Senior Lecturer of Historical-Systematic Theology, Philippine Baptist Theological Seminary, Baguio City, Philippines

T. LAINE SCALES, Professor of Social Work and Baylor Master Teacher, Baylor University, Waco, Texas, USA

MALKHAZ SONGULASHVILI, Professor of Comparative Theology, Ilia State University, Tbilisi, Georgia

BRIAN TALBOT, Extraordinary Researcher, Faculty of Theology, North-West University, South Africa, and Minister, Broughty Ferry Baptist Church, Dundee, Scotland

C. DOUGLAS WEAVER, Professor of Baptist Studies and Chair, Department of Religion, Baylor University, Waco, Texas, USA

FOREWORD

"You are not to warble from the top of a tree, like an invisible nightingale," the great English Baptist preacher of the Victorian age, Charles Haddon Spurgeon, told the students at his college, "but to be a man among men." Spurgeon repeatedly made the point about the way in which the students should behave when they became ministers. They must not attempt to be gentlemen. "Manliness," he wrote, "must not be sacrificed to elegance." They must avoid imitating the manners of the Church of England, which Spurgeon stereotyped as requiring "fine deportment and genteel propriety." Instead, they must talk in "a natural and hearty style." Spurgeon himself habitually signed his letters "yours heartily." He spoke his mind, cultivated a no-nonsense image, and admired Luther for his swashbuckling approach to debate. Spurgeon contrasted the manliness he admired with femininity. When speaking in the pulpit, his students must avoid enunciation that was "lady-like, mincing, delicate, servant-girlified." They should shun "the perfumed prettiness of effeminate gentility." Here was a female antithesis to the ideal male comportment of ministers of the gospel. The choice between manly and womanly approaches, Spurgeon believed, had potent consequences. Working men, he claimed, abhorred the "artificial and unmanly ways" of ministers. "If they saw us," he went on, "in the pulpit and out of it, acting like real men, and speaking naturally, like honest men, they would come around us."[1] The success of the gospel in nineteenth-century England was tied to developing manly qualities. Spurgeon placed enormous weight on cultivating masculinity.

In early twentieth-century America, Helen Barrett Montgomery, one of the outstanding Baptist women of her generation, reflected on the proper role of women in the world. In her *Western Women in Eastern Lands* (1910) she wrote of the huge improvement in the status of women in the West during the nineteenth century. At its opening they had been restricted to a "cribbed, cabined, and confined sphere," but a "new spirit of women's emancipation" had gradually spread. She celebrated the growth of the "Woman's Right" movement in the United States from its beginnings at a convention in Seneca Falls in 1848 up to her own day. "They asked for woman the right to have personal freedom," she explained, "to acquire an education, to earn a living, to claim her wages, to own property, to sue and be sued, to make contracts, to testify in court, to obtain

---

[1] Charles Haddon Spurgeon, *Lectures to My Students* (Grand Rapids, MI: Zondervan, 1955), 168, 299, 300, 299, 112, 123, 167.

a divorce for just cause, to possess her children, to claim a fair share of the accumulations during marriage, *to vote*." The last item was italicized because, unlike all the other freedoms, it had not yet been achieved in 1910 but had to wait another decade. What had been gained over the previous century in the West remained to be reached in Eastern lands where missionaries served. Montgomery wanted to release Eastern women from "the caste of sex" that severely limited the roles they could occupy. In her view, the Bible alone could foster so profound a transformation. It was already making a new world, different from "a man's world, hard, cruel, bitter toward the weak." Montgomery, though a feminist of the first wave, still adhered to stereotypes about women as well as men, for she argued that the new world would equally not be "a woman's world, weak, sentimental, tasteless." Yet she contended that the new world was to be "a world of humanity" in which "all the qualities that serve to mark the human shall have free course and be glorified."[2] Her aspiration was an age when the gospel would enable women to take their place as the equals of men. "Jesus Christ," she told the Baptist World Alliance in 1923, "is the great Emancipator of woman."[3]

Spurgeon's depiction of manly behavior and Montgomery's prospect of female equality were striking instances of Baptist constructions of gender. They were describing realities in their day but also projecting ideals for imitation. Those are the themes of the essays in this book. They address topics between the seventeenth and twentieth centuries and, in a few cases, extend into the twenty-first century. They deal with issues in Britain, the United States, Canada, Nigeria, Russia, Romania, Georgia (in the Caucasus), China, Japan, the Philippines, and Australia. Sixteen concentrate primarily on women, three on men, and four are broader studies of gender relations. All are papers prepared for the ninth International Conference on Baptist Studies that was to have been held in 2021 but which could not take place because of the COVID-19 pandemic. They contribute significantly to a fuller understanding of the varying relationships of believers, both women and men, in the Baptist churches of the world over the centuries.

David Bebbington
Baylor University
October 2022

---

[2] Helen Barrett Montgomery, *Western Women in Eastern Lands* (New York: Macmillan, 1910), 8, 7, 9–10, 72, 73–74.

[3] William T. Whitley, ed., *Third Baptist World Congress, Stockholm, July 21–27, 1923* (London: Kingsgate, 1923), 99.

INTRODUCTION

What does it mean to be a gendered person within a specific cultural context? The pages of this book analyze global Baptists' responses to this question in historical perspective. The term *gender* describes culturally constructed roles of femininity and masculinity. Baptists have both influenced and been influenced by concepts of gender within the variety of cultures around the world in which they find themselves. In addition, Baptists have formed their own religious subcultures with unique gender expectations. In some contexts, for example, Baptist women are expected to cover their heads during worship services led by men; in others, Baptist women lead worship with heads uncovered while men listen. The chapters in this book explore the fascinating ways that global Baptists have constructed gender roles.

The study of gender as a category of analysis in historical studies began in the 1970s, influenced by the second wave of feminism. Women's history dominated the field of gender studies for its first decades; more recently, critical studies have turned to gender itself as a category for analysis.[1] In recent years transgender and non-binary identities have challenged scholars of gender to think of gender as more complex and along a continuum. These newer disruptions of binary gender are outside the scope of this volume but merit address in future publications.

Traditional Baptist historiography largely ignored gender, focusing instead on institutions run by leading men. Leon McBeth once quipped, "If any of you men ever want to get away from women, here is one way you can do it: just get into the pages of Baptist history. Women will not bother you there."[2] Baptist historians—especially women—began writing about women's history in the latter decades of the twentieth century, influenced by the broader trend in historiography. This was especially true of Baptist historians in Western contexts, which were most influenced by the feminist movement.[3] Books with titles such as *Women in Baptist Life* and *The New Has Come* were published, with the greatest

---

[1] For more information, see "Gender and History," in Anna Green and Kathleen Troup, *The Houses of History* (Manchester: Manchester University Press, 2016), 262–73.

[2] H. Leon McBeth, "Perspectives on Women in Baptist Life," *Baptist History and Heritage* 22, no. 3 (July 1987): 9.

[3] Most Baptist historians in the late twentieth century also lived in Western contexts.

number of publications coming from researchers of Southern Baptists in the United States.[4] Into the present day, historians continue studying Baptist women, although much work remains to be done. Studies of Baptist men and masculinity, however, are scarce. *Baptists and Gender* thus fills a gap in scholarship, with chapters that explore Baptist constructs of both femininity and masculinity over the past four hundred years. This volume is also global in scope, analyzing Baptists from Australia to Nigeria and thus revealing important insights that studies focused on North America (or Europe) overlook.

With twenty-three chapters, this book is organized chronologically as well as geographically. The majority of chapters discuss the twentieth and twenty-first centuries, when gender roles became a significant topic for global Baptists as a result of the second wave of feminism. Yet others analyze Baptists and gender in earlier centuries. Several of these focus on Baptists in England in the seventeenth and eighteenth centuries.

We begin with some of the earliest Baptist texts and hymns to explore gender. In his analysis of John Bunyan's *The Pilgrim's Progress*, Matthew James Gray challenges the common belief that Bunyan had a negative view of women and their role in the church. Instead, he describes Bunyan's gender views as a "pilgrimage" and a "journey," rather than a "swamp of scandal" and "denominational controversy." Gray proposes that Bunyan's views are best understood as being in a state of flux, indicating a struggle with the topic, and that his expressions of women grow more favorable over time. To support this idea, Gray explores Bunyan's choice to include a female protagonist in his story and provides examples of egalitarian ideas within Bunyan's work.

Lon Graham's chapter explores the gendered nature of church discipline in eighteenth-century English Baptist life. Using the 1781–1801 book of College Lane Church, Northampton, he argues that the church disciplined women more harshly than men, and with fewer opportunities for the women to speak in their own defense. However, Graham demonstrates that the church's pastor, John Ryland Jr., supported and valued women in his own writings. Graham explains this divergence by appealing to the English concept of politeness, through which women were held to a higher standard than men.

Both Michael Haykin and Peter Morden explore themes related to noted Baptist hymnwriter Anne Steele. Haykin analyzes Steele's use of language related to colors. Steele frequently describes green meadows and foliage, more sparingly

---

[4] H. Leon McBeth, *Women in Baptist Life* (Nashville: Broadman Press, 1979); Anne Thomas Neil and Virginia Garrett Neely, *The New Has Come: Emerging Roles among Southern Baptist Women* (Washington, DC: Southern Baptist Alliance, 1989).

using other chromatic terms to describe natural features like flowers and the sky. She also repeatedly references the color black when describing sin, as was common at the time. In her writings, Steele poetically links colors with the worship of God, using chromatic language to praise the creator.

Peter Morden analyzes the nineteen of Steele's hymns that were included in Spurgeon's *Our Own Hymn Book*, which was published in 1866 and widely used. These hymns were shaped by Steele's evangelical Calvinism, emphasizing God's sovereignty as well as human responsibility. Several of them also focused on personal suffering, a topic with which Steele was familiar. Yet her hymns also urged worshipers to find joy in Jesus, a theme that Spurgeon likewise emphasized. Steele's hymn writing influenced the theology of many in the Spurgeonic tradition.

Several authors write about Baptists in the nineteenth century, especially in the British empire. Rosalind Gooden probes the life of Silas Mead, a South Australian Baptist minister who advocated for the ministry of women. Mead urged churches to appoint women as deaconesses who would assist the minister. His own church took this step in 1868. He also promoted the ministry of Emilia Baeyertz, a woman evangelist. Mead likewise encouraged women to serve as missionaries, with women from his own congregation (and others) departing to serve in India. Gooden argues that the lives of Mead's daughters served as the final component of his legacy.

In his chapter, Gordon Heath explores two leaders regarded as heroes by Baptists in the late nineteenth-century British empire: Queen Victoria and Major-General Charles George Gordon. He analyzes publications of Baptists from Britain, Australia, Canada, South Africa, and New Zealand that mention these two individuals. He argues that these Baptists considered Queen Victoria and General Gordon exemplars of Christian virtue, soothing the consciences of those who doubted the goodness of the empire. Heath also demonstrates that Baptists viewed the two leaders as ideal examples of femininity and masculinity.

From the entire British empire, Adam Rudy narrows the focus of his historical inquiry to Canada while still examining Baptist publications. He analyzes *The Canadian Missionary Link*, a Baptist women's publication, from 1878 to 1890. Rudy demonstrates that Canadian Baptist women, shaped by their Victorian context along with their interpretation of the Bible, saw missions as a special, gendered role they could fill. They emphasized "woman's work for woman" overseas, especially among Hindu women in India. They thus exemplified the way that women's roles were gradually expanding within the Victorian milieu.

A gripping story of a terrible incident provides the basis of the chapter by Chaves and Parsons about the rape of Baylor University student Antônia Teixeira in the 1890s and the attempted cover-up. Reviewing various historical documents and tracking the work of the journalist William Brann, the authors highlight several instances where morality and ethics were abandoned in favor of preserving not only the status and reputation of Rufus Burleson, who was the president of Baylor at the time, but also that of the university itself. Ultimately, Chaves and Parsons argue for a widened view of Baylor's history and a deepened understanding of justice at every level, one that includes and listens to the voice of Antônia Teixeira from beyond the grave.

Matthews A. Ojo draws upon various historical records from both the Foreign Mission Board of the Southern Baptist Convention and a Baptist girls' school to create an important sketch of the ideas and values underlying the educational and religious training of girls in Nigeria. Ojo contends that although the provision of female education in Nigeria was a major step forward for the country, the prevalence of traditional views of women as societally subordinate and the general lack of resources for education slowed down any forward progress. Ojo demonstrates that it was not until the mid-1950s that both the government and the Baptist churches in Nigeria began to invest heavily in education, which in turn enhanced the flourishing of Nigerian women.

The majority of the chapters in this volume focus on Baptists in the twentieth and twenty-first centuries, periods in which questions of gender were at the forefront of both church and society in many contexts. Several feature Baptists in Europe. Miriam Dobson's contribution highlights gender dynamics and conflicts within the Moscow Congregation of Evangelical Christians Baptists in the 1950s and 1960s, using two case studies. She demonstrates that the Soviet state was unable to impose unity on Evangelical Christian Baptists through pastoral authority; laywomen played an active role in gendered church controversies. Divergent opinions over divorce and remarriage, along with generational conflict, affected the church during this period. Women from the congregation wrote letters and poems, collected signatures, and distributed anonymous notes, among other actions, to express their opinions.

George Hancock-Stefan's chapter utilizes a historical lens to analyze the movement of the Romanian Baptist denomination before and after communism, as well as after Romania entered the European Union. More specifically, Hancock-Stefan details the Romanian Baptist response to Romania's shift away from previously held traditional views on marriage and family and towards a more liberal, progressive view that affirms the LGBTQIA+ community and their relationships. This chapter does well in presenting both a historical overview of Romania and the ways in which Romanian Baptists have felt both liberated and oppressed in their struggle for traditional family values and beliefs.

4

Keith Jones's chapter highlights the ministry of Margaret Jarman, a groundbreaking British Baptist leader. Jarman was the first woman to study for a theology degree at Spurgeon's College. At different times throughout her life, she served as a deaconess, pastor, spiritual director, and staff member for the Baptist Union of Great Britain. She also led the union as its vice president and later president. Even more remarkable was Jarman's commitment to religious community. In 1983, feeling led to a life of prayer, she became an oblate of the Community of St. Mary the Virgin. Jarman later helped establish the Community of the Prince of Peace, a Baptist residential community. In 2001 she was consecrated as a hermit, all while remaining within the Baptist tradition.

In his chapter, Malkhaz Songulashvili utilizes a historical lens to analyze the first consecration of a female bishop in the country of Georgia. Songulashvili asserts that three major factors contribute to the groundbreaking inclusion of women into the episcopate in Georgia: the delayed recognition of the life and legacy of the female apostle St. Nino, the rise of egalitarianism during the pre-Soviet and Soviet eras in Georgia, and the subsequent way that egalitarianism began to express itself in the leadership opportunities for females in the Georgian Orthodox Church.

Brian Talbot examines the published sermons of Walter Mursell, a Baptist minister who served in Paisley, Scotland. In his sermons, Mursell instructed young people on "ideal manhood," which he characterized as "a positive virtue, an aggressive activity." He encouraged young men to take action, avoid temptations, maintain physical health, and seek spiritual growth. During World War I, Mursell preached on the high cost of war and urged his congregation to rise to the challenges before them. Throughout his ministry, he extolled the virtues of masculinity to his audiences.

Seth Dowland also focuses on masculinity in his chapter, which moves in context to North America. Dowland analyzes the football program at the University of Chicago around the turn of the twentieth century. Although the game was rather brutal at the time, the Baptist founders of the university, along with coach Amos Alonzo Stagg, believed it was an essential part of forming the strength and character of Christian young men. Stagg led a successful career at the university, coaching generations of white, male, Christian students in the sport that he thought would advance their faith and their race.

Continuing on the subject of masculinity and manhood, Malcom Foley's chapter narrows the focus a bit further in the US, examining the work of the prominent Black Baptist pastor William Bishop Jones. In his investigation of Jones's work, Foley seeks to extrapolate an understanding of Black manhood during the lynching era, posing the brilliant question: "What did it mean to be a Black man in a society that sought to define Black manhood not only from outside of Black communities but particularly with an eye toward the destruction of Black male life?" Foley expertly draws from the historical figure to shine a favorably hopeful and holy light on both Black manhood and Black womanhood.

Melody Maxwell's chapter analyzes oral histories of eight women ordained in Atlantic Canada between 1976 and 1987 with an emphasis on relationships. These women were some of the first ordained by a Canadian evangelical denomination. Maxwell demonstrates that they generally came from families committed to faith, although they had few female ministerial role models. Those who were married at times stepped down from ministry responsibilities in order to care for family members; those who were single faced their own challenges and opportunities. Multiple interviewees described their congregations as becoming like family, demonstrating the importance of their relationships.

Taylor Murray likewise profiles Canadian Baptist women, but he features those of the Regular Baptists, a fundamentalist denomination organized in the 1920s. Murray demonstrates that the women who founded the Women's Missionary Society of the Regular Baptists of Canada were empowered by this role; despite their fundamentalist beliefs, they initiated and led a significant ministry endeavor. The chapter details the creation of this society from a split within the woman's missionary movement, including the new society's independence and its advocacy of women ministering abroad—striking characteristics within its fundamentalist context.

Northern Baptist women and their work with immigrants to the United States is the subject of T. Laine Scales's chapter. Focusing on the decade between 1908 and 1918, Scales demonstrates the ways women missionaries avoided preaching in their evangelistic efforts, because that was considered to be for men only. Instead, they used particularly feminine methods of evangelism through home visits and establishing industrial schools and settlement houses. The goal was to win converts to Christ, but also to Americanize new immigrants who would be future citizens and leaders.

Ken Manley contributes a chapter on Australian Baptist poet and novelist Marion Downes, whose work "celebrated the place of women in Australian society." Downes's experiences at Collins Street Baptist Church informed her writing; in fact, one of her characters was based on the church's pastor. Downes wrote multiple love stories with religious themes. In addition, her poems featured topics such as war, nature, women's roles, and spirituality. Downes's writings sometimes espoused ideology that could arguably be characterized as feminist.

Eiko Kanamaru explores the life of Akiko Matsumura, an influential leader of Baptist women in Japan who deserves more recognition than she has received for promoting women's public role in the kingdom of God. Kanamaru uses Matsumura's original writings to provide a biography, including her pursuit of education, conversion, study of Greek, and leadership role within women's organizations. As Matsumura connected with the Japan Baptist Convention, she faced adversity because of her gender, and at times her Japanese identity. Her role is described as one that sought not to destroy the current state of the church, but to assimilate the efforts of women seeking to add to the kingdom of God.

Francis Jr. S. Samdao analyzes the historical movement of Filipino women from pagan priestesses to contributing leaders and pastors in the Baptist community in Western Visayas. The roles of women on both sides of the Baptist mission (the female Baptist missionaries and the Filipino women they educated) are highlighted for the purpose of "elucidating a cultural and spiritual evolution of Visayan women." Samdao's chapter brings long overdue recognition to the historical contributions of Filipino women to the body of Christ.

Douglas Weaver's chapter details the missionary efforts of Mary Crawford and her participation in the Shantung Revival during the first half of the twentieth century. Weaver provides a well-documented case for the important roles that Mary Crawford and others played in what has been considered as one of the greatest Baptist revivals to date. By highlighting the valiant efforts of Crawford and other female Baptist missionaries in contrast to the patriarchal pushback from Southern Baptist individuals and institutions, Weaver expertly demonstrates the value that women bring to the table when they unabashedly share the Gospel in both word and deed.

Although these essays cover a diverse chronological and geographical range of Baptist history, several themes emerge from them. The first is that of exemplary Baptist women leaders, who pioneered new roles in circumstances in which it was unusual for women to do so.[5] Women such as Anne Steele, Margaret Jarman, Rusundan Gotziridze, Marion Downes, Akiko Matsumura, and Mary Crawford undertook significant endeavors which Baptists should remember; no Baptist history is complete without the stories of women such as these. More than one of these women found their voice through writing either prose or poetry at times when women were not allowed to speak from a pulpit. Even more found missions work to be a role that was both denominationally acceptable and vocationally fulfilling. In the early centuries of the Baptist movement, Western

---

[5] Compare this to Gerda Lerner's "compensatory history." See Lerner, *The Majority Finds Its Past: Placing Women in History* (New York: Oxford University Press, 1979).

women led in promoting missions as well as in traveling to far-flung mission fields, where non-Western women proved vital to the cause of the Christian faith by serving in roles such as "Bible women." In the late twentieth and early twenty-first centuries, Baptist women from countries around the globe embarked in missions leadership to and from everywhere. Even today, missions remains an admired and generally non-contested role for Baptist women to fill.

Yet the essays in this volume also remind us that Baptist women, like Baptists in general, have been and are a diverse group. In some contexts, such as the Philippines, Baptist women regularly preach and pastor congregations. In others, such as among the Regular Baptists of Canada, women assumed a submissive and supportive role. In Georgia, a woman served as a Baptist bishop; in Russia, Baptist women could not lead churches, but they played an important role in church conflicts. In general, Baptist women have assumed more expansive roles over time, particularly with the advent of the women's movements of the mid-twentieth century. This has especially proven true in the West.

This volume on Baptists and gender is concerned with more than Baptist women, however. Several essays reflect on men and masculinity among global Baptists. Some Baptist men, such as Silas Mead, advocated for women; others, such as those involved in the Antônia Teixeira affair, took advantage of them. In general, Baptists profiled in this volume advocated for a rugged masculinity that included physical activity and strength. They used mediums such as sermons to convey their views to others. Some Baptist men and women took a more activist stance than others; not all, in hindsight, were on the side of justice.

The study of Baptists and gender also includes varied understandings of sexual as well as gender identities. This is especially true for analyses of Baptists in more recent years. George Hancock-Stefan's chapter, for example, discusses Romanian Baptists' views of LGBTQIA+ issues. It is our hope that future volumes on Baptist identity will further explore the subjects of sexual and gender identities, which have become pressing topics in the twenty-first century, especially in the West. Much history of Baptists and gender remains to be written.

For the history that has been written in this volume, we are grateful. We thank especially the contributing authors for their excellent analyses and the time they have dedicated to this project. We are indebted to David Bebbington and the continuation committee of the International Conference on Baptist Studies for their work in assembling this astute group of scholars, even though issues related to the COVID-19 pandemic meant that ICOBS did not take place in 2021 as planned. We are glad to present most of the papers that were scheduled for that gathering in this volume. We extend special thanks to the graduate assistants at Baylor University who spent hours of careful work copyediting each submission: Kevin Scott, Sean Powell, and Hayden Lott. We are grateful to Susan Shaw for reviewing portions of the Introduction for us. Gratitude is also due to the financial supporters of this volume: the Department of Religion of Baylor University in Waco, Texas, USA and the Acadia Centre for Baptist and Anabaptist Studies of Acadia University in Wolfville, Nova Scotia, Canada. Finally, we thank the team at Mercer University Press—including Marc Jolley, Joseph Payne, Marsha Luttrell, and Mary Beth Kosowski—for their work in the production and promotion of this book. We are grateful for the global community that has made the idea of this volume a reality.

Melody Maxwell
T. Laine Scales
Fall 2022

PART ONE

BAPTISTS IN THE SEVENTEENTH AND

EIGHTEENTH CENTURIES

BAPTISTS IN ENGLAND

THE SHIFTING PORTRAYAL OF WOMEN IN BUNYAN'S *THE PILGRIM'S PROGRESS*

Matthew James Gray

John Bunyan was one of the most prolific Baptist authors during the English Restoration period, and gender issues frequently emerged in his literature. Between 1678 and 1679, he made significant alterations between the first and second editions of Part I of *The Pilgrim's Progress*, and many of these revolved around the role of women. In 1680, in the fifth edition of his autobiographical *Grace Abounding to the Chief of Sinners*, Bunyan discussed his views of women extensively. In 1683, Bunyan wrote *A Case of Conscience Resolved*, a very negative response to London Baptist leaders, who had publicly endorsed women meeting separately from male leaders. But then in 1684, he published Part II of *The Pilgrim's Progress*, which had a female hero, Christiana. While easily perceived as having a negative view of women having authority or voice, a more thorough analysis of Bunyan's writings unveils a complex sense of flux in his views of this topic. Ultimately, his views gradually evolved, developing a nuanced connection between gender and congregational *communitas*.

Unsurprisingly, Bunyan's writings have frequently been analyzed by gender historians. These assessments have usually been negative for several reasons. For example, Bunyan describes women as a threat in the fifth edition of *Grace Abounding*, claiming that "the common Salutation of women I abhor, 'tis odious to me in whomsoever I see it. Their company I cannot away with. I seldom so much as touch a woman's hand, for I think these things are not so becoming of me."[1] In Part II of *The Pilgrim's Progress*, Christiana and her fellow female pilgrim, Mercy, are met on the road by two men who threaten to "make Women of you."[2] After the women resist and cry out for help, a male Reliever comes to save them. He soon asks, "I marvelled much when you was entertained at the Gate above, being ye knew that ye were but weak Women, that you petitioned not the Lord there for a Conductor: Then might you have avoided these Troubles and Dangers."[3] Several historians, especially N. H. Keeble, have seen the

---

[1] John Bunyan, *Grace Abounding to the Chief of Sinners*, Fifth Edition (London, 1680), 125–26.

[2] John Bunyan, *The Pilgrim's Progress... Wherein Is Set Forth the Manner of the Setting Out of Christian's Wife and Children (Part II)* (London, 1684), 32.

[3] Bunyan, 33.

Reliever's response as placing the responsibility for a potential rape upon the women victims, rather than upon the male attackers.[4]

Qualification

Yet at other points in his writings, Bunyan seems to have a very positive view of women. In fact, despite the overall negative tone of the work, Bunyan starts *A Conscience Resolved* by conceding at the outset that to God men and women are equal, and that "the love of Women in Spirituals (as well as Naturals) oft times outgoes that of Men."[5] And of course, despite controversy about certain aspects, Bunyan does make Christiana the hero of *The Pilgrim's Progress*, Part II. So, how do we reconcile these two sides to Bunyan? At once misogynist and egalitarian? By simply realizing they do not occur "at once" at all. These writings span over a decade, and Bunyan's attitudes within them are intimately tied to his circumstances at each point: circumstances in his personal life, or within his denomination itself.

Changes from 1st to 2nd Edition

In examining Bunyan and gender, the history of *The Pilgrim's Progress*'s publication proves invaluable. The first edition of Part I was published in 1678 and was significantly shorter than the second edition, published just a year later in 1679. For the most part, the second edition became the definitive edition of the work, and the first edition was largely forgotten. This perhaps explains why, to my knowledge, no other scholars have ever compared the two, despite significant differences between them. Specifically, gender had been virtually ignored in the first edition of 1678, but that changed significantly from that point on. Almost all of the additions Bunyan made to the second edition have to do with women and are largely negative. For example, in the first edition the villain, Giant Despair, is unmarried.[6] In the second, he is married to Mrs. Diffidence, and

---

[4] N. H. Keeble, "'Here Is Her Glory, Even to Be under Him': The Feminine in the Thought and Work of John Bunyan," in *John Bunyan & His England, 1628–1688*, ed. Anne Laurence (Continuum International Publishing Group, 2003), 142. See also Thomas R. Cole, *The Journey of Life: A Cultural History of Aging in America* (Cambridge: Cambridge University Press, 1992), 46; Michael Davies, *Graceful Reading: Theology and Narrative in the Works of John Bunyan* (Oxford: Oxford University Press, 2002), 335–36; Tamsin Spargo, *The Writing of John Bunyan* (Milton, UK: Taylor & Francis Group, 1997), 124.

[5] John Bunyan, *A Case of Conscience Resolved* (London, 1683), 4.

[6] John Bunyan, *The Pilgrim's Progress from This World, to That Which Is to Come*

continually does "as his Wife had bidden him."[7] In fact, Diffidence becomes the prime motivator behind Despair's torture of Christian and Hopeful, which is also more elaborate than in the 1678 first edition. She even orders Despair to make Hopeful and Christian commit suicide.[8] Technically, Diffidence is a superfluous addition—Bunyan could have chosen to have Despair alone torture them. Bunyan adds Diffidence to represent disorder within a believer's emotions, through the similitude of a disordered marriage.

By far, the best example of these gendered additions is none other than Christian's wife. While in Part II of *The Pilgrim's Progress* she will become the heroic Christiana, in the 1678 first edition she barely exists at all. There, Christian simply leaves his family to begin his pilgrimage, without discussion or interaction.[9] However, in the 1679 edition, the period before his departure is greatly elaborated. Christian tells his wife and children that he is distressed about the impending destruction of their city, but they dismiss this as "some frenzy distemper." His nameless wife also tries to discourage him from leaving, by ridicule and neglect.[10] Thus the wife evolves in the two editions, from being virtually inconsequential in 1678, to in 1679 becoming a threat to salvation.

The wife's soteriological threat is further elaborated upon in later interactions in the 1679 edition. Bunyan added a discussion about Christian's wife with Mr. Worldly Wiseman. Wiseman asks Christian if he has a wife and children, to which he replies, "Yes, but I am so laden with this burden, that I cannot take that pleasure in them as formerly: methinks, I am as if I had none."[11] Wiseman suggests Christian ease his burden by going to the town of Morality, and "thou mayest send for thy wife and Children to thee to this Village, where there are houses now stand empty."[12] Central, then, to Morality's danger for Christian is the temptation of his wife. When Christian cannot reach the village because Mount Sinai is too high, he meets Evangelist again, who reminds Christian of Luke 14:26, where Jesus calls His followers to hate their family in comparison to their love of Christ.[13]

Delivered Under the Similitude of a Dream, 1st ed. (London, 1678), 152.

[7] John Bunyan, *The Pilgrim's Progress from This World, to That Which Is to Come Delivered Under the Similitude of a Dream*, 2nd ed. (London, 1679), 202.

[8] Bunyan, 197.

[9] Bunyan, *The Pilgrim's Progress*, 1678 ed., 2–3.

[10] Bunyan, *The Pilgrim's Progress*, 1679 ed., 3.

[11] Bunyan, 17.

[12] Bunyan, 23.

[13] Bunyan, 27. Luke 14:26 (Geneva): "If any man come to me, and hate not his father, and mother, and wife, and children, and brethren, and sisters: yea, and his own

Later, when Christian arrives at the Beautiful inn, he is met by four sisters: Discretion, Piety, Prudence, and Charity, "the Virgins of this place."[14] Once again, the 1679 version is expanded to include discussion of Christian's wife and children.[15] Charity, who does not talk at all in the 1678 edition, interrogates Christian about whether he had taken seriously his wife and children's plight: why had he not brought them with him? Had he prayed for them? Had he explained their immanent destruction?[16] Christian asserts that he had, but that, "why, my Wife was afraid of losing this World; and my Children were given to the foolish delights of youth: so…they left me to wander in this manner alone."[17] Charity replies, "if thy Wife and Children have been offended with thee for this, they thereby shew themselves to be implacable to the good, and thou hast delivered thy soul from their blood."[18]

What was the motivation behind this shift, with women being portrayed as a threat? Bunyan explicitly explained why he now saw women as a threat, in the fifth edition of *Grace Abounding*, published one year later in 1680. Specifically, in 1674 he had ridden a horse with a young woman straddled behind him, Agnes Beaumont, while taking her to a congregational meeting in Gamlingay, Cambridgeshire.[19] This resulted in accusations of sexual impropriety being leveled against him. This explains his response that he seldom touched so much as a woman's hand. Anne Dunan-Page has argued that another reason Bunyan was susceptible to accusations of sexual impropriety was precisely because he was a Baptist; their "dipping" of women was often perceived by the wider English public as bathing with them.[20] Richard Greaves, a Bunyan biographer and gender historian himself, argues that Bunyan's emphatic negativity in *Grace Abounding* "is not evidence of misogyny, but reflects an acute reaction against the slings and

---

life also, he cannot be my disciple."

[14] Bunyan, *The Pilgrim's Progress*, 1678 ed., 51; Bunyan, *The Pilgrim's Progress*, 1679 ed., 70.

[15] Bunyan, *The Pilgrim's Progress*, 1678 ed., 58.

[16] Bunyan, *The Pilgrim's Progress*, 1679 ed., 77–80.

[17] Bunyan, 79.

[18] Bunyan, 80.

[19] Kathleen Lynch, "'Her Name Agnes': The Verifications of Agnes Beaumont's Narrative Ventures," *ELH* 67, no. 1 (April 1, 2000): 71–98, https://doi.org/10.2307/30031907; Agnes Beaumont, "The Singular Experience and Great Sufferings of Mrs. Agnes Beaumont," in *An Abstract of the Gracious Dealings of God, with Several Eminent Christians, in Their Conversion and Sufferings*, by Samuel James (London, 1760).

[20] Anne Dunan-Page, *Grace Overwhelming: John Bunyan, 'The Pilgrim's Progress' and the Extremes of the Baptist Mind* (Bern: Peter Lang, 2006), 90.

arrows that threatened his reputation."[21] The same could well explain his alterations between the first and second editions of *The Pilgrim's Progress*. It seems likely that the "horse-riding" scandal broke some time before the second edition was published, and Bunyan's concerns about his own reputation found their way into his writing at the time. Part of Bunyan's literary charm is his expressive vulnerability, the way he so comfortably integrates his own emotions into his writings. It would be entirely consistent if, feeling frustrated at how this incident with a woman had damaged his reputation, that frustration permeated his writing in this period.

Of course, Bunyan's writings do contain strong expectations of classic gender roles. On the other hand, Bunyan's writings also show that he moved further towards a more egalitarian view of women over time, which is consistent with the views of women among much of the Baptist community by that point. For forty years they had insisted that both men and women had the right and responsibility to take ownership of their faith through baptism. And Bunyan's *A Conscience Resolved*, written in 1683, two years after *The Pilgrim's Progress's* revision, indicates that in London Baptists were going even further.

Bunyan writes *A Conscience Resolved* in reply to "Mr. K," identified as one of the leaders of the Baptists in London. The specific identity of Mr. K is difficult to ascertain, but the most likely candidates would be Hanserd Knollys, William Kiffen, or Benjamin Keach, some of the most illustrious Baptist pastors in the period.[22] Mr. K was responding to an incident from 1681, where Bunyan had discouraged women-only prayer meetings within his congregation at Bedford. Consequently, Mr. K had written a refutation of Bunyan's decision. In his response, Bunyan included Mr. K's arguments for women having meetings. Mr. K offered several reasons for the women's being able to run prayer meetings autonomously, without a pastor presiding over them. Many of his arguments were pneumatological, derived from the Spirit's endorsement of female Biblical figures, such as Miriam in Exodus 15:20–21: "And the same Spirit of Christ that was in her, is also in all his Servants." Mr. K goes on "If God hath in Gospel times promised the powring out of his Spirit to Women, to that very end that they may pray together apart from Men, Then it is not only their Liberty, but Duty to Meet and Pray together."[23] Here, Mr. K is citing the Geneva Bible's wording of Acts 2:17, that the God would "powre" (i.e., pour) His Spirit upon

---

[21] Richard L. Greaves, *Glimpses of Glory: John Bunyan and English Dissent* (Stanford: Stanford University Press, 2002), 310.

[22] Greaves, 480–81.

[23] Bunyan, *A Case of Conscience Resolved*, 6–7.

"maydes."[24] Such divine endorsement was also evident in the London Baptists' most significant argument—an experiential one: "Cannot many women that have used this practice, by experience, say, they have met with the Lord in it, and have found blessed returns of prayer from God, both to themselves and the Church, wherein God hath owned them? Therefore what God hath Born Witness to, and approved of, let no Man deter you from."[25]

This experiential argument is particularly important, because it shows that this was not merely a theoretical position for the Baptists. Instead, many women within Baptist congregations were already meeting, without men, for worship and prayer, and were being encouraged by Baptist leaders to do so. Indeed, this is Bunyan's chief criticism of those leaders. Admittedly, Mr. K seems to have been hesitant to discuss Bible passages commonly identified with negative views of women's voice, such as 1 Corinthians 11, 1 Corinthians 14, and Eve's role at the Fall in Genesis 2–3. Indeed, Bunyan cited such passages, especially the story of Eve, in his arguments against Mr. K.[26]

Yet only one year later, in Part II of *The Pilgrim's Progress*, he de-emphasized Eve's complicity in the Fall: "For as Death and the Curse came into the World by a Woman [Eve in Genesis 3], so also did Life and Health; God sent forth his Son, made of a woman (Galatians 4)."[27] Bunyan now surmised that "Women therefore are highly favoured, and shew by these things that they are sharers with us in the Grace of Life."[28]

Therefore, Bunyan's overall view of women seems inconsistent and potentially difficult to decipher. There could be several potential reasons for this. Perhaps he somehow held these positive and negative views continually in tension. Perhaps he was torn between acceding to the negative view of women in wider society and the more positive view prevalent within his own denomination. Or perhaps he shifted his stance in the wake of circumstances. When under the stress of scandal, he exaggerated a disdain of women. But when confronted with the London Baptists' arguments, he had to change his mind—not at first, to be sure, but within a year or so.

Some might argue, and have, that Part II of *Pilgrim's Progress* is not a positive representation of women, as discussed earlier. However, the claim by Keeble

---

[24] Théodore de Bèze, ed., *The Bible: That Is, the Holy Scriptures Contained in the Olde and Newe Testament* (London: Christopher Barker, 1587).

[25] Mr. K, in Bunyan, *A Case of Conscience Resolved*, 6–7.

[26] Bunyan, 15.

[27] Bunyan, *The Pilgrim's Progress, Part II*, 148.

[28] Bunyan, 149.

and others that Bunyan was placing the blame for rape upon the woman fails to recognize the overall purpose of the work itself. Their argument rests on the assumption that Part II is primarily designed to be a woman's story. It is not. While there are certainly aspects of the story that are about the role of women, it is, like Part I, primarily the story of any Puritan, male or female.[29] In Part II of *The Pilgrim's Progress*, the attack upon Christiana and Mercy comes just after they enter through the Wicket Gate, Bunyan's metaphor for anybody entering the Christian life. He places this pericope into the narrative to make a more general, non-gender-specific point: the newly converted believer tends to be idealistic and consequently underestimates the temptations they will soon face.[30] Christiana and Mercy's need for a protector is a metaphor for *every* Christian's need to be in Christian community, and especially under sound leadership, irrespective of gender. Far from being an attempt to disempower women, then, Bunyan uses Christiana and Mercy in this pericope as role models for any new convert, just as Part I's hero, Christian, was a role model there. Greaves asserts that this very example shows the danger of isolating gender from the wider context and purpose of the writer, suggesting, "such readings, in my judgment, overemphasize gender and accord insufficient weight to…the change in emphasis [between Part I and Part II] from individual to communal. The second part is about much more than gender."[31]

Nonetheless, while it remains true that Part II is about more than gender, it does provide insights into Bunyan's shift towards viewing the role of women in churches more positively. Firstly, it reveals that a woman can have a role at all. When Christiana first feels compelled to leave the City of Destruction, she is visited by two friends, Mrs. Timorous and Miss Mercy. Mrs. Timorous tries to convince Christiana not to leave, saying, "For if he [her husband, Christian], tho' a man, was so hard to put to it, what chanst thou being but a poor Woman do?"[32] Even Keeble and Breen emphasize this as a positive aspect of Bunyan's view of women, because Christiana's departure effectively denies the validity of Timorous's argument, an argument that was certainly dominant at the time in England.[33] Furthermore, the young woman Mercy's decision to join Christiana on her pilgrimage distances her from the prime identity marker for a young woman

---

[29] Greaves, *Glimpses of Glory*, 500.

[30] Bunyan, *The Pilgrim's Progress, Part II*, 33–34.

[31] Greaves, *Glimpses of Glory*, 505n75.

[32] Bunyan, *The Pilgrim's Progress, Part II*, 16.

[33] Keeble, "Here Is Her Glory," 136; Margaret Soenser Breen, "The Sexed Pilgrim's Progress," *Studies in English Literature, 1500–1900* 32, no. 3 (July 1, 1992): 448.

in that period, being a father's daughter. She is autonomous, identified outside of any family affiliation. She is herself. While Christiana and Mercy in part exemplify overcoming the sense of inadequacy that any new believer will experience, the gender implications are significant. Bunyan is encouraging women to dismiss wider social expectations if those expectations hinder the Christian life. This theme is prevalent throughout the text.

Bunyan also endorses a woman's rejection of a suitor in Part II of *The Pilgrim's Progress*, when Mercy is courted by Mr. Brisk, "a man of some breeding, and that pretended to Religion."[34] While Mercy has a "fair Countenance," Brisk is primarily attracted to her because she is hardworking, making hosiery for the poor. Assuming she makes these things for personal profit, Brisk says, "I will warrant her a good Huswife."[35] Once Mercy discovers that Brisk's faith is insincere, she uses her pious generosity to discourage Brisk's courtship. Mercy is then warned by a female catechist along the way, Prudence, that few men will want to marry her, given her piety. To this, Mercy replies, "if no body will have me, I will dye a Maid, or my Conditions shall be to me as a Husband. For I cannot change my Nature, and to have one that lies cross to me in this, that I purpose never to admit of, as long as I live."[36] Bunyan here gives women the right to reject spouses, based on their own high religious standards, even validating them not getting married at all.

Of course, Mercy eventually does get married. Keeble claims this is Bunyan's way of forcing her under the traditional patriarchal structures.[37] But this fails to see the main motivation behind Mercy getting married at this point. It is Christiana's decision for Mercy to marry her son, Matthew. Thus, Matthew is reduced to being merely a mechanism for Mercy's integration into Christiana's family. Mercy is less identified as now being Matthew's wife, as she is now Christiana's daughter. Indeed, Matthew is defined primarily as being under Christiana's authority and is frequently portrayed as subordinate to women, such as Christiana and Prudence. Moreover, he is never portrayed as having authority over a woman, least of all over Mercy, his wife. Mercy is a far more impressive character than her husband, Matthew.

In fact, if Christiana's story is compared to that of her husband, Christian from Part I, she is often far more impressive than he. For example, whereas Christian was significantly hampered by the Slough of Despond at the beginning of

---

[34] Bunyan, *The Pilgrim's Progress, Part II*, 80.
[35] Bunyan, 81.
[36] Bunyan, 82.
[37] Keeble, "Here Is Her Glory," 144.

his journey, Christiana and Mercy cross it easily.[38] Admittedly, Keeble complains that Christiana's journey culminates in arriving at the same Celestial City that her husband arrived at and argues that this subordinates her story into Christian's.[39] However, Christiana's motivation for going there is not so much to follow her husband, but to receive eternal life.

Furthermore, Christiana's entry into the Celestial City is, again, significantly more impressive than Christian's. Whereas Christian is assailed by terror as he crosses the Jordan, Bunyan explicitly represents Christiana's crossing as peaceful and full of assurance. Indeed, all the other pilgrims gather around Christiana to hear her wisdom before she leaves. Christiana bestows advice upon both male and female pilgrims there.[40] Christiana's death gives her an authoritative voice over the whole congregation. None of the male characters are given this authoritative voice, at all.[41] Even their pastor, Mr. Greatheart, fades from any authority he may have gained in the journey, in the wake of Christiana's dying words.[42]

In fact, throughout the narrative, the male pilgrims are often portrayed as weaker than the women, for example, Mr. Much Afraid and Mr. Fearing. As Kathleen Swaim has said of these characters, "these are not gendered tendencies, they are human tendencies."[43] In Part II of *The Pilgrim's Progress*, weak males like Mr. Much Afraid and Mr. Fearing are designed by Bunyan to actually redefine the nature of weakness. Weakness is no longer about being male or female, afraid or brave. It is defined as separating one's self from community.

This raises the issue of Bunyan's insistence upon having strong leadership. Some have complained because of the whole group of pilgrims coming to have a male leader, a pastor, Mr. Greatheart. But his qualification to be their guide and protector is not so much that he is a man, but that he knows the way to the Celestial City.[44] His strength is derived from his reliance upon God, not his gender, as Breen has recognized.[45] Nonetheless, strong the pastor must be, because he is the primary mechanism for Bunyan's highest priority, community.

---

[38] Bunyan, *The Pilgrim's Progress, Part II*, 21.

[39] Keeble, "Here Is Her Glory," 142.

[40] Bunyan, *The Pilgrim's Progress, Part II*, 214–15.

[41] Bunyan, 217–18.

[42] Greaves, *Glimpses of Glory*, 506.

[43] Kathleen M. Swaim, "Mercy and the Feminine Heroic in the Second Part of Pilgrim's Progress," *Studies in English Literature, 1500–1900* 30, no. 3 (July 1, 1990): 397.

[44] Greaves, *Glimpses of Glory*, 501.

[45] Breen, "The Sexed Pilgrim's Progress," 444.

This ultimately reveals the connection between *A Conscience Resolved* and Part II of *The Pilgrim's Progress*. It is not simply that Bunyan wrote negatively about women in 1683 and then wrote positively about them in 1684. There is a consistent theme running through both texts: that isolation from the wider Christian community, and especially from pastoral leadership, is dangerous. If Greaves is correct that Part II of *The Pilgrim's Progress* is more about community than gender, the same could well be said of *A Conscience Resolved*. Certainly, there are negative views of women in Bunyan's arguments in *A Conscience Resolved*. However, he is more concerned that they will be isolated from the wider congregation and leadership than that they are women. This is hardly surprising given that communion—the experience of Christian unity—was a significant facet of Bunyan's ecclesiology.

Bunyan's view of gender is therefore, itself, a pilgrimage—a journey. It evolves along that journey, often in reaction to the heroes and villains, hills and valleys he encounters along the way. From the swamp of scandal to the storm of denominational controversy, Bunyan ultimately emerges as an advocate for women sharing voice and status, always within Christian community together.

CHURCH DISCIPLINE AND GENDER IN EIGHTEENTH-CENTURY ENGLISH BAPTIST LIFE

Lon Graham

On October 16, 1792, the case of a "Mrs. Camm"[1] was brought before the church at College Lane in Northampton.[2] She was charged with "acts of imprudence & sin" and giving "but little Satisfaction or Pleasure to your Pastors or Fellow Members."[3] The letter written to her notes that she had been a member longer than any other woman then living.[4] She had, apparently, been trouble to the church for some time, although the record never specifies her crimes, preferring instead simply to refer to a general sinfulness by which she "grieved & dishonored" the church.[5] In one meeting, a decision was made: she was excluded from their fellowship, and the church "disown[ed] all church relation" to her.[6]

Mrs. Camm's case illustrates important aspects of the discipline of women at College Lane, namely, that the charges, though always portrayed as serious, were often vague, and discipline could be swift, with very little deliberation

---

[1] Her first name was Mary. She had been married to a Pratt and was widowed. She married John Camm on September 25, 1787 (*Northamptonshire, England, Church of England Marriages, 1754–1912*, Northamptonshire Record Office, 154).

[2] This church has been known as both College Lane and College Street. The name most commonly used in the time period under examination was College Lane, so that will be the name used in this study. For more information on this church, see John Taylor, *History of College Street Church, Northampton: with Biographies of Pastors, Missionaries and Preachers; and Notes of Sunday Schools, Branch Churches and Workers: Illustrated with Portraits and Drawings* (Northampton: Taylor & Son, Dryden Press, 1897).

[3] John Ryland Jr., *College Lane: Church Book, 1781–1801* (Northamptonshire Record Office), 136.

[4] The letter notes that she belonged to "the Old Church" and "was in Fellowship with Mr Ryland sen[r] came to Northampton" (Ryland Jr., *Church Book*, 138). John Collett Ryland came from Warwick to Northampton in order to assume the pastorate of College Lane in 1759.

[5] Ryland Jr., *Church Book*, 136. She was encouraged to abstain from the Lord's supper in 1786 for conduct that was "in many respects very disagreeable," though the details of her ill conduct are not specified (Ryland Jr., 94).

[6] Ryland Jr., 137.

recorded. This chapter will examine the 1781–1801 church book of College Lane in order to demonstrate that these aspects of the discipline of women were not restricted to Mrs. Camm and that men did not experience the same severity, indicating a divergence of treatment between men and women. It will also investigate the role that the eighteenth-century culture of politeness played in College Lane's treatment of women.

1781–1801 Church Book

The 1781–1801 church book of College Lane was chosen for several reasons. First, it presents a more complete picture of church meetings than is found in other church books. Mark Burden and Anne Dunan-Page, in their study of the church books of the dissenting churches, note that many such books often show signs of neglect (e.g., gaps in coverage), censorship (both contemporary and by a later hand), and degradation over time.[7] The earlier years of College Lane records suffer from some of these issues. For example, the book that covers the pastorate of John Collett Ryland, which lasted from 1759 until 1785, has gaps in coverage, during which time either no important church meetings were held, or they simply were not recorded. The latter seems more likely.[8] When John Ryland Jr. was ordained as a minister in 1781, he also took on the responsibility of keeping the church book, which resulted in a more consistent and fuller account.[9] For this reason, the church book of 1781–1801 contains helpful insight into the practice of church discipline at College Lane.

Second, College Lane was an influential church in the Northamptonshire Baptist Association, especially during the years under consideration. It was from this association that the Baptist Missionary Society was birthed, and ministers in the association during these years included both Rylands, Andrew Fuller, John

---

[7] Mark Burden and Anne Dunan-Page, "Puritans, Dissenters, and their Church Books: Recording and Representing Experience," *Bunyan Studies: A Journal of Reformation and Nonconformist Culture* 20 (2016): 17–18.

[8] The church book from Ryland Sr.'s tenure also includes his musings on open communion, a minority position to which both he and his son held. For more information on Ryland Sr. and open communion in the College Lane record books, see Lon Graham, "John Collett Ryland, Daniel Turner, and *A Modest Plea*," *Baptist Quarterly* 52 no. 1 (2021): 34–42.

[9] A study of Ryland's record keeping reveals a man who was fastidious in keeping track of his own life and activity. The Northamptonshire Record Office also has Ryland Jr.'s "Text Book," in which he recorded every sermon he ever preached, complete with date, place, and scripture passage.

Sutcliff, and Robert Hall Sr.[10] The importance of College Lane in its region and association was highlighted by James Culross, who referred to the pastor of the church as a "Baptist bishop."[11]

Finally, much of the research on women in Baptist life focuses on the seventeenth century, while the pivotal period of the late eighteenth and early nineteenth centuries has not seen as much attention. Part of the reason for this lack of attention on the contribution of women is that, according to John Briggs, the "opportunities for women to participate in church life seem to have shrunk by the early eighteenth century."[12] Though opportunities for public ministry waned, nevertheless, there is room for investigating the place and portion of women in Baptist life in that important time frame, which saw the rise of a missionary impulse in the formation of the Baptist Missionary Society in 1792 and a shift in theological emphases, led largely by Andrew Fuller. The focus on women at College Lane from 1781 to 1801 is an attempt to fill a lacuna in the research.

Church Discipline at College Lane: Case Studies

The 1781–1801 church book records sixteen separate cases of church discipline which resulted in exclusion. Of these seventeen cases, ten involved women alone, two involved women with men, and four involved men alone. At the outset, then, the balance is tipped against women, with far more women coming under exclusionary discipline than men. It might be objected that there were more women members than men, which would result in more cases for women. While

---

[10] Fuller, Sutcliff, Ryland Jr., and Hall Sr. were all pivotal to the Baptists giving a positive answer to the "modern question" and beginning to engage in the missionary task: Fuller through his theological writings, Sutcliff through the Prayer Call of 1784, Ryland Jr. through his preaching and leadership, and Hall Sr. through his *Help to Zion's Travelers* (Bristol: William Pine, 1781).

[11] James Culross, *The Three Rylands: A Hundred Years of Various Christian Service* (London: Elliot Stock, 1897), 76.

[12] John Briggs, "She-Preachers, Widows and Other Women: The Feminine Dimension in Baptist Life since 1600," *Baptist Quarterly* 21 no. 7 (July 1986): 342. Carolyn DeArmond Blevins argues that as Baptist life became more structured, women began to be pushed to the side (Carolyn DeArmond Blevins, "Women and the Baptist experience," *Baptist History and Heritage* 51 no. 1 [2016]: 91). She notes that women began to be referred to merely as the "wife of" someone. This entailed less freedom of speech and expression for women, less agency, and a greater social pressure to conform.

it is true that there were more women members than men at College Lane, it is equally true that the church did not have over twice as many men members, which would be required for this objection to be sustained.

In order to see the differences in how men and women were treated in disciplinary cases, it is necessary to find two cases in which a man and a woman engaged in similar sinful behavior. Fortunately, there are the cases of John Mitchell and Jane Minstrell. On March 12, 1784, John Mitchell was charged with being "very ready to run into evil Company & to indulge himself in drinking more than was becoming a Christian, & is now charged with downright Intoxication."[13] At that meeting, the church agreed to a precautionary measure: have him withdraw from the Lord's table until they could examine the affair. Nine days later, another meeting was held, with Mitchell present, where he was allowed to make his case. Witnesses were brought against him, and he was allowed a defense. No decision was reached, and the case was deferred to still another day. Four additional meetings were devoted to Mitchell's case. At the sixth meeting, the church voted to exclude Mitchell from their communion. Six meetings over four months were given to hearing John Mitchell's case of discipline over public drunkenness.

The case of Jane Minstrell presents a far different process, though with the same outcome. Minstrell was charged with the "practice of privately indulging a taste for strong drink so as to have a very visible Effect upon your body, & sometimes to unfit you for the duties of a Servt., & much more for the duties of a Christian."[14] The charge is similar to that against Mitchell, with one important difference: Mitchell's sin was public, while Minstrell's was largely private.[15] Because Minstrell's sin was private, the church book says, she was not immediately disciplined. There were, apparently, instances in which she was admonished and warned, but these are only hinted at in the church book.[16] Whereas Mitchell's case was given several months and church meetings to resolve, Minstrell's case was resolved in one meeting. In the same meeting she was charged, convicted, and excluded. She was neither able to make a case for nor defend herself. In some ways, the church meeting appears to have been a mere formality.

---

[13] Ryland Jr., *Church Book*, 80.

[14] Ryland Jr., 98–99.

[15] According to the church book, Mitchell's sin took place in a public house in view of many witnesses, including members of the church (Ryland Jr., 81).

[16] This is also in contrast to how cases with men were handled: often, the events of private meetings of admonishment were recounted, at least in brief summation.

The deliberation of the Mitchell case and the swiftness of the Minstrell case indicates that College Lane had far more patience with men than with women. The case of James Hewitt may serve as an example of the church's patience with men.[17] The church book records that James and Elizabeth Hewitt had "occasionally discover'd much disaffection to the pastor of this Church ever since the time of his ordination" and "had often express'd their dissatisfact". with his Min^ry [ministry] in a bitter and unbecoming spirit."[18] They were excluded from the church on February 7, 1790, and Ryland Jr. was ordained on June 8, 1781, meaning that there was an almost ten-year period of forbearance. In January 1790, the deacons of the church had apparently run out of patience with the Hewitts. The precipitating incident that led to their exclusion was a conversation that Mr. Hewitt had with another church member in which he harshly criticized Ryland Jr., charging that Ryland Jr. "doth not preach the gospel" and that he is a "linsey-woolsey preacher."[19] Both of the Hewitts had an attachment to John Collett Ryland, Ryland Jr.'s father and predecessor at College Street. Mr. Hewitt is quoted in the church book as saying, "As to the young one he is none of my pastor." He claimed that he "never had owned him for his pastor and he never wou'd."[20]

The deacons of the church attempted to meet with the Hewitts, but Mr. Hewitt refused to meet with anyone from the church except in his own house, which was objectionable to the deacons, since Hewitt had "heretofore threatened to turn one & another out, if they did not speak exactly to his own mind."[21] While the time from the precipitating incident to the time of exclusion was less than a month, much activity was packed into those few weeks: a lengthy church meeting in which, unusually, the conduct of the deacons toward the people under discipline was questioned; a "letter of admonition" was written and sent; a Friday meeting of twenty-seven male members was held; a church meeting in which formal charges were made and agreed to; and a final meeting at which a letter of exclusion was approved and sent. There was, in the case of the Hewitts,

---

[17] While both James and his wife Elizabeth were excluded, the record book makes it clear that James was the one who committed much of the discipline-worthy acts.

[18] Ryland Jr., *Church Book*, 106.

[19] "Linsey-woolsey" was a slang term that meant "neither one thing nor the other" (John Stephen Farmer and William Ernest Henley, eds, *Slang and Its Analogues Past and Present*, 7 vols. [1896] 4:204). Hewitt seems to have meant that Ryland Jr. was a "nonsense" preacher (F. Sturges Allen, *Allen's Synonyms and Antonyms* [New York: Harper and Brothers, 1920], 295).

[20] Ryland Jr., *Church Book*, 106–7.

[21] Ryland Jr., 107.

much more deliberation and even introspection devoted to their case than was usual in the church book. They were given many opportunities to meet with the church, which they refused.

While the eventual discipline was enacted rather swiftly, the Hewitts, and Mr. Hewitt especially, was allowed to engage in such behavior without interference for many years. Even when discipline was enacted, the church moved with unusual deliberation, self-awareness, and something approaching self-censoriousness. For the women, however, discipline was always swift. Typically, one church meeting was given over to the discipline of women, while men were given three or four meetings before the decision to exclude. While the church book referenced attempts to reprove the women in private before the meeting to exclude, the same is also said of the men, and they received more time, attention, and deliberation in their disciplinary cases.

A Complex Picture: College Lane and John Ryland, Jr.

The differences between the ways men and women under church discipline were treated at College Lane might lead one to believe that women simply were not valued as were men. However, there are indications that the picture is more complex than that. In particular, the presence and role of John Ryland Jr. at College Lane should be considered as a way of more fully understanding the story of the place of women at College Lane. Ryland Jr. was the church recorder, pastor, son of the beloved former pastor, and long-time member of the church; as such, his influence can hardly be overestimated. The course of discipline would have been approved by him, as evidenced by his signature on letters of exclusion sent to persons under discipline. Ryland Jr.'s view and treatment of women is not as one-dimensional as the discipline cases at College Lane might suggest. This may be seen in his correspondence with and support of women.

Ryland's extant correspondence with women reveals a man who treated them as equals and valued their contributions. One letter is especially revealing of his attitude toward women. After the death of Andrew Fuller in 1815, Ryland wrote to Maria Hope, who organized ladies' auxiliary branches for the Bible Society in Liverpool.[22] In the letter, he updated Hope on the progress of his biography of Andrew Fuller, for which she had given an account of Fuller's first

---

[22] John Ryland, "Letter to Maria Hope," Tutt Library, Colorado College. The letter is undated, but it was written after Fuller's death on May 7, 1815 and before the publication of Ryland's memoir of Fuller the following year.

religious impressions. He shared missionary intelligence relating to Lee Compere. He also solicited Hope's assistance with a delicate situation in Jamaica relating to the planters on the island who opposed the work of the Baptist Missionary Society. He wrote to her in much the same way he wrote to men: as an equal and a co-laborer in a common work.[23]

Ryland also valued the spirituality of women. Writing in the preface of a work by Susanna Anthony, Ryland said, "We cannot but consider Miss ANTHONY as a female PEARCE; and not inferior to him in spirituality."[24] "Pearce" was Ryland's deceased friend Samuel Pearce, whom he held in the highest regard.[25] Equating Anthony with Pearce was, therefore, no small commendation. Ryland also recognized and appreciated the contributions of women to the work of missions. He wrote in the same preface,

> In the late extraordinary exertions for imparting the gospel to the heathen, your sex has borne an honourable part. They have not only generously contributed of their substance, and been unweariedly assiduous in accommodating those who have embarked in the important undertaking; but many of them have cheerfully left their country and their kindred, and with their husbands, encountered its perils; nor have they been less useful in their spheres of action than their companions.[26]

Ryland also encouraged the literary contributions of women. Writing to his friend John Saffery, he included a note at the end, encouraging Saffery's wife, Maria Grace Saffery, in her writing: "I wish Mrs. Saffery w^d employ her pen more

---

[23] In a preface to a work telling the stories of faithful Christian women, Ryland wrote, "it is one of the glories of christianity, that it knows neither jew nor greek, bond nor free, male nor female; but considers all as one in Christ Jesus. As fellow-heirs of the same grace, we feel interested in your edification" (John Ryland Jr., Andrew Fuller, and John Sutcliff, "Dedication for *An Illustrious Example of Female Piety in the Life and Experience of Miss Susanna Anthony*," New and Improved Edition, compiled by Samuel Hopkins [London: Wightman and Cramp, 1830], vii).

[24] Ryland Jr., Fuller, and Sutcliff, "Dedication," ix.

[25] Ryland referred to Pearce as his "invaluable Bro^r." (John Ryland Jr., "Letter to John Saffery," October 22, 1799, Angus Library and Archive) and "a burning & ſhining Light" (John Ryland, "Sermon Notes: John 14:18: Funeral Sermon for Samuel Pearce," October 20, 1799, Bristol Baptist College Archives). In his funeral sermon for Pearce, Ryland says, "I kn. not a Wid^w. who c^d. lose more by the removal of a husband, I scarcely kn. a Ch. who c^d. lose so much in the Loſs of a Pastor."

[26] Ryland Jr., Fuller, and Sutcliff, "Dedication," xi.

for Christ, her Talent ought not to be hid in a napkin."[27] Ryland Jr. valued the public voice of women, as was also seen in the practice at College Lane of giving experiences before the church. When a person joined the church, they had to give an account of their spiritual experience before the congregation. Men as well as women were allowed to give their experience before the congregation. The descriptions given of both betray no degradation of the testimony of women.

English Politeness and Church Discipline

One is left with a variety of observations. On the one hand, the opinions and contributions of women were valued, at the very least, by the pastor of College Lane, John Ryland Jr., and public testimony to their spiritual experiences was received gladly by the congregation. On the other hand, women were treated with stricter discipline when they were perceived as straying from the norms and rules established and maintained by the community. In other words, women were valued, honored, and their voices heard when they supported the existing structures, beliefs, and authorities. However, when they strayed from their path, the authority and the power of the institution was brought to bear on them swiftly. An explanation for this may be found in the concept of politeness in English society.

Lawrence Klein provides a helpful summary of the use of politeness as a lens through which to see and interpret England in the eighteenth century.[28] He writes, "politeness was extensive in reach and formative in effect. Like 'honor' or 'godliness' for earlier periods, 'politeness' helps us map the culture broadly conceived."[29] Politeness came to be a way in which the structure of society was held together—indeed, the way in which civilization was passed on.[30] Soile Ylivuori has taken up the research into politeness and demonstrated the ways in which English politeness affected women in the seventeenth and eighteenth centuries. She writes, "women were, firstly, represented as the naturally polite sex. Corresponding to their more delicate bodies compared to men, women's natural

---

[27] John Ryland Jr., "Letter to John Saffery."

[28] Lawrence E. Klein, "Politeness and the Interpretation of the British Eighteenth Century," *The Historical Journal* 45 no. 4 (December 2002): 870: "Politeness was an important eighteenth-century idiom. Indeed, it was one of the myths of the age." Klein's thesis has continued to be developed and challenged. See the summary of recent works in Rosalind Carr, "A Polite and Enlightened London?" *The Historical Journal* 59 no. 2 (2016): 623–34.

[29] Klein, "Politeness," 877.

[30] Klein, 878.

character was respectively thought to be more soft, complaisant, and agreeable—which were all qualities essential for politeness."[31] Women, as the "naturally polite sex," were, therefore, tasked with civilizing English society, namely, the men and children. On civilizing children and the household, she explains,

> Women's moral discipline was also thought to have broader consequences. The domestic woman had a duty to her husband and family to bring up her children into responsible citizenship or pious housewifery, to set an example to her servants and guide them in their religion, and to manage the household with frugality and diligence. Therefore, as the whole English nation was thought to rely on women's moralising effect, unblemished morality became practically a civic duty for all elite women, as well as a natural quality.[32]

It is not difficult to see, then, why College Lane would hold women to a stricter standard. Ryland himself saw women as the more naturally polite sex, even if he did not use that exact language, saying,

> The best part of [the pagan literature] is mere natural accomplishment; and much of it is base and vicious. There is nothing in it of that pure chastity, of that sweet modesty; or, as the scriptures term it, "shame-facedness," which courts not to be seen; of that meekness, mildness, gentleness, sympathy and goodness, which is the ornament of human nature, and the peculiar glory of women.[33]

If women were the wall that held England from falling into incivility, then, when a woman engaged in what was considered unlawful speech and conduct, it was more than merely an indiscretion, as it might have been understood in a man. It was a danger to society. To use a modern analogy, women functioned as both the steering and brakes for society; if the steering and brakes of a car fail, then the whole car is in danger of crashing. Or, to use a picture from a contemporary work aimed at the refinement of young ladies, "A young Lady without

---

[31] Soile Ylivuori, *Women and Politeness in Eighteenth-Century England: Bodies, Identities, and Power* (New York: Routledge, 2018), 39.

[32] Ylivuori, 208–9. On civilizing men: "Only women who possessed virtue, modesty, and gentleness would lead men into 'the decencies of life, the softness of love, the sweets of friendship' and 'the nameless tender charities that pervade and unite the most virtuous form of cultivated society'" (Ylivuori, 39).

[33] Ryland Jr., Fuller, and Sutcliff, "Dedication," viii.

Piety, and a religious Reverence towards Heaven, is a kind of Monſter in the World."[34]

Conclusion

The people of College Lane confessed themselves to be walking "together in the profession of all Gospel Doctrines; and in an Attendance on all Gospel Ordinances; and in the Practise and Discharge of all Relative Duties as the Lord ſhall enable" them,[35] and they no doubt believed wholeheartedly that they were doing that in each case of church discipline. However, the values, commitments, and expectations of the broader cultural emphasis on politeness, and its role in the lives of women, played an important yet unacknowledged role in the church's treatment of over half of their church body. While this period in Baptist history was one during which old practices and beliefs were being reexamined,[36] this particular practice and belief took longer to examine, perhaps because it was unacknowledged. It is difficult to examine a conviction that one does not know one has.

---

[34] Abbe D'Ancourt, *The Lady's Preceptor, or, a Letter to a Young Lady of Distinction upon Politeness*, 3rd ed. (London: J. Watts, 1745), 5, cited in Ylivuori, *Women and Politeness*, 209.

[35] Ryland Jr., *Church Book*, 2.

[36] Specifically, beliefs related to the "modern question" and practices including the offer of the gospel in preaching were being reevaluated, most notably by Ryland and his friends, Andrew Fuller and John Sutcliff.

"A THOUSAND BEAUTEOUS DYES": ANNE STEELE AND THE GOD OF COLOUR[1]

Michael Haykin

The publication of Isaac Newton's (1643–1727) *Opticks* in 1704 not only revolutionized the way that colour was perceived by science, but also rejuvenated the world of colour for poetry after an era in which poets, under the influence of Cartesian inner reflection, had neglected its potency for their craft.[2] The Scottish poet James Thomson (1700–1748) well typifies this rejuvenation. *The Seasons*—especially *Summer* and *Spring*, which Thomson wrote over the course of 1727 and 1728—clearly views the world through Newtonian eyes and reveals Thomson to be "undoubtedly the great literary colorist" of the first half of the eighteenth century.[3] Now, one of those who deeply appreciated Thomson's poetic classic, *The Seasons*, was Anne Steele (1717–1778), by common reckoning the most significant Baptist hymnwriter of the long eighteenth century.[4] Her poem

---

[1] For help with this essay, I would like to express my profound thanks to Prof. Timothy Whelan of Georgia Southern University.

[2] Marjorie Hope Nicolson, *Newton Demands the Muse: Newton's Opticks and the 18th Century Poets* (1946, Princeton: Princeton University Press, 1966), 19, 22; Timothy Campbell, "Literature and the Performing Arts" in Carole P. Biggam and Kirsten Wolf, ed., *A Cultural History of Color in the Age of Enlightenment*, A Cultural History of Color, vol. 4 (London: Bloomsbury Academic, 2021), 131–36.

[3] Campbell, "Literature and the Performing Arts," 135. See also the argument of Nicolson, *Newton Demands the Muse*, 43–49.

[4] On Steele as a hymnwriter, see especially Karen Smith, "The Community and the Believers: A Study of Calvinistic Baptist Spirituality in Some Towns and Villages of Hampshire and the Borders of Wiltshire, c.1730–1830" (DPhil dissertation, Regent's Park College, University of Oxford, 1986); Sharon James, *In Trouble and in Joy: Four Women Who Lived for God* (Darlington, UK: Evangelical Press, 2003), 115–64; J. R. Broome, *A Bruised Reed: The Life and Times of Anne Steele* (Harpenden, UK: Gospel Standard Trust Publications, 2007); Nancy Jiwon Cho, "'The Ministry of Song': Unmarried British Women's Hymn Writing, 1760–1936" (PhD thesis, Durham University, 2007), 43–84; Cynthia Y. Aalders, *To Express the Ineffable: The Hymns and Spirituality of Anne Steele* (Milton Keynes, UK, Colorado Springs, and Hyderabad, India: Paternoster, 2008); Priscilla Chan, *Anne Steele and Her Spiritual Vision: Seeing God in the Peaks, Valleys and Plateaus of Life* (Grand Rapids, MI: Reformation Heritage Books,

"In a Dirty Cold Village" recalls the way that the Steele household sought to "shorten the dull winter nights" by reading the poetry of Thomson or Alexander Pope (1688–1744) or Edward Young (1683–1765). The poem depicts the family seated around "a good fire of od'riferous Peat," as one of them read to the others by candlelight from either Thomson or these other two poets. It was "scarce needful to mention," Steele added, that "all sit delighted with sober attention" when the works of these men were read.[5] Although Steele used chromatic terms less often than Thompson, her poetry and prose demonstrate that she shared his delight in colour.

"All the Varyed Colours"

Like Thomson, Steele was fascinated by the seasons, especially spring, which she once called the "Queen of seasons."[6] It was in the springtime that the fields near "Grandfathers," the spacious Steele home in Broughton, Hampshire, were carpeted with "flowers of a thousand beauteous dyes"[7] and this "beauteous queen" was

> Drest in a robe of lively green
> That cheers the gazing eye:
> Green is the ground, but o'er it spread,
> Wrought with inimitable skill,
> Beyond description's boldest quill,
> By Nature's animating hand,
> A various rich embroidery glows;
> And though the work no real error knows,
> All with the nicest care exactly plann'd;
> The tints in seeming, sweet confusion lie;

2012); and Joseph V. Carmichael, *The Sung Theology of the English Particular Baptist Revival: A Theological Analysis of Anne Steele's Hymns in Rippon's Hymnal*, Monographs in Baptist History, vol. 15 (Eugene, OR: Pickwick Publications, 2021).

[5] Steele, "[In a Dirty Cold Village]," lines 3–6, 19–24, in Julie B. Griffin, ed., *Nonconformist Women Writers, 1720–1840* (London: Pickering & Chatto, 2011), 2:147. For a list of Steele's reading, see Aalders, *To Express the Ineffable*, 183–85.

[6] Steele, "Ode to Spring, written in March," line 1 in Griffin, ed., *Nonconformist Women Writers*, 2:1. In a letter that Steele wrote to her brother William Steele on May 16, 1755, she told him that "Autumn almost rivals the charms of Spring" (Griffin, 2:284).

[7] Steele, "Ingratitude Reproved," line 8 in Griffin, 1:227.

Here shines the purple, there the red,
Here yellow, snowy white, and azure's lovely dye.[8]

Three of the six hues named here—red, yellow, and "snowy white"—virtually never appear in the rest of Steele's literary corpus.[9] As for purple, Steele used it to describe the robe that was put on Christ, the coming of evening, a "purple cluster" of the grape vine, and wine's "rich vintage" [that] flows in purple streams."[10] The "lovely dye" of azure appears more frequently and that with reference to heaven and even terrestrial meadowlands. Detailing the evening sight of an "azure plain," Steele wrote of "unnumber'd beauties" that "inspire my breast with wonder and delight."[11] Properly, though this chromatic term should be associated with the sky, and so it is understandable that reference is made to the "azure canopy of Heaven."[12]

Of all the chromatic terms mentioned in this stanza, it is green that Steele most frequently used and in which she clearly found special pleasure.[13] During spring and summer the meadows near her home were "array'd in smiling green"[14] and the one who dressed them receives their silent praise:

---

[8] Steele, "Ode to Spring," lines 52–64 in Griffin, 2:2–3. Cf. Anne Steele, Letter to Mary Steele Wakeford, undated (Griffin, 2:329): "all the varied colours of the blooming spring."

[9] For a reference to "spotless white," see Steele, "To a Flower," line 6 in Griffin, 2:6. White is also implied in the lines "Thy sovereign mercy can bestow,/A heart more pure than falling snow" ("Psalm 51," lines 27–28 in Griffin, 1:304), an allusion to the statement in Isaiah 1:18 that God can make the sins of the repentant as "white as snow." Steele used yellow in a letter to her stepmother, Anne Cator Steele (1689–1760), where she referred to a "yellow gown" (Letter to Anne Cator Steele, May 21, 1739, in Griffin, 2:264). By contrast, of all the colours, it was "the golden light" of yellow that most entranced Thomson (Nicolson, *Newton Demands the Muse*, 45–46).

[10] Steele, "Redeeming Love," line 88 in Griffin, ed., *Nonconformist Women Writers*, 1:37; Letter to William Steele, IV, June 28, 1736, in Griffin, 2:260; "Psalm 105," lines 97–98 in Griffin, 1:331; and "Psalm 104," line 54 in Griffin, 1:327.

[11] Steele, "An Evening Meditation," lines 42–43 in Griffin, 1:161. For a similar use of the phrase "azure plain," see her "A Rural Hymn," line 100 in Griffin, 1:64.

[12] Steele, "Recovery from Sickness," line 47 in Griffin, 1:236. See Nicolson, *Newton Demands the Muse*, 44, for the distinction between azure—a sky-blue—and blue. In her poem on Psalm 104, Steele spoke of the heavens as a "radiant curtain of celestial blue, / Adorn'd with stars and suns" (Griffin, ed., *Nonconformist Women Writers*, 1:326).

[13] The same was true for Thomson: see Nicolson, *Newton Demands the Muse*, 44.

[14] Steele, "Meditating on Creation and Providence," line 17 in Griffin, ed., *Nonconformist Women Writers*, 1:34.

Ye lovely, verdant fields,
In all your green array,
Though silent, speak his praise,
Who makes you bright and gay…[15]

The poetess herself, as she surveys "with pleasing rapture" these meadows of "smiling green in rich embroidery drest," is likewise inspired "with wonder and delight."[16] And given the pleasure she derived from the colour green, it is no surprise that Steele envisaged this hue to be prominent in the world to come:

The Heavenly Hills crown'd with immortal green
Display a Paradise of endless Bliss.
There fairer scenes than Eden ever knew!
Fairer than all luxuriant Fancy paints![17]

Other colours like brown, blue, and crimson, appear sparingly in Steele's writings. Brown, for example, is found once in the verb "embrown." Steele told one of her correspondents that "Winter is coming, cold, joyless Winter!" When it does, "no fragrant blossoms shall perfume the air,…nor Autumn shall embrown the ripening field, nor paint the blushing fruit."[18] Then, the blue sky is a means by which the beauty of Steele's God is displayed to her soul:

…my soul would see her Saviour God,
The living source of all that's fair and good:
His beauties, though at humble distance, view
And trace him in the scenes his pencil drew.
…His beauty glitters in the pearly dew,
And smiles amid the bright etherial blue
Which paints yon spacious arch…[19]

As for crimson, a striking employment of this colour occurs in relation to the death of Christ:

---

[15] Steele, "A Rural Hymn," lines 48–51 in Griffin, 1:62.
[16] Steele, "An Evening Meditation," lines 37–38, and 43 in Griffin, 1:161.
[17] Steele, "A Prospect of Life," lines 47–50 in Griffin, 2:131.
[18] Steele, Letter to Mary Steele Wakeford, undated, in Griffin, 2:291.
[19] Steele, "On Reading Mr. Hervey's Meditations," lines 59–62 and 71–73 in Griffin, 1:174.

Stretch'd on the Cross the Saviour dies;
Hark! his expiring groans arise!
See, from his hands, his feet, his side,
Runs down the sacred crimson tide![20]

J. R. Watson rightly sees here the influence of Isaac Watts (1674–1748), namely, his most famous hymn, known to modern congregations as "When I Survey the Wondrous Cross."[21] Originally written by Watts in 1707 as a communion hymn, this hymn appeared in his *Hymns and Spiritual Songs* with the title "Crucifixion to the World by the Cross of Christ" and a subtitle reference to Galatians 6:14.[22] Watts's hymn called upon the singer/hearer to meditate with the mind's eye upon the crucified Jesus and to "see from his Head, his Hands, his Feet,/Sorrow and Love flow mingled down" (stanza 3). For the Christian, this death—graphically described as "His dying crimson"—means that the believer must reckon himself or herself as "dead to all the Globe" (stanza 4).[23] The influence of Watts's wording, even to the use of crimson, which Steele normally never uses in relation to the death of Christ, is obvious. Yet it is noteworthy that, diverging from the emphases of Watts's hymn, Steele stresses that life and salvation issue from the "sacred crimson tide":

But life attends the deathful sound,
And flows from every bleeding wound;
The vital stream, how free it flows,
To save and cleanse his rebel foes![24]

---

[20] Steele, "A Dying Saviour," lines 1–4 in Griffin, 1:154.

[21] J. R. Watson, "Eighteenth-Century Hymn Writers," in R. Lemon, E. Mason, J. Roberts, and C. Rowland, ed., *The Blackwell Companion to the Bible in English Literature* (Oxford: Blackwell Publishing, 2009), 336–37. See also Cho, "The Ministry of Song," 77.

[22] For a critical edition of this hymn, see Selma L. Bishop, *Isaac Watts, Hymns and Spiritual Songs 1707–1748: A Study in Early Eighteenth Century Language Changes* (London: Faith Press, 1962), 353.

[23] From 1757 onwards this stanza was regularly omitted from hymnals. For the date, see Donald Davie, *The Eighteenth-Century Hymn in England* (Cambridge: Cambridge University Press, 1993), 40.

[24] Steele, "A Dying Saviour," lines 5–8 in Griffin, ed., *Nonconformist Women Writers*, 1:154. For one other use of crimson in this way, see Steele, "God's Omnipresence," in Griffin, 2:237: "Life flows amid the crimson tide / Which issued from the wounded side / Of Jesus when, for guilty man, he suffer'd, groan'd and died!

"Stained with Black Enormous Blotts"

There is one chromatic adjective, though, that Steele employed with great frequency, namely, black. In line with a tradition of associating sin with blackness—a tradition that reaches back to the second century though it has no biblical precedent[25]—Steele used black to describe humanity's fallen state. All sins are "black rebellions," "vile ingratitude" in the face of divine grace and numerous blessings of God.[26] So even though our lives be "unstain'd with black enormous blotts [*sic*],"[27] yet, since in "our first parent's crime we fell" and are now "Deep ting'd with all the seeds of ill,"

Black o'er wrath-devoted heads
Avenging justice frown'd;
While hell disclos'd her deepest shades,
And horrors rose around.[28]

It is noteworthy that Steele not only depicted sin as black, but here also divine judgment. Steele used the same chromatic term in this latter regard when she asked, "'Thy fierce displeasure who can bear?' 'Tis death array'd in black despair."[29] The solution to this horrific situation is Christ's "Redeeming Blood"—as already noted—where sinners, "though black with guilt and stain'd with sin," can find total cleansing and where their "lusts expire beneath the flood."[30]

Steele also used black to speak of the challenges that Christians face. From personal experience she knew that the walk of faith was not free from doubt and "black Melancholy."[31] As she asked, "And can my vile ungrateful heart / Still

---

[25] See Michael A. G. Haykin, "'I Am Black and Beautiful': Blackness and the Patristic Exegesis of Song of Songs 1:5" in his and Barry H. Howson, ed., *Reading Scripture, Learning Wisdom: Essays in Honour of David G. Barker* (Peterborough, ON: Joshua Press, 2021), 159–170.

[26] Steele, "On the 17th February a Day Appointed for General Prayer Etc.," lines 7, 9, 13–14 in Griffin, ed., *Nonconformist Women Writers*, 2:103. "Deep" is the "dye" of a person's sins, according to "Psalm 51," line 33 in Griffin, 1:305.

[27] Steele, "Epitaph," line 3 in Griffin, 2:146.

[28] Steele, "Redeeming Love," lines 13, 15, 17–20 in Griffin, 1:36. In an undated letter, Steele described Adam's sin as a "black rebellion" (Griffin, 2:289).

[29] Steele, "Psalm 88," lines 45–46 in Griffin, 1:315.

[30] Steele, "Hebrews 6:9 Version 1," lines 17–18, 20 in Griffin, 2:114.

[31] Steele, "[Thus in a Careless Hour I Trifling Wrote]," line 12 in Griffin, 2:150.

harbour black distrust and fear?"[32] Ultimately, though, her trust was in Christ's intercessory prayer for her among his people that was greater than all of her "black despairing thoughts."[33] Indeed, at the approach of the "eternal God…black doubt and gloomy fear / Retreat like mists before the rising sun."[34]

The one main positive employment of blackness in Steele's corpus is in her use of the phrase "sable veil of night." The moon and stars, she wrote in "Meditating on Creation and Providence," "deck the sable veil of night, / And speak their Maker's praise."[35] Again, in "Ingratitude Reproved," Steele declared, these "radiant orbs" that "deck the sable veil of night" display God's "wonderous [sic] glory."[36]

"Speak Sweet Conviction"

If Steele did not utilize individual chromatic hues as prolifically as James Thomson did in *The Seasons*, she nevertheless saw in the colours of nature a powerful witness to the existence and transcendence of the God of the Bible, who, for her, was clearly the God of colour who had filled this earth with rich chromatic hues. If the heavenly inhabitants in the "sable veil of night" praise their Maker, so do "a thousand beauteous dyes" that fill the human sight during the day. In "The Voice of the Creatures" Steele contrasted human painting with divine colouring to make this point:

> The flowery tribes, all blooming, rise
> Above the faint attempts of art;
> Their bright, inimitable dyes
> Speak sweet conviction to the heart.[37]

---

[32] Steele, "Complaining at the Throne of Grace," lines 33–34 in Griffin, 1:132. For an excellent discussion of these doubts and suffering in Steele's life, see Aalders, *To Express the Ineffable*, 102–35.

[33] Steele, "The Intercession of Christ," line 9 in Griffin, ed., *Nonconformist Women Writers*, 1:77.

[34] Steele, "The Wish," lines 11, 26–27 in Griffin, 1:252.

[35] Steele, "Meditating on Creation and Providence," lines 31–32 in Griffin, 1:34.

[36] Steele, "Ingratitude Reproved," lines 19–21 in Griffin, 1:228.

[37] Steele, "The Voice of the Creatures," lines 25–28 in Griffin, 1:60. The verb "paint" and its cognates bear a negative connotation more often than not. See Steele, "The Desire of Knowledge a Proof of Immortality," lines 28–29 in Griffin, 1:220; Steele, "Pleasure," lines 5–8 in Griffin, 1:231; Steele, "Wishing for Real Pleasure," lines 10–18 in Griffin, 2:59; Steele, "Acquaintance with God the Supreme Good," lines 14–15 in

God employs the colours that adorn the various flowers of the field to speak "sweet conviction" to the human heart, bearing witness to his existence and power. Nature's colours constitute divine speech to fallen humanity.[38]

In the poem "Ingratitude Reproved," Steele thus called upon her heart to respond to this colourful witness with praise:

Ye lovely offspring of the ground,
Flowers of a thousand beauteous dyes,
You spread your Maker's glory round…

My God, shall every creature join
In praises to thy glorious name,
And this ungrateful heart of mine
Refuse the universal theme?
Well may the stars and winds, the birds and flowers,
Reprove the heart that brings not all its powers.[39]

From the frequent occurrence of the phrase "a thousand beauteous dyes" or something akin to this in Steele's writings, it is obvious that this phrase was a favored way by which she sought to capture the colourful beauty of the world around her home and village.[40] In her "Ode on a Rural Prospect in June," the link between colour and the worship of its creator is even more obvious:

Every plant, and every flower
Speak his wisdom, goodness, power:
With sweet attractive lustre how they shine!
Ye beauteous scenes, 'tis yours to show
The hand from whence your blessings flow:

Griffin, 2:224; Steele, "[How Long Shall Courts]," line 2: "false painted pleasures," in Griffin, 2:142.

[38] The wording of this sentence was suggested by a comment made by Prof. Kirk Wellum of Toronto Baptist Seminary in a sermon that he preached at Muskoka Bible Centre, Huntsville, Ontario, on July 11, 2021.

[39] Steele, "Ingratitude Reproved," lines 7–9, 25–30 in Griffin, 1:227–228.

[40] See Steele, "A Rural Hymn," lines 58, 82 in Griffin, 1:63; Steele, "An Evening Meditation," lines 42–43 in Griffin, 1:161; Steele, "Desiring a Taste of Real Joy," line 7: "beauteous colours," in Griffin, 1:109; Steele, Letter to William Steele, IV, June 28, 1736, in Griffin, 2:260.

To wonder, love, adore, and praise be mine!

While yonder wide-extended fields,
With eager gaze my eye surveys;
The scene a thousand beauties yields,
A thousand blessings claim my praise.[41]

Here Steele moves from colour ("sweet attractive lustre") to beauty ("beauteous scenes" and "a thousand beauties") and finally to adoration ("To wonder, love, adore, and praise be mine!" and "A thousand blessings claim my praise"). For Steele, colour, when rightly understood, is a pathway to worship.

Coda

Steele was well aware that these colourful beauties of nature, these "shining dyes,"[42] were transient: "the colours fade, the lovely form decay."[43] But such was not the final word about colour. When Steele's stepmother, Anne Cator Steele, died in 1760, Steele penned a poem for her half-sister, Mary Steele Wakeford (1724–1772) and asked her to imagine meeting her mother in glory:

Urania, come, thy fairest colours bring,
Present the dear departed to our view.[44]

Protestant tradition had taken over the figure of Urania, who was the ancient Muse of Astronomy, as the Christian Muse. She thus appeared, for example, in John Milton's *Paradise Lost*, where Steele probably first encountered this literary idea.[45] But even Urania is not up to this task of "painting" the triumphant saints:

But not thy noblest strokes, thy sweetest force,
In equal colours e'er can represent
A soul made perfect in the realms of light,

---

[41] Steele, "Ode on a Rural Prospect in June," lines 39–48 in Griffin, 2:29.

[42] Steele, "To Belinda," line 15 in Griffin, 1:202. For a similar use of "glowing colours," see Steele, "The Death-Watch," line 12 in Griffin, 1:186.

[43] Steele, "To Belinda," line 18 in Griffin, 1:202.

[44] Steele, "To Amira on the Sudden Death of Her Mother," lines 36–37 in Griffin, 2:26.

[45] Griffin, ed., *Nonconformist Women Writers*, 1:367n36.

And in her Saviour's lovely image drest.
Nor can thy tints, though borrow'd from the sky,
Describe the vigorous life, the active joy
Which animates a citizen of heaven.
Urania, drop thy pencil…[46]

Although the colours of heaven and its holy inhabitants cannot be caught on any terrestrial canvas, they, like this world's entire spectrum of created hues, bear witness to the glory of God.

Steele obviously took great delight in the colouring of this world. And surely it is correct to say that she anticipated that the delight that God has in filling this earth with colour will be replicated in the world to come—a realm of light and rich chromatic hues.

---

[46] Steele, "To Amira on the Sudden Death of Her Mother," lines 43–50 in Griffin, 2:27.

"JESUS OUR SUPREME DELIGHT": THE HYMNS OF ANNE STEELE IN C. H. SPURGEON'S *OUR OWN HYMN BOOK*

Peter J. Morden

On Sunday, January 14, 1866, the Victorian "Prince of Preachers," Charles Haddon Spurgeon (1834–1892), delivered a sermon at the Metropolitan Tabernacle in London based on Psalm 147:16–18, verses which, in the Authorized Version, include the words: "He casteth forth his ice....who can stand before his cold? He...melteth them: he causeth his wind to blow, and the waters flow." Spurgeon preached about the different ways God brought "frost" and "thaw" in both creation and salvation. At the heart of his message, he quoted four stanzas from Anne Steele (1716–1778), the premier Baptist hymnwriter of the eighteenth century, using John Rippon's *Selection of Hymns*, the highly influential hymnal which the church used in public worship at that time.[1] It was as he expounded on the theme of salvation that he cited Steele's lines:

Stern winter throws his icy chains,
Encircling nature round:
How bleak, how comfortless the plains,
Late with gay verdure crown'd!

The sun withdraws his vital beams,
And light and warmth depart:
And drooping lifeless nature seems
An emblem of my heart—

My heart, where mental winter reigns
In night's dark mantle clad,
Confined in cold inactive chains;
How desolate and sad!

---

[1] John Rippon, ed., *A Selection of Hymns*...28th ed. (London, 1828) in which Steele's composition, entitled "Winter," is number 506. It was included in the first edition of Rippon's hymnal, published in 1787, and in subsequent editions.

Return, O blissful sun, and bring
Thy soul-reviving ray;
This mental winter shall be spring,
This darkness cheerful day.

Spurgeon applied these words to his hearers: "Poor sinner….Perhaps the Master has sent a frost to you, and you think it will never end. Let me encourage you to hope….Steele's words will just suit your mournful yet hopeful state."[2] Spurgeon's vast congregation—at that time the largest in the world—were thus encouraged to receive freshly the "light and warmth" of God's love.

1866 was a significant year in the worshipping life of the Metropolitan Tabernacle as it saw the publication of a new hymn book, edited by Spurgeon himself, which was to be used instead of Rippon's *Selection* in their services. *Our Own Hymn Book* appeared in October and was warmly received by a wide range of evangelical churches who appreciated Spurgeon's biblically orthodox, experiential piety.[3] Yet it was among Spurgeon's particular constituency, especially the churches that were served by former students of the Pastors' College he had founded in 1856, that its influence was strongest.[4] The majority of these churches quickly abandoned Rippon's *Selection*—which had enjoyed a resurgence in sales due to Spurgeon's support—in favor of *Our Own Hymn Book.* This became the new hymnal of choice for those who identified with the Spurgeonic tradition. The book went through multiple editions and after Spurgeon's death the compilers of his *Autobiography* recorded that his hopes for it had been "fully realized."[5] The appearance of a *Supplement to Our Own Hymn*

---

[2] C. H. Spurgeon, *Metropolitan Tabernacle Pulpit (MTP)*, 12.670, January 14, 1866, 33.

[3] See, e.g., the enthusiastic review of the *Wesleyan Times* which Spurgeon reprinted verbatim in *The Sword and The Trowel (ST)* (London: Passmore and Alabaster, 1865–92), October 1866, 474–76.

[4] See C. H. Spurgeon, *Autobiography: Compiled from His Diary, Letters, and Records…*, 4 vols. (London: Passmore and Alabaster, 1897–99), 3:320–21. For the college, see Peter J. Morden, *"Communion with Christ and His People": The Spirituality of C. H. Spurgeon (1834–92)* (Eugene, OR: Wipf and Stock, 2014), 199–203.

[5] C. H. Spurgeon, *Autobiography*, 3:320. There were new editions in, e.g., 1867, 1868, 1873, and 1885. These were essentially reprints. In this chapter I have cited from the first edition: C. H. Spurgeon, ed., *Our Own Hymn Book: A Selection of Psalms and Hymns for Public, Social and Private Worship (OOHB)* (London: Passmore and Alabaster, 1866).

Book in 1898 testified to the work's enduring popularity and helped extend the life of the original compilation.[6] Moreover, and as the hymnal's editor had planned, the book was used by many to augment family and personal devotions. Spurgeon's colporteurs facilitated its widespread distribution by going house to house selling the book alongside other Spurgeonic literature. *Our Own Hymn Book* had a deep impact and also cast a long shadow, shaping and helping give expression to the faith of many.

Given Spurgeon's obvious appreciation of Steele, it is little surprise that her hymns feature strongly in his hymnal. True, he included only nineteen of Steele's compositions, whereas Rippon had used fifty-two.[7] But Steele still featured more prominently in *Our Own Hymn Book* than any other eighteenth-century Baptist writer, and Spurgeon's regard for her work is evident.[8] The last forty years have seen a welcome revival of scholarly interest in Steele, with the quality and importance of her work increasingly recognized.[9] Her influence was especially strong in Particular Baptist churches, although it extended far and wide, mediated through her published works and some especially important eighteenth-century hymnals in which her verses were prominent.[10] These included the pioneering Bristol *Collection* of hymns, which was the first Baptist hymnbook;[11] and Rippon's *Selection*, which saw remarkable success.[12] However, whilst Rippon's hymnal was dominant in English Calvinistic Baptist churches in the first quarter

---

[6] *Supplement to Our Own Hymn Book* (London: Passmore and Alabaster, 1898).

[7] The nineteen hymns are 143, 199, 324, 326, 367, 388, 390, 423, 461, 482, 496, 616, 622, 623, 657, 669, 696, 837, 862.

[8] Cf. *MTP*, 35.2071, May 1, 1884, 107.

[9] See, e.g., Cynthia Y. Aalders, *To Express the Ineffable: The Hymns and Spirituality of Anne Steele* (Milton Keynes: Paternoster, 2008); J. R. Broome, *A Bruised Reed: The Life and Times of Anne Steele* (Trowbridge: Gospel Standard, 2007); Priscilla Chan, *Anne Steele and Her Spiritual Vision* (Grand Rapids, MI: Reformation Heritage, 2012); Nancy Jiwon Cho, "'The Ministry of Song': Unmarried British Women's Hymn Writing, 1760–1936" (PhD thesis, University of Durham, 2007), 43–84.

[10] For Anne Steele's works, see *Poems on Subjects Chiefly Devotional*, 2 vols. (Bristol: W. Pine, 1760). A third volume, *Miscellaneous Pieces in Verse and Prose*, was published alongside these in 1780.

[11] John Ash and Caleb Evans, eds., *A Collection of Hymns Adapted for Public Worship* (Bristol: W. Pine, 1769). Sixty-two of Steele's compositions are included.

[12] Joseph V. Carmichael, *The Sung Theology of the English Particular Baptist Revival: A Theological Analysis of Anne Steele's Hymns in Rippon's Hymnal* (Eugene, OR: Wipf and Stock, 2021), examines "Rippon's Steele," analysing her fifty-two hymns included in the *Selection*.

of the nineteenth century, it was gradually abandoned in favor of newer works that were cheaper, easier to navigate, and included more recent compositions alongside the older hymns, as was seen in the case of the Metropolitan Tabernacle.[13] This essay shows one way—through the popularity of *Our Own Hymn Book*—that Steele's influence extended into the mid to late nineteenth century and considers the nature of that influence. The following analysis of the nineteen hymns considers three important themes.[14]

Evangelical Calvinism

Steele's theology was shaped by her adherence to Particular (Calvinistic) Baptist principles, especially as they were expressed at her chapel at Broughton, Hampshire, which was pastored by her father, William Steele. This church was firmly committed to particular redemption and other Calvinistic tenets. Working squarely within this theological framework, Anne Steele wrote that God is "sovereign" over all things, including salvation. Only God's "sovereign love" can "melt the stubborn soul" and bend it to his "divine control."[15] Put simply, the sinner's only hope is "sovereign grace."[16]

It is little surprise that Spurgeon included lines such as these in his hymnal, as he was well known as a doughty defender of Calvinism. His Calvinistic commitments were not quite as straightforward as is sometimes supposed, and they shifted somewhat in the course of his ministry. Nevertheless, he was avowedly a Calvinist throughout his life.[17] This was unusual in the later nineteenth century which, as Ian Sellers states, increasingly saw the "tide" of opinion "running against religious particularism of any form."[18] *Our Own Hymn Book*, with sections and subsections with titles such as "Predestination in Connection with Grace," "The Covenant," and "The Work of Grace as a Whole," helped fan into flame a limited but nevertheless significant revival of Calvinistic theology and spirituality. Steele's own expressions of Calvinistic sentiments took their place in the new hymnal, helping give shape and voice to the beliefs and piety of this new generation.

---

[13] *ST*, October 1866, 474–76.

[14] Prayer is another theme that could have been treated explicitly. On this, see, e.g., "Advocate," *OOHB*, 367.

[15] "Making God a Refuge," *OOHB*, 388, v.6.

[16] "Jesus," *OOHB*, 388, v.4.

[17] For discussion, see Morden, *Spurgeon*, 39–43.

[18] Ian Sellers, "John Howard Hinton, Theologian," *Baptist Quarterly* 33, no. 3 (July 1989), 123.

Given this stress on God's sovereignty, it might be supposed that Steele's hymns have little space for human responsibility. Yet this is not the case. In one of the hymns included in *Our Own Hymn Book*, she sets out the gospel of God's love expressed through his son. The hymn includes a strong stress on the gospel as the "mercy" of God. Only he can "draw" "reluctant hearts" to himself. Thus, the sovereignty of God in salvation is firmly underscored. But the hymn also sounds a complementary note, one of invitation (indeed, it is placed by Spurgeon in his subsection headed "Gospel Invitations"). God invites sinners to come to him. The only appropriate human response is to hear and "obey" the "gracious call" and trust in Jesus. Indeed, such a response should be made without "delay."[19] Divine sovereignty and human responsibility are thus held in careful balance.

This twin stress—on God's sovereignty on the one hand and human responsibility on the other—locates Steele in the broad stream of invitational Calvinism within which many earlier, seventeenth-century Particular Baptists had stood. Just one representative is John Bunyan, whose vigorous evangelistic ministry was indicated by the title of one of his treatises, *Come and Welcome to Christ Jesus*.[20] Yet this outwardly focused, "moderate" Calvinism saw even greater expression in the fusion of Calvinistic doctrine with the evangelistic impulses of the eighteenth-century evangelical revival. Steele was certainly shaped by the revival, with its influence mediated by, for example, her friendship with the evangelical president of the Bristol Academy, Caleb Evans. Forces associated with the revival began to flow into Baptist life from the 1730s onwards, although slowly at first. By the 1760s, the movement was giving many Calvinistic Baptist congregations a significant transfusion of life, bringing renewal to declining churches. Spurgeon also stood firmly in this tradition; hence *Our Own Hymn Book* contains many compositions exhorting men and women to come to Christ and put their faith in him. Steele and Spurgeon shared a basic commitment to an understanding of Calvinism that saw no contradiction in emphasising human responsibility alongside divine sovereignty.

Faithful Suffering

The second theme to consider is Steele's response to suffering. Many biographical sketches highlight her own personal suffering, sometimes in ways which stretch the available evidence beyond the breaking point. The story of the

---

[19] "The Saviour Calls," *OOHB*, 496.

[20] This work was first published in 1678.

drowning of her supposed fiancé in 1737, the day before their wedding, has often been told. This is despite the absence of firm evidence that Steele and the man in question, James Elcombe, were actually engaged.[21] Although she did know him, his death is unlikely to have affected her to the extent that is often claimed. The sensationalized accounts of this supposed incident were especially prevalent during the Victorian period.[22] Nancy Cho is justified in her comment: this 'story of thwarted love" reveals less about Steele and more about Victorian "ideologies concerning marriage, such as the notion that a single woman could not be complete."[23] Yet, as Cho demonstrates, the "notion that a single woman could not be complete" does not appear to have been held by Steele herself. She turned down a marriage proposal from Baptist pastor and fellow hymnwriter Benjamin Beddome five years after Elcombe's death and expressed a reluctance to marry at all in a letter to her half sister, Mary Steele Wakeford.[24] It is probable that remaining single was a deliberate choice, made in part to give her the time and space to develop her writing. In respect of friendship, she was at the center of a rich circle of friends which included her close-knit extended family and drew on the wider network of Particular Baptist life in Hampshire and West Country.[25] This was both intellectually stimulating and socially satisfying. The Steeles as a family were financially secure; her father was a successful timber merchant whose customers included the British navy, so he was able to pastor the Broughton congregation without remuneration. After his death in 1769 Anne was welcomed into her brother's comfortable home. Thus, the picture of Anne Steele as the lonely, heroic sufferer, written in significant degree to align with Victorian sensibilities, needs thorough revision.

Nevertheless, in a number of ways Steele's life was not easy. She experienced prolonged bouts of physical illness, faced the death of well-loved family members, and was bedridden for the final years of her life. Unsurprisingly, then, the reality of personal suffering surfaces in her published work, including hymns

---

[21] The story probably first appeared in Joseph Ivimey, *A History of the English Baptists* IV (London: Taylor Hinton, 1830), 312. The evidence against it includes a letter in the Steele family papers. See J. R. Watson and Nancy Cho, "Anne Steele's Drowned Fiancé," *British Journal of Eighteenth-Century Studies* 28 (2005), 117–21.

[22] See, e.g., Emma R. Pitman, *Lady Hymn Writers* (London: Thomas Nelson, 1892), 67–70.

[23] Cho, "Women's Hymn Writing," 47–48.

[24] Benjamin Beddome to Anne Steele, December 23, 1742 (STE 3/13 [i]); Anne Steele to Mary Steele Wakeford. "Silvania" and "Amira" Letters (STE 3/10 [iii]), Angus Library, Regent's Park College, Oxford.

[25] Cf. Cho, "Women's Hymn Writing," 48.

Spurgeon incorporated into *Our Own Hymn Book*. One composition, "Making God a Refuge," encourages worshippers to persevere in prayer through times of suffering.[26] Another hymn, "The Request," reinforces this point, with the first stanza concluding, "let this petition rise." This second hymn also gives additional guidance for those who suffer. There is a resignation to the will of God expressed in the line, "low at Thy feet my soul would lie." Spurgeon's placing this hymn at the head of his section "Peace and Resignation" seems appropriate. This is not fatalism, though; rather, it is a belief that in the presence of the Savior and in submission to him is safety. It is here that "eternal life is found." Further, the time of suffering should impel the faithful believer to greater commitment: "The blessings of Thy grace impart / and make me live for Thee."[27] The concern is not to understand the "Why?" of suffering. As far as this goes, the hymnwriter is content to rest in the providence of God. Rather, the hymn focuses on the question "How?" Specifically, how does someone respond well in the midst of suffering? Such a response will be authentic, with the worshipper willing to admit to doubts and fears. Yet it will also be faithful, clinging onto God and living only for him. Those who sang Steele's lines were invited to make this authentic, faith-filled spirituality their own.

How can the "resignation" of which Steele speaks (we might say "contentment") and the radical commitment she calls for be sustained through the storms of suffering? She urges the worshipper to look to God and the gospel for inspiration and strength. Eternal realities, she declares, far outweigh all of earth's potential joys and also serve to put suffering in perspective. The third and fourth stanzas of "The Request" expand on this theme:

Eternal life Thy words impart;
On these my fainting spirit lives;
Here sweeter comforts cheer my heart,
Than all the round of nature gives.

Let earth's alluring joys combine,
While Thou art near, in vain they call;
One smile, one blissful smile of Thine,
My gracious Lord, outweighs them all.[28]

---

[26] "Making God a Refuge," *OOHB*, 622.
[27] "The Request," *OOHB*, 669, vs. 1, 5, 2.
[28] "The Request," *OOHB*, 669, vs. 3–4.

Many of Steele's lines extol the beauty of the natural world, but here, rather than highlighting its splendour or using it as a metaphor for salvation, she contrasts nature with the very presence of God himself. All "the round of nature"—the yearly rhythm of the seasons which was so important to her—is as nothing compared to one smile from the face of God. Through the pursuit of God, a humble yet confident faith could be nurtured.

Steele's genius is, in the view of this present writer, highlighted here. She does not expound Christian themes in a formulaic way, nor does she major on subjective experience. Rather she fuses orthodox belief with ardent piety in ways that are both intensely personal and appropriate for congregational singing. Moreover, she has the ability to be both authentic, giving expression to pain, fears, and doubts; and hopeful, affirming the faithfulness of God. Thus, her hymns often lead worshippers on a journey, in this case a journey through suffering. She takes seriously both the human condition and the goodness of God and gives worshippers the words that enable them to do the same.

Joy in Jesus

Consequently, although the reality of suffering is woven into the fabric of much of Steele's writing, it is a mistake to portray her as a gloomy writer, for she wrestles with the issue in such a way as to put it in larger perspective and show the triumph of faith and hope. Further consideration of her corpus reinforces the view that her writing is in fact characterized by life and warmth, peppered with words such as "bliss" and "rejoice." As already noted, Steele enjoyed rich, satisfying friendships, a dimension of her life to which her extant correspondence gives eloquent testimony.[29] Moreover, a focus on God and his goodness, especially as this is revealed in Jesus, permeates her writing and leads to expressions of heartfelt joy. It is this theme—joy in Jesus—that is considered in the remainder of this chapter. It is much in evidence in the Steele hymns selected for *Our Own Hymn Book*. One example is hymn 388, which is simply entitled "Jesus." The lines pour out praise to God for Christ's incarnation and atonement. The hymn is quoted here in full:

Jesus, in Thy transporting name,
What blissful glories rise!
Jesus! the angels' sweetest theme,
The wonder of the skies!

---

[29] Cf. Cho, "Women's Hymn Writing," 44–45; 48–53.

Didst Thou forsake Thy radiant crown,
And boundless realms of day,
Aside Thy robes of glory thrown,
To dwell with feeble clay.

Victorious love! Can language tell
The wonders of Thy power,
Which conquered all the force of hell,
In that tremendous hour?

Is there a heart that will not bend
To Thy divine control?
Descend, O sovereign Love, descend,
And melt the stubborn soul! [30]

The inadequacy of language to tell God's story ("Can language tell / The wonders of Thy power?") is one of the recurring—and innovative—themes of Steele's writing.[31] This hymn contains some beautifully crafted phrases, not least in the description of the incarnation, with God in Christ coming to "dwell with feeble clay." Thus, the incarnation is illuminated in telling poetic detail. The gospel is further unfolded as the cross is expounded. Steele held firmly to the doctrine of penal substitution as the primary way to understand the atonement, as did Spurgeon.[32] But here the complementary stress on Christ's victory over "all the force of hell" is set forth. Reflection on Christ's person and work engenders a spirit of praise, one which pervades the hymn. Focusing on Jesus results in profound transformation and gives rise to "blissful glories."

These emphases are woven into the fabric of almost all the Steele hymns in *Our Own Hymn Book*. Jesus is the source of "true pleasure"; contemplation of him leads to "bliss"; a sight of his "glories all divine" will surely call forth his people's praises.[33] This joy in Jesus will be "everlasting," based as it is on the

---

[30] "Jesus," *OOHB*, 38. Steele's original had seven stanzas. See *Poems…Chiefly Devotional*, 163–65.

[31] Cf. Aalders, *Express the Ineffable*, e.g., 4, 66.

[32] For Steele, see, e.g., "Redemption by Christ Alone," in Broome, *A Bruised Reed*, pt. 2, "Hymns of Anne Steele," 71, 284. For Spurgeon, see, e.g., *MTP*, 27.1611, July 31, 1881, 425–36.

[33] "Penitence and Hope," *OOHB*, 616, v. 3; "Goodness of God," *OOHB*, 199, v. 5; "King of Saints," *OOHB*, 390, v. 2.

unchanging character of God and the sure promises of his word.[34] What greater encouragements could there be to "look up…with cheerful eye" and share in this "joy divine"?[35] Such joy is to be personally expressed and shared with others, in corporate praise, prayer, and outreach. All those who "love the Saviour's name" should "joy to make it known."[36] Steele compositions not included in *Our Own Hymn Book* offer many further examples.[37] Yet it is likely that Spurgeon was especially drawn to her Christ-centered expressions of joy since this was one of the keynotes of his own life and ministry.[38] If so, his selection helps to highlight a vital yet neglected theme in Steele's hymnody, for the stress on joy through knowing and worshipping the living Christ is not always given the prominence it deserves in expositions of her writing. It is likely that the ways her life was redrawn to fit the Victorian convention of the lonely female sufferer have shaped a reading of her hymns that has accentuated her struggles and downplayed what is a central theme—joy in Jesus—so that it is minimized or even lost altogether. Yet her hymns repeatedly exude joyful praise to God. Those who sing them are exhorted to concentrate on Jesus and to make him their "supreme delight."[39]

Spurgeon himself suffered greatly, both physically as Steele had done and—it appears unlike Steele—mentally, struggling for most of his life with clinical depression.[40] Yet he challenged himself to maintain the joy which came through worship of Jesus and urged others to do the same. When he preached on the parable of the lost sheep on a Sunday in 1884, he spoke of the overwhelming joy he believed Jesus himself felt as he came to this world and then suffered on the cross. How might these events, which were the cause of so much suffering, occasion joy for Jesus? The answer is that the incarnation and atonement were deeply purposeful: Jesus came "out of boundless love" and died in order that men and women might be saved. It was what his life and passion accomplished in salvation history that gave Jesus such joy, and this was a joy that all who came to the Lord could share. Such joy—deep, overflowing, and eternal—is part of a Christian's birthright and an authenticating hallmark of true Christian experience. To close

---

[34] "Heavenly Teaching," *OOHB*, 482, v. 4.

[35] "Advocate," *OOHB*, 367, vs. 1, 3.

[36] "King of Saints," *OOHB*, 390, v. 1.

[37] The 1817 edition of *Poems…Chiefly Devotional* contains the following occurrences of relevant words: "joy" (forty-six times), "joys" (twenty-nine), "joyful" (nine), "bliss" (twenty-four), "blissful" (twenty-five).

[38] See Morden, *Spurgeon*, e.g., 286–95.

[39] "Redeeming Love," *OOHB*, 423, v. 3.

[40] He probably had bipolar disorder. On this and Spurgeon's physical ailments, see Morden, *Spurgeon*, 258–85.

the service, Spurgeon announced they would sing the four stanzas of the hymn, "Jesus," which have just been cited.[41] Joy in Jesus, a neglected but crucial dimension of Steele's hymnody, found fresh expression through these lines as they were sounded out once again. For Steele and for Spurgeon alike there was no higher theme.

Conclusion

As has been shown, Anne Steele's hymns in *Our Own Hymn Book* balance divine sovereignty and human responsibility, thus helping Christian believers articulate a dynamic that is at the heart of evangelical Calvinism, a tradition with which both Steele and Spurgeon identified. Her lines also helped worshippers give voice to their experience of suffering and articulate what an appropriate response to that suffering might be. The vital importance of hymnody in shaping the theology and spirituality of congregants has long been recognized. Most likely, this was even more the case in dissenting chapels than in Anglican churches, as "hymnody (as opposed to The Book of Common Prayer) provided a collective theology and identity."[42] Thus Steele's "sung theology" was surely more influential in molding the lived experience of Christian believers than the writings of many better-known theologians. This influence certainly extended to those who identified with the Spurgeonic constituency.

Steele's best-known hymn begins with the line "Father of mercies, in Thy word," and is included in *Our Own Hymn Book* under the title "Heavenly Teaching." It expresses a belief in the Bible as God's word and contains the stanzas:

Oh may these heavenly pages be
My ever dear delight;
And still new beauties may I see,
And still increasing light.

Divine instructor, gracious Lord,
Be Thou for ever near:
Teach me to love Thy sacred word,
And view my Saviour there.[43]

---

[41] *MTP*, 30.1801, September 28, 1884, 526 [qtd.], 527. For the hymns sung, see 528.

[42] Cho, "Women's Hymn Writing," 70.

[43] "Heavenly Teaching," *OOHB*, 482, vs. 3–6.

Once more, we see Steele writing about joy and Jesus, exploring the interplay between the two. The Bible is God's word; its pages are "heavenly," "sacred," and her "ever dear delight." What is the central reason for this delight, this joy? It is that in the Scriptures Jesus, "my Saviour," is seen. Anne Steele once received a letter from Mary Steele Wakeford which declared, perceptively: Jesus is the "hero of your poetry."[44] It is this Christ-centered joyful devotion which represents the greatest theme of Steele's writing, one which was passed on to new generations of worshippers through the pages of Spurgeon's hymn book.

---

[44] Mary Steele Wakeford to Anne Steele, November 10, 1757, "Silvania" and "Amira" Letters [xiii].

PART TWO

BAPTISTS IN THE NINETEENTH CENTURY

BAPTISTS IN THE BRITISH EMPIRE

SILAS MEAD'S ADVOCACY OF WOMEN

Rosalind Gooden

South Australia was a unique colony in the settlement of Australia, priding itself on its differences. To quote Ken Manley: "The South Australian colony was established in 1836. It was a point of considerable pride that the colony was never 'stained' by the stigma of being a convict settlement."[1]

A key figure in the establishment of that colony was George Fife Angas, a Baptist deacon and an English businessman, who worked with his inspiration for a colony that would become "the headquarters for the diffusion of Christianity in the Southern Hemisphere"—a colony of civil and religious liberty. He encouraged dissenters to migrate. Adelaide became known as the City of Churches, and South Australia was termed a Paradise of Dissent by historian Douglas Pike.[2] As journalist Rex Jory wrote, "the fight against religious persecution and discrimination, the encouragement of freedom and religious diversity, is one of the proudest achievements of the City of Churches."[3]

In general, though, Baptists in South Australia initially remained in small, squabbling, separating groups, or worshipped with the Congregationalists until 1861 and the arrival of Silas Mead from Stepney/Regents Park. He made the significant difference.[4]

Silas Mead, MA LLB, arrived in Adelaide on July 12, 1861 in order to become the minister of a new church in Adelaide, to be built within the surveyed city square mile. It was and is known as Flinders Street Baptist Church (FSBC). With twenty-six initial members (ten men and sixteen women) the church planned a building to seat seven hundred, and Mead stayed to minister there for thirty-six years until he moved to Harley College in London, and then to Perth, Western Australia.

---

[1] Ken Manley, *From Woolloomooloo to "Eternity": A History of Australian Baptists* (Milton Keynes: Paternoster, 2006), 44.

[2] Douglas Pike, *Paradise of Dissent*, 2nd ed. (Melbourne: Melbourne University Press, 1967).

[3] Rex Jory, "City of Churches Has Been Twisted…," *The Advertiser*, June 21, 2021, 20.

[4] A group of nine are collaborating to produce Mead's biography.

In this essay, I will examine three specific areas in which Mead advocated and utilized the ministry of women and encouraged others to follow his example while at FSBC.

Women Deaconesses

Firstly, Mead viewed deaconesses as officers, ministers of the church. On Good Friday, April 10, 1868, Mead was invited to speak at the opening for a new Baptist building at Morphett Vale. He spoke on the subject of "Women's Work in the Church." He said:

> Women's work in Churches, like everything else in reference to the Bible, had been perverted. Women had always worked for Jesus until the day of His crucifixion, and they were the first to welcome Him from the grave. The Apostle Paul in his journeyings was helped in his work by the sister members of the Christian Church, and in his time, there were female deacons....What was wanted was a clear recognition of the services of the sister members. Woman in no case ought to usurp the authority of man and do work that he is able to do. There were many ways in which women could make themselves useful—in hospital work, teaching in Sunday-schools, and as Bible-women speaking personally in the homes of the people.[5]

The report of that meeting quoted Mead as also saying he would "that all our [South Australian Baptist] churches had two or more sisters appointed as deaconesses to take a loving oversight over the young female members."[6] He also thought that the women ought to help the pastor in his visiting duties, working, not in the place of their minister, but with him.

At the FSBC members' meeting that very same month, William Kyffin Thomas (newspaper proprietor, secretary, and one of the founding deacons)[7] presented a notice of motion:

> That the Church appoint by ballot six sisters for one year, whose duty it shall be to exercise spiritual oversight over the whole Sisterhood of the Church, with the concurrence of the Pastor, such elected sisters to

---

[5] *South Australian Register,* April 25, 1868, 6; See also *Truth and Progress,* August 1868, 156–60, for his thinking on this issue. These resources are available from Archive Digital Books Australasia.

[6] *South Australian Register,* April 25, 1868, 6.

[7] Thomas's wife and three daughters were founding members of the church, and his younger daughter was one of the first Sunday school scholars.

have no charge or authority in connection with the business matters of the Church.[8]

The motion was passed unanimously in June.[9]

In August of 1868, Mead published in the South Australian Baptist paper *Truth and Progress* a detailed analysis of the scriptural and historical work of deaconesses. He concluded by advocating four aspects for their ministry:

1. To give all proper attention to sisters about to be immersed.

2. To visit the sick, the poor and the friendless, especially of the church and congregation.

3. To give special heed to the younger sisters, and to catechumens, i.e., those standing at the threshold of the church and needing instruction.

4. To prayerfully and lovingly watch over the whole sisterhood of the church, with a view to its spiritual growth in grace, blameless consistency of life, and individual usefulness in the Master's service.[10]

At the July 1868 FSBC members' meeting, five women were elected to serve in this role. They were required to signify their acceptance in writing by the next meeting and—due to a tie for the sixth—a further deaconess needed to be nominated and elected. Mead did counsel the church meeting that "with regards to Mrs Mead[11] it was unnecessary for numbers to record any votes for her, as on account of her relationship to the pastor, she already virtually filled such an office: therefore, if any members thought of voting for her, they had better substitute some other name."[12]

Following these deaconesses' appointments, the members discussed appointing in addition to their existing deacons a group of elders—whose "special duty [was] to visit the male members and attend exclusively to spiritual work."[13] So gender-based ministries were to be equivalent. A year later the deaconesses were elected for three years, and lists were drawn up for pastoral care. But it does not seem that the proposed election of the office of elder with these pastoral

---

[8] FSBC Members Minutes, April 29, 1868, 121, State Library of South Australia.

[9] FSBC Members Minutes, June 3, 1868, 123.

[10] *Truth and Progress*, August 1868, 160.

[11] Ann Mead had come out from Somerset to marry Silas in 1863, and they had six children before her untimely death in 1874. At the time under discussion, she already had three children.

[12] FSBC Members Minutes, July 1, 1868, 129.

[13] FSBC Deacons Minutes, July 29, 1868, 57.

responsibilities occurred for ten years, until 1878, after Mead's trip to England following his wife Ann's death. This concept was suggested early but took time to develop.

For the counselling of enquirers at services, the pastor also suggested the desirability of two men and three women joining him to stay behind after services.[14] The Mrs. Beeby, Leyburn, and Glandfield were appointed for such duties; these women were also deaconesses.

My one disappointment is that at the farewell to Mead from FSBC in 1897 no woman was invited to speak. There were other compelling issues at the time.

A Woman Evangelist

Secondly, Mead enthusiastically utilized and endorsed the ministry of a woman evangelist, Emilia Baeyertz.[15]

In September 1880, Rev W. C. Bunning of Geelong, the fraternal visitor from the Victorian Baptist Union, attended the South Australian Baptist Association meetings held in Adelaide. His topic was evangelism, and Bunning spoke of his experience with the work of Baeyertz, whom he had baptized five years earlier at Aberdeen Street Baptist Church.

Emilia Aronson, a Welsh woman, had been sent to her sister in Australia to recover her health following the breakdown of her Jewish marriage arrangements in 1864. There she met and fell in love with Charles Baeyertz, an Anglican bank manager. Without telling her family, she married him in 1865 on the condition that he would never attempt to convert her. Her family disowned her. Emilia and Charles had two children, Charles and Marion. Her husband died from a shooting accident in 1871, and it was only after his death that she became a follower of Jesus. Gradually, she and others recognized her unique gifts and her effectiveness as an evangelist.[16]

---

[14] FSBC Members Minutes, November 12, 1873, 192.

[15] For more on the evangelistic work of Emilia Baeyertz, see Robert Evans, *Emilia Baeyertz, Evangelist: Her Career in Australia and Great Britain: An Historical Study and a Compilation of Sources* (Hazelbrook, NSW: Research in Evangelical Revivals, 2007); John Walker, "The Baptists in South Australia, 1863–1914," (hons. diss., Flinders University, Adelaide, 1990) 35–44; and Elizabeth Wilson, "Totally Devoid of Sensationalism: Mrs. Baeyertz, the 'Jewish Lady Evangelist from Melbourne,'" *Tasmanian Historical Research Association Papers and Proceedings* 49, no. 3 (September 2002): 153–66. See also Betty Baruch and Amanda Coverdale, *This is My Beloved: The Story of Emilia Baeyertz, Jewish Christian Lady Evangelist* (Nunawading: Emilia Baeyertz Society, 2017).

[16] Baruch and Coverdale, *This is My Beloved*.

Bunnings knew of Baeyertz's story and ministry in Melbourne, particularly among young women working in factories, and had seen her in action in crusades in Geelong and Ballarat. He stated his conviction "that Mrs. Baeyertz would probably consent to pay a visit to Adelaide if she was invited."[17] The next day an *ad hoc* committee, including Mead, on a social picnic at Mount Lofty at the close of the assembly meetings, sent the suggested invitation.[18]

Within days, Baeyertz arrived in Adelaide by ship.[19] Mead organized three weeks of special events at FSBC, at which Baeyertz spoke to meetings for both men and women. The church was not large enough for the final meeting, so Mead booked the Adelaide Town Hall, where over two thousand people attended.[20] A contemporary report chronicled:

> Her first service was held in Flinders-street Baptist Church…when the place was crowded. She created a good impression, and has continued to deepen it through the series of services. Meetings have been held in North Adelaide, Norwood, and Parkside Baptist Churches, which were crowded to excess.[21] She also held meetings in the Town Hall, when about 2,000 persons were wedged into the building, and hundreds had to go away. Beside her Sunday services, she has conducted week night meetings, and held special afternoon gatherings for women and girls.[22]

Mead was often on the stage with Baeyertz at many of her meetings, commending her to the audiences. He was there at the first meeting at North Adelaide on November 23, 1880.[23] On another occasion, Mead preached in the morning service and Baeyertz preached in the afternoon service of the first Sunday gathering at Parkside Baptist Church, which Mead had constituted in October 1880.[24]

---

[17] *Truth and Progress,* October 1, 1880, 120.

[18] *Truth and Progress,* October 1, 1880, 120.

[19] There was no rail travel at that date between Melbourne and Adelaide; 1887 was the first train.

[20] *South Australia Register,* November 29, 1880, 4.

[21] Norwood and Parkside Baptist churches had been formed from members of FSBC.

[22] *Truth and Progress,* January 1, 1881, 8.

[23] *Truth and Progress,* December 1, 1880, 135.

[24] *Truth and Progress,* January 1, 1881, 3; *Truth and Progress,* November 4, 1880, 124.

On Tuesday, December 7, 1880, Baeyertz held a farewell tea meeting at FSBC for converts and those who had been restored to fellowship. After tea more than 120 converts assembled in an allotted portion of the church, with the remainder of the building filled with an audience mostly of well-wishing Christian friends. It was an impressive sight. The majority of them were, "young, only twenty or thirty being apparently over twenty years of age. Some ten or twelve were men, two or three of whom were of middle age....There may have been twenty lads and boys, the remaining number comprised fourteen to twenty women, and the rest were girls."[25]

The next day on the wharf, as the ministers farewelled Baeyertz, they handed her a letter endorsing her work among them. They wrote: "We are equally confident...in testifying not only to our esteem for you as a sister in Christ Jesus, but to our conviction that God has eminently endowed you with gifts for the setting forth of His precious truth both to Christians and Non-Christians."[26]

Demonstrating their satisfaction with her ministry, the ministers concluded their letter with: "You know...how ardently we entertain the hope of your returning to labour afresh in and around Adelaide as well as in the country districts."[27]

Mead reported to the Baptist Association Baeyertz's imminent return later in 1881.[28] Baeyertz and her two children came back to South Australia in August 1881, and she ministered in various Baptist congregations until the end of 1883. Regular news reported details of her addresses, attendances, and converts' testimonies. Reporters were particularly careful to inform readers of her lack of sensationalism and her femininity. They referred to her messages as full of "pathos and intense earnestness" and called them Bible readings rather than sermons.[29] But no matter how her efforts were described, in a place with a burgeoning women's suffrage movement, Baeyertz was seen as a public evangelist. It is worth noting that South Australian women obtained both the vote and the right to sit in parliament by 1894, second only to New Zealand.[30] Women's rights were accepted here more readily than elsewhere.

---

[25] *Truth and Progress*, January 1, 1881, 8.

[26] *Truth and Progress*, January 1, 1881, 8.

[27] *Truth and Progress*, January 1, 1881, 8.

[28] *Truth and Progress*, August 1881, 88.

[29] *South Australian Register*, November 29, 1880, 4.

[30] Women from FSBC played leadership roles in these achievements. Rosetta Birks (William Kyffin Thomas's youngest daughter) and Isabella Whiting were both well-

Baeyertz was used by a wide range of churches, Baptist and others, to hold evangelistic events in the tradition of visiting evangelists of that time, and for eighteen months she particularly served Baptist churches in South Australia. John Walker, South Australian Baptist historian, concludes, "over the next thirty years no other evangelist gained the acceptance and exposure which Mrs. Baeyertz had enjoyed among South Australian Baptists in the final decade of the nineteenth century."[31]

Following Baeyertz's return to Victoria, she moved on to evangelistic crusades in other colonies, including New Zealand, and eventually to ministry in both the United States and England. She did not return to Adelaide for further ministry even when she revisited Australia in 1905 for crusades in Western Australia, Victoria, and Tasmania.[32] Mead was to be one of those who endorsed her ministry in Perth, although he was overseas for much of her time in Western Australia.[33]

Women as Missionaries

Thirdly, the first two Australasian Baptist missionaries, Marie Gilbert and Ellen Arnold, were sent out from Mead's Flinders Street Baptist Church. The two schoolteachers left for India in October of 1882, and a further nine women departed before the first man (also from Flinders Street) was sent.[34]

From his arrival in 1861, Mead was a missions enthusiast. Missions were on both his mind and heart. He had studied with missionary applicants under Joseph Angus, a previous Baptist Missionary Society secretary. He had also seen the formation of the South Australian Baptist Missionary Society (SABMS) in 1864. For eighteen years that organization supported national preachers, evangelists, and booksellers; and towards the end of that period it also supported Bible women. Mead visited India to see this work in 1874.

Zenana missions work had developed in India as a targeted attempt to reach women who were segregated into quarters (or zenanas) in their homes and were unreachable by the standard missionary methods of outdoor market preaching. Such work had been started initially by missionary wives visiting homes and was

---

known in suffrage and temperance circles.

[31] Walker, "The Baptists in South Australia," 41.

[32] For detail of her wider ministry see Evans, *Emilia Baeyertz, Evangelist*.

[33] *The Western Australian*, August 30, 1904, 6.

[34] Rosalind Gooden, "'Mothers in the Lord:' Australasian Baptist Women at the Intersection of Cultural Contexts 1882–1931" (PhD diss., Tabor College of Higher Education, Adelaide, 2016).

gradually augmented by single women recruited for the task. As a contextual response to cultural restraints, it developed rapidly, but often was only loosely linked to the work being done by the men. Women's work was thought to be for women. The Baptist Zenana Mission (BZM) was formed by Baptist women in 1867 in the midst of these significant developments in Calcutta and other centers.

For South Australian Baptists, the availability of women and not men missionary applicants posed unexpected issues. Mead had regularly articulated the need for the workers; the offers they received were initially from single women. John Price, Secretary of the SABMS and a close friend and collaborator of Mead, wrote in 1892, a decade after the events:

> It was felt that the proposal involved a new departure of great importance and one which called for thoughtful deliberation and earnest prayer....The vote was not entirely unanimous. The resolution that was passed was brief but definite—"That this Society take up Zenana work at Furreedpore."[35] No step in the history of the mission has been more momentous. It has completely revolutionized our methods, more than doubled our sphere of operations, and at home it has created an opening for splendid service which consecrated Christian women have gladly availed themselves of.[36]

Gilbert had originally been a member of Aberdeen Street Baptist Church, Geelong, and had been recommended by Bunning to the BZM in England, but those plans had been frustrated by the failure of Victorian Baptists to finance her travel and allowances in Bengal. She and her mother moved to Adelaide, where Mead recruited Arnold to accompany her to the mission field. The two women had been colleagues at teachers' college. They were farewelled at a special meeting at Flinders Street Baptist Church at the same time as Emilia Baeyertz was in South Australia. Neither woman sat on the platform of that historic meeting, and Mead read their statements of call to the packed congregation.

Gilbert and Arnold spent their first year in Calcutta learning Bengali, observing the work of the BZM missionaries while a house was built for them at Faridpur. They transferred to the South Australian station early in 1884.

---

[35] Furreedpore was later know as Faridpur.

[36] John Price, Silas Mead, and Samuel Vincent, *The Centenary Volume 1792–1892: The South Australian and Tasmanian Baptist Missions at Furreedpore and Pubna* (Adelaide: WK Thomas, 1892), 14.

However, by mid-year Arnold's health necessitated her repatriation to Adelaide; Gilbert remained in Faridpur.

Arnold's sea travel to Sydney enabled her to recuperate, and while in that city, she was present for the formation of a zenana mission society. However, the mission's medical gatekeepers would not allow her to return to India as soon as she felt she had regained health. Instead, Mead and Arnold planned a tour for her to visit all the colonies. Mead requested ministry for her in Baptist churches and Sunday schools in order to encourage the formation of missionary societies and to recruit personnel, finance, and prayer support.[37] Arnold was most probably the most well-known Baptist woman in Australasian churches, for New Zealand was included in her crusade, and the formation of the New Zealand Baptist Missionary Society was credited to her visit. Arnold recruited four others to join her, and they became the Australian Baptist missionary icons, "the five barley loaves."

Eleven women were sent from Baptist churches in Australasia to Bengal, India, before the first man, Arthur Summers (also from FSBC), joined them. A decade later Mead's son, Cecil, also joined them.

Generations of women missionaries testified to the support, interest, and prayers of Mead. Bertha Tuck, another FSBC missionary, wrote of Mead's advocacy for all missionaries:

Have any missionaries left Australasian shores without Mr Mead's sympathy, prayers and blessing?…Not only was Mr Mead ever on the look-out for recruits, but also he earnestly sought to help those who went forth to realize what a holy, happy and dignified service they were called to.[38]

Edith King, one of the early women from Western Australia, wrote:

To us missionaries Mr. Mead was always kind and sympathetic, and it was always a help to talk to him about one's own work, for he entered into it so heartily, and made one feel that he was more than merely interested. I shall never forget some of Mr. Mead's prayers….How he

---

[37] See the letter Mead wrote to ministers and Sunday School superintendents in each colony, published in *Truth and Progress,* January 1885, 17–18; and *New Zealand Baptist,* January 1885, 10–12.

[38] Bertha Tuck, "The Late Rev Silas Mead MA LLB," *Our Bond,* November 1909, 1–3.

used to pray for a spiritual awakening to come to India, for the dead bones to live![39]

Conclusion

Undoubtedly, Mead enabled women to have a vital contribution as deaconesses in the thirty-six years he was pastor at Flinders Street Baptist. In addition, his organization of the initial visit of Emilia Baeyertz to speak to mixed audiences as well as meetings for women was practical proof of the contention that she was gifted of God and therefore should be given opportunities to exercise her spiritual gifts. The sending of women missionaries to India also resulted in a response to the Gospel in what today is Bangladesh.[40]

Final proof for Silas Mead's advocacy of women was found in the education and lives of his daughters. He had four—Lilian, Gertrude, Blanche, and Flora. Sadly, Flora, the youngest, as a thirteen-year-old, died of typhoid just weeks after the death of her stepmother in 1886.

Blanche married A. S. Wilson, the first minister of the Perth Baptist Church. Rebecca Hilton has written of her as a Baptist minister's daughter, wife, and mother in the coming biography of Silas Mead.

Gertrude was one of the early women medical students of the University of Adelaide Her contributions to medicine, to the newly formed Western Australian University Senate, and to the care of children and the aged are noteworthy. Her part in church and mission gave evidence of her adherence to Silas's values. She is honored by a street named after her in Canberra, the federal capital of Australia.

Lilian left her university studies to support her father. She was invited to give a significant paper on "Awakened Women" to the Women's Christian Temperance Union in 1895; she dedicated it to her father, and her words reflected his views.[41] She went with him to England and was active in the Christian Endeavour movement. She married Crosbie Charles Brown, a tutor at Harley

---

[39] "Goalundo Mission," *West Australian Baptist,* November 15, 1909.

[40] See Jess Redman, *The Light Shines On* (Melbourne: ABMS, 1982); Tony Cupit, Ros Gooden, and Ken Manley, *From Five Barley Loaves: Australian Baptists in Global Mission, 1864–2010* (Preston, VIC: Mosaic Press, 2013).

[41] Adelaide was one of the first universities in the world to admit women students, a move made when Silas was a member of the University Senate. A donation that could have gone for theological training where Mead was tutoring was used instead for the actual founding of the university. Lilian S. Mead, *The Awakened Woman* (Adelaide: Hussey and Gillingham, 1895), 201–2.

College. Lilian wrote three books and ran an international guest house for overseas students studying in the UK.

Silas Mead was a man ahead of his time, recognizing women's potential and facilitating their ministries.

QUEEN VICTORIA AND GENERAL GORDON:
HEROES IN THE AGE OF EMPIRES[1]

Gordon L. Heath

Two of the larger-than-life figures within the British empire's late nineteenth-century panoply of heroes were Major-General Charles George Gordon (1833–1885), often referred to as Chinese Gordon for his involvement in suppressing a rebellion in China, and Queen Victoria (1819–1901), who reigned from 1837 to her death in 1901. Upon his death, General Gordon was described as "the nearest approach to that one Man, Christ Jesus, of any man that ever lived."[2] Vying for accolades of divinity was Queen Victoria. Upon her death it was stated, "were we in the habit of deifying monarchs, we would not, in Queen Victoria, have the worst example of history for such exaltation."[3] Both Gordon and Queen Victoria were heroic figures in the age of empires, a period coinciding with the New Imperialism, and it is the intersection of heroes, religion, gender, and empire that is the focus of this research. This chapter will detail the devotion of Baptists to such heroes, but it will also delve into the role such heroes played in Baptist life. More specifically, it will address the role these two heroes played in the imagination and discourse of the churches living in the age of empires.

The New Imperialism

Throughout the nineteenth century, Baptists (along with other Nonconformists[4]) increasingly identified with the empire and its aims, and by the end of the

---

[1] Thank you to Ken Manley, Rosalind Gooden, Bill Sumners, Taffey Hall, Adam McCulloch, Emily Burgoyne, and Lindsay Walker for helping me gain access to archival sources during the difficulties of the COVID-19 pandemic. Thank you as well to Brad Faught for pointing me to secondary literature on late nineteenth-century heroes.

[2] John M. MacKenzie, "Heroic Myths of Empire," in *Popular Imperialism and the Military, 1850–1950*, ed. John M. MacKenzie (Manchester and New York: Manchester University Press, 1992), 127.

[3] Rev. A. Carman, "The Empire's Noble Queen," *Christian Guardian*, January 30, 1901. Immediately following this statement Carman noted that the Queen would have fought such exaltation of herself. Gordon L. Heath, "'Were We in the Habit of Deifying Monarchs': Canadian English Protestants and the Death of Queen Victoria, 1901," *Canadian Evangelical Review* (Fall 2005–Spring 2006): 72–97.

[4] Nonconformists had neither a static nor monochrome view of empire. See David

nineteenth century there was a potent mix of theological, racial, and imperial assumptions among Baptists within the empire. More specifically, assumptions regarding God's providence, Anglo-Saxon superiority, the benevolence of the empire, and the advance of missions under the Union Jack undergirded and colored every decision made regarding war. That was especially the case during the period known as the New Imperialism.

New Imperialism was marked by a dramatic intensification of imperial expansion and conflict between the end of the Franco-Prussian War (1870) and the start of the First World War (1914).[5] Its origins have often been linked to the Berlin Conference of 1884, where Europeans parceled out much of Africa. Baptist commentary reveals support for the surging imperial vision. As one commentator wrote regarding the conference,

> The blessing of civilization long bestowed in rich abundance in Europe and North America, and in measure in Asia and South America, seem now destined to overflow, flood with a new life and light the long oppressed, dark continent, with its swarthy races so long victimized by every nation possessed of ships and colonies. Never before in the annals of history of our race, has such a hopeful prospect exalted for the inhabitants of an uncivilized region brought for the first time into contact with strong and civilized peoples.[6]

Optimism towards the motives and mandate of nations involved in the Berlin Conference is also evident in a brief article extolling Belgium's King Leopold II's missionary passion for the Congo.[7] Hopes were high and confidence abounded, for it was believed that through the spread of European empires injustices were to end, slavery was to be abolished, and "black men and whites" were to be "equal before the law."[8] For many, the empire most able to bring

---

Bebbington, *The Nonconformist Conscience: Chapel and Politics, 1870–1914* (London: George Allen and Unwin, 1982).

[5] Harrison M. Wright, ed., *The "New Imperialism": Analysis of Late Nineteenth-Century Expansion* (Lexington, MA: D. C. Heath and Company, 1961).

[6] "The Results of the Berlin Conference," *Canadian Baptist*, July 23, 1885.

[7] "King Leopold and Africa," *Messenger and Visitor*, January 28, 1885. While Baptists could not have known it at the time, Leopold's rule in the Belgium Congo became atrocious and one of the worst examples of exploitation and abuse in Africa. See Adam Hochschild, *King Leopold's Ghost: A Story of Greed, Terror, and Heroism in Colonial Africa* (Boston: Houghton Mifflin, 1998).

[8] "The Results of the Berlin Conference," *Canadian Baptist*, July 23, 1885.

about such manifold blessings was the empire to which they already proudly belonged.

While there was widespread support for the empire, there was no uniform idea as to what belonging to the empire meant. Imperialism in the late-Victorian empire enveloped a wide and diverse range of sentiments, and it was that ambiguity that was a part of its strength.[9] Yet that ambiguity is one of the problems that confronts historians who attempt to make sense of the whole imperial movement.[10] It is also important to observe that imperialism among Baptists in the empire was not deemed to be necessarily at odds with national or regional identity. Nationalism and imperialism went hand in hand, and, for many, were not considered to be mutually exclusive.[11]

The Churches

Baptists in Britain, Australia, Canada, South Africa, and New Zealand—hereafter referred to as BACSANZ Baptists—are the focus of this research. David Armitage provides a helpful reminder of the breadth and power of ideological convictions to unite disparate parts of the empire,[12] and commentary in Baptist periodicals provides glimpses of the shared imperialism among BACSANZ Baptists in the late nineteenth century.[13] Evangelicals had been "hitching a ride for

---

[9] Carman Miller, *Painting the Map Red: Canada and the South African War, 1899–1902* (Montreal and Kingston: McGill-Queen's University Press, 1998), 4.

[10] Robert Page, "Carl Berger and the Intellectual Origins of Canadian Imperialist Thought, 1867–1914," *Journal of Canadian Studies* 5 (August 1970): 40.

[11] Barbara R. Penny, "Australia's Reactions to the Boer War—A Study in Colonial Imperialism," *Journal of British Studies* 7, no. 1 (November 1967): 97–130; Carl Berger, *The Sense of Power: Studies in the Ideas of Canadian Imperialism, 1867–1914* (Toronto: University of Toronto Press, 1970); Philip Buckner, "Whatever Happened to the British Empire?" *Journal of the Canadian Historical Association* 4 (1993): 3–32; Keith Sinclair, *A Destiny Apart: New Zealand's Search for National Identity* (Wellington: Allen and Unwin, 1986); James Belich, *Paradise Reforged: A History of the New Zealanders from the 1880s to the Year 2000* (Honolulu: University of Hawaii Press, 2001); Ian van der Waag, "War Memories, Historical Consciousness and Nationalism: South African History Writing and the Second Anglo-Boer War, 1899–1999," in *One Flag, One Queen, One Tongue: New Zealand, The British Empire and the South African War*, ed. John Crawford and Ian McGibbon (Auckland: Auckland University Press, 2003), 180–204.

[12] David Armitage, *The Ideological Origins of the British Empire* (Cambridge: Cambridge University Press, 2000).

[13] Contrary to the argument of J. G. A. Pocock in *The Discovery of Islands: Essays in British History* (Cambridge: Cambridge University Press, 2005) that local regions could

the gospel" for a number of decades, taking advantage of the spread of empire when it suited their purposes.[14] BACSANZ Baptists were convinced that the missionary enterprise and the alleviation of suffering had benefited from the spread of European empires. National and imperial identities were also fused with evangelical convictions and imperatives.[15] Or, to use the words of Douglas Cole, the shared "Britannic nationalism" in many ways was merged with evangelical (Baptist) identity and purpose.[16]

Baptists were firmly embedded within their culture, and their displays of imperialism indicate significant support for popular imperialism. The degree to which they supported popular expressions of imperialism indicates an affinity with the "masses" that suggests a closing of the gulf between evangelicals and the wider culture.[17] While that fusion of Baptist identity and purpose with popular

---

be understood without reference to empire, BACSANZ Baptists saw their individual and collective history as an integral part of British history, rooted not just in patterns of migration but also in shared ideological convictions.

[14] This is Stuart Piggin's phrase. See Stuart Piggin, "The American and British Contributions to Evangelicalism in Australia," in *Evangelicalism: Comparative Studies of Popular Protestantism in North America, the British Isles, and Beyond, 1700–1990*, ed. Mark Noll, David Bebbington, and George Rawlyk (Oxford: Oxford University Press, 1994), 294.

[15] Gordon L. Heath, *A War with a Silver Lining: Canadian Protestant Churches and the South African War, 1899–1902* (Montreal and Kingston: McGill-Queen's University Press, 2009).

[16] Douglas L. Cole, "Canada's 'Nationalistic' Imperialists," *Journal of Canadian Studies* 5 (August 1970): 44–49. David Bebbington's recent global history of Baptists does place the global communion of Baptists in an imperial context. He suggests that Baptists within the empire were often amenable to its benefits, but his focus on imperialism is secondary. Robert E. Johnson's introduction to the global Baptist community is even more explicit regarding Baptist life and growth in the British Empire, but while his work places the Baptist experience in the vicissitudes of empire, he pays little attention to the imperial assumptions among adherents of that global community. See David Bebbington, *Baptists through the Centuries: A History of a Global People* (Waco: Baylor University Press, 2010); Robert E. Johnson, *A Global Introduction to Baptist Churches* (Cambridge: Cambridge University Press, 2010).

[17] Bebbington minimizes the affinity of evangelicals and popular culture and claims that the greatest influence on evangelicals was high culture (intellectual movements such as the Enlightenment). He writes, "popular culture in the sense of secular ways of life probably exerted its greatest influence by repulsion, creating a gulf between the churches and the mass of the people. The high cultural movement of the Enlightenment, in the third place, provided the intellectual framework within which early Evangelicals

imperialism was nurtured by an international network of Baptist newspapers,[18] those same papers reveal that the imperial idea in the various colonies was far from homogeneous; rather than uniform it was imagined, elastic, and contested, often meaning "different things to different people."[19] Critical voices inside and outside the churches were raised against the expansion of imperial rule. There were tensions as well among Baptists related to empire, not surprisingly since they were, among other things, dissenters who had a deeply rooted aversion to the state privileging, promoting, or coercing in matters of faith. Despite—and because of—their willingness to be involved in the empire-building enterprise (a commitment that led to a drift from dissenting convictions[20]), there remained a need to assuage a nagging conscience when faced with the moral ambiguities of imperialism.

This chapter argues that the stellar and heroic lives of General Gordon and Queen Victoria not only provided idealized views of being male and female, but also acted as a salve to the conscience by demonstrating the Christian virtues of two of the most prominent imperial leaders of the age, and, by association, the virtues of empire as well. In a manner similar to chivalrous and noble medieval heroes, their alleged honorable conduct "cast a sheen of glamour and nobility over the reality of bloody wars."[21] John MacKenzie's description of the purpose of heroes is central to this argument: "Imperial heroes developed instrumental power because they served to explain and justify the rise of the imperial state, personified national greatness and offered examples of self-sacrificing service.…Their moral force might serve to assuage the tensions induced by the

---

operated." See David Bebbington, "Evangelicalism and British Culture," *Perichoresis* 6, no. 2 (2008): 153.

[18] Gordon L. Heath, *The British Nation is Our Nation: The BACSANZ Baptist Press and the South African War, 1899–1902* (Milton Keynes: Paternoster, 2017).

[19] Duncan Bell, *The Idea of Greater Britain: Empire and the Future of World Order, 1860–1900* (Princeton: Princeton University Press, 2007), 7. See also Hilary M. Carey, *Empires of Religion* (Houndmills, UK: Palgrave, 2008); and Carl Berger, *The Sense of Power: Studies in the Ideas of Canadian Imperialism, 1867–1914* (Toronto: University of Toronto Press, 1970).

[20] Gordon L. Heath, "Dissenting Traditions and Politics in the Anglophone World," in *The Oxford History of Protestant Dissenting Traditions*, vol. 5, *The Twentieth Century: Themes and Variations in a Global Context*, ed. Mark P. Hutchinson (Oxford: Oxford University Press, 2018), 62.

[21] Margaret MacMillan, *War: How Conflict Shaped Us* (New York: Random House, 2020), 51.

political and economic consequences of their actions."[22] Governments were involved in the "invention of traditions"—including that of the creation of particular types of heroes—that served the purposes of society and the state.[23] And public services such as funerals were ideal moments for what H. V. Nelles calls "acts of self-invention of a national consciousness."[24] Religious groups were often willing participants in the process, aiding and abetting the creation of national heroes.

There were heroes that were widely known in nineteenth-century Britain, with publications on figures such as missionary-explorer David Livingstone being "the mother's milk of Christian Sunday schools and missionary teaching."[25] Baptists had their own heroes of the faith, such as famous missionaries like William Carey or A. V. Timpany. However, General Gordon and Queen Victoria were a fusion of martial, imperial, and Christian heroism, and Baptists throughout the empire identified much in them that resonated with their own religious identity and purposes. Consequently, they saw in such heroes idealized virtues worthy of emulating and extoling. Baptist commentary and constructions of Gordon and Victoria served many purposes, such as reinforcing gender roles, or stemming the tide of what they saw as social decay, but, as will be argued below, it also assuaged a nagging conscience in the age of empires by providing a moral imprimatur for the empire. In other words, the alleged impeccable conduct of Gordon and Victoria provides one explanation for Baptist support for and partnership with the empire.[26] Joanna Lewis' comments about the "structure of feeling" that idealized imperial heroes mesh well with this argument, for, as she argues, the idealized language surrounding heroes was a "key reason why criticism

---

[22] MacKenzie, "Heroic Myths of Empire," 114–15.

[23] Eric Hobsbawm, "Introduction: Inventing Traditions," in *The Invention of Tradition*, ed. Eric Hobsbawm and Terence Ranger (New York: Cambridge University Press, 2012), 1–14; Eric Hobsbawm, "Mass-Producing Traditions: Europe, 1870–1914," in *The Invention of Tradition*, ed. Eric Hobsbawm and Terence Ranger (New York: Cambridge University Press, 2012), 263–308; Benedict Anderson, *Imagined Communities: Reflections of the Origin and Spread of Nationalism* (New York: Verso, 1991).

[24] "Commemoration as an act of self-invention" is Nelles's expression. See H. V. Nelles, *The Art of Nation-Building: Pageantry and Spectacle at Quebec's Tercentenary* (Toronto: University of Toronto Press, 1999), 12.

[25] Joanna Lewis, *Empire of Sentiment: The Death of Livingstone and the Myth of Victorian Imperialism* (Cambridge: Cambridge University Press, 2018), 254.

[26] There are many reasons for Baptist support for empire—views of providence, patriotism, missions, and race being just some—but this research focuses on the role of imperial heroes in the shaping of Baptist attitudes to the empire.

about imperial violence, exploitation and abuse was always muted."[27] Before proceeding further, however, a few comments on definitions and sources are in order.

Definitions and Sources

Heroes. While many definitions and studies of heroes focus on the qualities of the individual in question, this research takes its lead from C. Cubitt and others who shift attention to ways in which the person was deemed to be heroic. Cubitt's definition is focused on the meaning associated with the figure: "A hero is any man or woman whose existence…is endowed by others, not just with a high degree of fame and honour, but with a special allocation of imputed meaning and symbolic significance—that not only raises them above others in public esteem but makes them the object of some kind of collective emotional investment."[28] Such a view of heroes allows for a shift away from analyzing if they were actually great to the question of "why did a past society raise this individual as a hero?"[29] As Max Jones argues, that shift allows for a recalibrating of research of heroes to focus on how the person has been appropriated, or what he calls the "collective emotional investment generated about an individual."

> If we follow Cubitt…we must attempt to assess the level of "collective emotional investment" generated about an individual, a task which can be executed by studying a range of concrete indicators. Cubitt displaces the male warrior from his position at the core of the OED's heroic ideal. Both men and women can be heroes under Cubitt's definition, as it is the level of collective emotional investment which matters, not the possession of characteristics primarily associated with male warriors.[30]

That emphasis on the meaning of a person is echoed in Victoria Smith's comments on Queen Victoria. Smith argues that the Queen "did not only carry one symbolic meaning. Rather, her importance stemmed from the way in which various groups and individuals were able to project different, and sometimes

---

[27] Joanna Lewis, *Empire of Sentiment: The Death of Livingstone and the Myth of Victorian Imperialism* (Cambridge: Cambridge University Press, 2018), 254.

[28] As quoted in Max Jones, "What Should Historians Do with Heroes? Reflections on Nineteenth- and Twentieth-Century Britain," *History Compass* 5, no. 2 (2007): 441.

[29] Jones, "What Should Historians Do with Heroes?" 441.

[30] Jones, 441.

contradictory, meanings onto her."[31] That concern for projected meanings is critical to identifying the churches' discourse on Gordon and Victoria.

Imperial heroes such as Gordon were commonly male. As a result, it may seem odd identifying Queen Victoria as a hero, since she was not a soldier. Yet being the head of state of an empire—with the title Empress of India—makes one a decidedly imperial personage. It could also be argued that referring to her as a hero is justified because of the way in which her reputation was socially constructed and appropriated. As Tine Van Osselaer and Alexander Maurits note, "heroic individuals are analyzed as instruments of propaganda, and as 'a site on which a range of cultural attitudes and social practices can be examined,' meaning that a hero could be seen as the embodiment of virtue and a role model who inspired imitation and veneration."[32] The Queen was certainly portrayed as worthy of imitation, and thus, while not a soldier she was an imperial hero nonetheless.

Sources. Support among the churches for imperial expansion can be seen throughout the churches' newspapers in the later part of the nineteenth century, but, quite naturally, imperial zeal was heightened during moments of crisis or celebration, such as the death of General Gordon (1885), the Golden Jubilee (1887), the Diamond Jubilee (1897), and the death of Queen Victoria (1901). This research is based primarily on sermons, editorials, official statements, poems, artwork, and letters to the editor contained in the religious periodicals of BACSANZ Baptists during those specific events.

Increasingly throughout the nineteenth century, newspapers became a forum for expressing public opinion.[33] The role of newspapers in the shaping of public opinion is widely recognized. For instance, the New Journalism was linked to the New Imperialism, and John A. Hobson, one of the most prominent late-Victorian opponents of imperialism, was concerned about the power of the press in promoting imperialism.[34] While there were limitations on what

---

[31] Victoria R. Smith, "Constructing Victoria: The Representation of Queen Victoria in England, India, and Canada, 1897–1914" (PhD diss., Rutgers University, 1998), 376.

[32] Tine Van Osselaer and Alexander Maurits, "Heroic Men and Christian Ideals," in *Christian Masculinity: Men and Women in Northern Europe in the 19ʰ and 20ʰ Centuries*, ed. Yvonne Maria Werner (Leuven: Leuven University Press, 2011), 94.

[33] Stefanie Markovits, "Rushing into Print: 'Participatory Journalism' during the Crimean War," *Victorian Studies* 50, no. 4 (Summer 2008): 559–86.

[34] John A. Hobson, *Imperialism: A Study* (New York: James Pott & Company, 1902).

influence the press could have on its readers, it did have the power to set agendas, mobilize, stereotype, confer status, manipulate, socialize, and legitimize.[35] Keith Sinclair argues that "it is difficult to exaggerate the importance of newspapers in stimulating national sentiment. They create a sense of community. They enable us to sense—to feel that we *know*—what other members of our community, quite unknown to us as individuals, are doing."[36] John MacKenzie has noted how in Britain there was no pressing need for government agencies to be involved in imperial propaganda, for a number of non-governmental agencies were enthusiastically doing it for them.[37] MacKenzie was not necessarily referring to Christian denominations, but the extent to which they supported and promoted imperialism, national identity, and civic responsibility, as well as who were (or should be) the nation's heroes, indicates that BACSANZ Baptist newspapers were one of those non-governmental agencies. The international network of Baptist papers also played a role in nurturing imperial loyalties, what Simon Potter refers to as "diverse connections" and "complex webs of communication" that "forged links between each of the settler colonies"[38] or what Carl Bridge and Kent Fedorowich call the "plethora of networks" that acted as "cultural glue" which "held together" the British world.[39]

---

[35] Paul Rutherford, *A Victorian Authority: The Daily Press in Late Nineteenth-Century Canada* (Toronto: University of Toronto Press, 1982), 7–8. See also John George Bourinot, *The Intellectual Development of the Canadian People: An Historical Review* (Toronto: Hunter, Rose & Company, 1881), 83; Denis Judd and Keith Surridge, *The Boer War* (New York: Palgrave Macmillan, 2002), chapter 19; Peter Harrington, "Pictorial Journalism and the Boer War: The London Illustrated Weeklies" in *The Boer War: Direction, Experience and Image*, ed. John Gooch (London: Frank Cass, 2000), 224–44.

[36] Keith Sinclair, *A Destiny Apart: New Zealand's Search for National Identity* (Wellington: Allen and Unwin, 1986), 138.

[37] John M. MacKenzie, *Propaganda and Empire: The Manipulation of British Public Opinion, 1880–1960* (Manchester: Manchester University Press, 1984), 2–3.

[38] In his analysis, though, Potter did not mention the religious press. See Simon J. Potter, "Communication and Integration: The British and Dominions Press and the British World, c.1876–1914," *Journal of Imperial and Commonwealth History* 31, no. 2 (2003): 191. See also Simon J. Potter, "Communication and Integration: The British and Dominions Press and the British World, c. 1876–1914," in *The British World: Diaspora, Culture and Identity*, ed. Carl Bridge and Kent Fedorowich (London: Frank Cass, 2003), 190–206.

[39] Carl Bridge and Kent Fedorowich, "Mapping the British World," in *The British World: Diaspora, Culture and Identity*, ed. Carl Bridge and Kent Fedorowich (London: Frank Cass, 2003), 6. Also Carl Bridge and Kent Fedorowich, "Mapping the British

A final word from David Cannadine concerns the context of ritual. The discourse and descriptions in the religious press regarding funerals and jubilees point to meaning. The actual rituals may stay the same over time, but the meaning being ascribed to such ritual may evolve from context to context. As Cannadine writes, "for if, indeed, cultural forms are to be treated as texts, as imaginative works built out of social materials, then it is to an investigation of those social materials and of the people who—consciously or unawares—do the building, that our attention needs to be directed, rather than to an intricate and decontextualized analysis of the texts themselves."[40]

The advantage for historians accessing such literature seems readily apparent; the content in the papers "tell us a lot about the writers themselves, their motives, their aspirations, their prejudices and their sources of information" and they "bring to light the *mentalité* of the contemporary protagonists, in a way few other sources can."[41] Editorial selection regarding what is, or is not, printed does as well. All that is to say that the religious newspapers of BACSANZ Baptists are a rich treasure of material for accessing contemporary views of heroes, in particular the role of Gordon and Victoria in soothing the consciences of those dissenters who were ardent supporters of empire.

Two Victorian Heroes

As the toppling of statues of historical figures indicates, heroes are culturally manufactured icons whose appeal waxes and wanes according to the *zeitgeist* of the age. Referring to how Lytton Strachey in his *Eminent Victorians* (1918) ridiculed the Victorian pantheon of heroes such as Gordon, Lawrence James states, "yesterday's heroes and prophets [can] became today's figures of ridicule."[42] Yet

---

World," *Journal of Imperial and Commonwealth History* 31, no. 2 (2003): 6.

[40] David Cannadine, "The Context, Performance and Meaning of Ritual: The British Monarchy and the 'Invention of Tradition' c. 1820–1977," in *The Invention of Tradition*, ed. E. Hobsbawm and T. Ranger (New York: Cambridge University Press, 1992), 162.

[41] Paul Auchterlonie, "From the Eastern Question to the Death of General Gordon: Representations of the Middle East in the Victorian Periodical Press, 1876–1885," *British Journal of Middle Eastern Studies* 28, no. 1 (May 2001): 23.

[42] Lawrence James, *The Rise and Fall of the British Empire* (New York: St. Martin's Griffin, 1997), 429. Brad Faught, among others, claims that Strachey's work was a "misinformed polemic." See C. Brad Faught, *Gordon: Victorian Hero* (Washington, DC: Potomac Books, 2008), x.

in the late nineteenth century distain for imperial personages was marginal, and few questioned the heroic figures of General Gordon and Queen Victoria.

Both Gordon and Victoria were figures deemed worthy of emulation and veneration in life and in death. Their deaths, and Victoria's two Jubilees, were widely recognized events inside and outside the empire, with outpourings of public outrage (over government bungling that led to the death of Gordon); lamentation and mourning over the loss of iconic figures; and exuberant celebrations over the life, witness, and ideals of two imperial figures who self-identified as Christians.

What follows is a summarizing of public BACSANZ Baptist responses to the two deaths and two Jubilees in order to demonstrate how widespread the support was for the two figures. They were not marginal figures, and, as the following examples indicate, their lives and example resonated with Baptists throughout the empire.

General Gordon. On a cold Sunday evening in February 1885, congregants in First Baptist Church, Montreal, listened as Rev. Dr. Wheaton Smith waxed on about the life and heroics of General Gordon, who had recently been killed deep in the Sudan in the hot and dusty city of Khartoum. The text was John 12:24 (KJV): "Verily, verily, I say unto you, except a corn of wheat fall into the ground and die, it abideth alone: but if it die, it bringeth forth much fruit." The application being made was that Gordon's death would spark an outpouring of imperial zeal that would lead to the eventual capture of the Sudan, bringing in its wake the manifold blessings of British imperial rule: "England had drawn the sword, and justice should be done to humanity. The talismanic name of Gordon would electrify the forces of mankind" and "regiments without number...could be enlisted to march to the Soudan and suppress the inhuman Madhi."[43] Those across the Dominion who missed the Sunday sermons could learn about

---

[43] "General Gordon," *Canadian Baptist*, February 26, 1885.

78

Gordon's exploits and death in articles, editorials, poems, and maps in the denominational press,[44] as well as the secular press.[45]

Baptist churches around the empire shared in the grief, and, in like manner, commemorated Gordon's death. The *New Zealand Baptist* reported that "eulogies on General Gordon have been multiplied beyond measure. It were *[sic]* superfluous for us to add another to the number" (and then went on to offer one anyway).[46] The British *Freeman* likewise noted public reactions and the extensive number of memorial services.[47] The Australian *Victorian Freeman* praised Gordon's faithfulness, linking his life to that of medieval knights and his death to the ancient martyrs.[48] British Baptist commentary echoed the medieval chivalry motif and praised his self-sacrifice.[49]

Though Gordon was dead, his memory was kept alive in a variety of ways. For instance, in the following years the pages of the *New Zealand Baptist* illustrate how he was commemorated in hymns, sermons, exhortations, editorials, and illuminated lantern talks in the evening.[50] His "come quickly" was applied to

---

[44] "Map of the Egyptian Soodan *[sic]* and Abyssinia," *Canadian Baptist*, March 19, 1885; *Religious Intelligencer*, February 13, 1885; "English and Foreign," *Religious Intelligencer*, February 13, 1885; *Religious Intelligencer*, February 27, 1885; "English and Foreign," *Religious Intelligencer*, June 12, 1885; "A General's Excuses," *Religious Intelligencer*, June 19, 1885; "News of the World," *Christian Messenger*, November 5, 1884; "Beyond the Sea," *Christian Messenger*, November 19, 1884; "News of the World," *Christian Messenger*, November 19, 1884; "News of the World," *Christian Messenger*, November 26, 1884; "News of the World," *Christian Messenger*, December 3, 1884; "Beyond the Sea," *Christian Messenger*, December 3, 1884; *Messenger and Visitor*, February 11, 1885; "British and Foreign," *Messenger and Visitor*, February 11, 1885; "British and Foreign," *Messenger and Visitor*, February 18, 1885; "British and Foreign," *Messenger and Visitor*, February 25, 1885; *Canadian Baptist*, February 12, 1885; "Death of General Gordon," *Canadian Baptist*, September 12, 1884; *Canadian Baptist*, February 19, 1885.

[45] Paul Auchterlonie, "From the Eastern Question to the Death of General Gordon: Representations of the Middle East in the Victorian Periodical Press, 1876–1885," *British Journal of Middle Eastern Studies* 28, no. 1 (May 2001): 5–24.

[46] *New Zealand Baptist*, March 1885.

[47] *Freeman*, March 20, 1885.

[48] F. J. W., "Faithful General Gordon," *Victorian Freeman*, March 1885; Dawson Burns, "Gordon," *Victorian Freeman*, June 1885; "For the Grave of Gordon," *Victorian Freeman*, June 1885.

[49] "General Gordon," *Freeman*, February 13, 1885.

[50] "Mount Eden," *New Zealand Baptist*, January 1896; "Dunedin," *New Zealand Baptist*, September 1898; "Mosgiel," *New Zealand Baptist*, September 1899; "Baptist

recruitment for Sunday School teachers.[51] A "splendidly-bound copy" of *The Life of General Gordon* was deemed a suitable reward for the New Zealand captain of a cricket and football club.[52] A hymn book (referred to as a "relic") actually used by Gordon was sold for £30 to raise money for a school.[53] Attempts to commemorate his life in statues were noted,[54] and the advance of the British once again up the Nile was followed—often with reference to redeeming the death of Gordon.[55]

Almost a decade and a half later, Gordon's death was avenged when the British, under the leadership of Major-General Kitchener, captured Khartoum (September 2, 1898). That battlefield success that made Kitchener famous allowed for the expansion of British imperial rule in the Sudan. As the following announcement of the victory in the *Canadian Baptist* indicates, it was also seen to redeem the tragedy of Gordon's death.

> Following the advance up the Nile and the capture of Khartoum and Omdurman, comes a proposition from the victorious General that a college and medical school be established at Khartoum in memory of General Gordon. The whole to cost about $300,000, which General Kitchener thinks the British public would gladly provide. Such a memorial would avenge the murder of Chinese Gordon in a spirit akin to his own, and would show the barbaric tribes of the Nile tributaries the great difference between the religion of Christ and the cruel fetishism of the Mahdi.[56]

Even the oft-anti-British[57] American Baptist *Watchman* (Boston) reported on the British victory, linking the battlefield success with the memory of

---

Union of Tasmania," *New Zealand Baptist*, May 1885; "Melbourne," *New Zealand Baptist*, June 1886; *New Zealand Baptist*, March 1887; John Clifford, "Cant: a Letter to Young Men," *New Zealand Baptist*, September 1888.

[51] "Wellington," *New Zealand Baptist*, April 1885.

[52] A. V. G. Chandler, "The Tale of a Chinaman," *New Zealand Baptist*, August 1900.

[53] "Chit Chat," *New Zealand Baptist*, March 1899.

[54] *New Zealand Baptist*, August 1890; "Chit Chat," *New Zealand Baptist*, May 1900.

[55] "Chit Chat," *New Zealand Baptist*, July 1898; "Chit Chat," *New Zealand Baptist*, August 1898; "Temperance Notes," *New Zealand Baptist*, January 1899; "Chit Chat," *New Zealand Baptist*, February 1899; "A Notable Prayer," *New Zealand Baptist*, September 1899; "England and Egypt," *New Zealand Baptist*, August 1907.

[56] "Editorial Note," *Canadian Baptist*, September 22, 1898.

[57] Gordon L. Heath, "Canadian and American Baptist Self-Perceptions in the Age

Gordon: "General Gordon was deserted by the Gladstone Government and left to perish at Khartoum, but his work lives, and his insight of the situation and his superb self-devotion have inspired the action of Great Britain and Sir Herbert Kitchener's masterly generalship."[58] These responses to the recapture of Khartoum reveal how the memory of Gordon had lingered within the churches. It is also worth noting that his memory was also invoked in the Great War.[59]

Queen Victoria. The fact that Queen Victoria was dearly loved by most of her subjects in Britain in her later years seems to be beyond dispute.[60] The reaction to her Golden Jubilee indicates that her subjects in the peripheries were also quite enamored with her—perhaps even more so—as well as with the empire associated with her rule.[61]

---

of Imperialism," in *Mirrors & Microscopes*, ed. Douglas Weaver (Milton Keynes: Paternoster, 2015), 87–109.

[58] *Watchman,* September 8, 1898.

[59] "A Good Soldier," *New Zealand Baptist,* February 1915; "Our Bible Class Unions," *New Zealand Baptist,* October 1915; "Among the Churches," *Canadian Baptist,* October 29, 1914; "The Girdle of Truth," *Canadian Baptist,* January 25, 1917.

[60] The books on Queen Victoria are too numerous to list here. For an ever-so-brief look at a few sources, see the following biographies: Elizabeth Longford, *Victoria R.I.* (London: Weidenfeld and Nicolson, 1964); Christopher Hibbert, *Queen Victoria: A Personal History* (Cambridge, MA: Da Capo Press, 2001); and Carolly Erickson, *Her Little Majesty: The Life of Queen Victoria* (New York: Simon and Shuster, 1997). For a discussion of the Queen's popularity, as well as contemporary criticisms of the Queen, see Richard Williams, *The Contentious Crown: Public Discussion of the British Monarchy in the Reign of Queen Victoria* (Aldershot, UK: Ashgate, 1997). For reaction to her death, see Jerrold M. Packard, *Farewell in Splendor: The Passing of Queen Victoria and Her Age* (New York: Dutton, 1995).

[61] For a brief survey of how Canadians in general have been loyal to the British monarchy, see Robert M. Stamp, *Kings, Queens and Canadians: A Celebration of Canada's Infatuation with the British Royal Family* (Markham, ON: Fitzhenry & Whiteside, 1987).

Golden Jubilee (1887)[62] Queen Victoria's Golden Jubilee (June 20, 1887) kicked off a month of celebrations and special services. The planning was extensive throughout the empire, as the *New Zealand Baptist* indicates:

> The Jubilee Day in Auckland will be long remembered by old and young. It was observed as a close holiday, and everyone was prepared to do honour to our most gracious and beloved Queen. The city and harbour were gaily decorated with flags, etc., and at night the illuminations were excellent, the main thoroughfares being crowded to excess with those anxious to see. The only church illuminated was the Tabernacle, and by many was considered one of the best (if not the best) illuminations in the city. It consisted of the letters V.R. over the words "JUBILATE DEO," in three-feet block letters in gas jets, and had a most brilliant effect. Owing to the position of the Tabernacle, it could be distinctly seen for miles, and from the North Shore across the harbour was plainly visible. It was kept alight from five o'clock to ten, and was admired by thousands.[63]

The various Baptist periodicals provide glimpses into the wide-ranging responses of the churches to the empire-wide commemorative events, including commentary, prayers, poetry, official statements, and loyal addresses.[64] British

---

[62] An interesting foil for the role of media in Queen Victoria's Golden Jubilee is a study of the media during Elizabeth II's Golden Jubilee. See Claire Wardle and Emily West, "The Press as Agents of Nationalism in the Queen's Golden Jubilee: How British Newspapers Celebrated a Media Event," *European Journal of Communication,* 19, no. 2 (2004): 195–214.

[63] "The Queen's Jubilee at the Tabernacle Auckland," *New Zealand Baptist*, August 1887.

[64] "Her Majesty's Coronation," *Canadian Baptist*, June 9, 1887; "The Year of Jubilee," *Canadian Baptist*, June 23, 1887; "The Queen's Jubilee," *Canadian Baptist*, June 23, 1887; "British and Foreign," *Religious Intelligencer*, May 25, 1887; "A Waste-Basket Item," *Canadian Baptist*, June 16, 1887; *Canadian Baptist*, June 23, 1887; "Fifty Years a Queen," *Religious Intelligencer*, June 22, 1887; "Manitoba's Future," *North West Baptist*, June 1, 1887; "The Reign of Victoria," *Religious Intelligencer*, May 4, 1887; "The Year of Jubilee," *Canadian Baptist*, June 23, 1887; "The Jubilee," *Religious Intelligencer*, June 22, 1887; "Foreign Missions During the Reign of Queen Victoria," *New Zealand Baptist*, June 1887; *New Zealand Baptist*, June 1887; "Auckland," *New Zealand Baptist*, July 1887; "Cambridge," *New Zealand Baptist*, August 1887; "Nelson," *New Zealand Baptist*, August 1887; "Wellington," *New Zealand Baptist*, August 1887; "The Queen's Jubilee at the Tabernacle Auckland," *New Zealand Baptist*, August 1887; "The Queen's Jubilee," *Victorian Freeman*, April 1887; "The Queen's Jubilee," *Victorian Freeman*, May 1887;

Baptist commentary was marked by both appreciation and criticism. There was concern expressed over the "mixture of worldly pomp and religious services"[65] that seemed to be more about "glorifying the Queen rather than the King of kings."[66] Yet the expansion of Christianity at home and abroad was noted as a boon of her reign,[67] and the character of the Queen was extolled amidst calls for "thanksgiving."[68] Australian Baptists supported the Queen's Jubilee New Testament Fund—an effort in conjunction with other denominations and the Bible Society to distribute to every school age child a penny New Testament with the Queen's autograph on the inside cover,[69] as well as supported a widows' relief fund to commemorate the Queen's Jubilee.[70] In one of the more unique ways of commemorating the Jubilee, a New Zealand missionary happily reported in the *New Zealand Baptist* that she had taken part in a baptismal service in Ceylon that included a new baptismal tank "erected in honour of Her Majesty's Jubilee."[71] That zeal for the Queen was exceeded a decade later in the Diamond Jubilee.

Diamond Jubilee (1897). Britain had another opportunity to celebrate its greatness in 1897, despite a nagging sense of uncertainty and insecurity due to the rising power and ambition of nations such as Germany and the United States.[72] Between June 19 and June 24, 1897, the empire was fixated on celebrating the sixtieth anniversary of Queen Victoria's accession to the throne. Tributes to the Queen flowed from friend and foe around the world. The highlight

---

"Report of Executive Committee Meeting," *Victorian Freeman*, June 1887; "Notes and Comments," *Victorian Freeman*, July 1887; "To the Queen's Most Excellent Majesty," *Victorian Freeman*, July 1887; "The Nonconformists and the Queen," *Freeman*, June 24, 1887; "The Jubilee at the Abbey," *Freeman*, June 24, 1887.

[65] "The Nonconformists and the Queen," *Freeman*, June 24, 1887.

[66] "The Jubilee at the Abbey," *Freeman*, June 24, 1887.

[67] "Progress of Religion During the Queen's Reign," *Baptist Magazine*, June 1887.

[68] "The Jubilee at the Abbey," *Freeman*, June 24, 1887.

[69] "The Queen's New Testament Jubilee Fund," *Victorian Freeman*, May 1887; "The Queen's Jubilee Testament," *Victorian Freeman*, June 1887.

[70] "The Queen's Jubilee," *Victorian Freeman*, May 1887.

[71] "Good News from Ceylon," *New Zealand Baptist*, February 1888.

[72] See Denis Judd, *Empire: The British Imperial Experience from 1765 to the Present* (London: Fontana Press, 1997), 136, 139; Lawrence James, *The Rise and Fall of the British Empire* (New York: St. Martin's Griffin, 1994), 201–2; Paul Kennedy, *The Rise and Fall of the Great Powers: 1500–2000* (New York: Random House, 1987), 226–32. For contemporary concerns expressed in the denominational press, see "Twentieth Century Problems," *Canadian Baptist*, January 3, 1901.

of the Jubilee celebrations was on June 22, when the royal procession, with fifty thousand troops from the various regions of the empire, made its way from Buckingham Palace to St. Paul's Cathedral. The *Times* remarked: "History may be searched, and searched in vain, to discover so wonderful an exhibition of allegiance and brotherhood among so many myriads of men....The mightiest and most beneficial Empire ever known in the annals of mankind."[73]

Baptists shared in the zeal for Queen and empire, with commentary and services surpassing the response to the Golden Jubilee. The *South African Baptist* provides a description of commemorative events.

> In common with the Christian assembly at large, our services on Sunday, June 20th, particularly the evening, were dedicated to Praise and Thanksgiving for the glorious reign of our most gracious Queen. Mr. Heard taking for his subject "The True Woman."...On this day, too, the Wesleyans held their Sunday School Anniversary, and at the afternoon gathering, the other Sunday Schools attended by invitation, such service being the last public appearance of the Rev. A. Graham, who in an interesting discourse dwelt on the life of "Our Queen."[74]

Reporting of the Jubilee in the denominational press was extensive, providing readers with commentary, news, notes, and pictures of the celebrations.[75] Denominations and clergy crafted loyal addresses, and prominent speakers exhorted the faithful to thank God for the reign of Victoria and the spread of empire under her rule.[76] It was a time of heightened patriotism, and the Australian

---

[73] As quoted in Judd, *Empire*, 132.

[74] "Pietermaritzburg," *South African Baptist*, August 1897.

[75] "Sixty Years," *Religious Intelligencer*, June 16, 1897, 4; "A Patriotic Sermon," *Religious Intelligencer*, June 30, 1897; "Editorial Notes," *Canadian Baptist*, July 15, 1897; What Victoria Has Seen," *Religious Intelligencer*, June 16, 1897; BCOQ Resolution, "The Victorian Order of Nurses in Canada," *Canadian Baptist*, April 22, 1897; "Editorial Notes," *Canadian Baptist*, May 27, 1897; "Editorial Notes," *Canadian Baptist*, June 3, 1897; Peter W. Gordon, "The Victorian Era," *Messenger and Visitor*, June 2, 1897; "Victoria's Reign," *Messenger and Visitor*, June 23, 1897; "The United Empire," *Messenger and Visitor*, June 30, 1897; "British Colonization," *Messenger and Visitor*, April 28, 1897; "Mr. Depew on the Jubilee," *Messenger and Visitor*, July 28, 1897; "The Diamond Jubilee," *Queensland Baptist*, June 1, 1897; "Long Live the Queen!" *Southern Baptist*, June 17, 1897; J. E. W., "Victoria the Good," *Southern Baptist*, June 17, 1897. See supplement with pictures in *Southern Baptist*, June 17, 1897.

[76] *North West Baptist*, July 1, 1897; "Our English Letter," *South African Baptist*, August 1897; "The Diamond Jubilee," *New Zealand Baptist*, July 1897; "The Address to

Southern Baptist cautioned, "he would be a very rash man who dare to utter a word indicative of relaxed attachment to the Throne of Britain."[77] British Baptist commentary extolled the Queen as perhaps the "most Christian of all the monarchs who have reigned within and over British Isles."[78] Poets created verse to praise the godly Victoria and her benevolent reign.[79] Special Jubilee church services were held throughout the empire.[80] Ministry efforts such as missions or support for a woman's hospital were tied to the commemoration of the Queen.[81] Money was raised to purchase commemorative medals for children in Sunday Schools.[82] One lamentation during the festivities was that a local orphanage was short of funds because of so many appeals for Jubilee money from the pockets of citizens.[83]

The discourse surrounding the Diamond Jubilee abounded with late nineteenth-century optimism. Yet that optimism faced a challenge when, only four years later, Queen Victoria died.

Death (1901). The death of Queen Victoria on January 22, 1901 was a shock for a nation embroiled in a nasty and seemingly intractable war in South Africa. The "strength and extent of the global response to Queen Victoria's death was on an unprecedented scale,"[84] and Baptist responses were immediate and ubiquitous. Among British Baptists her death was lamented, with news reports,

---

Her Majesty," *Queensland Baptist*, November 1, 1897.

[77] "The Diamond Jubilee," *Southern Baptist*, June 3, 1897. See also Dr. Clifford's comments on the need for imperial loyalty and the value of empire in "Dr. Clifford's Visit to Melbourne," *Southern Baptist*, June 17, 1897.

[78] C. Williams, "Queen Victoria," *Freeman*, June 18, 1897.

[79] "A Hymn of National Praise," *New Zealand Baptist*, July 1897.

[80] "Chit Chat," *New Zealand Baptist*, July 1897, 100; "Otago and Southland Auxiliary of the Baptist Union," *New Zealand Baptist*, July 1897; "Hanover St., Dunedin," *New Zealand Baptist*, July 1897; "Auckland," *New Zealand Baptist*, August 1897; "Wellington," *New Zealand Baptist*, August 1897; "Dunedin," *New Zealand Baptist*, August 1897; "N. E. Valley," *New Zealand Baptist*, August 1897; "Jamestown, St. Helena," *South African Baptist*, September 1897; "Launceston," *Southern Baptist*, June 3, 1897; "South Australia," *Queensland Baptist*, August 2, 1897; "Toowong," *Queensland Baptist*, July 1, 1897.

[81] "The Jubilee and Missions," *Southern Baptist*, April 29, 1897; "The Queen's Shilling," *Southern Baptist*, March 18, 1897.

[82] "Petrie Terrace," *Queensland Baptist*, May 1, 1897.

[83] "Dr. Barnardo's House," *New Zealand Baptist*, August 1897.

[84] John Wolffe, *Great Deaths: Grieving, Religion and Nationhood in Victorian and Edwardian Britain* (New York and Oxford: Oxford University Press, 2000), 225.

sermons, and eulogies providing the necessary coverage of her passing.[85] It was virtually the same in the peripheries of empire.[86] The *Canadian Baptist* printed an account of the services held in Toronto,[87] along with the text of a tribute delivered at Jarvis Street Baptist Church.[88] It also reprinted the Baptist Convention of Ontario and Quebec's executive resolution expressing sorrow and sympathy over the loss of the Queen.[89] A message by Alexander Maclaren in Manchester was printed.[90] Dr. Thomas' tribute to Victoria captured the essence of all of those tributes when he proclaimed that the "name of Queen Victoria will go down the ages with a fragrance that no precious ointment could produce."[91] Her death led to outpourings of sadness as well as memorial church services among Australian Baptists.[92] New Zealand Baptists were grieved to hear of Queen

---

[85] "The Queen Gone Home," *Baptist Times and Freeman*, January 25, 1901; "The Death of the Queen," *Baptist Times and Freeman*, January 25, 1901; "The Illness of the Queen," *Baptist Times and Freeman*, January 25, 1901; "Prayer for the Queen," *Baptist Times and Freeman*, January 25, 1901; "Our Beloved Queen Is Dead," *Baptist Times and Freeman*, January 25, 1901; "Death of the Queen," *Baptist Times and Freeman*, February 1, 1901; Rev. Alexander Maclaren, "Christ's Ideal of a Monarch," *Baptist Times and Freeman*, February 1, 1901; "Our New Sovereign," *Baptist Times and Freeman*, February 1, 1901; "Our Late Beloved Queen," *Baptist Times and Freeman*, February 8, 1901; Alexander Maclaren, "In Memoriam: Queen Victoria," *Baptist Times and Freeman*, February 8, 1901; "The Funeral of the Late Queen," *Baptist Times and Freeman*, February 8, 1901; "Patriotic Declaration," *Baptist Handbook 1902*, 110; "The King," *Baptist Times and Freeman*, March 22, 1901; "Nonconformists and the King," *Baptist Times and Freeman*, March 22, 1901.

[86] Heath, "'Were We in the Habit of Deifying Monarchs,'" 72–97.

[87] The three churches were College Street, Jarvis Street, and Dovercourt Road. See "The Queen's Funeral," *Canadian Baptist*, February 7, 1901.

[88] "Dr. Thomas' Tribute to the Queen," *Canadian Baptist*, February 14, 1901.

[89] *Canadian Baptist*, February 28, 1901.

[90] Alexander Maclaren, "In Memoriam: Queen Victoria," *Canadian Baptist*, February 28, 1901.

[91] "Dr. Thomas' Tribute to the Queen," *Canadian Baptist*, February 14, 1901.

[92] "The Death of the Queen," *Southern Baptist*, January 31, 1901; "Our Beloved Queen," *Southern Baptist*, January 31, 1901; "Queen Victoria," *Southern Baptist*, January 31, 1901; "And Yet We Cannot," *Southern Baptist*, January 31, 1901; "One Painful Factor," *Southern Baptist*, January 31, 1901; "Young People," *Southern Baptist*, January 31, 1901; J. B., "The Death of Our Great and Good Queen," *Southern Baptist*, January 31, 1901; "The People's Lament," *Southern Baptist*, February 14, 1901; "The Remains of Our Late Beloved Queen," *Southern Baptist*, February 14, 1901; "The Memorial Service," *Southern Baptist*, February 14, 1901; "The Memorial Services," *Southern Baptist*,

Victoria's death.[93] The *South African Baptist* let it be known that Baptists in the far flung outpost of empire mourned the loss:

> As those far off from the central seat of power, at the southernmost fringe of Her Majesty's African dominions, it is our sad privilege to pay our last act of homage to Her august personality, and bring our wreath, bedewed with affectionate tears, to her bier. By multitudes of loyal hearts, of exiled home-born sons, of colonial-born brothers and sisters, and of various child-like native peoples, Victoria the Great and Good was loved and revered in this bright, weird land."[94]

Besides the obvious racial overtones that betray problematic assumptions about the so-called "child-like" natives, such language reveals an attachment to the monarchy and British identity that ensured colonial loyalty in the midst of a time of transition.

February 14, 1901; "The Queen's Statue," *Southern Baptist*, February 14, 1901; "The Queen," *Southern Baptist*, March 14, 1901; "Her Majesty Led in Prayer," *Southern Baptist*, April 17, 1901; "Our Late Kind Queen," *Southern Baptist*, April 17, 1901; "Our Gracious Queen," *Queensland Baptist*, February 1, 1901; "United Service," *Queensland Baptist*, March 1, 1901; "The Children's Service," *Queensland Baptist*, March 1, 1901; "All Denominations," *Queensland Baptist*, March 1, 1901; "Was Queen Victoria a Roman Catholic?" *Queensland Baptist*, March 1, 1901; "Topics of the Month," *Baptist*, February 1, 1901; "The Queen's Religion," *Baptist*, February 1, 1901; "Memorial Sunday," *Baptist*, February 1, 1901; "Queen Victoria and the Second Advent," *Baptist*, June 2, 1901; "Annual Report of the Executive," *Baptist Yearbook, 1901–1902*, 16; "City Tabernacle," *Queensland Baptist*, March 1, 1901; "Charters Towers," *Queensland Baptist*, March 1, 1901; "Petrie Terrace," *Queensland Baptist*, March 1, 1901; "Toowong," *Queensland Baptist*, March 1, 1901.

[93] "In Memoriam," *New Zealand Baptist*, February 1901; "Sympathy with the Royal Family," *New Zealand Baptist*, March 1901; "Chit Chat," *New Zealand Baptist*, April 1901; "Royal Funeral Parade at Sea," *New Zealand Baptist*, June 1901. For brief summaries of memorial services in Baptist churches, see "Oamaru," *New Zealand Baptist*, March 1901; "Invercargill," *New Zealand Baptist*, March 1901; and "Ponsonby," *New Zealand Baptist*, March 1901.

[94] "V.R.J.," *South African Baptist*, February 1901. For the Baptist Union's official expression of loyalty, see "Baptist Union of South Africa," *South African Baptist*, June 1901.

Saintly Heroes as Moral Imprimatur

The empire-wide popularity of Gordon and Victoria as detailed above was due to a variety of factors, but the focus now shifts to what purpose they played in Baptist life and thought. Heroic figures are constructed for a reason, and they served a function in communities as small as a local church or as large as an empire. The interest here is how their function intersected with the imperialism of the day: what role—whether conscious or not—did they play in the discourse and imagination of BACSANZ Baptists?

The empire under Victoria's tenure was understood to have brought progress in literacy, communication, science, social reform, transportation, electricity, canals, trade, religion, music and arts, tax reform, criminal laws, photography, and home comforts (e.g., soaps, glassware, sewing accessories, and washboards). Such developments led Canadian imperialist George R. Parkin to argue a "special capacity for political organization may, without race vanity, be fairly claimed for Anglo-Saxon people."[95] There was more than just material progress, however, for under the rule of Victoria the spread of missions had dramatically expanded. For churches enthused with the late-Victorian passion for missions, the fusion of imperial growth and missionary expansion was further cause for celebration. In other words, the empire advanced justice through its myriad benefits and benevolent rule and furthered missions through the safe conduct provided to missionaries. But what about the seedy underbelly of imperial expansion? What about the growing chorus of critics, both domestic and international? What about the jingoistic celebrations of imperial victories that shocked Victorian sensibilities? And what about the propriety of advancing the faith in the wake of empire?

The heroic figures of Gordon and Victoria served the purpose of not only demonstrating what type of manhood and womanhood was necessary for nation/empire building (thus guaranteeing a righteous empire, God's blessing, and a future), but they also acted as a moral imprimatur for the empire. Their godly lives acted as a model for citizens and a salve for consciences: there might be unsavory figures or abuses of empire, but the empire could be trusted and supported because of the godly character—and subsequent influence—of its leaders.

Ideal Male and Female. The widespread popularity of General Gordon and Queen Victoria was noted with pleasure, for it was comforting to know that

---

[95] George R. Parkin, *Imperial Federation: The Problem of National Unity* (London: MacMillan and Co., 1892), 1.

Christian convictions were embraced by the highest officials of the empire. It was believed that the Christian identity of the empire and its providential calling made it imperative that its leaders be above reproach. Thus, the godly character of heroes such as Gordon and Victoria acted as leaven, a model, and a prophetic witness. In death they had lived up to the evangelical concern for *ars moriendi* (the art of dying).[96] In the words of John Wolffe, there was a "visual didacticism" to portrayals of Gordon and Victoria,[97] and Baptists seized the day to promote the ideal man and woman.

Basic expectations of Baptist piety revolved around things such as Bible reading, discipline, moral purity, temperance, sabbath keeping, Sunday school attendance, support for missions, and charity. And both Gordon and Victoria were deemed to be stellar examples in those aspects of piety that transcended being either male or female. But there were specific male and female codes that were also a part of the iconization of such heroes.

Male. First, the ideal male. There was significant anxiety in Britain about the condition of the empire at the end of the nineteenth century, and much of the imperial zeal was reaction to feelings of insecurity about Britain's continued dominance. There was also a fear that Britain's decadence threatened the empire and that the superiority of the Anglo-Saxon race would be lost. A popular conviction was that war and soldierly qualities could solve some of the empire's problems and reverse the corrosive influences of an increasingly materialistic society; in that sense imperialism was perceived by many to be "an antidote to the evils of contemporary social life."[98] Consequently, as John Tosh notes, overseas threats contributed to the convergence of the language of empire and the language of manliness.[99]

In many Victorian papers, war and soldiering were idealized.[100] Writers emphasized the heroic nature of battle but glossed over death, maiming, and the

---

[96] Mary Riso, *The Narrative of the Good Death: The Evangelical Deathbed in Victorian England* (London and New York: Routledge, 2015).

[97] Wolffe, *Great Deaths*, 14.

[98] Carl Berger, *The Sense of Power: Studies in the Ideas of Canadian Imperialism, 1867–1914* (Toronto: University of Toronto Press, 1970), 253. See also Anne Summers, "Militarism in Britain before the Great War," *History Workshop Journal* 2, no. 1 (1976): 111.

[99] John Tosh, *Manliness and Masculinities in Nineteenth-Century Britain* (Harlow, UK: Pearson Education, 2005), 193–94.

[100] For instance, see Wilkinson, *Depictions and Images of War in Edwardian Newspapers, 1899–1914*; R. T. Stearn, "War and the Media in the 19th Century: Victorian Military Artists and the Image of War, 1870–1914," *RUSI: Royal United Services Institute*

horrific nature of war. Heroes for boys could be the ardent explorers of unknown hinterlands, but soldiers were often portrayed to be the ideal heroic figures. Since the Crimean War and the suppression of the Indian Mutiny, soldiers in the empire had provided examples of Christian heroism, and "abundant hagiographical literature" had flooded the press.[101] Soldiers such as Gordon were the modern-day heroes, the ones commonly portrayed in pictures and stories as people to emulate.[102] And they were the ones whose piety and devotion were called upon to defend the outposts of empire: "Responses to Livingstone's death established the preconditions for powerful reactions to Gordon's: the model of the great hero standing and dying alone in the face of the natural and human perils of Africa had now been firmly anchored in the public mind."[103]

The language of manliness and piety intersected in notions of muscular Christianity, a late-Victorian emphasis on physical health, moral character, Christian faith, and vigorous engagement in public affairs.[104] It was a movement that resisted common assumptions that "religious indifference was…an equally normal part of manhood"[105] and rejected notions that Christianity was mainly for women by offering "an arena where male virtues and powers could be used

---

for Defence Studies, Journal 131, no. 3 (September 1986): 55–62.

[101] Summers, "Militarism in Britain before the Great War," 117. See also Olive Anderson, "The Growth of Christian Militarism in Mid-Victorian Britain," *English Historical Review* 86, no. 338 (1971): 46–72.

[102] John Clifford, "Cant: a Letter to Young Men," *New Zealand Baptist*, September 1888, 139–40; "Mount Eden," *New Zealand Baptist*, January 1896, 10–11. The military aspect of Gordon was downplayed in some commentary, though: "The true grandeur of men lies not in the outer but in the inner life. His career is not one to the taste of the Christian, nor the example it affords one to be held up for emulation." See "General Gordon," *Freeman*, February 13, 1885, 97.

[103] Wolffe, *Great Deaths*, 145.

[104] Donald E. Hall, *Muscular Christianity: Embodying the Victorian Age* (New York: Cambridge University Press, 2006); Clifford Putney, *Muscular Christianity: Manhood and Sports in Protestant America, 1880–1920* (Boston: Harvard University Press, 2009); Nick Watson and Stuart Weir, "The Development of Muscular Christianity in Victorian Britain and Beyond," *Journal of Religion & Society* 7 (2005): 1–21; Stuart J. Smyth, "Muscular Christianity," *Asia Journal of Theology* 14, no. 1 (2000): 68–81; William Winn, "Tom Brown's Schooldays and the Development of Muscular Christianity," *Church History* 29, no. 1 (1960): 64–73.

[105] Yvonne Maria Werner, "Studying Christian Masculinity, An Introduction," In *Christian Masculinity: Men and Women in Northern Europe in the 19th and 20th Centuries*, ed. Yvonne Maria Werner (Leuven: Leuven University Press, 2021), 9.

for religious purposes."[106] Gordon's life exemplified such a code of manhood, and portrayals of Gordon reinforced specific idealized notions of manhood. In fact, his life was deemed to be a testament against accusations that "Christianity…[was] a weak thing."[107] With "virtually every facet of society teaching boys that the warrior was the ultimate masculine ideal, there could be little mistake about the message."[108] That being the case, faith and soldiering were reconciled, for the example of Gordon demonstrated that one could serve in the imperial army but also embody Christian piety. He was a "Christian knight" fighting for the right.[109] Not long after his death he was referred to as a "soldier-saint"[110] and a "martyr,"[111] a striking fusion of the secular and sacred, a "blurring between metaphor and literal truth in the matter of fighting,"[112] linking the martial activities of the empire's soldiers with the faith: "The response to Gordon's death boosted the tendency already apparent in the response to Livingstone's for a Christian concept of martyrdom to blend almost imperceptibly into a more diffuse ideal of dying for the cause of the nation and the Empire."[113]

Female. Second, the ideal female. The Queen was considered to have embodied "womanhood in its gentlest, purest, most regal, most endearing forms."[114] Or, quite simply, she was the "true woman."[115] In the decades preceding Victoria's death, the defining characteristic of the monarchy had shifted from one marked by martial skills to one marked by a "more domestic and spiritual emphasis."[116] Part of that shift was due to the Queen's domestic interests, and part

---

[106] Werner, "Studying Christian Masculinity," 13.

[107] *New Zealand Baptist*, March 1885.

[108] Mark Moss, *Manliness and Militarism: Educating Young Boys in Ontario for War* (Toronto: Oxford University Press, 2001), 20.

[109] Dawson Burns, "Gordon," *Victorian Freeman*, June 1885.

[110] "Stanley and Emin Pasha," *New Zealand Baptist*, March 1890; "General Gordon Again," *New Zealand Baptist*, August 1908; "A Good Soldier," *New Zealand Baptist*, February 1915.

[111] "General Gordon Again," *New Zealand Baptist*, August 1908. See also F. J. W., "Faithful General Gordon," *Victorian Freeman*, March 1885.

[112] J. R. Watson, "Soldiers and Saints: The Fighting Man and the Christian Life," in *Masculinity and Spirituality in Victorian Culture*, ed. Andrew Bradstock, Sean Gill, Anne Hogan, Sue Morgan (Houndsmills, UK: Macmillan Press, 2000), 10–26.

[113] Wolffe, *Great Deaths*, 150.

[114] J. E. W., "Victoria the Good," *Southern Baptist*, June 17, 1897.

[115] "Pietermaritzburg," *South African Baptist*, August 1897.

[116] Ian Bradley, *God Save the Queen: The Spiritual Dimension of Monarchy* (London: Darton, Longman & Todd, 2002), 121.

was due to her strong Christian faith. The Queen took her faith seriously, and for that reason churches saw her as an ideal Christian monarch and woman. Not only did Victoria embody all the religious idealism behind the establishment and maintenance of the British Empire,[117] but she also embodied all that a Christian woman was to be and do.[118] She was, as one British Baptist commentator declared, more than just a queen; she was "a true woman."[119]

Nineteenth-century clergy consciously sought to shape conceptions of gender through ministerially written obituaries,[120] and it was through those obituaries (and memorial sermons that acted as such) that the churches used the death of Queen Victoria to capitalize on a great opportunity to present the Queen one last time as the ultimate example of Christian womanhood. In the words of one Australian commentator, "she was a great woman and a good woman, who loved justice, and followed after righteousness. It can be said of her what could not be said, probably, of any other sovereign the world has ever known, that she lived and died without reproach."[121] Victoria was perceived to be a *Christian* Queen above worldly mudslinging and moral compromise, and, while her subjects could not be a queen like her, her subjects could model her Christian virtues in home and in the workforce.

The Queen was both a mother and empress, thus straddling the domestic and public spheres. And because of that, her example was even more compelling.

---

[117] For the past 150 years, the "monarchy has embodied and personified the values of duty, service, self-sacrifice, stability, dignity and moral principle." See Bradley, *God Save the Queen*, 120.

[118] Support for imperialism was not just a male phenomenon, for imperial attitudes were held by a significant number of women at the end of the nineteenth century. More research needs to be done on the support for the empire among Baptist women not just in organizations such as the Imperial Order Daughters of the Empire but also among church women's groups, especially within the predominantly women-run mission agencies. For a discussion of women in general and attitudes to empire, see Joanne Trollope, *Britannia's Daughters: Women of the British Empire* (London: Pimlico, 1983); Eliza Riedi, "Women, Gender, and the Promotion of Empire: The Victoria League, 1901–1914," *The Historical Journal* 45 (September 2002): 569–99; Cecilia Morgan, "History, Nation, and Empire: Gender and Southern Ontario Historical Societies, 1890–1920's," *The Canadian Historical Review* 82 (September 2001): 491–528.

[119] "Our Beloved Queen Is Dead," *Baptist Times and Freeman*, January 25, 1901.

[120] Marguerite Van Die, "'A Woman's Awakening': Evangelical Belief and Female Spirituality in Mid-Nineteenth-Century Canada," in *Canadian Women: A Reader*, ed. Wendy Mitchinson et al. (Toronto: Harcourt Brace, 1996), 52.

[121] "Topics of the Month," *Baptist*, February 1, 1901.

Victoria was understood to have maintained a virtuous life despite the constant and seductive pressures of power in the upper echelons of society and had established an impeccable moral standard. In fact, it was argued that her personal influence was so powerful that she had retarded moral degeneracy in government and high society, and, instead, had "lifted up" the nation's "moral status."[122] Unlike many of the men in power, her life was considered an example of true Christian virtue. And for a church that was concerned with the decline of traditional morals, and the increase of women's participation in the public sphere, Victoria's virtuous life and dedication to family were no small matter. Her commitment to character, motherhood, home, and empire was considered to be just the type of role model needed for the nation's ills. And her example was thought worthy of emulation by both women and men.[123]

Provided a Moral Imprimatur. The focus on the impeccable character of General Gordon and Queen Victoria was fused to troubling questions about imperialism's potent and pervasive mix of race, social Darwinism, paternalism, trusteeship, providence, nationalism, jingoism, hubris, and missions. Despite the link between the spread of empire and missions—a link central to Baptist support for empire[124]—it was clear that empire-building was a nasty business at

---

[122] "The Diamond Jubilee," *Queensland Baptist*, June 1, 1897.

[123] Whether male or female, her example was stated the ideal for which to strive: "We each have a work given us to do—not, indeed, to carry a sceptre, but some duty in life, it may be apparently insignificant. It is for us, not simply to do our work well, as it was done by our predecessors, but to raise the ideal and ennoble it for our successors. Let the field labourer and the gentlemen, the artisan and the merchant, seek to elevate his vocation and raise his employment to a higher level....In the lowliest position in which a child of God can be placed, there is ever scope for a great life." See "The Funeral of the Late Queen," *Baptist Times and Freeman*, February 8, 1901.

[124] Brian Stanley argues, "if you wish to mobilize Baptists (and evangelicals as a whole) on an issue that divides the nation down the middle politically, the way to do it is to persuade them that liberty to preach the gospel is at stake." And the advance of the empire was often framed with that very issue in mind. Stanley also proposes that British missionaries in the later nineteenth century entered the political arena to protect their interests. It was assumed, Stanley argues, that British imperial control could best bring about the much-needed stability and rule of law (not to mention commerce and technology) that would aid the work of the missionaries. BACSANZ Baptists defended imperial expansion when deemed necessary for the expansion of the gospel. Brian Stanley, "Baptists, Antislavery and the Legacy of Imperialism," *Baptist Quarterly* 42 (October 2007): 289. See also Brian Stanley, *The Bible and the Flag: Protestant Missions and British Missions and British Imperialism in the Nineteenth and Twentieth Centuries* (Leicester, UK: Apollos, 1990),

times and consequently it had its ardent critics. Little Englanders in Britain were alarmed at the rapid expansion of empire. Jingoistic calls for imperial armies to "paint the map red" were disquieting to those wishing for a less ambitious and rapacious approach to foreign expansion. French Catholics in Canada were wary of getting embroiled in far-flung imperial adventures. During the conflict in South Africa there were intense, sustained, and widespread domestic and global criticisms of the empire, something especially troubling for those convinced of its righteousness.[125]

Baptists were not always Pollyanna when it came to the empire's failings, for they often lamented the sins of empire. John Clifford, president of the Stop the War Committee in Britain during the war in South Africa, is one example of how Baptists found the empire wanting at times. However, myriad other examples of criticisms can be seen throughout discourse on the empire. Questions were raised about the justice of military campaigns in places such as the Sudan[126] or South Africa.[127] The corruption of imperial figures such as Cecil Rhodes was lamented, with his version of false imperialism contrasted with true

---

chapter 5; James G. Greenlee and Charles M. Johnston, *Good Citizens: British Missionaries and Imperial States, 1870–1918* (Montreal and Kingston: McGill-Queen's University Press, 1999); Heath, *A War with a Silver Lining*, chapter 5; and Heath, *The British Nation is Our Nation*, chapter 7.

[125] Bernard Porter, *Critics of Empire: British Radicals and the Imperial Challenge*, 2nd ed. (London: I. B. Tauris, 2008); Arthur Davey, *The British Pro-Boers: 1877–1902* (Cape Town: Tafelberg Publishers Limited, 1978); Paul Laity, "The British Peace Movement and the War," in *The Impact of the South African War*, ed. David Omissi and Andrew S. Thompson (HoundsMill, UK: Palgrave, 2002), 138–56; Alan Jeeves, "Hobson's *The War in South Africa: A Reassessment*," in *Writing a Wider War: Rethinking Gender, Race, and Identity in the South African War, 1899–1902*, ed. Greg Cuthbertson, Albert Grundlingh, and Mary-Lynn Suttie (Athens: Ohio University Press, 2002), 233–46; Bernard Porter, "The Pro-Boers in Britain," in *The South African War: The Anglo-Boer War 1899–1902*, ed. Peter Warwick (Burnt Mill: Longman, 1980), 239–57; David Nash, "Taming the God of Battles: Secular and Moral Critiques of the South African War," in *Writing a Wider War: Rethinking Gender, Race, and Identity in the South African War, 1899–1902*, ed. Greg Cuthbertson, Albert Grundlingh, and Mary-Lynn Suttie (Athens: Ohio University Press, 2002), 266–86.

[126] "Christian Statesmanship," *Canadian Baptist*, February 26, 1885; "Who Is to Blame?" *Freeman*, February 13, 1885; "The Mahdi," *Freeman*, March 20, 1885.

[127] For details on the range of Baptist support and criticism of the justice of the war in South Africa, see Heath, *The British Nation is Our Nation*, chapter 6.

imperialism.[128] The alarming rise of militarism was bemoaned.[129] The link between the advance of missions and empire was increasingly questioned in light of the Boxer Rebellion in China.[130] In theory, imperial heroes could be taken to task. Despite what was deemed to be his godly character, some suggested that General Gordon was partly responsible for his demise: "Of the three chief qualifications of a noble soul, courage, goodness and wisdom, he possessed the first two in a very eminent degree."[131] Even loyalty to the monarchy was stated to be contingent on the character of the monarch (but, fortunately for Baptists, it was argued, Victoria's godly character made loyalty a certainty): "With us loyalty is a religious duty which can only cease when a monarch has proved his or her utter unworthiness for rule. But because our Queen is so worthy of her people's reverent loyalty, with all the heartiness of a religious conviction we yield it."[132]

The notion that the empire was God's providential tool to spread Christianity around the globe cut both ways, for while God's promise was to bless the

---

[128] Baptist commentary on Cecil Rhodes's death was mixed. There were positive reviews of his life, and of the scholarships established after his death, as well as criticism of his various schemes and motives. See "The Cecil Rhodes Scholarships," *Messenger and Visitor*, April 30, 1902; "Rhodes and the Races," *Messenger and Visitor*, April 16, 1902; "Cecil Rhodes Educational Scheme," *Messenger and Visitor*, April 16, 1902; "Talmage and Rhodes," *Free Baptist Banner*, April 1902; "Cecil Rhodes," *Messenger and Visitor*, April 2, 1902; "The Transvaal War," *Baptist Times and Freeman*, November 10, 1899; "Mr. Robinson's Views," *Baptist Times and Freeman*, January 19, 1900; "Mid-way through the War," *Baptist Times and Freeman*, January 19, 1900; "The Friends and Peace," *Baptists Times and Freeman*, July 20, 1900; "A Baptist Missionary and Mr. Rhodes," *Baptist Times and Freeman*, April 19, 1901; "Wheresoever the Carcass Is," *Baptist Times and Freeman*, March 30, 1900; "Was the Hon. Cecil Rhodes," *Southern Baptist*, April 12, 1900.

[129] "Deeds That Marred the Empire," *Southern Baptist*, June 17, 1897. See also Heath, *The British Nation is Our Nation*; and Heath, *A War with a Silver Lining*.

[130] Gordon L. Heath, "When Missionaries Were Hated: An Examination of the Canadian Baptist Defense of Imperialism and Missions during the Boxer Rebellion, 1900," in *Baptists and Mission*, ed. Ian M. Randall and Anthony R. Cross (Milton Keynes, UK: Paternoster, 2007), 261–76; James G. Greenlee and Charles M. Johnston, *Good Citizens: British Missionaries and Imperial States, 1870–1918* (Montreal and Kingston: McGill-Queen's University Press, 1999), chapter 3.

[131] "General Gordon and the Late Government," *Freeman*, October 9, 1885. See also *New Zealand Baptist*, March 1885; *Baptist Magazine* 78 (1885). The *Baptist Magazine* admired Gordon, but believed he was responsible for his own demise. See Wolffe, *Great Deaths*, 147.

[132] "The Diamond Jubilee," *Southern Baptist*, June 3, 1897.

empire when it lived up to its high calling, it was also true that God promised to bring judgment when it failed to live up to the high expectations of righteousness.[133] In that sense, the example of Gordon and Victoria was a vivid reminder to the faithful to live godly lives so that the empire would continue to experience God's blessing. To use the words of Baptists, they were to work to see the nation and empire "exalted by righteousness."[134]

However, despite any minor character flaws common to the human condition, the other aspect to their godly lives was to provide legitimacy for the empire, even when (and perhaps especially when) its critics railed against the sins of empire. The impeccable lives of Gordon and the Queen were considered evidence that, despite the sins of some, the empire remained a force for good. Their lives provided a moral imprimatur for an empire with many detractors. As the following examples demonstrate, their heroic virtues were considered to have shaped, demonstrated, confirmed, and guaranteed the righteousness of the empire.

For instance, writers considered Gordon an example of the best of the best, and he embodied ideal imperial leadership. His was a life of sacrifice for the good of others, one who "working righteousness, serenely stood Champion-elect of right and human good."[135] And, as one author noted, that godly character acted as a corrective to abuses.

> Show and luxury, the spending of much time and money on eating, drinking, dressing, were offensive to him; he preserved an almost Spartan simplicity. Like a fresh breeze from off the sea on a sultry day, health-giving, inspiriting is the record of this phase of his career; and in these days of feverish greed for profits, of ruinous competition in home, and dress, and table, of growing luxury, the corrective it affords is trebly welcome."[136]

The idealized life of Gordon is clearly illustrated by an elegy crafted by English Baptist minister Dawson Burns. Burns emphasized Gordon's courage, defense of others, the exemplary quality of his life, and the "working righteousness"

---

[133] In this regard, Baptists were not alone among evangelical Protestants. For a discussion of the connection between righteousness, sin, and the support for (and criticism of) empire in Britain, see David Bebbington, "Atonement, Sin, and Empire, 1880–1914," in *The Imperial Horizons of British Protestant Missions, 1880–1914*, ed. Andrew Porter (Grand Rapids, MI: Eerdmans, 2003), 14–31.

[134] "National Exaltation," *Canadian Baptist*, April 3, 1884.

[135] Dawson Burns, "Gordon," *Victorian Freeman*, June 1885.

[136] *New Zealand Baptist*, March 1885.

that benefited those under the empire's sway. The poem was published in Britain and in Australia.[137] It reads in part:

> He lived not for the honour men could give;
> For him, to win applause was not to live;
> When Duty called, he knew no doubt or fear;
> No peril held him from her sacred sphere.
> One task he set himself—what most to do,
> By work severely strict, and just, and true.
> His love of man to trust in God was bound;
> He drew his courage from a faith profound.
> And, working righteousness, serenely stood
> Champion-elect of right and human good.
> No ancient hero more heroic rose,
> No Christian knight more pitied human woes;
> And, seeking not the fame men's breath imparts,
> He gained high place in all men's thoughts and hearts.
> Speeding to save far-off Nile-washed Khartoum,
> He held back day by day its dreaded doom;
> …
> To live or die, as may be, yet maintain,
> As Gordon did, a name without a stain!

That "name without a stain" led many to conclude that an empire led by such godly people was, in a relative sense, also without a stain.

The discourse surrounding the Queen was even more pointed when it came to noting how her personal character had shaped the empire. The poem "Victoria" expresses well the connection between the character of the Queen and the nature of the empire. Bessie R. Cogswell wrote it in Wolfville, Nova Scotia, Canada, in response to the death of the Queen. Portions of it read as follows:

> Reigns by example fair,
> Influence fell-far and near,
> For righteousness.
> God's holy Word her guide,
> Her trust "The Crucified,"

---

[137] Dawson Burns, "Gordon," *Freeman*, March 20, 1885; Dawson Burns, "Gordon," *Victorian Freeman*, June 1885.

Over her Empire wide,
She reigned to bless.

In countless hearts she reigns –
Still her pure life restrains –
Her good deeds live.
She reigns wrongs to redress,
To make earth's sorrows less,
Still, still for righteousness,
Victoria reigns.

"Defender of the Faith,"
Faithful e'en unto death,
Our Christian Queen.
Still over land and sea,
'Gainst slavery, tyranny,
She reigns majestically,
Empress and Queen.

So shall old England's might,
Wielded for God and Right,
Still stronger grow.
Her Empire still extend,
Her supremacy ne'er end,
Jehovah's power, her Friend,
Will foes o'erthrow.[138]

A hymn written by Mr. Driver, Dunedin, New Zealand, was sung in a number of Baptist churches on the Diamond Jubilee Sunday. It too noted the character of the Queen and the example for the empire. A portion reads:

For Thy goodness to our Queen
Who these sixty years hath been
Tenant of an ancient throne,
Wearer of a splendid crown;
Sovereign Lord of earth and heaven,
Unto Thee all praise be given.

---

[138] Bessie R. Cogswell, "Victoria," *Messenger and Visitor*, May 22, 1901.

For the pureness of her life,
Both as ruler and as wife;
For the bright example, good,
Of her royal widowhood;
Thanks to Thee, our Gracious Lord,
We with joyful lips accord.[139]

Such praise was ubiquitous. Victoria was portrayed as one who "frowned on vice and smiled on virtue" and "discourage[d] war and promote[d] peace"—the net result being a reign marked by growth "in intelligence, in civilization, in freedom, in religion."[140] The "splendor" of the Queen's reign was considered to be "more marvelous" than King Solomon's reign.[141] Her wise rule had brought "inestimable blessings" to the empire.[142] The Queen's purity had an incalculable impact on the character and conscience of the empire, and had, it was argued, "an influence to hold the world in peace as perhaps never before was embodied in any human being."[143] The Queen had "been characterized by the highest nobility, which is purity of life and conduct" and that "royalty of character" had an impact on establishing an empire of "righteousness and truth and meekness."[144] One British commentator noted that she governed the nation and empire by the "golden rule of the Sermon on the Mount," something "unheard of in kingcraft."[145] Elsewhere it was stated that "the beauty of her character, and the purity of her court, and the justice of her administration have shed a halo over the whole realm" and that the "scepter of her motherhood and wifely devotion is one of the greatest forces for good today in all the homes of the Empire."[146] Upon her death prominent Baptists eulogized her as a profound godly influence that shaped the character of the nation and empire. For instance, John Clifford declared she was

---

[139] "A Hymn of National Praise," *New Zealand Baptist*, July 1897.

[140] C. Williams, "Queen Victoria," *Freeman*, June 18, 1897.

[141] "Memorial Sunday," *Baptist*, February 1, 1901.

[142] *Minutes of the Free Baptist General Conference of New Brunswick (1901)*, 61.

[143] "The Queen," *Messenger and Visitor*, January 23, 1901. See also H. P., "Honour the King," *Victorian Freeman*, July 1887; "Long Live the Queen!" *Southern Baptist*, June 17, 1897; and A. Metters, "The Princess Who Became Queen," *Southern Baptist*, June 17, 1897.

[144] "Our English Letter," *South African Baptist*, August 1897.

[145] "Our Beloved Queen Is Dead," *Baptist Times and Freeman*, January 25, 1901.

[146] "The Death of Our Great and Good Queen," *Southern Baptist*, January 31, 1901. See also *Victorian Freeman*, June 1887.

one of the "most influential forces [for good] operating among us;"[147] Thomas Spurgeon declared in a sermon at the Metropolitan Tabernacle that Queen Victoria knew "how to be Imperial without being imperious;"[148] and Principal W. J. Henderson at Bristol Baptist College declared that her godly rule led to "a great enrichment of…liberties, a great increase in…material and temporal advantages, and an improvement in the moral religious life of the nation."[149] Finally, in the words of the *Baptist Times and Freeman* editor, "The spring of [her reign] has been the recognition of the regality of conscience, which, flowing from her throne as a clear crystal river, has brought life and strength to all the institutions of the land."[150]

In all those references, and more,[151] the character of General Gordon and Queen Victoria was highly touted and the pervasive influence of that character on the morality and conduct of the empire was assumed. As a result, those two imperial heroes demonstrated (and taught) the type of character that would keep the empire faithful to its ideals, but also confirmed the essential goodness of the empire. Their character was a stamp of authenticity on the genuine Christian character of the empire, a sort of moral imprimatur that lent an air of legitimacy to the empire. Their lofty character did not justify imperial abuses; in fact, their conduct was a rebuke to those who abused the responsibilities of imperial rule. What their examples really accomplished was to provide heroic figures that embodied the ideals of the empire—ideals that pointed to a telos of empire that was for the good.

Conclusion

The lives of General Gordon and Queen Victoria were a fusion of martial, imperial, and Christian heroism, and Baptists identified much in them that resonated with their own religious identity and purposes. The commentary on General Gordon and Queen Victoria in the late-Victorian Baptist press was extensive,

---

[147] "Dr. Clifford at Westbourne Park Chapel," *Baptist Times and Freeman*, February 1, 1901.

[148] "Mr. Spurgeon at the Metropolitan Tabernacle," *Baptist Times and Freeman*, February 1, 1901.

[149] "Principal Henderson at Coventry," *Baptist Times and Freeman*, February 1, 1901.

[150] "Our Beloved Queen Is Dead," *Baptist Times and Freeman*, January 25, 1901.

[151] For instance, see "Our Gracious Queen," *Queensland Baptist*, February 1, 1901; "Topics of the Month," *Baptist*, February 1, 1901, "Queen Victoria," *Messenger and Visitor*, January 30, 1901.

particularly around the Jubilees and their deaths. The purpose of this chapter has been to examine the role that such heroic figures played in the Baptist imagination.

Both Gordon and Victoria were deemed to have embodied the ideals of Christian citizenship and imperial virtues. Their godly conduct was understood to have stemmed the tide of societal moral decay as well as the corruption of imperial ideals. The didactic purpose behind the coverage of the Jubilees and funerals, and ensuing memorializing, seems obvious, with idealized notions of male and female codes fused to Christian virtues and imperial aims writ large. In an empire believed to be doing the work of God, such purity was necessary for God's continued blessing.

But more was going on than just teaching the faithful about godly living. This chapter also argues that the heroic lives of Gordon and Victoria acted as a salve to the conscience by demonstrating the Christian virtues of the most prominent imperial leaders of the age. The New Imperialism was just that—new— and its intensity led to doubts, ambiguity, uncertainty, and criticisms. Yet reminders of the Christian identity of the empire's leaders acted as a moral imprimatur for the empire. Consequently, with such godly heroes whose virtue had allegedly shaped the very essence of the empire, the empire—despite its faults— could legitimately be supported with a good conscience.

"THE VERY NATURE OF WOMAN HAS FITTED HER FOR THIS WORK": CANADIAN BAPTIST WOMEN AND MISSIONS, 1878–1890

Adam Rudy

The nineteenth century has been called "the great century of Protestant missions," and Canadian Protestants were caught up in the missionary zeal of the time.[1] For them it aligned nicely with their nation-building work to shape Canada into "the Lord's Dominion."[2] In a sense, foreign missions had the same goal, but on an international scale. Speaking of American and British Baptists, David Bebbington notes that not only were Baptist missions very successful, but that missions were "the most significant achievement of the Baptists."[3] This statement was no less true of Canadian Baptists. Lorraine Coops observes that "foreign missions captured the minds, hearts, and pocketbooks of thousands of Canadians, and every Protestant denomination sponsored missionary work in Asia, South America, and Africa. Women in particular vigorously answered the call to help 'spread the word' in foreign lands."[4] Alongside male-dominated missionary societies, groups of women formed their own missionary societies and were thus

---

[1] Kenneth Scott Latourette, *The Great Century, A.D. 1800–A.D. 1914* (New York: Harper, 1941), 1. However, Brian Stanley shows that in terms of numbers, the twentieth century was greater than the nineteenth for Protestant missions. See Brian Stanley, *The Bible and the Flag: Protestant Missions and British Imperialism in the Nineteenth and Twentieth Centuries* (Leicester: Apollos, 1990), 83–84.

[2] See Phyllis Airhart, "Ordering a New Nation," in *The Canadian Protestant Experience*, ed. George A. Rawlyk (Montreal: McGill-Queen's University Press, 1990), 98–138; Robert Wright, "Canadian Protestant Tradition," in *The Canadian Protestant Experience*, ed. George A. Rawlyk, (Montreal: McGill-Queen's University Press, 1990), 139–97; and, Neil Semple, *The Lord's Dominion* (Montreal: McGill-Queen's University Press, 1996).

[3] David Bebbington, *Baptists through the Centuries* (Waco: Baylor University Press, 2010), 232.

[4] Lorraine P. Coops, "Shelter from the Storm," in *Aspects of the Canadian Evangelical Experience*, ed. George A. Rawlyk (Montreal: McGill-Queen's University Press, 1997), 210.

able to participate in "a larger scheme of affairs than had ever been available to them."[5]

In September 1878, a new Canadian newspaper was born. Taking the name *The Canadian Missionary Link*, it was a newspaper edited and managed by women, for women who were passionate about foreign missions. The founders hoped it would be "something which connects," bringing into greater unity and effectiveness regional missionary societies.[6] As they began with one thousand subscribers, little did these Baptist women know that this essay would be a feature of the Canadian print landscape until 1927.[7] While the newspaper's stated purpose was to bring unity and sympathy to the various Baptist women's missionary societies in Canada, it also provided a forum for the women who edited the paper to present a public articulation of what they saw as the ideals of Christian womanhood.[8]

The Canadian Missionary Link (henceforth *The Link*) focused primarily on the Canadian Baptist Mission in the Telugu region of India. However, other mission fields were included, as well as home mission news, news from missionary societies and circles, letters from missionaries, excerpts from other missionary magazines and newspapers, speeches, hymns, poetry, and even a children's column. In this sense it was in keeping with the broader religious print culture of Canada and the larger English-speaking world. Gordon Heath argues that Canadian religious newspapers in the Victorian era played a critical role in the

---

[5] Wendy Mitchinson, "Canadian Women and Church Missionary Societies in the Nineteenth Century: A Step Towards Independence," *Atlantis: Critical Studies in Gender, Culture & Social Justice* 2, no. 2 (1977): 59.

[6] "Our Paper," *The Canadian Missionary Link*, September 1878, Canadian Baptist Archives, 1.

[7] *The Canadian Missionary Link* ran from 1878 to 1927. In 1890 a Canadian Baptist newspaper concentrating on home missions was started: *The Baptist Visitor*. It ran until 1927, at which point it merged with *The Link* to form the *Link and Visitor*, which ran until 2013, when it became known as *live* (yes, all lowercase) which, at the time of writing, is still actively published. Thanks to Adam McCulloch, archivist at the Canadian Baptist Archives, Hamilton, Ontario, for providing me with this information.

[8] The original editors were Mrs. J. H. Rose and Mrs. Freeland. By 1880, Mrs. J. H. Rose was no longer listed as an editor. Mrs. Freeland continued and was joined by Miss Jane Buchan. In 1885 both these women resigned their trust to other hands. Coincidentally this occurred in the wake of the sudden death of A. V. Timpany, who had persuaded Mrs. Freeland to start *The Link* back in 1878. The editorship of *The Link* was taken over by Mrs. Newman, her first issue being September 1885. See "Farewell," *The Canadian Missionary Link*, July 1885, 84, for Mrs. Freeland's farewell address.

nation-building work of the Protestant churches.[9] And indeed, their prominence supports this claim; as Merrill Distad notes, the religious press was the largest single genre in Canada, making up at least one-fifth of nongovernment imprints.[10] Denominational (and nondenominational) newspapers were a crucial instrument in shaping public opinion, as Heath points out, and though there were limitations on the press's influence, it "did have the power to set agendas, mobilize, stereotype, confer status, manipulate, socialize, and legitimize."[11]

Bearing in mind the power of the religious press in Canada and the high view of missions in the late nineteenth century, this essay examines *The Link* to demonstrate how Canadian Baptist women elucidated their belief in woman's special role in missions. Relying on biblical interpretation, they articulated ideals of Christian womanhood in a Victorian framework. This essay thus provides a domestic perspective, albeit one informed by reporting from overseas missionaries.

Biblical Interpretation, Ideals of Womanhood, and Missions

Late nineteenth-century evangelical gender roles were shaped by a traditional yet also uniquely Victorian biblical interpretation, though they were undergoing gradual change. Jocelyn Murray, for example, notes that passages in Paul's letters that appeared to restrict women from public ministry were taken very seriously.[12] This was further reinforced by a more general interpretation of Genesis which promoted the notion that women were naturally inferior to men, intended by God to be subordinate to men, and therefore unfit for leadership.[13] Muir and Whiteley argue that a common conception of woman characterized her as being both temptress and saint, and that this mythology was informed, supported, and

---

[9] Gordon L. Heath, "Forming Sound Public Opinion: The Late Victorian Canadian Protestant Press and Nation-Building," *Journal of the Canadian Church Historical Society* 48 (2006): 114.

[10] Merrill Distad, "Newspapers and Magazines," in *History of the Book in Canada*, vol. 2, ed. Patricia L. Fleming and Yvan Lamonde (Toronto: University of Toronto Press, 2005), 299–300.

[11] Heath, "Forming Sound Public Opinion," 112.

[12] Jocelyn Murray, "Gender Attitudes and the Contribution of Women to Evangelism and Ministry in the Nineteenth Century," in *Evangelical Faith and Public Zeal: Evangelicals and Society in Britain 1780–1980* (London: SPCK, 1995), 98.

[13] Murray, "Gender Attitudes," 98.

sanctified by scripture passages.[14] Acknowledging how Victorian and evangelical notions of womanhood had become deeply intertwined, Alison Bucknall claims that appeals to Scripture produced a Mary and Martha typology, which conveniently emphasized the Victorian values of domesticity and spirituality, respectively.[15]

In *The Link*, though, the restrictive passages of Paul's epistles were rarely mentioned, and a portrayal of woman was offered that differed from the mythology suggested by Muir and Whitely, perhaps because it was offered by women rather than men. Typology was a common tool in describing the ideals of womanhood. Mary and Martha, as Bucknall notes, were prominent. But so were Eve, Miriam, Deborah, Esther, Priscilla, and Mary Magdalene, to name a few.[16]

In seeking to answer the question "have we as Christian women, any commission given us by Christ, to spread the Gospel message from pole to pole?" one writer looked to Mary Magdalene, writing:

> Christ seemed to understand that the timid, shrinking nature of woman, needed a special revelation—a special request; and this, with the message given her formerly by the angels—to "go tell the brethren and Peter, that Christ is risen,"—is enough for Mary. She hastens to publish "glad tidings." And shall we hide the story of our Father's love, and the condescension of our Jesus in veiling the glory which he had with the Father before the world was, and coming to earth to redeem mankind—millions of whom are perishing for lack of knowledge?[17]

In a similar way, an archetypal understanding of Eve was used by the president of the Women's Baptist Missionary Union of the Maritime Provinces who, in an address printed in *The Link*, described how the Foreign Missionary Board,

---

[14] Elizabeth Muir and Marilyn Whiteley, "Canadian Women's Work," in *Changing Roles of Women Within the Christian Church in Canada,* ed. Elizabeth Muir and Marilyn Whiteley (Toronto: University of Toronto Press, 1995), 7.

[15] Alison M. Bucknall, "Martha's Work and Mary's Contemplation? The Women of the Mildmay Conference and the Keswick Convention 1856–1900," *Studies in Church History* 34 (1998): 408.

[16] For examples, see "Woman's Commission," *The Canadian Missionary Link,* November 1878, 1; "Our Sisters in India," *The Canadian Missionary Link,* December 1880, 13–14; "Woman's Mission," *The Canadian Missionary Link,* February 1881, 31; "Address of the President," *The Canadian Missionary Link,* October 1885, 15–16; "Women and Missions," *The Canadian Missionary Link,* June 1886, 111–13; "Consecration," *The Canadian Missionary Link,* January 1879, 1.

[17] "Woman's Commission," *The Canadian Missionary Link,* November 1878, 1.

run by men, had "recognized in us true help-meets, laboring side by side with them in the true God-given relations established in Eden."[18] She went on to argue that Canadian Baptist women can and should be inspired by "many noble examples of courage and devotion furnished us by our infallible guide—Scripture."[19]

Coupled with the sense of a special commission for women from Christ himself was the idea that woman was by nature timid, tender, and kindly, making her well-suited to what Sharon Cook has called "Christian nurture."[20] Nurture entailed interpreting, inculcating, and monitoring morality, as well as child-rearing, and, was generally considered the evangelical woman's greatest task.[21] The notion of woman being timid, tender, and kindly was not seen as a drawback but rather as being related to a special commission for women by Christ himself. When this was coupled with "earnestness, and steadfastness of purpose, also a spirit of prayer, consecration and self-denial," women could accomplish a great deal.[22] Foreign missions provided ideal opportunities for their abilities and fervor. One writer explained the need in foreign mission fields:

> For centuries, the women of these lands have been degraded, ignorant, immured from the every-day world—condemned to a bondage worse than slavery; and that *caste* has reared its adamantine walls so high between them and all that is bright, beautiful and happy, that now, only women, *Christian women, with their kindly hearts and tender fingers*, can find a crevice in this wall, or turn the key and fling open wide the doors to the Heathen homes.[23]

This statement epitomized, first, the fact that these Baptist women saw an active ministry for women in foreign missions, and second, that the feminine

---

[18] "Address of the President," *The Canadian Missionary Link*, October 1885, 15–16. The president's name is not noted in *The Link*.

[19] "Address of the President," *The Canadian Missionary Link*, October 1885, 15–16.

[20] Sharon Cook contends that the notion of Christian nurture was a major component of the ideal womanhood articulated by evangelicals in the late nineteenth century.

[21] Sharon Anne Cook, "Beyond the Congregation: Women and Canadian Evangelicalism Reconsidered," in *Aspects of the Canadian Evangelical Experience*, ed. George A. Rawlyk (Montreal: McGill-Queen's University Press, 1997), 407.

[22] "Woman's Commission," *The Canadian Missionary Link*, November 1878, 1.

[23] "Woman's Commission," *The Canadian Missionary Link*, November 1878, 1. Emphasis added.

qualities of kindly hearts and tender fingers, thought to be nurturing features that complemented the task bestowed by Christ upon women, were crucial to their mission work.

Rhonda Anne Semple argues that gendered notions of women's roles in religion and society contributed to the creation of a specific mission rhetoric, namely, "woman's work for woman."[24] This phrase came to represent woman's special contribution to missions. Semple claims that women played a central role in conflating the professional and the private in mission practice. She notes, "whereas women were initially constrained to such personal work in their homes, increasingly their 'at home' connections refocused mission practice on the social transformation of people's lives."[25] In *The Link*, this process of change was acknowledged. One writer, identified only as E. M. Upham of Montreal, described woman's outlook: "In the past woman's sphere was said to be in the home," she stated, "but times have changed, spheres have enlarged, woman is stepping out of the old beaten track and forming new lines of action. Not that the home has ceased to be her sphere, but other paths are open to her in connection with it."[26] The notion that nineteenth-century women expanded their "sphere" on the basis of activities that were natural extensions of ideal womanhood, such as Christian nurture, caregiving, teaching children, and nursing, is common in the historiography.[27] Upham's statement above seems to confirm that there was at least some truth to this and that some women were aware of the changes.

Positing a different perspective, Carmen Neilson Varty contests claims that women's work in charity and social reform challenged the boundaries between public and private spheres. She contends that these arguments are fundamentally flawed in their assumption that these spheres are actual spaces. Varty argues,

---

[24] This appears to have become a common phrase in the 1880s. While its origins are unclear, it may have derived from an article by Isabel Hart entitled "Woman's Work for Heathen Women," *Canadian Methodist Magazine*, vol. 12, 1880, 266–67, or an article by Mrs. J. L. Harvie entitled "Woman's Work for Woman in Heathen Lands," *Canadian Methodist Magazine*, vol. 18, 1883, 53. Of course, it also could have been common parlance in Britain and made its way across the Atlantic via the broad nineteenth-century network of Protestant literature.

[25] Rhonda Anne Semple, *Missionary Women: Gender, Professionalism, and the Victorian Idea of Christian Mission* (Rochester: The Boydell Press, 2003), 2.

[26] "Women and Missions," *The Canadian Missionary Link*, June 1886, 111.

[27] For some examples of scholars who hold this position, see Delia Davin, "British Women Missionaries in Nineteenth-Century China," *Women's History Review* 1, no. 2 (1992): 259; Bucknall, "Mildmay and Keswick," 408; Murray, "Gender Attitudes," 97.

rather, that the public sphere is a linguistic and discursive process. This meant that by seeing their work in Christian terms, these women "successfully argued that their acts were righteous, disinterested, and thus, justifiable in the realm of the rational public sphere."[28] Unfortunately, Varty fails to define the cornerstone of her argument: a "linguistic and discursive process." Finally, it is also important to note David Bebbington's suggestion that the church functioned as a type of third sphere, overlapping the public and private.[29] Under the auspices of Christian service and the notion of woman being a caregiver, women could undertake not just practical work such as feeding the poor and visiting the sick, but could also organize themselves into groups to tackle larger issues such as widespread alcohol abuse. Participation in foreign missions, then, was the next logical step.

Rather than a linguistic and discursive process, Upham's writing indicated a view of public and private spheres as social spaces, but spaces that were somewhat malleable and rooted in Scripture. Upham wrote, "Woman's mission in the world is to be helpful. This is as old as the creation of Mother Eve."[30] She argued that women were especially well-suited to missions and were uniquely gifted to spread the gospel because of woman's intuitive reception of Scripture. Upham wrote:

> Foreign missions have not opened a new sphere so much as extended the old one. Here is a work which calls for her to act in all her womanly dignity—to exercise her gifts of patience, sympathy, and love. The very nature of woman has fitted her for this work—has called her to it. She is peculiarly susceptible of religious truths, discerns them intuitively as the Bible presents them to her, questions not, argues not so much as believes. The Bible appeals specially to faith and thus touches woman in a strong point. Perhaps education, habits of thought, her position in life largely sheltered from deception and scepticism, have given her greater trust and less inclination to view things critically and doubtingly; perhaps her intimate relations with children give her unconsciously lessons of faith and trust, developing in her the childlike teachableness.[31]

---

[28] Carmen Neilson Varty, "'A Career in Christian Charity': Women's Benevolence and the Public Sphere in a Mid-Nineteenth Century Canadian City," *Women's History Review* 14, no. 2 (2005): 253.

[29] Bebbington, *Baptists through the Centuries*, 164.

[30] "Women and Missions," *The Canadian Missionary Link*, June 1886, 111.

[31] "Women and Missions," *The Canadian Missionary Link*, June 1886, 112.

In case she had not yet convinced all of her readers, Upham emphasized woman's uniqueness in understanding Scripture by citing several biblical women who she considered among the most touching examples of faith. This list included Ruth, Esther, Hannah, Elizabeth, the Syrophoenician woman, Mary of Bethany, and the company of women who were the last at the cross and the first at the tomb. Finally, she connected this biblical understanding of womanhood with missions:

> If truth has entered the heart of woman…she cannot be loyal to her Master and sit idle while others are without the knowledge of Christ, the sin-bearer, and she does not. The first instincts are to bring others into the same joy and peace which she possesses; the darkness, the superstition, the degradation, the miseries of the dusky sister over the seas have been mute appeals in her tender, loving heart; she could not enjoy all the blessings, direct and indirect results of Christianity, and see her sisters, though afar, pass through this "vale of tears" to an eternity of tears, when Christ stands ready to wipe away all tears, and has prepared mansions where "there shall be neither sorrow nor crying."[32]

"Woman's work for woman" was also built on the notion of a worldwide sisterhood. This concept implied that Christian women of western nations were responsible for bringing the gospel to their "benighted sisters."[33] Indeed, this woman's work for woman was deemed to be of the utmost importance, as the president of the Women's Baptist Missionary Union of the Maritime Provinces stated at their annual meeting in 1885: "This work of missions had come to a point where it could do little more until the citadel of superstition—the home––had been reached—*woman only can reach it.*"[34] In large part, this was in response to the realization that in some mission fields, indigenous women were in special need of the "civilizing" elements of missions. In describing the needs of the foreign mission fields, one writer provided an extended discussion about the moral depravity of the Hindus, noting especially the terrible treatment of women

---

[32] "Women and Missions," *The Canadian Missionary Link*, June 1886, 112.

[33] "Address of the President of the Women's Baptist Missionary Union of the Maritime Provinces," *The Canadian Missionary Link*, 15–16. *The Link* was replete with poetry and hymns that used the idea of a worldwide sisterhood. Other examples include "Hymn for Missionary Workers," *The Canadian Missionary Link*, January 1882, 41; "Sisters," *The Canadian Missionary Link*, May 1882, 1; and "The Macedonian Call," *The Canadian Missionary Link*, December 1884, 1.

[34] "Address of the President of the Women's Baptist Missionary Union of the Maritime Provinces," *The Canadian Missionary Link*, 15–16. Emphasis in the original.

in that culture by comparison to women in Europe and North America.[35] The writer decried the fact that "the influx of civilization and religious light from the New World has fallen on men alone. It has had no means of reaching the hidden retreats where the women dwell. The only rays of light that have penetrated there have been carried by missionary women."[36]

Canadian Baptist women were especially interested in the Hindu cultural practice of zenanas.[37] This, in itself, was rooted in the conviction that "women make the home," which was, of course, derived from the Victorian understanding of woman's role as being primarily focused on home life. As a letter written by a male missionary printed in *The Link* noted, "when the wife and mother is converted, the influence extends to the whole household."[38] Zenanas were high-caste Hindu dwellings which forbode the entrance of males who were not part of the immediate family.[39] Karen Smith has suggested that to Western eyes, women living in zenanas were essentially being held in captivity in their own homes, and in desperate need of the freedom provided by the gospel.[40] An article in *The Link* described the zenana as "little better than a luxurious prison," which could only be infiltrated by Christian women.[41] Thus, the unique calling of women as interpreted in Scripture, noted above, was buttressed by the belief that women's role in the home as primary teacher and monitor of morality applied to non-Western cultures too. As one article in *The Link* described it:

---

[35] "A Cruel Deed! Heroic Women!" *The Canadian Missionary Link*, March 1887, 81. For other examples, see "Practical Consecration," *The Canadian Missionary Link*, July 1887, 128; "Address," *The Canadian Missionary Link*, October 1887, 14; and "Work for 1888," *The Canadian Missionary Link*, January 1888, 58.

[36] "Needs of the Foreign Field," *The Canadian Missionary Link*, April 1881, 41.

[37] This was not original to Canadian Baptist women. Zenana work, and the notion that this was mission work that only women could participate in, originated with the British Baptist Missionary Society's work in India. The first English woman to gain access to a zenana seems to have been Elizabeth Sale, in 1854. Marianne Lewis publicized zenanas in 1866 with the publication of a treatise titled "A Plea for Zenanas." Soon the Baptist Zenana Mission was formed, and that work took on official status. Canadian Baptist women followed in these footsteps. See Karen E. Smith, "Women in Cultural Captivity: British Women and the Zenana Mission," *Baptist History and Heritage* 41, no. 1 (Winter 2006): 30–41, for a more extensive treatment of this.

[38] "Home Influence," *The Canadian Missionary Link*, January 1883, 40.

[39] Smith, "Women in Cultural Captivity," 31.

[40] Smith, "Women in Cultural Captivity," 31.

[41] "Native Christian Women at Work in India," *The Canadian Missionary Link*, December 1883, 1.

And this work, the bringing of life and light and salvation into the homes of thousands and thousands of our Indian sisters, can never be done except we, the women of Christian lands, do it. These women can never even hear the name of Christ unless we teach them, or unless native women of India, Christianized, trained and sent by us, carry the good news into their secluded homes.[42]

Writing in *The Link* in May 1882, Mrs. Murray Mitchell answered the question "what is a Zenana?" by contrasting India's homes with Canadian homes. She wrote,

What above all else constitute the strength and glory of our country? Certainly our Christian homes. But poor India has no home,—or rather it has a divided home, and no home-life. 'Home sweet home!' No place like home!'—these are words which have no echo in India: they touch no chord in a Hindu's heart. Ere long, however, this boon will be given to India through the influence of our Zenana work; we shall, with God's help, train the women; and the women make the home.[43]

Meanwhile, an article describing the zenana work done in Calcutta acknowledged that "it is not possible to educate men in the highest sense, nor raise the moral and social standard effectually, while women are debarred from sharing equal advantages."[44] For Canadian Baptist women writers and readers of *The Link*, "woman's work for woman" was how Western missionary work would effect ultimate change.

Conclusion

This essay has demonstrated that *The Link* was a forum for the delineation of Christian womanhood that was uniquely designed by God and commissioned by Christ. I have argued that Canadian Baptist women interpreted Scripture to express what they believed to be the ideals of womanhood. From Scripture they drew the conclusion that woman had been given a special commission by Christ for evangelism, and this commission was confirmed in how God had designed woman. What they considered the dire plight of women in India, and other parts of the world, was construed as work best suited to women. Zenanas, in particular, were a prominent area of Canadian Baptist women's interest.

---

[42] "Zenana Work," *The Canadian Missionary Link*, January 1885, 37.
[43] "What is a Zenana?" *The Canadian Missionary Link*, May 1882, 68.
[44] "Zenana Mission Work," *The Canadian Missionary Link*, January 1883, 34–35.

What is clear from examining the primary themes in *The Link*'s first twelve years is that Canadian Baptist women had successfully created a public platform from which they could not only further support and cultivate their passion for foreign missions, but could also share with others how they understood their place in the church during the heyday of nineteenth-century Protestant missions. Their view of woman, indeed of themselves, was not negative but upward and forward looking, acknowledging how the role of woman in Victorian society had begun to shift, if ever so slightly, and how even the strength of gender norms could not impede a fruitful life of Christian ministry.

BAPTISTS IN THE UNITED STATES

THE RAPE OF ANTÔNIA TEIXEIRA: RACISM, SEXISM, AND XENOPHOBIA AT BAYLOR AND BEYOND[1]

João Chaves and Mikeal C. Parsons

The story of Antônia Teixeira's rape at Baylor represents not only another instance in which powerful men used their resources in an attempt to establish official legacies and institutional memories, but it also reveals ways in which the global presence of Baptist educational institutions partnered with Baptist missions in the perpetuation of intersectional, transnational violence. When missionary Z. C. Taylor brought Brazilian-born Antônia Teixeira to Waco, Texas, to be educated at Baylor University in 1892, the SBC mission in Brazil was over a decade old. Although Southern Baptist missions to Brazil began in 1860, when Thomas Bowen left Nigeria to spend one contentious year in the country, it was only after the Civil War that the sustained phase of that mission started. With the Southern loss, Confederate exiles went to Brazil, forming Baptist churches in Confederate colonies. Because Brazil remained a slaveholding country until 1888, Southerners moved to Brazil with the dream of reconstructing the Old South in Latin America.

The confederacy is still celebrated in Brazil today—particularly in the cities where the *Confederados* formed their White supremacist evangelical enclaves—but the goal to rebuild the antebellum South in Brazil mostly failed. Southerners were disappointed that Brazilian racial imagination did not follow the norms to which Confederate immigrants were accustomed. The formation of Confederate enclaves itself was a function of White Southern anxiety towards Brazilian racial mixing as well as of their commitment not only to White supremacy writ large—something from which Brazil was not lacking—but also to the particular ways in which White supremacy expressed itself in the antebellum slaveholding "Land of the Free." It was in this context of Confederate ethnic enclaves that the first Baptist churches in Brazil were formed and where the first Brazilian-born Baptist pastor—the father of Antônia Teixeira—was baptized and ordained.

---

[1] Portions of this chapter are adapted, with permission, from Mikeal C. Parsons, "Rufus Burleson and the Brazilian Girl," *Baptist History & Heritage* 56, no. 1 (March 2021): 26–38.

Antônia was the daughter of Antônio Teixeira de Albuquerque (1840–1887). Albuquerque had been consecrated as a Catholic priest in 1871, but in 1878, under the preaching and influence of a Presbyterian minister, he left the Catholic church. In 1880, he joined up with the Baptists and was on the same day baptized and ordained as the first Brazilian-born Baptist minister.[2] In 1882, Albuquerque teamed with Baptist missionaries William Bagby and Z. C. Taylor to organize the first Baptist Church of Bahia. Together, Taylor and Albuquerque published the "Rules of Order and Regulations for the Church" in 1883.

Antônia was the *primogênita*, the firstborn daughter of Antônio Albuquerque and Francisca de Jesus.[3] Five years after Albuquerque's death, when Antônia was eleven or twelve years old, Taylor brought her to Waco.[4] Rufus and Georgia Burleson, President and First Lady of Baylor University, offered to take Antônia in, furnishing her with "board, tuition, books and clothing." Rufus Burleson also promised to "teach her housekeeping as requested, on Saturdays, mornings, evenings when not conflicting with her studies."[5] In return for the efforts, all Burleson asked "was that the girl would become…useful in the cause of religion and education in Brazil."[6] Antônia was not the only Brazilian to study in the segregated South. Other Brazilian Baptists came to the Southern US at the end of the nineteenth century to study—most prominently William Bagby's mentee F. F. Soren, who would become the first president of the Brazilian Baptist Convention and whose son would be the first president of the Baptist World Alliance from the Global South. However, Antônia may have been the first Brazilian Baptist woman to study in the United States.

At the end of her first term at Baylor in 1893 Antônia received passing marks in reading (80) and penmanship (78), but "deficient" grades in Arithmetic (70) and Orthography (70).[7] Her grades appeared to be marginal when judged

---

[2] Betty Antunes de Oliveira, *Antônio Teixeira de Alburquerque: O Primeiro Batista Brasileiro—1880: Uma Contribuicao para a Historia dos Batista No Brasil* (Rio de Janeiro, 1892), 77, appendix 2.

[3] Antônio and Francisca married on September 7, 1878 in Recife, the capital of Brazil's northeastern state of Permambuco (Antunes de Oliveira, *Antônio Teixeira de Alburquerque*, 10). Antônia's date of birth is uncertain, but presumably she was no younger than eleven and no older than twelve when she travelled to the US.

[4] Taylor had written the Foreign Mission Board immediately after Teixeira's death asking that it help financially support Teixeira's *orfaos*, orphans (Antunes de Oliveira, 67).

[5] Rufus Burleson, "The Brazilian Girl and Baylor University," William Cowper Brann Collection Box 2, Folder 7, Texas Collection, Baylor University.

[6] Burleson, "The Brazilian Girl."

[7] Report card for Antônia Teixeira, Baylor University, Spring term, 1893. Brann

by a system designed to assume and measure excellence via a number of linguistic, cultural, racial, and class biases. Still, Antônia's conduct grade was "100"; she received no "Demerits" for that term. At the least, she began to fulfill part of Baylor's goal for female education, which was "to encourage character, piety, and the thirst for education in the female students of Baylor."[8] Antônia's place in her new world, however, soon took a sharp and devastating turn. Antônia's host, Rufus Burleson, failed in helping her navigate the tragic series of events soon to follow, choosing instead to attempt to protect his own family, reputation, and the Baylor "brand." It is perhaps past time to re-tell Antônia's side of the story and to examine more closely Burleson's role in the episode dubbed by him, "The Brazilian Girl and Baylor University."

The Incident

In early 1895, it was discovered that Antônia was pregnant. Burleson wrote: "We immediately wrote to Galveston, Dallas and Ft. Worth to find some safe Reformatory where she could be placed," but they finally settled on entrusting her to the care of a local woman, Mrs. Ollie Jenkins, who "had some skill in reforming 'fallen women.'"[9] Critics would later charge that the Burlesons had "attempted to conceal her condition from the general public; and she was placed in a private house, no steps being taken to discover the responsible man."[10]

Antônia's condition, however, soon drew public attention, first by a "nervy justice of the peace" who "proceeded to investigate the matter."[11] Antônia named Steen Morris as her assailant, accusing him of rape. Steen Morris, age twenty-seven, was the brother of Rev. S. L. Morris, publisher of a Baptist monthly, *The Guardian*, who was son-in-law of Rufus and Georgia Burleson.[12] According to

---

Collection Box 2, Folder 7. The report card explains the grading system: "The above grades are upon a basis of 100 for perfection in recitation and deportment, regardless of time. If less than 75, he is Deficient; if less than 60, Bad. A Student who receives 20 Demerits in a term of five months is publicly notified his standing is bad, and when his Demerits amount to 50, he is sent home or otherwise severely punished. Rufus C. Burleson, D.D., L.L.D., President."

[8] Quoted from the historical marker, "Georgia Burleson and Early Female Education at Baylor," on Baylor's campus.

[9] Burleson, "The Brazilian Girl."

[10] John Randolph, "The Apostle of the Devil: A Biography of William Cowper Brann," (PhD diss., Vanderbilt University, 1939) 139.

[11] *Brann the Iconoclast: A Collection of the Writings of W.C. Brann in Two Volumes, with Biography by J.D. Shaw*, vol. 1 (Waco: Herz Brothers, 1911), 323.

[12] S. L. Morris was married to Hallie Burleson, the Burlesons' only daughter.

Antônia, Morris, after drugging her, sexually assaulted her on or around November 1, 1894. At the time of the attack, Morris was also a boarder in the Burleson home and took his meals with the family. On January 13, 1895, Steen Morris married Nettie Torry.[13] Antônia claimed she told Georgia Burleson of the assault, but Morris denied the story and nothing was done. Teixeira reported she was then attacked twice more (dates unspecified).[14]

The story hit the Waco *Morning News* on June 16, 1895. Rufus Burleson linked Antônia with an unnamed Baylor student, calling charges of rape against Steen Morris "preposterous" and denying that Antônia had ever complained to Mrs. Burleson. Steen Morris's brother, S. L., had accused Antônia of being sexually involved with a Black servant. Two days after the newspaper article, Antônia gave birth prematurely to a White male child, disproving the latter charges, with their underlying racist and misogynist undertones.[15] Initially, a District Court Judge, L. W. Goodrich, dismissed the charges as "groundless and without a particle of evidence."[16]

The case did not end here, however. A talented muckraking journalist, William Cowper Brann, had recently settled in Waco and started a journal called *The Iconoclast*, which eventually reached a circulation of one hundred thousand.[17] Brann took a keen interest in Antônia's story, criticizing Baylor and Burleson at every turn. He charged that Burleson had relegated Antônia to a "scullion maid" in the "kitchen curriculum," ignoring her education, a fact supported, Brann claimed, by the preliminary trial in which it was determined her academic progress was "unsatisfactory."[18] Brann was incensed by Judge Goodrich's dismissal of the case, writing:

> Poor Antônia! Miserable little waif, adrift among the Baptist wolves. She can now beg money of the publicans and sinners to carry her to her native land, and there lay her ill-begotten babe on her old mother's breast—as her diploma from Baylor! She can seek sanctuary in the Catholic Church—which her fond parents left to tread a primrose

---

[13] Morris was buried in Jena, Louisiana.

[14] Charles Wellborn, "Brann vs. the Baptist—Violence in Southern Religion," *Christian Ethics Today* 72, no. 33 (2001): 14–18.

[15] The child, three pounds at birth, did not survive long.

[16] Burleson, "The Brazilian Girl."

[17] For more on Brann, see Charles Carver, *Brann and the Iconoclast*, 2 vols. (London: T. Nelson, 1958) and, more recently, Eric S. Ames, *Hidden History of Waco* (History Press: Charleston, SC, 2020).

[18] Randolph, "The Apostle of the Devil," 139.

path to Christ—and there find help and human sympathy…but Baylor college will stink forever in the nostrils of Christendom—it is "damned to everlasting fame."[19]

Despite having the case dismissed, Burleson was losing the battle of public opinion. So he decided in August 1895, after consulting the Board of Trustees, to publish a statement, clarifying his and Baylor's role in the Antônia Teixeira controversy. He was primarily concerned to counter attacks by critics, who charged that "Baylor University is an unsafe place to educate young ladies."[20] Burleson feared the incident could cause Texas Baptists to withdraw their daughters from enrollment in the school.[21] Burleson countered: "I can and do challenge any school in or out of Texas, Catholic or Protestant, to show purer brighter jewels than the daughters of Baylor University."[22]

Brann, for his part, took issue with Burleson's account of the incident, charging that only when Antônia's pregnancy became a matter of public knowledge did he [Burleson] bother to respond:

> It was then that the reverend president of Baylor rushed into print with a screed branding her as little better than a public bawd in short dresses, who to this day refers to him as "gran'pa!" It was then that all the power of Baylor was exerted, not to ferret out the criminal and bring him to the bar, but to forever blacken the character of the little orphan.[23]

In at least one crucial respect, Brann's essays proved more convincing than Burleson's. In September 1895, one month after the publication of "The Brazilian Girl and Baylor University" and the district judge's initial ruling, a charge of rape was brought against Steen Morris. The specific charge reads: "On or about the 1st of November, in the year of our Lord eighteen hundred and ninety-four…one Steen Morris, did then and there, in and upon Antônia Teixeira, a

---

[19] "Baylor in Bad Business," *Complete Works of W.C. Brann*, 12 vols. (New York: Brann Publishers, 1919), 2: 32–33. Brann's hyperbolic rhetoric, as evidenced in this quotation, made it easier for Burleson and his Baylor allies to dismiss Brann's critique (some of which is insightful and convincing) as "vile slander."

[20] Burleson, "The Brazilian Girl."

[21] Burleson's fear was not completely unfounded: by some accounts, more than thirty women did withdraw from the university in the immediate aftermath (John Nova Lomax, "The Apostle of the Devil," *Texas Monthly*, June 3, 2016).

[22] Burleson, "The Brazilian Girl."

[23] Carver, *Brann and the Iconoclast*, 2:324.

woman, make an assault and did then and there, by force. Threats, and fraud, and without the consent of the said Antônia Teixeira, ravish and have carnal knowledge of the said Antônia Teixeira."[24] On September 28, 1895, Steen Morris was arrested and placed in jail.[25] The trial was delayed for several months. During that time, Brann claimed both Burleson and Taylor (who had originally brought Antônia to Waco) attempted to get her to change her testimony.[26] The trial was finally held in mid-1896 and resulted in a hung jury. Seven jurors voted for conviction; five voted for acquittal. The case was carried over to the next term of court.[27]

Before the retrial could take place, however, Antônia signed a sworn affidavit recanting her testimony and claiming the relationship with Morris was consensual.[28] Soon after signing this affidavit releasing Steen Morris from all charges, Antônia Teixeira left Waco.[29] Brann, predictably but also not without cause, raised questions of impropriety: "When Capt. Blair (Morris's attorney) asks the court to dismiss the case…let him be required to state why the drawer of the remarkable document purchased Antônia's ticket, and who furnished the funds."[30]

The Aftermath

Events subsequent to the Teixeira-Morris case have garnered as much or more attention than the case itself. Much of the attention has centered on the (mis)fortunes of Brann and his adversaries. Brann soon broadened his attack on the university, claiming that "Texas Baptists…believe it better that their daughters should be exposed to its historic dangers and their sons condemned to grow up in ignorance than that this manufactory of ministers and Magdalens should be permitted to perish."[31]

---

[24] "The State of Texas vs. Steen Morris. Indictment. Filed September 28, 1895." Brann Collection Box 2, Folder 7.

[25] "Sheriff's Return," Brann Collection, Box 2, Folder 7.

[26] Carver, *Brann and the Iconoclast*, 2:321.

[27] Randolph, "The Apostle of the Devil," 172.

[28] Affidavit of Antônia Teixeira, August 11, 1896, R. L. Allen, Notary Public, McLennan County, Texas, Texas Collection, Baylor University.

[29] Lomax ("The Apostle of the Devil") claims Antônia left the very same day that she signed the affidavit.

[30] *The Iconoclast Complete Works* (September, 1896), 6:8; cited by Wellborn, "Brann vs the Baptist," 17.

[31] *The Iconoclast Complete Works*, 10:64.

Brann had finally gone too far. Brann met his demise on April 1, 1898 in a gun duel on South Fourth Street with real estate developer and Baylor supporter Tom Davis, in which each man fatally wounded the other.[32]

It is, of course, impossible to retry the rape case of Steen Morris. But it is possible to retell Antônia's story and to examine the actions and behavior of Rufus Burleson, President of Baylor University, as evidenced in his pamphlet, "The Brazilian Girl and Baylor University." Specifically, Burleson engaged in what we, today, would call "victim blaming." According to the United Nations Girls' Education Initiative, victim-blaming occurs "when it is assumed that an individual did something to provoke the violence by actions, words, or dress."[33] Some of Burleson's own contemporaries came to similar conclusions, albeit without the benefit of such theorizing. Consider, for example, the "nervy justice of the peace" who began the investigation, or the seven jurors who—despite the power, wealth, and prestige Baylor and its officials wielded in late nineteenth-century Waco (and Texas generally)—still voted to find Morris guilty of rape. Consider also the fact that this incident is widely held (including, apparently by Burleson himself) to be a central cause of the Board of Trustees transitioning Burleson from President to Emeritus shortly after the whole affair ended.[34]

Note also that the title of Burleson's pamphlet depersonalizes Antônia. She is not Antônia, or Antônia Teixeira; she is "the Brazilian girl." Next, note that Burleson's victim blaming is rooted in racism and xenophobia. Quoting Taylor, Burleson reported that "the three besetting sins of Brazilians are lust, a want of veracity and honesty."[35] Presuming these bigoted stereotypes to be true, Burleson presumed that Steen Morris was innocent of all charges and that Antônia Teixeira brought on herself, through her "actions or words," whatever shame and hurt that accompanied her pregnancy by some other unknown male.

It is not remarkable that Steen was acquitted; it is remarkable that seven White male jurors, at that time, found him guilty. Burleson, however, refused to even entertain the possibility of a relationship between Antônia and Morris,

---

[32] Brann Collection, Box 2, folder 6.

[33] https://www.ungei.org/website/how-avoid-victim-blaming.

[34] Lomax, "The Apostle of the Devil." Also, see below.

[35] All Burleson quotations in the remainder of the essay are taken from Burleson's pamphlet. That Taylor was entirely capable of slandering the entirety of the Brazilian population is evidenced in his personal correspondence. See for example Taylor's letter to "Misses Wilcox and Stenger," dated May 1, 1895. The Brazilian people are "idolatrous Catholics, the masses ignorant and superstitious" (Z. C. Taylor Correspondence, International Mission Board Archives).

consensual or coerced. He claimed: "on her single testimony an honorable young man was thrown into jail, and his young wife, and aged parents and family made inexpressibly miserable."[36]

But Morris was never fully exonerated; in the best-case scenario for him, he was morally guilty of an extramarital affair that he apparently refused ever to acknowledge. Burleson rather chose to intimate that Antônia was boy crazy. By innuendo, Burleson sought to shift blame for Antônia's situation squarely to her. As Brann pointed out, no attempt, so far as we know, was made by Burleson to determine the identity of the man (if not Morris) who had impregnated Antônia.

Burleson also attempted to distance Baylor from responsibility for this young woman who was thousands of miles away from her home in a foreign land with strange customs and a different language. Antônia, Burleson claimed, was never an official "ward" of Baylor University. Instead, he and Mrs. Burleson took personal responsibility for Antônia, efforts he attempts to monetize by asserting they spent $320 on her in room, board, and clothing. In return, they received domestic services from Antônia that "would have been dear at $1.00 a month" after deducting "the trouble and annoyance of teaching her what to do, and seeing that she did it."[37]

Burleson's literary efforts in the pamphlet were mostly exerted in defending the Baylor "brand" and reassuring Texas Baptists that their daughters were safe at Baylor. At the least, Burleson was guilty of inhospitable treatment of the daughter of a distinguished and lauded national who was the first ordained Brazilian Baptist minister who helped establish the first Baptist congregation in Brazil outside the confines of Confederate colonies.

Finally, there is no doubt that race played a significant role in these events. The racial composition of nineteenth-century Brazil was complex. Brazil is similar to the US in terms of racial taxonomy, Brazilian Whites (who the missionaries sometimes called "Portuguese") were perceived as elites, Afro-Brazilians (who the missionaries sometimes called "Africans") were still mostly enslaved until 1888, and there were many mixed options in between. The mixing of races in Brazil caused anxiety among missionaries for several decades—Z. C. Taylor himself refused to marry Brazilians of different races on at least one occasion, a decision he proudly defended. Antônio Teixeira was well-received in the Confederate colony of Santa Barbara, where he was baptized by a Southern American. It is highly unlikely that the Santa Barbara church would welcome someone whom they perceived as Black as they did Teixeira. That said, this does not mean that

---

[36] Burleson, "The Brazilian Girl."
[37] Burleson, "The Brazilian Girl."

US missionaries saw White Brazilians as equals—but they certainly didn't see them the way they saw Black Brazilians or Brazilians of mixed races. This means that even if Antônia was "White" in Brazil, it doesn't mean she was "White" in Texas—and the story of Whiteness in the US, with its own complexities, inclusions, and exclusions, also reveals the fluidity of how race is constructed around shifting geographic, chronological, ethnic, and economic boundaries.

Evidence that Antônia may not have been perceived as "White" can be found in Burleson's comment that Antônia had a seat at the dinner table, but "preferred to wait and talk with the servants, as her Pastor, John the Baptist, who baptized her was a negro preacher."[38] Before the rape, Antônia occupied a liminal space in terms of racial identity. On the one hand, she was accepted, at least initially, as a student at Baylor, indicating she was, to some degree, counted as White. But Antônia worshipped in one of the Black Baptist churches in Waco and was a domestic servant in the Burleson household. From that perspective, she was clearly perceived as "non-White." Can one imagine Burleson relegating the daughter of a prominent *White* Baptist preacher to the role of domestic servant? After her pregnancy and charges of rape against Morris, Antônia was moved decisively out of the White space she had tenuously occupied (and lost whatever few "White" privileges she had previously enjoyed). Brann recognized that Antônia, as a foreigner and now unambiguously reckoned a person of color, stood little chance of surviving well when challenging the power dynamics of the Baylor machinery.[39]

Conclusion

Steen Morris, who got off scot-free, presumably returned to his life of privilege.[40] One can only speculate regarding the damage inflicted on young Antônia.[41]

---

[38] Burleson, "The Brazilian Girl."

[39] This is not to suggest that W. C. Brann was some liberal progressive ahead of his time in terms of race relations. *The Iconoclast* was filled with venomous anti-Catholic, anti-Jewish, and racist rhetoric.

[40] Little is known yet about Steen Morris (February 4, 1867–March 3, 1911). He and Nettie Torry migrated to Louisiana; they had three children. He is buried in Nolley Memorial Methodist Cemetery in Jena, La Salle Parrish, Louisiana.

[41] Antônio Teixeira's biographer apparently did not even know her name: "First-born daughter. Her name is unknown. She was born in Alagoas. It is said she married a North American, and went to live in the United States of America. In 1915, she tried to get close again to her relatives in Brazil, however unsuccessfully. Nothing else is known of her, or if she has descendants"; Antunes de Oliveira, *Antônio Teixeira de Alburquerque,*

Brann, as we learned, was shot down in the streets of Waco in 1898. The year before, on June 10, 1897, Baylor's Board of Trustees resolved to transition Burleson out of the President's office, designating him President Emeritus of the university for life. Burleson reluctantly accepted the position. The Teixeira affair was not mentioned publicly, but Burleson partly blamed it on what he considered his premature removal from office.[42] Soon after his death, efforts were made to rehabilitate Burleson's reputation, which had been stained by Antônia's mistreatment and abuse. A Baylor committee (that included a young Pat Neff, who would later serve as Texas governor and Baylor President) commissioned a statue of Rufus Burleson to be erected in the quadrangle surrounded by Old Main, Georgia Burleson Hall, Carroll Science Building, and Carroll Library and Chapel. The purpose here has been to retell Antônia's story from a different perspective and to give a fuller picture of Rufus Burleson, the man. Rufus Burleson is, not without reason, an admired and revered figure at Baylor and in Texas Baptist life. This episode surely represents the nadir of his career.[43] It is imperative that we recognize and acknowledge Antônia's story as paradigmatic of the institutional racism of Baylor (and other institutions). In this case, the racism was entangled with sexism, that together have too often taken a tremendous toll, albeit in different ways, not only on our Black brothers and sisters, but on our Brown brothers and sisters as well. Beyond the grave, Antônia Teixeira still cries out for justice; who will answer?

23.

[42] Lomax, "The Apostle of the Devil." Burleson was already in his seventies when the Teixeira incident occurred.

[43] *The Baylor University Commission on Historic Representation: Final Report* (December 2020), 47, recommended to the Baylor University Board of Regents and Administration that the Burleson Quadrangle be renamed and that the Burleson statue be moved to "a less prominent location." In addition to Burleson's connections to the "Lost Cause" movement, the Report (46) also cited "issues regarding the treatment of Antônia Teixeira, a young woman entrusted to the care of the Burleson family during Rufus Burleson's presidency whose rape and controversy surrounding the related criminal case contributed to Burleson's retirement as Baylor President in 1897." On July 18, 2022, the Burleson statue was removed from the Quadrangle.

BAPTISTS IN THE MAJORITY WORLD

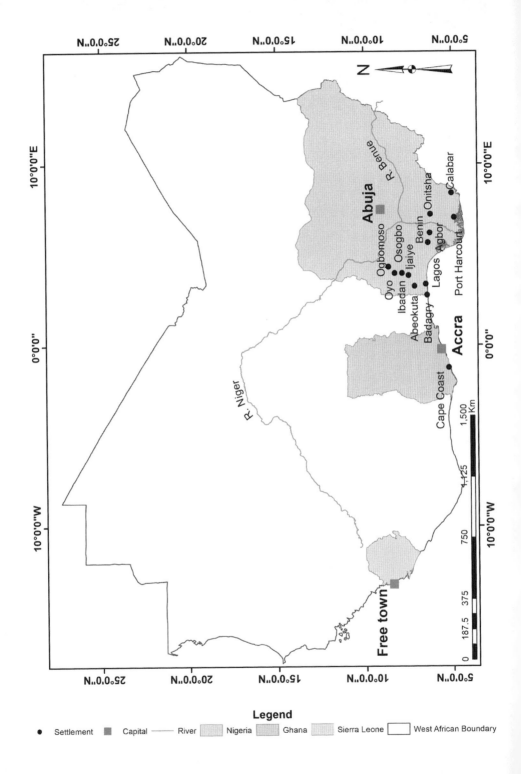

SOUTHERN BAPTIST CONVENTION MISSIONS AND FEMALE EDUCATION IN NIGERIA

Matthews A. Ojo

This essay examines the activities of Southern Baptist Convention missionaries in Nigeria, with particular focus on their endeavors to provide education to females at the elementary, secondary, and vocational levels from the mid-nineteenth century until the 1950s. This essay argues that although the provision of female education from the late nineteenth century was a radical intervention in the social emancipation that Southern Baptist missions and other Protestant missions envisaged for various African societies among which they worked, traditional perception of females as a subordinate social class by traditional African societies and by Western societies, and lack of human resources to teach in the schools, retarded the progress of female education until the 1950s.

In the nineteenth century, Western education, comprised of mostly elementary education and later vocational training and secondary education, constituted one of the important tools for Christian evangelization in Africa.[1] While adults showed reluctance to abandon their traditional African religion, children were more receptive to the Gospel through schooling. Southern Baptist missions were among the first three major Christian organizations that laid the foundation of Western education in Nigeria in the nineteenth century, and the churches controlled the provision of educational institutions unhindered until the 1920s when the British colonial administration began to regulate formal educational institutions. In the nineteenth and early twentieth centuries, Baptist mission work and its educational endeavors were concentrated in Western Nigeria, the autochthonous home of the Yoruba people, one of the largest ethnic groups in Nigeria.

---

[1] Magnus O. Bassey, "Missionary Rivalry and Educational Expansion in Southern Nigeria, 1885–1932," *The Journal of Negro Education* 60, no. 1 (Winter 1991): 36–46. See also Brendan Carmody, "Conversion and Schools in Chikuni, 1905–39," *Africa: Journal of the International African Institute* 58, no. 2 (April 1988): 193–209; and Felix K. Ekechi, "The Holy Ghost Fathers in Eastern Nigeria, 1885–1920: Observations on Missionary Strategy," *African Studies Review* 15, no. 2 (September 1972): 217–39; and Sonia F. Graham, *Government and Mission Education in Northern Nigeria 1900–1919* (Ibadan: Ibadan University Press, 1966).

Western missionaries in the nineteenth and early twentieth centuries were mostly men, though their wives accompanied them. Mary Slessor, a single woman who was appointed by the Scottish United Presbyterian Church to Calabar, Southeastern Nigeria, in August 1876, was an exception.[2] The preference for men was a reflection of the patriarchy of Western and African societies in those centuries.

I am drawing my facts from records of the missionary activities of the Foreign Mission Board of the Southern Baptist Convention in Nigeria and records of the Baptist girls' schools in Nigeria. Some pertinent questions to ask are: what ideas and values were embedded in the training of girls in the nineteenth and early twentieth in Nigeria? To what extent did female education on the Western model promote any fundamental shift in the status and role of women in Nigerian society in early twentieth century? And to what extent did formal Western education provide females with opportunities for social and material benefits beyond the strict evangelical goal of conversion?

An Overview of Southern Baptist Missions in Nigeria

Sustained Christian evangelization in Nigeria began in September 1842 when the Wesleyan Methodist Missionary Society and the Church Missionary Society (Anglican), in response to a plea from some freed slaves who had settled in Badagry, a coastal town in Southwestern Nigeria, sent resident missionaries to Badagry, and to Abeokuta, the next major town in the interior.[3]

Thomas Jefferson Bowen, the pioneer missionary of the Foreign Missions Board, Southern Baptist Convention, USA, landed in Badagry on August 5, 1850 and later moved to Abeokuta. He worked alone in Abeokuta until 1853 when on his return from a furlough, an additional three missionaries accompanied him. Bowen and his wife later moved to Ijaiye, another major town in the interior and in 1855 to Ogbomoso, a much bigger town, where his preaching laid the foundation of a strong Baptist work in the town, which had become the fulcrum of Baptist work in Nigeria. Additional Baptist missionaries came to Yorubaland in the 1860s, and despite a short break from 1869 to 1875, caused by

---

[2] Jeanette Hardage, "The Legacy of Mary Slessor," *International Bulletin of Missionary Research* 26, no. 4 (October 2002): 178–81. See also J. H. Proctor, "Serving God and the Empire: Mary Slessor in South-Eastern Nigeria, 1876–1915," *Journal of Religion in Africa* 30, no. 1 (February 2000): 45–61.

[3] J. F. Ade Ajayi, *Christian Missions in Nigeria: 1841–1891* (London: Longmans, 1965), 25–52. See also E. A. Ayandele, *The Missionary Impact on Modern Nigeria: 1842–1914* (London: Longmans, 1966), 283–304.

the American Civil War, the work progressed rapidly, partly fueled by competition with the Anglicans who also concentrated their efforts in this same geographical area.[4] By the close of the century, hundreds of converts were won and Baptist churches were planted in about twenty towns in Southwestern Nigeria, the result of hard work, heroism, persistence, and divine favor.

The Beginnings of Baptist Female Education, 1842–1879

Although preceded by the Methodists and Anglicans who had started some form of schooling for their workers and emigrants from Sierra Leone in 1843 and 1847 respectively,[5] the provision of female education by the Baptists started modestly. First, in January 1854, Mrs. Laurenna Bowen, wife of the pioneer Baptist missionary, started the instruction of a Yoruba girl, Mosibi, in sewing and reading at Ijaiye. At the end of the same month, Mrs. Bowen began a Sunday School for seventeen boys and girls.[6] Equally significant was Mrs. Sarah Harden, the wife of an African American Baptist missionary stationed in Lagos, who on January 17, 1859 began a girls' school with four pupils in the Baptist compound in Lagos.[7]

Generally, in this first period of endeavor in Western education, few girls were trained in the residences of the missionaries. Evidence indicates that some of the girls, who were trained alongside boys in the day schools, excelled in their studies. Although there was no school building, and neither was there any formalized curriculum, the pupils were taught reading, writing, arithmetic, and sewing. Schooling was free, and the children regularly received gifts of clothes, books, and pencils from the missionaries.

---

[4] S. Ademola Ajayi, *Baptist Work in Nigeria, 1850–2005: A Comprehensive History* (Ibadan: Book Wright Publishers, 2010). See also T. J. Bowen, *Adventures and Missionary Labours in Several Counties in the Interior of Africa from 1849 to 1856,* 2nd ed. (London: Frank Cass, 1968); and Collins Travis, *The Baptist Mission of Nigeria, 1850–1993: A History of the Southern Baptist Convention Missionary Work in Nigeria* (Ibadan: Associated Book Makers, 1993).

[5] Sarah Tucker, *Abeokuta or Sunrise Within the Tropics* (New York: Robert Carter & Brothers, 1854), 136, 189–90.

[6] Cecil Roberson, "A Chronology: A List of Dates and Events Relative to the History of the Baptists of Nigeria, West Africa," typewritten manuscript, 1970, Nigerian Baptist Theological Seminary (NBTS) Library, Ogbomoso, 7.

[7] Cecil Roberson, "Baptist Female Education Until 1910," *Nigerian Baptist Historical Documents*, 1965, NBTS Library, Ogbomoso, 1–2. See also Cecil Roberson, *A History of Baptists in Nigeria, West Africa: 1849–1935*, typewritten manuscript, 1970, NBTS Library, Ogbomoso, 64.

The Domestic Value of Female Education, 1880–1927

By the 1880s, the training of girls began to go beyond rudimentary training in the homes of missionaries, and planned training programs with standard curricula were put into place, albeit slowly. Although there was an increased awareness of the education of girls, this awareness was developed on the philosophy that female education was of domestic value in the evangelization program. From the 1880s, the philosophy of the education of female children was to prepare them "for the duties of life as wives to the male converts."[8] C. E. Smith, a Southern Baptist missionary in Nigeria about 1900, argued that "I think it will be a fine thing to have a girls' training institution school that the wives of our young men might be suitable helpmeets for the their husbands in the work."[9] Eventually, Baptist missionaries during this period focused their attention on the domestic value of preparing girls as prospective Christian wives for male converts and also for the girls to assume their domestic roles as good Christian mothers in the homes.

It was the expediency of the time that partly demanded such an approach. For example, in the late 1850s in Abeokuta, there were instances of persecution when the women betrothed to men who had converted to Christianity were withdrawn by the brides' parents on account of the abandonment of traditional Yoruba gods.[10] Equally in Onitsha, Eastern Nigeria in the 1890s, it was very difficult getting marriageable girls for the male converts because the senior men who were in African traditional religions exercised control over bride wealth and marriage partners, and they were not kind to the Christians.[11] Consequently, this domestic value of female education shaped the curriculum in the few female institutions that were established at this time. The training consisted of reading, writing in Yoruba and English, and sewing, knitting, or dressmaking. In comparison, boys were taught English, poetry, arithmetic, geography, hygiene, and also Latin, the subject for the enlightened minds at that time.

The earliest effort of the Baptists to promote any formal female education was the Baptist Girls' Institute established in Oyo in August 1902. The school operated on the ground floor of the mission house and was placed under the supervision of Rev. and Mrs. S. G. Pinnock, the resident missionaries. As a tool

---

[8] F. Deaville Walker, *The Romance of the Black River* (London: Church Missionary Society, 1931), 213.

[9] Roberson, "Baptist Female Education," 1.

[10] Tucker, *Abeokuta or Sunrise Within the Tropics*, 171–72.

[11] Misty L. Bastian, "Young Converts: Christian Missions, Gender and Youth in Onitsha, Nigeria 1880–1929," *Anthropological Quarterly* 73, no. 3 (July 2000): 145–58.

in the evangelization of the Yoruba people, it was aimed at producing indigenes who would be trained to preach and teach.[12] The school received the unanimous approval of all Baptist missionaries since it was meant to serve all the Baptist stations, hence it was supported by regular mission appropriation. Barely a year after its establishment, there were twenty pupils in the school.[13] A report by S. G. Pinnock in 1905 indicated that eleven out of seventeen pupils had passed an examination.[14] However, despite its steady growth, the school came to an abrupt end on June 7, 1909, when the paramount ruler, the Alaafin of Oyo, exiled the Pinnocks from the town over a lingering feud. The school was then left in the care of Mrs. Carrie Lumbley, who had relocated to Oyo after the death of her missionary husband in the late 1890s. In late 1909, Mrs. Lumbley also moved to Abeokuta due to loneliness and difficulty getting girls to come to the school.[15]

This school reopened in Abeokuta in early January 1910 under the leadership of Mrs. Lumbley at the missionaries' residence at Ago-Ijaiye, a community of Abeokuta.[16] A group of four girls who were brought from Oyo, and a few from the new station, were assembled in the lower rooms of the mission residence. By the end of 1910, there were fourteen pupils, growing to twenty in 1911.[17] The Foreign Mission Board sought to recall Mrs. Lumbley from the mission field, but her insistence to continue the missionary assignment alone brought about the change in the operation of the Baptist work in Nigeria. Eventually the success of Mrs. Lumbley with the school in Abeokuta facilitated the appointment of single female missionaries to Africa.

In 1912, the paramount ruler of Abeokuta donated two plots of land to the school at the suburb of Idi Aba because the mission was not immediately responding to Lumbley's request for expansion. Subsequently, decisions were made to raise the standard of the school and to make it gradually self-supporting.[18] Thereafter, churches and individuals within and outside the country who were fascinated by the phenomenal activities and growth of the school began to support it generously. As a pioneering female school in the interior of Yorubaland, the significance of the school broke the cultural jinx against female

---

[12] Roberson, "Chronology," 85. See also "Minutes of the Baptist Mission of Nigeria, 1850–1940," January 19, 1909, NBTS Library, Ogbomoso.

[13] Cecil Roberson, *A History of Baptist Mission, Ishokun, Oyo: 1856–1925*, typewritten manuscript, 1972, NBTS Library, Ogbomoso, 22.

[14] Roberson, "Baptist Female Education," 2.

[15] Roberson, 6.

[16] Roberson, 5.

[17] Roberson, *A History of Baptists in Nigeria*, 292.

[18] Roberson, 293.

education among the Yoruba people. In fact, the school became an evangelizing force among the pupils as they interacted and witnessed in the community. More importantly, the school set a pattern for girls' education in years to come.

In the early years, the curriculum consisted of reading, writing, and some domestic subjects such as sewing and knitting. However, by the 1940s, the school had grown to become a full secondary school offering secular subjects tailored towards providing functional and integrated education. Its elementary section also attracted many female pupils.

Another important Baptist female institution, the Elam Iyawo School at Shaki, in northwestern Yorubaland, pursued vigorously the domestic education which some of the missionaries had advocated for since 1900. The school was established first at Abeokuta by Miss N. C. Young as a class for prospective brides in 1933. It was formally opened at Shaki on April 17, 1934 and renamed Elam Memorial Baptist Iyawo Girls' School.[19] The pioneer teachers were two female missionaries and two Nigerian women. On the first day of enrollment, there were six girls, and by the end of that year, nine girls were on the roll. The number rose to eighteen in 1935, and by June 1964 when the record was terminated, 842 females had attended the school.[20] Not all the young women finished their sessions as some withdrew for unstated reasons.

This school was established as a school for training housewives for male converts. The students were taught the general principles of housekeeping, the care of children, and equally they were impressed with the ideals of being good housewives. Its success could be seen in the fact that several indigenous preachers and church workers were anxious to marry from among the trained women who came from different parts of the country where Baptist work had been established.

During this period, other Christian missions did not fare better in female education. For example, Methodist Girls' High School established in Lagos in 1879 as the third secondary institution in the country could not proceed for lack of teachers. There were only fifteen students in 1890, and thereafter the school was closed for almost twenty years. It was reopened in 1912 with 134 pupils graded into primary sections, intermediaries, and the high school sections. Even by 1920, there were only four teachers in the school—all women.[21] However, this school remained the only Methodist educational institution for girls until

---

[19] "Iyawo" is the Yoruba word for "wife."

[20] *Elam Memorial School Log Book*. NBTS Library, Ogbomoso.

[21] Mercy A. Oduyoye, *Leadership Development in the Methodist Church Nigeria 1842–1962* (Ibadan: Sefer, 1992), 54–55, 63–64.

the third decade of the twentieth century. In 1872, the Anglicans attempted a girls' school in Lagos, but it was not very successful.

Comprehensive Education for Females, 1928–1950s

The colonial government began to take more active interest in education after the amalgamation of the Northern Protectorate and the Southern Protectorate to create Nigeria as a single country. The Education Ordinance of 1926–27 for the whole country gave power to the government Education Department to close down any school that failed to meet certain minimum standards after inspections.[22] Indirectly, the Education Ordinance challenged Christian missions to improve the standards of their schools. A concerted opposition to certain sections of the Ordinance by some mission agencies invariably led to their coming together, and subsequently the formation of the Christian Council of Nigeria.

In response to the Ordinance, in April 1928, the Southern Baptist missionaries, operating then as Baptist Mission of Nigeria, accepted in principle the policy of receiving government grants-in-aid for its schools, an indication that the standards of Baptist schools would be upgraded to meet the standards set by the colonial administration. This decision was significant for the Southern Baptists who held on to the doctrine of separation of church and state. In January 1930, Baptist Mission of Nigeria decided to appoint a supervisor of Baptist schools in Western Nigeria, the first of its kind.[23]

With these developments, the girls' school in Abeokuta attained higher standards with more qualified teachers employed, and within the next decade it was offering secondary education. Hence, it became the flagship of Baptist female education in the country. This legacy was disrupted in 1975 when the Nigerian military government compulsorily took over the ownership of all elementary and secondary schools from the Christian missions.[24] By the new millennium, government had returned the school back to the Baptist Mission of Nigeria, which tried to salvage its old reputation.

Another advance in female education was the opening of a second institution for females in Lagos. Baptist Academy, a secondary school, opened

---

[22] Martins Fabunmi, "Historical Analysis of Educational Policy Formulation In Nigeria: Implications For Educational Planning And Policy," *International Journal of African & African American Studies* 4, no. 2 (July 2005): 1–7.

[23] Roberson, "Chronology," entries for April 13, 1928 and January 1, 1930, 191, 197.

[24] Austin Ahanotu, "The Nigerian Military and the Issue of State Control of Mission Schools," *Church History* 52, no. 3 (September 1983): 333–44.

November 1, 1886 and initially admitted mostly boys, though by the first decade of the twentieth century, some girls were also admitted.[25] However, the availability of a small number of female missionaries necessitated some consideration for another school to be devoted to the training of females.

The Reagan Memorial Baptist Girls' School, Lagos was opened on June 2, 1941 and named in memory of Miss Lucille Reagan, an American missionary who came to Nigeria in October 1921 and was appointed the vice principal and later principal of Baptist Academy, Lagos in June 1924 and May 1928 respectively. She died at Ogbomoso on July 12, 1937, as a result of a yellow fever attack.[26] The new school opened with a kindergarten as well as a primary section. It started on a temporary site, but on June 23, 1941, two school buildings were dedicated at its permanent site in the Yaba Estate.[27] The first building was erected with funds from Baptist women of Texas in memory of Miss Reagan. Right from its inception it received good patronage, hence it grew rapidly.

Miss Cora Ney Hardy became the principal in 1949 and admitted the first set of girls for secondary education in 1952.[28] Statistics showed a total enrollment of 145 girls in 1965 and 900 in 1976. The enrollment went up to 1,860 in 1977 as another school was merged with the school when government took over mission schools.[29] The subjects included cooking, sewing, housewifery, and domestic science. Baptist missionaries wanted to produce women who would play leading roles in building their nation, hence the school was well staffed. Reagan Girls' High School still exists as a major female institution in Lagos, and the ownership of the Baptists was restored in the 1990s.

The next major enterprise in female education was the Baptist Girls' High School in Agbor, Midwestern Nigeria, which was opened in 1946 as the first secondary school in that region. Its establishment was stimulated by Miss Ruth Walden, another female missionary who was concerned about girls' education in the Delta area of Nigeria. In 1940, a committee appointed by the Baptist Mission agreed to locate a girls' school at Agbor. In January 1947, nineteen girls were in standards three through five. There were two pioneer teachers, and in 1947, two missionaries, Willie Kate Baldwin and Mildred Crabtree, joined the staff, the

---

[25] Roberson, "Chronology," entry for November 1, 1886, 47.

[26] Roberson, entry for July 12, 1937, 222.

[27] Roberson, entry for June 23, 1941, 239.

[28] Historical Committee. *A Brief History of Reagan Memorial Baptist Girls' Secondary School, Yaba: Golden Jubilee (1941–1991)* (Lagos: Remckoye Press Ltd., 1991), 11.

[29] *A Brief History of Reagan Memorial Baptist Girls'*, 11, 13.

former serving as principal, and in 1948, Miss M. E. Yancey joined the staff. The number of students grew into the hundreds by the 1960s.[30]

Apart from operating as a full secondary school and providing a secular education, it also provided spiritual activities and involved the girls in denominational religious activities. In 1975, the school was taken over by the government and the name changed to Agbor Girls' Grammar School, and in 2012, it was handed back to the Nigerian Baptist Convention, successor to the Baptist Mission of Nigeria.[31]

By the 1950s, female education was progressing among Baptists, though slowly. The last endeavors for female education was the Baptist Girls' High School, Osogbo, which opened on January 1, 1956 with the same goal of creating more educational opportunities for girls.[32] It grew rapidly in the 1960s and 1970s until it was also compulsorily taken over by the government in 1975. Overall, at the end of the 1950s, four female schools were in operation. Each had an elementary school section which provided students for the secondary school branches. Each of the schools was headed by a Southern Baptist female missionary, and almost all the teachers with graduate degrees were missionaries. The schools provided comprehensive secondary education, while music and the school choirs were popular pastimes among the students. The schools operated boarding facilities, which was a platform to instill discipline and mainstream the Christian culture that was envisaged. The chapel was at the center of the religious activities of each school, and participation in the religious activities was compulsory. Furthermore, the schools received grants from the government after meeting certain criteria, and students paid some amounts as school fees, while infrastructures were provided from appropriations sent from the United States to the Baptist Mission of Nigeria.

Making a regional comparison of the number of secondary schools in Western Nigeria until the end of 1950 reveals the following. There were only nine secondary schools in Western Nigeria in 1913, and this grew to sixteen in 1940, rising to twenty between 1941 and 1945, and increased to twenty-two in 1950. By 1945, Baptists had four secondary schools, Anglicans had six, the Roman Catholics had one, and by 1950, the number of Baptist secondary schools had

---

[30] Ugochukwu Ezekiel Ezeimoh, "The Growth And Development Of Baptist Girls' High School, Agbor," unpublished Bachelor of Arts (History) degree essay, University of Benin, Benin City, Nigeria, August 2016, 24–25.

[31] Ugochukwu, "Growth and Development," 28–31.

[32] Roberson, "Chronology," 270.

increased to six, of which three were girls' schools.[33] Considering enrollment, there were a total of 1,281 students in 1940 in the region, rising to 1,895 in 1945 and to 4,563 in 1950. Adeyinka has argued that among other factors, the stringent conditions of the 1926–27 Education Ordinance, which set high standards and compulsory inspection for schools, initially slowed down the opening of more schools by Christian missions as they sought to bring their standards up to the required levels set by the government.[34]

In January 1955, the government of Western Nigeria, under the nationalist Obafemi Awolowo, introduced compulsory and universal elementary education in the region, and established hundreds of elementary schools in most towns and villages. Within a short time, the population of school pupils rose dramatically, and in the 1960s, a number of secondary schools and teachers' training colleges emerged to absorb the products from these schools. In response, the Baptists, under the leadership of Southern Baptist missionaries, invested much in broadening access to elementary education such that in almost every town where a Baptist church was established, a Baptist elementary school also operated alongside it. In general, the Baptist female institutions became springboards to raising the status and profile of females in the society, as some of the products of the Baptist female schools later acquired university degrees and assumed leadership positions in the administrative and educational spheres.

Conclusion

This essay has examined the activities of the Southern Baptist Convention missionaries with particular focus on their endeavors to provide education to females. After some success in their evangelistic program, the missionaries turned their attention to providing education for females, initially at the elementary level and later venturing into secondary education. The self-seeking domestic purpose, coupled with the patriarchal nature of nineteenth-century society both in the United States and in Southwestern Nigeria, did not allow the missionaries to see the full potential of female education. Indeed, the endeavor was also full of contradictions. First, there was a great disparity between the scope and quality of education for boys and girls. Second, there was a structural problem for the

---

[33] A. Ade. Adeyinka, "Local Community Efforts in the Development of Secondary Grammar School Education in the Western State of Nigeria, 1925–1955," *The Journal of Negro Education* 45, no. 3 (Summer 1976): 263–74. See also J. F. Ade Ajayi, "The Development of Secondary Grammar School Education in Nigeria," *Journal of the Historical Society of Nigeria* 2, no. 4 (December 1963): 517–35.

[34] Adeyinka, "Local Community Efforts," 263–65.

Southern Baptist Convention mission, which only engaged male missionaries for most of the nineteenth century and yet sought to promote female education. Third, European and traditional African gender biases about the status and roles of females in the society were important drivers in the conception of female education in Nigeria. Although there was little opposition to female education from the indigenous people, their response was rather poor arising from the traditional attitudes to females in the society.

Generally, Baptist female education until the 1930s was focused on character training and spiritual development and a consolidation of the evangelization work. Indeed, it was domestic in orientation, sustained by the wives of missionaries and later by single female missionaries, tailored to making females more subservient and subordinate to males as "Christian wives," and not fully conceived with sustainable development goals in mind. This perception began to change in the 1940s with the establishment of girls' secondary schools.

As change agents for a hundred years from 1842, Christian missions provided the direction of female education in the country. Although the number of schools for females and the enrollment was small, looking back, this innovation could be considered a major change in the cultural perspectives of the subordinate position of females in the society. The girls and women who attended the mission schools derived some prestige as educated women in what could be considered a hostile environment. Moreover, their sexuality—the moral purity of being chaste brides—and their potentials as good marriage partners further reinforced traditional African values of chastity as these women became potential role models to other women; an achievement of Christian missions' social goal of having women ready to live forever in monogamous relationships. Indirectly, Southern Baptist missionaries moved marriage to a central place in the new Christian culture.

Overall, Baptist missions and their foray into female education was a social innovation that set in motion social and political processes. These processes included women's empowerment through education, an agenda which has become an integral part of the social rights of women in the contemporary world.

PART THREE

BAPTISTS IN THE TWENTIETH AND

TWENTY-FIRST CENTURIES

BAPTISTS IN EUROPE

"FERMENT" IN THE CONGREGATION: GENDER DYNAMICS AND CONFLICT WITHIN THE MOSCOW BAPTIST CONGREGATION IN THE 1950S AND 1960S

Miriam Dobson

In the second half of the nineteenth century, new religious traditions emerged in the Tsarist Empire as the country experienced what one historian has called "Russia's lost Reformation."[1] From scattered beginnings, two significant Protestant groups emerged: the Baptists and the Evangelical Christians. In the first years of the Revolution, it almost seemed that the new Soviet state—intent as it was on the destruction of the Russian Orthodox Church—might seek accommodation with these so-called "sectarians."[2] As a result, certain forms of evangelism were possible in the 1920s: new Protestant congregations were established in more distant corners of the USSR and, with the aid of overseas missionaries, Pentecostalism spread.[3] But from the late 1920s onwards, Protestant communities and preachers endured sustained and violent persecution.[4] This article takes as its starting point the rather different set of strategies the Soviet state adopted during and after the Second World War. Perhaps unexpectedly, the state then sought to create a unified and centralized Evangelical Christian-Baptist church, with the Moscow Congregation of Evangelical Christians Baptists (hereafter MCECB) as its showcase institution.

---

[1] Sergei I. Zhuk, *Russia's Lost Reformation: Peasants, Millennialism, and Radical Sects in Southern Russia and Ukraine, 1830–1917* (Baltimore: Johns Hopkins University Press, 2004).

[2] Tat'iana Nikol'skaia, *Russkii protestantizm i gosudarstvennaia vlast' v 1905–1991 godakh* (Saint Petersburg: Evropeiskii universitet v Sankt-Peterburge, 2009) 51; S. N. Savinskii, *Istoriia evangel'skikh Khristian-Baptistov Ukrainy, Rossii, Belorussii. Chast' 2 (1917–1967)* (Saint Petersburg: Bibliia dlia vsekh, 2001), 14.

[3] Nikol'skaia, *Russkii protestantizm*, 69–75.

[4] A. I. Savin, "Repressii v otnoshenii evangel'skikh veruiushchikh v khode 'kulatskoi operatsii' NKVD," in *Stalinizm v sovetskoi provintsii 1937–1938gg.: Massovaia operatsiia na osnove prikaza no. 00447*, ed. M. Iunge, B. Bonvech, and R. Binner, 303–42 (Moscow: Rosspen, 2009).

This article uses the records of church leaders' meetings to explore how elusive this unity was to prove, even within the highly prominent and regulated MCECB. I take as a first case study a protracted conflict in the early 1950s sparked by divergent interpretations of scripture with regard to second marriages. This issue was of special importance for women who—as an overwhelming majority within the church—faced a deficit of suitable men. But as this and a later case from the MCECB indicate, the increased importance the state's new religious policy awarded to pastors, or the "ministerial personnel," as they were sometimes dubbed in official texts, did not prevent women from having a role in these conflicts. I uncover a vibrant culture of anonymous letter writing, petitioning, and rumor within the MCECB in which both female and male church members were active. I also show how on occasion certain older women contributed to, and even enflamed, discord, although this tradition seems to have weakened by the 1960s, as my second case study indicates. In these different ways, the pastors' authority in fact proved rather vulnerable.

Establishing Hierarchy, Seeking Unity: The Historical Background

After the persecution that had characterized religious life in the late 1920s and 1930s, the Second World War saw some reprieve for most religious groups in the USSR. Famously, in 1943, Stalin met with the three metropolitans of the Russian Orthodox Church.[5] Less famously, the Soviet state took a similar approach in its relations with other religious traditions. After Stalin's face-to-face with the three metropolitans, his deputies arranged similar meetings with the heads of other faiths and confessions.[6] They were now authorized to establish new ecclesiastical centers. For the Protestants, this meant that their two unions—the Union of Evangelical Christians and the Union of Baptists—were reestablished in a merged form and given a new remit as the All-Union Council of Evangelical Christians Baptists (AUCECB) in 1944.[7] At the same time, the Soviet government formed its own regulatory bodies for religious matters: the Council for the Affairs of the Russian Orthodox Church and its counterpart, the Council for the Affairs of Religious Cults (CARC), which oversaw the newly

---

[5] Steven Merritt Miner, *Stalin's Holy War: Religion, Nationalism, and Alliance Politics, 1941–1945* (Chapel Hill, NC: University of North Carolina Press, 2003).

[6] Eren Tasar, *Soviet and Muslim: the Institutionalization of Islam in Central Asia, 1943–1991* (New York: Oxford University Press, 2017), 46–55.

[7] Nikol'skaia, *Russkii protestantizm*, 123; Walter Sawatsky, *Soviet Evangelicals since World War II* (Kitchener: Herald Press, 1981), 78–104.

formed AUCECB.[8] The state had forged an infrastructure in which religious worship was permitted, whilst monitored, recorded, and (in theory) controlled by both state functionaries and church hierarchies.

The Soviet state was concerned about the evangelical resurgence that had taken place in the war and which seemed to be continuing in its wake. The officials who worked in CARC no longer wanted to use only repressive measures (such as arrest) to deal with the "problem" of evangelicals. Instead, they concluded, what was needed was a way to make the Protestants become more like the Orthodox, in terms of discipline and order at least; the new AUCECB was the tool to make this happen. CARC hoped to introduce a "clearly defined centralization and hierarchical system" to replace what was described as "the decentralization and anarchic existence of separate congregations." To this end, the new structure of the AUCECB included a layer of "senior pastors" [*starshie presvitery*], which CARC explicitly compared to the metropolitans and bishops of the Orthodox church.[9] A key CARC figure observed that the new structure gave much greater prominence to the "ministerial personnel" [*presviterskii sostav*], who were now responsible not only for spiritual leadership but the whole life of the congregation (a shift which he too described as the formation of an Orthodox-style "hierarchy"). The structure, he wrote, "entirely liquidates the sect's hazy 'democratism'" [*razplyvchatyi 'demokratizm'*], transferring much greater authority over congregational life into the hands of the pastors—pastors who were expected to accept CARC control.[10]

The state's objective in creating bodies such as the AUCECB was to reduce the complexity of the religious landscape. In the case of the Protestant tradition, they aimed to forge a single, umbrella organization. In addition to the merger of the Evangelical Christians and Baptists, the two major Pentecostal traditions were persuaded to join the AUCECB fold over the course of 1945 to 1947.[11] The chairman of CARC, I. V. Polianskii, referred to this process as *sliianie*, meaning fusion.[12] In Polianskii's view, a more unitary, streamlined religious institution would be easier to regulate, and more volatile, evangelical elements

---

[8] Nikol'skaia, *Russkii protestantizm*, 124–29.

[9] Rossiiskii gosudarstvennyi arkhiv sotsial'no-politicheskoi istorii (RGASPI) f. 17, op. 125, d. 506, ll. 17–22 (February 12, 1947), l. 19.

[10] RGASPI f. 17, op. 125, d. 506, ll. 26–65 (February, 1947), l. 40.

[11] T. K. Nikol'skaia, "Avgustovskoe soglashenie i pozitsii piatidesiatnikov v 40-50-kh. gg. XX v.," *Gosudarstvo, Religiia, Tserkov' v Rossii i za rubezhom*, no. 4 (2010): 124–33.

[12] RGASPI f. 82, op. 2, d. 498, ll. 48–49 (November 21, 1945), l. 48.

could be restrained. In the case of the MCECB, this coming together of Protestant traditions went further still; the building on Malyi Vuzovskii lane was not only home to the capital's congregation and the AUCECB headquarters but also housed the Seventh-Day Adventists.[13]

What does this all mean for gender dynamics within congregational life? Firstly, ordination as a pastor was only open to men, and so the enhanced role of the pastor gave men greater prominence in church life. Secondly, congregations were overwhelmingly, and increasingly, female. Reports produced by state officials frequently placed the proportion of women at between seventy and eighty percent, and sometimes even higher. This is a departure from pre-war communities, where male to female ratios seem to have been more even and women were more prominent in church life.[14] In an article I co-authored with Nadezhda Beliakova, we argued that in the postwar period women's opportunities were in many ways reduced—the position of deaconess almost disappeared, for example, and women appeared to preach rarely.[15] There were few calls for female ordination; in our reading of the archival record, the issue was not often raised. Even in tiny rural congregations that were almost exclusively female, women who took on leadership roles did so provisionally, expecting to hand their authority over to men as and when that became possible.[16] In our article Beliakova and I explored, however, some of the informal forms of authority women could take within these congregations and groups. In this piece I return to the informal agency women had in these communities, but this time with an explicit focus on moments of division and rupture.

The unity and peace that became cherished principles for the AUCECB and its leaders proved highly elusive. In fact, CARC officials had recognized almost from the outset the potential of the union to fracture and shatter. Describing in 1947 their goal of reducing ECB's "peculiar characteristics"

---

[13] Nadezhda Beliakova and Vera Kliueva, "'Kvartirnyi vopros tol'ko isportil ikh…': o konflikte vokrug odnogo molitvennogo pomeshcheniia v Moskve," *Istoriia* 7, no. 9 (2016).

[14] Nadezhda Beliakova and Miriam Dobson, *Zhenshchiny v evangel'skikh obshchinakh poslevoennogo SSSR. 1940–1980-e gg. Issledovaniia i istochniki* (Moscow: Indrik, 2015), 16–20.

[15] Nadezhda Beliakova and Miriam Dobson, "Protestant Women in the Late Soviet Era: Gender, Authority, and Dissent," *Canadian Slavonic Papers* 58 (2016): 117–40.

[16] For more on this, see Nadezhda Beliakova and Ekaterina Mironova, "Invisible Pastorship under Persecutions: Women in Evangelical Communities of Post-War USSR," in *Eight Essays on Russian Christianities*, ed. Igor Mikeshin, 108–31 (Saint Petersburg: Saint Petersburg Center for the History of Ideas, 2020).

[*ekstravagantnye osobennosti*] through the creation of a strong center, CARC leaders recognized the risk that this could create a new "split" [*otkol*], with schismatics striving to preserve the purity [*chistota*] of traditional Baptist practices. However, they believed that this possibility could safely be ignored because it was unlikely to occur in the near future and would probably involve only a very small minority of believers.[17] CARC leaders were right in a sense: a definitive split did not happen immediately. Yet the whole history of the AUCECB became a rather desperate quest to maintain this unity in the face of diverse threats. The inclusion of the Pentecostals in the AUCECB had been contentious from the outset, and in 1956, leading Pentecostal pastors recently released from prison convened an underground congress in Khar'kiv. They went on to form the Union of Christians of Evangelical Faith (KhVE), which was to give organizational structure to Pentecostals opposed to the merger with the AUCECB and to the suppression of important Pentecostal practices such as foot-washing and speaking in tongues.[18] Perhaps more dramatic and more unexpected for the AUCECB leaders was the 1961 rupture. Faced with new restrictions on church life, a group, initially called the "initiative group," condemned the AUCECB leaders for their concessions to the secular world, calling for the measures to be overturned, and for a new congress to be summoned to discuss these issues. By 1965, the "initiative group" had become the Council of Churches of Evangelical Baptists (the CCECB), and a new, rival church tradition was cemented.[19] Over the years the MCECB certainly lost members to both the Pentecostal and initiative movements, but there was never a decisive schism within the congregation. With the headquarters of the AUCECB and a whole team of pastors—not to mention the close attention of the capital's CARC officials—on hand, a unity of a sorts was maintained. But as this article will show, there were moments of quite significant discord, as recorded in the minutes and summaries of ministers' meetings. Church leaders wanted to preserve harmony within the congregation, but they also understood it to be their duty to protect their believers from sinfulness; at

---

[17] RGASPI f. 17, op. 125, d. 506, ll. 17–22 (February 12, 1947), 118–19.

[18] V. Kliueva and R. Poplavsky, "Russian Pentecostals: from the Soviet Union to Post-Soviet Russia," in *The Pentecostal World,* ed. Michael Wilkinson and Joerg Haustein (London: Routledge, 2023).

[19] For an overview of these divisions, see Nikol'skaia, *Russkii protestantizm,* 201–14; Walter Sawatsky, *Soviet Evangelicals since World War II,* 157–99. For a detailed account of the communications between the AUCECB and the initiative group, see A. Sinichkin, "Dialog mezhdu STsEKhB i VSEKhB 1961–1972 gg." *Put' bogopoznaniia: bogoslovsko-publitsicheskii zhurnal* 10 (2004): 40–80.

times, they could not agree on what this meant, or how these goals could be reconciled.

Congregations had various ways to try to discipline behavior that was either sinful or damaging to the congregation's unity. Pastors could engage church members susceptible to temptation in pastoral chats, offer public rebukes, or devote sermons to explaining and condemning particular behaviors.[20] Where these measures proved inadequate and a member had fallen into sin, the congregation could make the collective decision to excommunicate [*otluchit*] them. Excommunication could happen for various reasons, but common grounds were smoking and drinking alcohol, non-attendance at services, adultery, and, in some congregations, marriage to nonbelievers.[21] But excommunication itself could be a motor for further conflict: who was responsible for interpreting and applying the scriptures to real-life situations? In tricky cases, who was the final arbiter—the congregation or the pastor? Could external figures—such as the senior pastor for the region—have a say? As we shall see, the authority of the pastor was far from unchallenged, and informal practices such as slander, rumor, and refusing to take communion could be employed to weaken his standing. The shift in state policy during and after the Second World War had done much to enhance the standing and status of ordained men, but in the messy reality of congregational life, ministers did not speak with a single voice, and the positions they took were often contested.

Divorce and Remarriage (1951–52)

Let us take stock of the Moscow congregation, based on Malyi Vuzovskii lane in the very center of Moscow. In July 1950 membership stood at just over 3,300 with about another 300 or so members considered *priblizhennye*—those awaiting baptism.[22] Despite the size of the nineteenth-century church building, services were always crowded out. In an interview recorded in 2012, one woman who

---

[20] In 1969, A. I. Mitskevich gave an address to the AUCECB congress on the subject of excommunication. Mitskevich recommended caution in the use of excommunication and reminded his listeners of the other tools pastors held at their disposal to deal with sin and conflict within their congregations. Archive of the Russian Union of Evangelical Christians-Baptists (hereafter Archive of the RUECB), Box 9, File 3.

[21] On different reasons for excommunication, see Tsentral'nyi derzhavnyi arkhiv hromads'kykh ob'iednan' Ukrainy (hereafter TsDAHOU), f. 1, op. 24, d. 2741, ll. 199–277 (report from the CARC plenipotentiary for Ukraine, 1953), 217.

[22] Tsentral'nyi gosudarstvennyi arkhiv g. Moskvy (hereafter TsGAM) f. 3004, op. 1, d. 18, ll. 89–92 (Statistical information for the third quarter of 1950), l. 89.

moved to Moscow in 1950 as a young believer described the atmosphere she found at the church:

> When I arrived in Moscow, that is to the church in Moscow, I stood on the threshold, to go any further was absolutely impossible, and then I thought to myself, from now on I will come on hour earlier....I started to come an hour earlier so that I could get a place on the second floor, on the balcony, and I could see the choir, and all the preachers....Well nowadays everyone sits down in church, but of course then it wasn't possible to sit because the older people sat and us young ones didn't want to take up space. We were just happy that we had made it to God's house.[23]

As well as being exceptionally large and busy, the church was also of particular prominence: it was the showcase prayer house to which foreign visitors would be taken for a taste of the religious freedoms on offer in the Soviet Union. In 1950, for example, Protestant visitors from Belgium, England, and Australia were officially received.[24] The church's governing structures were also quite unusual as a result of its status. Whereas most registered congregations formed a committee of twenty members called the *dvadtsatka* [the twenty] comprised of the pastor, any deacons or preachers, and lay members, at the MCECB it was made up of the five members of the AUCECB's presidium, as well as the MCECB pastors, preachers, and senior AUCECB employees. The congregation had a significant cast of pastors and preachers, with varying degrees of experience and importance.[25] All this meant that the "ministerial personnel" were far more dominant than in other congregations. In 1950 the presidium of the AUCECB was composed of M. I. Zhidkov (president), A. V. Karev (general secretary), M. A. Orlov (vice-chairman), M. I. Goliaev (vice-chairman) and I. G. Ivanov (treasurer).[26] The five men played an important role both on the national and international stage but also within the life of the MCECB.

The congregation they ministered to was a growing one, with far more members joining than leaving. In the third quarter of 1950, for example, there

---

[23] Interview with V. (Moscow). Interview conducted by Miriam Dobson, July 7, 2012 (AHRC AH/I025883/1/10). This work was supported by the Arts and Humanities Research Council under Grant [AH/I025883/1].

[24] Gosudarstvennyi arkhiv Rossiiskoi Federatsii (hereafter GARF) f. 6991, op. 4, d. 6, l. 186.

[25] TsGAM f. 3004, op. 1, d. 93, ll. 32–33.

[26] Nikol'skaia, *Russkii protestantizm*, 41, 323–27.

were 138 new enrollments compared to 17 departures. Of those who joined the church, only 17 were men and 121 women; of these, more than half were widows or divorcees.[27] Many of these women came from provincial outposts, sometimes in search of employment; the church even acquired a reputation as the best place for elite Muscovites to acquire an honest servant.[28] In this short period of three months, the congregation saw three members excommunicated: an elderly couple because of their shouting matches [skloki], and a forty-eight-year-old woman for "slander" [kleveta] against Karev. She had spread rumors—both verbally and in written form—accusing him of adultery [blud].[29] As we shall see, this kind of ad hominem attack on the pastor was not unusual. As Alexander Popov wrote in his study of the AUCECB tradition,

> Insulting a pastor was a frequent reason for excommunication. At the same time, people who were excommunicated for this reason might consider themselves as heroes who dared to fight against evil in their leaders. The difference between abusive conduct and unmasking of evil-doers in the prophetic spirit was very unclear in the minds of many of the believers of that time.[30]

Given its strategic importance, size, and the close involvement of CARC in the workings of the presidium, it might be expected that the congregation would maintain discipline with relative ease. Yet several CARC reports for these years showed the potential for deep rifts to appear. As we shall see, the presidium of the AUCECB was itself bitterly divided. But it is also striking how ordinary members of the church—an overwhelmingly female cohort where women outnumbered men almost five to one—were ready to articulate their own criticism vis-à-vis their pastors.

This particular conflict began in 1951 when two female members of the congregation married divorced men. One woman was a member of the choir;

---

[27] Membership is given as 3,309. Of the 338 new members, 90 had been baptized whilst 48 had joined from other congregations. Of those who had been baptized, 51 were described as "workers," a category that included a variety of factory workers, manual laborers, caretakers, cleaners, railroad workers, shop workers, and nurses. TsGAM f. 3004, op. 1, d 18. Ll. 89–92.

[28] TsGAM f. 3004, op. 1, d. 24, ll. 34–37.

[29] TsGAM f. 3004, op. 1, d 18. ll. 89–92.

[30] Alexander Popov, "The Evangelical Christians-Baptists in the Soviet Union as a Hermeneutical Community: Examining the Identity of the All-Union Council of the ECB (AUCECB) through the Way the Bible Was Used in Its Publications," unpublished thesis, University of Wales and International Baptist Theological Seminary (2010), 228.

the other worked in the AUCECB canteen. A member of the presidium, Goliaev, considered the couples to be committing an act of adultery [*blud*]. Goliaev was deeply opposed to a church wedding being allowed, though Karev and Orlov were willing.[31] If this happened, he threatened, he would refuse any social contact [*obshchenie*] with whichever pastor performed the marriage; he would boycott the canteen (and no longer consider the woman in question a "sister"); and he would leave the council.[32] The AUCECB's leading brothers were in open conflict, and the reports record raised voices. Goliaev had support from several women who worked for the AUCECB, including the intriguing figure of V. M. Shcheglova, who refused to take communion for several months as her own symbolic act of protest. The small group ostracized the two couples and called for at least one of the newlywed women—the choir member—to be excommunicated [*otluchena*].[33] Much to their ire, Karev and Orlov refused to even contemplate excommunication on these grounds. The conflicts spilled out into the services. From the pulpit Goliaev denounced the marriage of divorcees. He described his own anti-divorce sermons as truthful and pure, and condemned others for preaching without regard to the scriptures. In turn, Orlov accused Goliaev of working himself into a frenzy [*isstuplenie*]: he "shouts with tears in his eyes and waving his arms."[34]

The records lay bare significant animosity between Orlov and Goliaev. The two pastors came from the different traditions of the AUCECB—Orlov had been leader of the Evangelical Christians in the 1930s, Goliaev was son of the Union of Baptists' last chairman—but there is little to suggest that this indicated a clear-cut confrontation between the two wings.[35] (At least initially, Goliaev had support from Ivanov who had belonged to the Evangelical Christian Union, for example.) The conflict does suggest, however, that even amongst the leading pastors of the AUCECB, there was quite significant divergence of opinion in terms of what represented sinful behavior in a believer's personal life, as well as quite distinct preaching styles. The guiding principle of the AUCECB was unity, but unity eluded them even within their own presidium. As one member of the congregation put it, "you preach peace and pray for peace, but we feel that there is

---

[31] TsAGM f. 3004, op. 1, d. 24, l. 119.

[32] TsAGM f. 3004, op. 1, d. 24, l. 120.

[33] For the proposal to excommunicate see TsAGM f. 3004, op. 1, d. 24, l. 121; on their refusal to greet the couples in question, see TsAGM f. 3004, op. 1, d. 24, l. 122.

[34] TsAGM f. 3004, op. 1, d. 24, l.121.

[35] Sawatsky, *Soviet Evangelicals*, 49.

no peace."[36] In 1954, Orlov and Goliaev were demoted from the presidium, leaving Zhidkov, Karev, and Ivanov in charge of "daily leadership."[37]

The case also confirms the vulnerability of the pastor. Despite their high standing, both Orlov and Goliaev came under attack from members of the congregation. Within a collective body numbering over three thousand, the passing of unsigned notes seems to have been common practice, and several of these notes came out against Goliaev's preaching style. One said that Goliaev had turned the pulpit into a "fairground show" [*balagan*] and made new members laugh, another that his sermons were like the "ramblings of a mad man" [*bred sumashedshego*]. A third accused him of transgressing scripture and cited Ephesians 4:29–31, verses that decried "unwholesome talk" and called for kindness, forgiveness, and compassion to others.[38] The following year, members of the congregation were still composing anonymous notes in which they expressed their sadness and weariness with Goliaev.[39] But in some quarters feelings also ran high against Orlov. By the spring of 1952, Orlov was speaking of a "campaign" being launched against him by Shcheglova, who worked in an administrative role in the AUCECB's office.[40] Whilst he had been absent from the church (through illness and work trips), she had "compromised" him in front of colleagues and choir members.[41] In the autumn of that year, even as Goliaev calmed, Shcheglova remained hostile to Orlov, calling him a bandit, drunkard, and unfit pastor.[42] Her distress was very real: she had known him in the 1920s when they had both worked in the Orel region, and she believed he had lost the sincerity and zeal of his youth, no longer offering the kind of spiritual and material support a pastor ought. For his part, Orlov believed that she, in cahoots with a former deaconess, was responsible for "agitating" against him.[43] He attributed her hostility to the fact that, following the death of his wife, he had rebuffed the proposal made by Ivanov's wife that he might marry Shcheglova.[44] In fact, he had married another member of the MCECB in 1948, something that may have made him more vulnerable to criticism, given that some within the ECB tradition believed that

---

[36] TSAGM f. 3004, op. 1, d. 29, l. 49.

[37] Sawatsky, *Soviet Evangelicals*, 179.

[38] TsAGM f. 3004, op. 1, d. 24, l. 122.

[39] TsAGM f. 3004, op. 1, d. 29, l. 50.

[40] *Bratskii vestnik* 2 (1979).

[41] TsAGM f. 3004, op. 1, d. 29, l. 49.

[42] TsAGM f. 3004, op. 1, d. 29, ll. 107.

[43] TsAGM f. 3004, op. 1, d. 29, ll. 107–108.

[44] TsAGM f. 3004, op. 1, d, 29, 49.

widowed pastors should not remarry.[45] Rumors were directed against him and other pastors, including of corruption and of adultery [*blud*].[46]

In the wake of war, family relations were unstable within Soviet society. Marriages had broken down during the years of separation and suffering; many spouses had died. It is hardly surprising that the question of who one could marry proved a sensitive one in these years, just as it had within the Russian Orthodox Church in the wake of the Revolution and Civil War.[47] The conflict at the Moscow central prayer house suggests that the AUCECB did not have a single, accepted view on issues that in this context were absolutely key for their (largely female, often single) membership, such as marriage, divorce, and remarriage. But it also shows that whilst power seemed to rest with the pastors, these men were sensitive to the ways in which accusations, slander, and rumor could deeply discredit them.

Generational Conflict (1964)

The late 1950s and early 1960s saw a new assault on religious life in the Soviet Union. Although the structures put in place during the Second World War to monitor and regulate the country's religious life remained in place, under Khrushchev's leadership the state took a range of new measures aimed to curb believers' activities, including arrests, the closure of places of worship, and a burst of anti-religious propaganda.[48] In December 1959, the AUCECB approved the

---

[45] For Orlov's biography, see the obituaries that appeared in *Bratskii vestnik*, issue 3, 1961, including one from his second wife, P. V. Orlova. The question of whether widowed pastors could remarry long remained a point of disagreement, some believers following Orthodox tradition in considering their remarriage sinful. On this, see Popov, "Evangelical Christians-Baptists," 150. For a case from the 1970s in which a congregation experienced a schism following their widowed pastor's remarriage, see the pastor's letter to the AUCECB leadership in Archive of the RUECB, Box 1, File 3, May 5, 1971.

[46] TsAGM f. 3004, op. 1, d. 29, l. 107.

[47] E. V. Beliakova, N. A. Beliakova, and E. B. Emchenko, *Zhenshchina v pravoslavii: Tserkovnoe pravo i rossiiskaia praktika* (Moscow: Kuchkovo Pole, 2011), 416–25.

[48] For recent scholarship on the antireligious campaigns, see Elena Zhidkova, "Antireligioznaia kampaniia vremen 'ottepeli' v Kuibyshevskoi oblast'," *Neprikosnovennyi zapas* 59, no. 3 (2008): 108–19; Irina Paert, "Demystifying the Heavens: Women, Religion and Khrushchev's Anti-religious Campaign, 1954–1964," in *Women in the Khrushchev Era,* ed. Susan E. Reid, Melanie Ilič, and Lynne Attwood, 203–21 (Basingstoke: Palgrave, 2004); Andrew B. Stone, "'Overcoming Peasant Backwardness': The Khrushchev Antireligious Campaign and the Rural Soviet Union," *Russian Review* 67 (2008): 296–320; Tatiana A. Chumachenko, *Church and State in Soviet Russia:*

"New Statutes" and "Letter of Instruction," which included the following pro-scriptions: no baptism before the age of thirty; no children at services; no visiting preachers; no gatherings at home; no charity to those in need.[49] This impacted church life at the MCECB, particularly for the younger generation. At the church on Malyi Vuzovskii lane, according to one church member, those under the age of thirty-five were dismissed from the choir, and young men were pre-vented from preaching. As elsewhere, some church members began to form or join new worship groups that sought to evade the new restrictions.[50]

In the early to mid-1960s, a rival to the AUCECB took shape in what was to become the Council of Churches of Evangelical Christians Baptists (CCECB). These newly formed communities were highly committed to ensuring their own "purity" [*chistota*]. One area where the two ECB traditions now diverged, for example, concerned marrying nonbelievers. The official AUCECB publication, *Bratskii vestnik*, was silent on this practice until *perestroika*, but it seems to have been accepted within the MCECB: the interviewee who arrived in Moscow in 1950, cited above, was married to a nonbeliever, for example, and this did not prevent her leading a full life within the congregation.[51] (It is worth noting that although unhappy, she did not contemplate divorce.)[52] In contrast, within CCECB congregations those married to nonbelievers faced excommunication.[53]

Russian Orthodoxy from World War II to the Khrushchev Years, ed. and trans. Edward E. Roslof (Armonk, NY: M. E. Sharpe, 2002); M. V. Shkarovskii, *Russkaia pravoslavnaia tserkov' i Sovetskoe gosudarstvo v 1943–1964 godakh: Ot "peremiriia" k novoi voine* (St. Petersburg, DEAN+ADIA-M, 1995); and Scott Kenworthy, "The Revival of Monastic Life in the Trinity-Sergius Lavra after World War II," in *State Secularism and Lived Religion in Soviet Russia and Ukraine*, ed. Catherine Wanner (Oxford: Oxford University Press, 2012), 117–58.

[49] Nikol'skaia, *Russkii protestantizm*, 201.

[50] Savinskii, *Istoriia evangel'skikh Khristian-Baptistov*, 223–24.

[51] Popov attributes *Bratskii vestnik*'s silence on the subject of marriage to nonbelievers to state pressure. See Popov, "Evangelical Christians-Baptists," 228. Elena Kondrashina reports that women who married nonbelievers might be excommunicated, but after a certain time they would "repent" in front of the congregation and be readmitted. Elena Kondrashina, "Uchastie zhenshchin v obshchinnoi zhizni protestantskikh tserkvei v SSSR (s 1945 po 1991 gg.)," *Gosudarstvo, religiia, tserkov'* 32 (2014): 151–71.

[52] Interview with V., AHRC AH/I025883/1/10.

[53] Interview with G. (Kyiv). Interview conducted by Miriam Dobson on June 6, 2013. AHRC AH/I025883/1/17. Before baptism in some CCECB congregations, girls would make a public vow not to wed a nonbeliever, but instead commit to Jesus. See Konstantin Prokhorov, "'Monashestvuiushchie' i khrista radi iurodivye v russkom

From the 1960s, the Moscow congregation keenly felt under threat from the CCECB and feared an exodus of members, particularly of younger members deeply affected by the restrictions imposed in 1959. When new internal conflicts emerged, church leaders were desperate to appease hostile factions and to keep their youth on board. They were also anxious to prove to their critics in the CCECB that their congregation was in fact disciplined and morally irreproachable. At times, the two ambitions proved difficult to reconcile, as in the 1964 case of a young assistant pastor's indiscretions.

At the MCECB in this period, the council (or "Brothers' Council," as it is tellingly called in the minutes) sometimes held open [*rashirennye*] meetings in order to "mobilize believers." On some occasions up to 150 members might attend, although, as we shall see, they continued to be almost exclusively dominated by the "brothers," particularly the leading pastors.[54] Several such meetings were held over the summer and autumn of 1964 to discuss the young assistant pastor accused of various inappropriate actions, from attending cinema and theatre (not even a sin, his supporters argued—don't we all have televisions?) to adultery in a church office (not true, they said).[55] The MCECB senior pastor also came under attack for defending him.[56]

As chairman of the MCECB Council, I. I. Motorin led the meetings, but in attendance were all the luminaries of the AUCECB, including the president Zhidkov, who intervened at several key moments in the discussions. What emerged from the meetings was a community bound by tight social ties, but also prone to painful division. In one meeting, a participant who had refused to join an attack on the younger preacher said of his colleagues: "I have prayed with them for nearly twenty years, we have shared both tears and happiness, but now we don't even greet one another. Now they call me other names: 'coward, traitor, betrayer, a toady.' It is my friends calling me these names because I refused to sign a dirty, slanderous petition against the pastor of our congregation."[57] The meetings tended to fracture along generational lines, with the most hostile attacks launched by older pastors. The assistant pastor's youthful allies were criticized

---

baptizme," in *105 let legalizatsii russkogo baptizma. Materialy mezhdunarodnoi nauchno-prakticheskoi konferentsii*, ed. N. A. Beliakova and A. V. Sinichkin (Moscow, RUECB, 2011), 24.

[54] TsAGM f. 3004, op. 1, d. 93, l. 33. A report from 1966 indicated that this practice of open meetings had recently been curtailed.

[55] TsAGM f. 3004, op. 1, d. 86, l. 23.

[56] TsAGM f. 3004, op. 1, d. 86, l. 23.

[57] TsAGM f. 3004, op. 1, d. 86, l. 28.

for their vocal defense of him and for showing inadequate respect for the senior pastors, including Zhidkov.[58] V. M. Koval'kov put it plainly: "Young people need to be removed from several church positions as they are very rude and do not behave correctly."[59] V. I. Lebedev worried that that if they took no action, the MCECB would appear to tolerate immoral and sinful behavior: "All the *initsiativniki* [members of the "initiative group"] are watching Moscow. That is why we need purity [*chistota*], there has to be a battle for purity."[60]

The case focused on the young assistant pastor and whether he should continue his position, or even be excommunicated. But several young women were also caught up in the scandal. In the minutes recording the four sessions devoted to this matter, the lists of attendees only include one woman—and she was the secretary. Yet these were held as "open" meetings, suggesting a wider audience, although there is little trace of their presence in the record. There is just one clue. In the second of the meetings, a young woman spoke out. She disputed the slur made at the previous meeting, when a senior minister made an insinuating comment about her having been caught in the church office with the assistant pastor during a service. Little was said in response to her objection, and the records suggest scant concern for the reputation of the women caught up in the case.[61] The young woman said no more. In 1964, there was no Shcheglova at the meetings, berating the pastors and launching her own campaigns to protect the congregation from sinful behavior. As we shall see in a moment, however, Shcheglova did get one fleeting mention.

As in the early 1950s, we see the wider congregation—which by the mid-sixties numbered almost five thousand—drawn into the conflict, albeit outside of the formal meetings.[62] Members compiled petitions both for and against the young preacher: one called for him to be excommunicated from the congregation, others for him to continue in his ministerial role. Although many of the assistant pastor's most vociferous supporters came from amongst the young deacons of the congregation, there was a letter from seventeen "elderly sisters" in his defense. With the levels of ferment [*brozhenie*] in the church at an all-time high—state officials warned church leaders to restore order—pastors once more

---

[58] TsAGM f. 3004, op. 1, d. 86, l. 25.

[59] TsAGM f. 3004, op. 1, d. 86, l. 26.

[60] TsAGM f. 3004, op. 1, d. 86, l. 38.

[61] TsAGM f. 3004, op. 1, d. 86, l. l. 26.

[62] In 1964, there were 4,808 baptized members of the MCECB. TsAGM f. 3004, op. 1, d. 93, l. 32.

found themselves under attack.[63] In the concluding remarks made at the final session on the matter, it was noted that "recently a significant number of anonymous letters and poems with blatant slander against long-standing brothers and other personnel of the Moscow church have been disseminated."[64] The authors of these texts were reminded that their actions undermined the authority of the church personnel and destroyed church unity; if they continued, they faced excommunication. Of especial concern was the circulation of a slanderous poem directed against a senior pastor in his sixties. Incensed, the pastor threatened to read the poem out loud from the pulpit at the next service. The poem, he noted, slandered him and another figure: "our elderly sister [*staritsa*], V. M. Shcheglova."[65] Although there is no record of her having participated in the discussions in the autumn of 1964, Shcheglova had still been caught up in the "agitation" overwhelming the church community. For the members of the younger generation who had apparently authored the verse in question, she had become the target. Her modes of operation and the authority she apparently wielded amongst the leading brothers of the Soviet evangelical movement now made her a figure of fun, at least for some of the church's younger members.

An oblique archival reference two years later suggests that Shcheglova continued to be a thorn in the side of the leading pastors. In 1966, the chairman of the MCECB visited the Moscow headquarters of the CARC and asked state officials there to discharge Shcheglova from her duties. The record of the meeting briefly notes, "she apparently holds a position on the staff of the religious center, and if he (the chairman) puts this question to the leadership, they will understand it incorrectly." In contrast, the CARC official "can do anything."[66] Once again, then, there was potential for conflict amongst the male leaders of the ECB community, and this time the congregation's chairman decided to circumvent his colleagues and appeal for intervention from the state.

Conclusions

This article focuses on two moments of discord within a single church community. In both cases, the conflicts were ultimately resolved. Although the MCECB certainly lost members to other movements and church communities, the congregation never experienced a major internal schism. Yet records of its leaders'

---

[63] TsAGM f. 3004, op. 1, d. 86, l. 37.
[64] TsAGM f. 3004, op. 1, d. 86, ll. 43–46.
[65] TsAGM f. 3004, op. 1, d. 86, l. l. 25.
[66] TsAGM f. 3004, op. 1, d. 93, l. 51.

meetings show that despite the shared goal of church unity, at the very heart of the AUCECB there was potential for significant friction.

The conflicts were highly gendered. In both cases, it was alleged that church members had sinned in their personal life: by marrying a divorcee, or by committing adultery. The male leadership—that "ministerial personnel" given new prominence and status in the postwar period—was responsible for discipline within the church community. At the MCECB this proved particularly challenging as the presence of the AUCECB headquarters and the size of the congregation meant that there was a large team of pastors and preachers, and their conflicting opinions on diverse matters laid bare the church's heterogenous heritage. The surviving records of their formal meetings suggest that the participation of women was relatively rare. At the meetings held in 1964, the young woman's bid to defend her reputation stands out, although her attempt to set the record straight gained little interest. A decade earlier, however, Shcheglova had taken a far more prominent and controversial role, in many ways propelling the campaign against the divorced women. According to Orlov, the AUCECB leaders "feared" her.[67] She appears representative of an older generation of women who had known a period of greater female activism within the church: she had attended the Bible courses in the 1920s, giving her knowledge and confidence; and between 1945 and 1960 she wrote more than twenty articles for the AUCECB's publication, a rare female voice on the pages of *Bratskii vestnik*.[68] But by the mid-1960s Shcheglova's authority had waned, certainly for the young generation who mocked her and for the chairman who wanted to dismiss her, even if his covert measures hinted that she still had some high-up supporters.

The disharmony displayed in 1951–1952 and 1964 was not confined to the leadership circles. With MCECB's three thousand-plus membership, the "democratism" state officials reviled as one of the more objectionable characteristics of Baptist life was never really viable there—certainly not in a formalized manner. Even open meetings could capture the perspective of only a small minority. Yet the congregation developed various practices for getting their voices heard: the writing of letters which passed judgement on the pastors' sermons; the dissemination of anonymous notes [*anonimki*]; the collecting of signatures for petitions; and the composition of satirical and offensive verse just discussed. Communication did not simply go one way, therefore: the ordained ministers might speak from the pulpit, but they could expect feedback. Although by the mid-sixties we do not seem to hear from outspoken women like Shcheglova, this

---

[67] TsAGM f. 3004, op. 1, d. 29, l. 50.

[68] She died in 1979, and her obituary was published in *Bratskii vestnik*, 2 (1979).

predominantly female congregation was hardly silent. Despite the enhanced role that the state wanted to give them after the Second World War, pastors were in fact quite vulnerable. The main tool at their disposal was the threat of excommunication, but in order to excommunicate a member some kind of collective consensus was needed. And as we have seen, that was not always so easy to achieve.

ROMANIAN BAPTISTS, GENDER ISSUES, AND THE EUROPEAN UNION: IMPORTANT QUESTIONS FOR OUR FUTURE

George Hancock–Stefan

For the 150th anniversary of the Romanian Union in 2018 and the 100th anniversary of the establishment of Great Romania, Vasile Boari was commissioned to gather top scholars for the publication of a magisterial book called *Cine sunt Românii? - Perspective Asupra Identității Naționale (Who Are We, the Romanians: Perspectives on Our National Identity).*[1] This text asks: who are the people of Romania? Who are they and how have they gotten to where they are today? Similarly, this article will examine who the Romanian people are religiously. It will then reflect on how those religious beliefs are affected by the legislation enforced by the European Union regarding marriage and gender.

After close to forty years of communism, Romania underwent political changes as a result of its 2007 entry into the European Union. Although Romania has historically been a politically and religiously conservative nation, this entry has forced Romania to adopt certain liberal values regarding marriage and gender. Understandably, as the values of the European Union grow more liberal, Romanian Baptists have become more vocal defending their traditional beliefs.

While this essay deals specifically with the Romanian Baptist response to the marriage and gender issues summarized by the Matić report voted into law in June 2021,[2] it is important to understand the Romanian Orthodox response

---

[1] Vasile Boari, ed., *Cine sunt Românii? Perspective Asupra Identitatii Nationale* (Cluj-Napoca, Editura Școala Ardeleană, 2019).

[2] To read a variety of perspectives on the Matic Report as well as its contents, see the European Parliament's "Sexual and reproductive health and rights in the EU, in the frame of women's health" presented by Fred Matić on May 21st, 2021, https://www.europarl.europa.eu/doceo/document/A-9-2021-0169_EN.html#title1; One of Us's "Statement European Federation One of Us against Matić 'Report," *One of Us*, June 16, 2021, https://oneofus.eu/statement-european-federation-one-of-us-against-matic-report/; St. Boniface Institute's "Analysis of the Matić Report," *St. Boniface Institute*, June 20, 21, https://www.boniface-institute.com/analysis-of-the-matic-report/; the European Parliamentary Forum's "European Parliament adopts landmark position on sexual and reproductive rights," *EPF*, June 24, 2021, https://www.epfweb.org/node/838;

as well. This is because Romania has largely been, and continues to be, Ortho-dox, while the Romanian Baptist denomination, together with other Neo-Protestant denominations, such as Pentecostals and Plymouth Brethren (also called evangelicals), makes up less than ten percent of the population. Thus, all the Christian denominations must work together if they want to engender change.

The following paper will be divided in four sections, with the goal of illu-minating the historical events that affect the current political and religious cli-mate of 2021 Romania, as well as the ways that Romanian Baptists have previ-ously and continually attempted to advocate for biblical family values despite increasing pressure from the EU.

Firstly, I will provide a brief and informative history of Romania. Secondly, to better understand the situation for Baptists in 2021 Romania, I will provide background on the tumultuous relationship between religion and politics within the country in the twentieth century due to the rise and fall of communism. This background will lead into a reflection on why Romania may have been so quick to join the European Union then and how the Union's liberal stance on marriage and gender is affecting contemporary Romanian Baptists now. Thirdly, I will discuss the controversies surrounding the creation of the Romanian Coalition for the Family as well as the coordination and ultimate failure of the Referendum of 2018, which supported an addendum to the Romanian Constitution. Lastly, I will specifically consider the actions of three Romanian Baptist leaders in the midst of these tumultuous struggles to defend traditional values.

By examining various actions and responses from the Romanian Baptists, the Romanian Orthodox, and the Coalition for the Family, we will see an alarm-ing trend as the increasingly liberal values of the European Union continue to be forced upon every country within its membership. Historically, Baptists have been against governmental restrictions, whether that government be composed of monarchs, communist comrades, or the European Union Parliament. How-ever, as we will explore, it is growing more difficult for Romanian Baptists to uphold their traditional biblical values.

---

and lastly, Joel Forster's "The European Parliament passes the controversial Matic report to promote 'free and legal abortion without barriers,'" *Evangelical Focus: Europe*, June 25, 2021, https://evangelicalfocus.com/europe/12213/the-european-parliament-passes-the-controversial-matic-report-to-promote-free-an-legal-abortion-without-barriers.

Who are the Romanian People?

So, to begin: who are the people of Romania? Romanians describe themselves as Latin people in the Slavic Ocean. Throughout Romania's millennial history, it has lost various territories to its neighbors, such as Hungary, Ukraine, Russia, and Bulgaria.

While linguistically, Romania is Latin, and most Latin countries practice Catholicism, it is an enthusiastically Orthodox country. Collectively, Eastern Orthodoxy has stayed faithful to the historic position of marriage being between one man and one woman. Numerically, the Moscow Patriarchate of Eastern Orthodoxy is the largest. Philosophically, the Moscow Patriarchate argues that the first Rome (Italy) is heretical, the second Rome (Istanbul) is in captivity, and the third Rome (Moscow) is the only free one. However, the Ecumenical Patriarchate from Istanbul has the greatest historical prestige.

The leadership of the Eastern Orthodox church is held by the Patriarch of Moscow, who presides over the largest group of ethnic Orthodox, namely Russians.[3] Each ethnic group is autocephalous, and the Patriarch of Constantinople is known as the Ecumenical Patriarch.

Despite a shared Orthodox heritage, the Romanians, not being ethnically Slavic and having negative past experiences with the Russians, are very reluctant to trust them, even if they are the "defenders" of their shared faith. However, there are political and economic interactions between Romania and Russia because they are geographical neighbors.

The Romanian Orthodox churches emphasize their nationalism. In contrast, the Romanian Neo-Protestants emphasize their internationalism. However, when it comes to the issues of biblical values, gender, and marriage, the Romanian Neo-Protestants are the same as their Romanian Orthodox brothers and sisters. As we will see, all the Christian denominations in Romania have been affected by the pressures of the European Union.

Joining the European Union

Once Ceausescu was eliminated in 1989, Romanian political leaders quickly decided to join the EU. At that time, the European Union had already long been established in an effort to prevent a Third World War. It developed into a union

---

[3] See Jeff Diamant's "Orthodox Christians in Central and Eastern Europe favor strong role for Russia in geopolitics, religion," *Pew Research Center*, May 11, 2017, https://www.pewresearch.org/fact-tank/2017/05/11/orthodox-christians-in-central-and-eastern-europe-favor-strong-role-for-russia-in-geopolitics-religion/.

without frontiers, with a single currency, a shared economic market headquartered in Brussels. As became evident later, the EU also created a system of values contrary to many moral and ethical values held by Christians.[4]

Romania applied for EU membership in February 1993 and became a full-fledged member on January 1, 2007. Gabriela Baicu, an economist at the Romanian Academy of Economic Studies in Bucharest, analyzed all requirements that Romania had to fulfill for the EU regarding its legal system, economic system, industries, and immigration policy. Baicu writes that Romania is still learning how to use the economic benefits of EU membership to their full advantage.[5] However, as I will elaborate on later, the overall benefits of EU membership are too beneficial to give up, despite the religious pressure. The resistance to this religious pressure exercised by the European Union and the Romanian government culminated in the formation of a Coalition, comprised of both Romanian Orthodox and Romanian Neo-Protestants.

The 2018 Referendum

The Coalition for Family was formed from thirty different organizations in 2016. It promotes the traditional idea of family, is against abortion, and sought to amend the Constitution of Romania's definition from a union being between two spouses, to a union being between a man and a woman. This was because the Coalition, along with other Romanian conservatives, believe that the original Constitution needed to be clarified as it *did* originally intend marriage to be between male and female spouses. However, because of the lack of specificity in the language, the Constitution could also be interpreted as supporting LGBTQIA+ marriages.[6] In 2016, the Coalition gathered three million signatures which were presented to the Romanian Parliament to advocate for the constitutional change to take place and for "spouses" to be replaced with "man and woman."

---

[4] For more information regarding the formation of the European Union, see Evrópustofa's "Why Was the EU Created?" *Evrópustofa: EU Info Centre*, August 19, 2015, https://eeas.europa.eu/archives/delegations/iceland/evropustofa/en/what-would-you-like-to-know/what-would-you-like-to-know/article/why-was-the-eu-created.html.

[5] See Gabriela Baicu's "Romania's EU Membership Was Slow to Be Appreciated But Now the Tide Is Turning," *Emerging Europe*, April 1, 2017 , https://emerging-europe.com/voices/romanias-eu-membership-slowappreciated-now-tide-turning/.

[6] At the time of this writing, these letters are in common use in English representing "Lesbian, Gay, Bisexual, Transgender, Queer, Intersex, Asexual (or allies) and people who identify as some other term."

Immediately upon hearing about this, a counter letter was drafted by the Romanian LGBTQIA+ community against this conservative proposal and was signed by over one thousand Romanian public figures. Soon it had an additional ten thousand online signatories. In response, American Christian organizations such as Liberty Counsel and Alliance Defending Freedom International submitted briefs to the Constitutional Court of Romania (CCR) seeking a Referendum. Additionally, the Orthodox Church of Romania (OCR) announced its official support for the Referendum. In July 2016, the CCR unanimously accepted the Referendum and sent it to the Romanian Parliament. However, LGBTQIA+ groups such as Accept, MozaiQ, and TRANSform protested in Romania's University Square in response.

Amidst these protests, the LGBTQIA+ groups called the Coalition for Family a hate group. Alternatively, the Coalition for Family called the LGBTQIA+ community an organization sponsored by outsiders, referencing the fact that LGBTQIA+ events are often largely attended by non-locals. The Southern Poverty Law Center accused various leaders of the Coalition for Family of being members of right-wing organizations. Eventually, the American Embassy sided with the LGBTQIA+ community and its protests. American newspapers such as *The New York Times* and *The Los Angeles Times* also publicly sided with the LGBTQIA+ community against the Coalition for Family.

Romanian political leaders were also very much involved in the discussion. President Klaus Iohannis called the three million who signed the Referendum Petition "obscurantists." Alternatively, the Prime Minister at that time, Dan Ciolos, and the socialist leader Liviu Dragnea sided with the traditional family definition.

The Referendum initiative was delayed in the Romanian Parliament for over two years. It was finally approved by the Senate on September 11, 2018 and took place on October 6–7, 2018. As the vote for the Reformation approached, the anti-Referendum's best strategic move turned out to be encouraging the electorate to just not show up to vote. The expectation was that over thirty percent of the electorate would vote for the Referendum; the shocking reality was that only twenty-one percent of the population showed up to vote, but around ninety percent of those who did voted in favor of the Referendum. Thus, the anti-Referendum's boycott campaign was successful. However, since the other seventy-nine percent of the electorate did not show up to vote, it is hard to put much stock in either side winning.

Cristina Grigore writes that "the Referendum upset individuals, beliefs, communities, and the society as a whole. Churches called for spiritual unity and made appeals to restore harmony and peace, reiterating the teaching on the family and marriage. Yet it was not enough."[7] Grigore lists three factors that contributed to the defeat: First, the secularization of the Romanian society which, while considered eighty percent Orthodox, did not come to vote as the Romanian Orthodox Church called them to do. This raises questions about the possibility that in Romania there are cultural Orthodox as there are cultural Catholics in the United States.[8] Secondly, the boycott against the Referendum was solidly international. Companies such as Coca Cola and Netflix participated in the boycott on behalf of the LGBTQIA+ organizations, with catchy slogans such as "We don't see any difference" and "Binging. It's your choice with whom you want to do it."[9] The final reason was that the Referendum was hitched to the wrong political party, which pushed for the soonest date possible, despite the Parliament's attempts to delay the vote.

Furthermore, all agree that the Referendum was poorly written. Instead of calling for a vote for marriage between a man and woman, it asked for people to vote *against* the Constitution which stated that marriage should be between two spouses. The Referendum became a negative vote *against* the Constitution versus a positive vote *for* the traditional, biblical perspective.[10]

One of the most profound questions that was raised after the 2018 Referendum hearkens back to Boari's text and the subject of Romanian identity: are Romanians Christians or Europeans first? Journalist Sorin Ionita answers this question indirectly, beginning his article as follows: "Dragnea, Romanian Orthodox Church and avantgarde of *militant Orthodox and Baptists* (author's emphasis) have been followed only by the 20% of the populists....It is a spectacular

---

[7] See Cristina Grigore's "Referendum on the family in Romania: the reasons for failure," *sir: agenzia d'informazione*, October 22, 2018, https://www.agensir.it/europa/2018/10/10/referendum-on-the-family-in-romania-the-reasons-for-failure/.

[8] For more on this notion of "cultural Catholics," see Laura R. Olson's "Joe Biden, Shepherd of Cultural Catholics?" *Georgetown University Berkley Center for Religion, Peace, & World Affairs*, October 22, 2020, https://berkleycenter.georgetown.edu/responses/joe-biden-shepherd-of-cultural-catholics.

[9] See Elena Brodeala's "Why Referendums on Human Right are a Bad Idea: Reflecting on Romania's Failed Referendum on the Traditional Family from the Perspective of Comparative Law," *The Comparative Jurist: William & Mary Law School's International and Comparative Law Blog*, November 11, 2018, https://comparativejurist.org/2018/11/11/why-referendums-on-human-rights-are-a-bad-idea-reflecting-on-romanias-failed-referendum-on-the-traditional-family-from-the-perspective-of-comparative-law/.

[10] Brodeala, "Why Referendums on Human Rights are a Bad Idea."

defeat and evidently not expected by both of these churches, but more shocking for the Orthodox hierarchy which is not used to the transparency of the public opinion."[11] Ionita argues that Romania is like France and that churches should no longer invoke God into politics. He says that the Romanian Orthodox Church and the Neo-Protestants have received an electoral slap to the face and have been put in their place by this Referendum—concluding that faith is one thing and politics is completely another.

Holdean responded to Ionita in May, asking what it means to be European, or to continue to be a part of the EU. Holdean argues that the EU is rapidly changing from a capitalist union to an ideological union in support of the LGBTQIA+ community. The EU wants all of its countries to accept marriages between homosexuals and does not grant allotted money to countries that do not support the LGBTQIA+ agenda. Ultimately, the EU and its major organizations are going to push for this agenda until it is completed.

Holdean concludes: "The progressivists have profited from the pandemic to destroy everything that was healthy and conservative in human societies, and Romania next to other countries from Central and East Europe (Poland and Hungary) is their target."[12]

While Holdean's position may seem reminiscent of fearmongering, various EU leaders feel that matters regarding certain topics, such as gender and sexuality, should not be solved at the country or national level, but at a higher level. In her article, Romanian Elena Brodeala argues against the Referendum, concluding: "if the RCC was not influenced by the attitudes of the broader public, who should decide on human rights when all national forums…agree on curtailing their protection? Should this perhaps be delegated to supra-national bodies?"[13] Clearly, Holdean is not entirely off-target as Brodeala is implying that the EU should make such decisions and prevent any countries from making an independent choice.

It is this confidence in supranational bodies' ability to dictate the future with which the Matić Report was presented and passed this summer, determining what the member countries have to do in order to maintain EU membership

---

[11] See Sorin Ionita's "De ce au fost învinși Dragnea și BOR la vot," *Contributors*, October 7, 2018, https://www.contributors.ro/invinsi-dragnea-bor-referendum/.

[12] See Marius Holdean's "Pe timp de pandemie, UE promovează intens agenda LGBT profitând de neatenția cetățenilor," *Sputnik: Moldova-România*, May 4, 2021, https://ro.sputnik.md/20210504/Pe-timp-de-pandemie-UE-promoveaza-intens-agenda-LGBT-profitand-de-neatentia-cetatenilor-34625541.html.

[13] Brodeala, "Why Referendums on Human Rights are a Bad Idea," 5.

and avoid penalty.[14] As previously discussed, the economic benefits of EU membership seem to be largely responsible for countries such as Romania deciding to stay within the EU. In view of the liberal trends of the EU, it is imperative for us to give space to traditionalist Christian perspectives.

Three Baptist Leaders

Before the issue of discordant values became so apparent, Romanian religious leaders were in favor of Romania joining the EU because they would gain unrestricted travel, become defended by the military, and benefit economically. As the Romanian government attempted to align with the European Union's moral and spiritual values, the clash between national and religious values became more evident.

As previously mentioned, Ionita is of the opinion that the Orthodox and Baptists are militant and should not mix politics and religion. However, the author disagrees with that position. Thus, we will conclude by looking at three Baptist leaders and how they have interacted with Romanian political leadership before the vote for the Referendum, as well as the position paper issued this summer by the Union of the Baptist Churches of Romania. By considering these three pastors and their positions, we shall see that the voice of the church should and can be heard even when national or continental majorities attempt to drown it out.

Dr. Iosif Ton. One of the leading Romanian Baptists is Iosif Ton. Educated at Oxford in 1978, he then returned to Romania, where he worked against the Ceausescu government. In 1982, Ton was exiled, and he became the President of the Romanian Missionary Society, as well as a pastor to the Romanian nation via his one-hour Radio Free Europe broadcasts on Sunday afternoons from 1983 to 1989. The first week after the fall of Ceausescu's government, Ton returned to Romania where he established Emmanuel University, the first evangelical university in the country.

In preparation for the 2018 Referendum, Ton wrote an article entitled "The Atheistic Marxism – or What Would the Romanians Choose at this Referendum."[15] In this article, Ton analyzes the ways the family has been regarded by the communists since the time of Marx and Lenin, through the Frankfurt School, which has become the ideology of the European Union.

---

[14] Holdean, "Pe timp de pandemie."
[15] Personal correspondence with the author via email, December 4, 2017.

Ton states that the three million signatories for the Referendum agreed with what Jesus says in Matthew 19:4–6: "*At the beginning the Creator made them male and female and said: For this reason, a man will leave his father and mother and be united to his wife and the two will become one flesh.*"

Ton concludes, "The Romanian people have to choose between Jesus Christ and Marx....Choosing to vote for a family made of a husband and a wife, we choose to declare Jesus Christ the rightful king of Romania."

Ton has also written about one of the most intriguing people in relation to the Referendum, Romanian President Klaus Iohannis. Iohannis belongs to the Lutheran Evangelical Church and courted the evangelical vote. Thus, as Iohannis became publicly *opposed* to the Referendum, Ton penned another article, "Righteousness in Love: President Iohannis, the Disappointment of the Evangelicals."

Ton writes, "Not only I, but all the Romanian evangelicals everywhere did everything possible to elect Mr. Iohannis as the first evangelical president of Romania....His attitude in the last months, not only frightens us, but surprises us in equal measure."

Ton continues, "when we shall inscribe in the Constitution that the family is made of a man and a woman, we are going to show to the whole world that we are the followers of Christ....We will not let anyone stop us, not even the President of the country."[16] As much as we appreciate Ton's enthusiasm, we can see that the Referendum vote ended quite differently. However, his assessment of Iohannis still seems correct.

Dr. Paul Negrut. Our next pastor also continues to write in the same tradition as Ton. Dr. Paul Negrut is the Senior Pastor of Emmanuel Baptist Church in Oradea, the largest Baptist church in Romania. He is also the President of Emmanuel University, the Christian university founded by Ton. In 1990 he was awarded the Torch of Freedom by Margaret Thatcher, and in 2000 he was knighted by the President of Romania, Emil Constantinescu, with the Order of Faithful Service for the preaching of the Word of God.

After the fall of the Ceausescu regime, Negrut became a part of the Romanian provisional government, but stayed in it for a short time, deciding that God had called him to be a preacher, not a politician.[17]

---

[16] See Iosif Ton's "Președintele Iohannis, dezamăgirea evanghelicilor!," *DREPTATE ÎN DRAGOSTE*, May 5, 2018, https://family2fam.wordpress.com/2018/05/05/incercarea-de-reinviere-a-comunismului/.

[17] See John Birnie's text, *Just Call Me Paul*, a biography of Paul Negrut's life, published in 2014 by the Slavic Gospel Association.

Negrut was interviewed by Ion Ciobota of *Agnus Dei* in March 2017.[18] The following are three highlights from the article describing the interview: Negrut pokes fun at the Romanian Parliament's inability to choose which branch should handle the Referendum. Additionally, as a psychologist, Negrut discusses sex as a blessing and a curse, and challenges the church to be involved in the formation of national thinking. Lastly, Negrut describes his experience interviewing American politicians, concluding that they agreed with the traditional Romanian evangelicals but would not admit it publicly for fear of angering their constituents.

Rev. Viorel Iuga. The last pastor we will consider is certainly not afraid to voice his opinions, whether it be via sermons, articles, letters, or podcasts. Viorel Iuga is the Pastor of Speranta (Hope) Baptist Church in Arad and the President of the Romanian Baptist Churches Union. For the past thirty years, Iuga has repeatedly preached and written on the subject of sex, staying within biblical parameters and emphasizing the sacredness of the traditional family.[19]

On October 18, 2018, Iuga wrote a letter to President Iohannis, saying, "you are not allowed to do it! In your position as the President of Romania, we want you to tell us clearly that you are on the side of the traditional family, that you are on the side of normalcy, and you do not want to leave behind your mandate as President of a country with more legalized sins."[20]

Iuga's theological reasons for his position are that God created the family, laws, and the church. By changing these, we challenge his sovereignty and profane his name. The President's reply to Iuga showed the disparity between his response and the majority of Christians in Romania.

In an interview, Iuga was asked, "how should a Christian respond to the problem of homosexuality and homosexuals?" He responded, "homosexuality, no matter how we turn the issue, is a sin. History draws our attention that whenever homosexuality is accepted and practiced it becomes the unleashing of the divine wrath. Homosexuals, though, are our neighbors and they are loved by God. We know and we should remember that they are beings for which the Lord Jesus Christ died. Like any other sins, they have the opportunity to repent and

---

[18] Agnus Dei blog, March 13, 2017, https://rodiagnusdei.wordpress.com/2017/03/13/suntem-normali-nu-suntem-fanatici-si-nu-suntem-homofobi/.

[19] See Viorel and Didina Iuga's Fundraising page at *Global Outreach International*, https://www.globaloutreach.org/giving/missionary-details/x-viorel-and-didina-iuga.

[20] See Rodi's article, "Viorel Iuga: Nu vă este permis!," *Agnus Dei*, October 18, 2016, https://rodiagnusdei.wordpress.com/2016/10/18/viorel-iuga-nu-va-este-permis/.

be freed from the power of sins, and homosexuals have the same."[21] Iuga continues to advocate for traditional values while also preaching love and salvation for the LGBTQIA+ community.

As mentioned previously, the vote in favor of the Matić Report in 2021 created an urgency for Romanian Baptists to preach more vigorously and create a denominational position paper on the subject. On July 18, 2021, Negrut gave a sermon in response to the vote, entitled: "The Sodomization of the United States, Europe and Romania Through Their Leadership." His conclusion was that the current political leadership in the United States, President Biden, the almost unanimous acceptance of the Matić Report by the European Union and President Iohannis, as well as the Romanian delegation, is God's punishment of the church for not standing up when issues regarding gender and sexuality became prominent.[22] Although seemingly extreme, Negrut's July 2021 sermon reflects the increasing concern that political leadership is directly impacting the spiritual health of these nations.

When we consider the extreme range of perspectives regarding the Referendum, it is clear that there is great division within the EU. On one side is Macron, the President of France and other political elites who pushed for the immediate acceptance and implementation of the Matić Report. On the other side are the Catholic Church in Poland, the Reformed and Catholic Church in Hungary, and the Orthodox and Baptists in Romania.

In 2021, the Council of the Christian Baptist Churches of Romania presented a position paper so that Romanian Baptist Churches would know how to handle various issues that may come before them due to Romania's continued EU membership (a similar position is held by the Romanian Evangelical Alliance, which is made up of the Baptist Union of Romania, the Pentecostal Union of Romania, and the Christian Evangelical Church of Romania). The document explains the rationale with four subheadings to outline main points:

> We are conscientious of the fact that if we are not acting now, our Baptist pastors will not be able to justify legally and explain adequately

---

[21] See George Danciu's "Adevărul.ro – INTERVIU cu Viorel Iuga – 'Oricum am întoarce-o, homosexualitatea este un păcat,'" *Armonia Magazine—USA*, October 31, 2016, https://armoniamagazineusa.com/2016/10/31/adevarul-ro-interviu-cu-viorel-iuga-oricum-am-intoarce-o-homosexualitatea-este-un-pacat/.

[22] The sermon can be viewed at Patrick Ovidiu's *YouTube* channel, entitled "Pastorul Paul NEGRUT despre SODOMIZAREA Americii, a Europei, a Romaniei prin CONDUCATORII lor," *YouTube*, July 18, 2021, https://www.youtube.com/watch?v=qv8keQyxdhc.

their doctrinal position, and professors in schools and universities, medical people, journalists and other professional categories who are Baptists, will not have a resolution from the Romanian Baptist Churches Union in case they need to make their appeal.

We reaffirm with all our conviction that an unborn child is still a child, and the life of the unborn child is a gift and a divine, inalienable right,

We reaffirm with all our conviction that all the orientations and deviant sexual behaviors are against the fundamental principles of Christian ethic,

We reject with all firmness all the ideologies that redefines the gender identity with the high price of destroying the bio-psycho-social unity and which promotes premarital orientations and practices, extramarital, homosexual, bisexual, and transgender,

We reject with all firmness every hermeneutical theory that ignores the principle of biblical interpretation strictly through the Bible under the illumination of the Holy Spirit.[23]

Questions for Romanian Baptists

The ideologies of the EU have placed Romanian Baptists and all traditional Romanian Christians at a historic crossroads. Two important questions Christians are facing relate to separation of church and state: If the LGBTQIA+ community believes that Christianity should not be taught in schools, why should the views of the LBTQIA+ community dominate? In addition, will people with different views from the now mainstream view that supports LBGTQIA+ be able to run for public office to make change?

Three additional questions are important for Romanian Christians to consider. First, there is no doubt that economically, politically, and militarily, Romania has gained a lot from its participation in the EU. However, is there a possibility that, despite these earthly gains, Romania as a country has forfeited its national soul?

---

[23] The Secretary General of the Baptist Union of Romania Ioan Ardelean sent the Position Paper directly to the author via email, entitled "Rezoluția Consiliului Uniunii Bisericilor Creștine Baptiste din România cu Privire la Sacralitatea Vieții și Demnitatea Ființei Umane în lumina Sfintelor Scripturi," on August 18, 2021; however, it should also be available via www.uniuneabaptista.ro.

Second, how should Romania best use its political structure and leverage? The Referendum has shown that neither the Orthodox Church nor the Baptists know how to advocate for themselves through the political system. Will Christians grow in their political skills, and will they learn and act more impactfully in the future?

Third, will the Christian believers of Romania need to prepare themselves to be persecuted once again? From 1945–1990, while Romanian believers suffered and were imprisoned for their faith in Christ, the believers in Western Europe lived as though nothing was happening. Now, under the Matić Report of 2021, will Western European Baptists become involved in the defense of their Eastern European Baptist brothers and sisters, rather than automatically supporting the policies of the EU?

To reconnect with Grigore, "the Referendum upset beliefs, communities, and the society as a whole. Churches called for spiritual unity and made appeals to restore harmony and peace, reiterating the teaching on family and marriage. Yet, it was not enough."[24] Thus, the twenty years since Romania joined the EU have been a struggle and a fight between the imposition of beliefs by the European Union, the support of the same by the leading Romanian politicians, and the consistent resistance by the Orthodox, Baptists, and other evangelicals who represent traditional Romanian values. Baptists, from their beginnings, have stood against governmental interference. Will they come to consider the European Union Parliament as oppressive as the monarchs and the communist comrades of the past? It remains to be seen if, within this decade, the nonacceptance of the EU's values will become considered worthy of persecution.

---

[24] Grigore, "Referendum on the Family."

MARGARET JARMAN, PIONEER IN
BAPTIST WOMEN'S MINISTRY IN ENGLAND

Keith Jones

Margaret Jarman was a remarkable woman within the British Baptist community, with a notable number of "firsts" to her name. She grew up in Hall Green, Birmingham, England's second city, attending the Solihull High School for Girls, obtaining her school certificate and leaving school to study at the Northamptonshire Institute of Agriculture with a view to working in the farming sector. She had grown up as part of Hall Green Baptist Church, but it was whilst at agricultural college that she attended Moulton Baptist Church, Northamptonshire, was converted at the age of eighteen, and was baptized as a believer. Having completed her training, she became a herdswoman on a farm and acquired a motorbike to get from her home to the farm.

However, a sermon at Hall Green on 2 Timothy 1:8–9 became a call to Christian service for Jarman. Whilst the Baptist Union of Great Britain and Ireland had theoretically ordained women to Christian ministry since 1918,[1] the reality was that in the 1950s most women in the isles were guided towards the Order of Baptist Deaconesses.[2] This order had been formed to direct single women to, principally, church-related social work, though by the 1950s most were serving as minister-equivalents in smaller churches, or in various forms of pioneer ministry.[3]

---

[1] *A Short History of Baptist Women in Ministry* (Didcot: Baptists Together, 2018). The name of this union has changed over the years as Baptist organizations in Scotland and Ireland have developed. In 1953 it was known as the Baptist Union of Great Britain and Ireland. It is now the Baptist Union of Great Britain, popularly known as "Baptists Together."

[2] Nicola Morris, *Sisters of the People: The Order of Baptist Deaconesses 1890–1975* (Bristol: Centre for Comparative Studies in Religion and Gender, 2002). It is always difficult to have a usable description of the islands off the northwest coast of Europe. Here I use the title offered by Professor Norman Davies in his important work *The Isles: A History* (London: Macmillan, 1999).

[3] Some of the deaconesses were married, though these were the exception. Deaconesses received a lower stipend than ordained ministers and were, therefore, cheaper to employ, a matter of shame, in retrospect, as many were placed in demanding situations. Today, British Baptists train and ordain many more women than in the 1960s

A Note on Women in Ministry from the 1600s

The first English General Baptists, led by John Smyth and Thomas Helwys, declared that there were two orders of ministry—bishops (men) and deacons (women and men).[4] This position represented a development beyond the Magisterial Reformers, but something short of the radical Anabaptists. Despite this limited starting point, as John Briggs has demonstrated, on various occasions from the 1600s onwards women exercised significant ministries in English Baptist churches.[5]

Dan Taylor, who was leader of the New Connexion of General Baptists in the late 1700s to the mid-1800s, encouraged the participation of women in the decision-making of the church, though his New Connexion did not go as far as ordaining women to the Gospel ministry.[6]

The Order of Deaconesses

As Karen Smith has observed, "our Baptist foremothers have continued to receive far less attention than our forefathers."[7] From 1890 there were women in the isles engaged in missional activity in areas of deprivation spurred on by the initiatives of the leading evangelical minister, F. B. Meyer.[8] The Order of Deaconesses was established as a substantial element of Baptist life in the isles.[9] Through time, the Order of Baptist Deaconesses moved beyond assisting ministers of larger urban churches in their outreach, to taking responsibility for mission and pioneering causes, often in challenging estate and urban settings.[10]

---

and 1970s. It is not at all unusual to have a woman exercising full ministerial leadership in a British Baptist church.

[4] See John H. Y. Briggs, "She-Preachers, Widows and Other Women: The Feminine Dimension in Baptist Life since 1600," *Baptist Quarterly* 31, no. 7 (July 1986): 337–52.

[5] Briggs, "She-Preachers," 339ff.

[6] Richard T. Pollard, *Dan Taylor (1738–1816): Baptist Leader and Pioneering Evangelical* (Eugene, OR: Pickwick Publications, 2018).

[7] Karen E. Smith, "Beyond Public and Private Spheres: Another Look at Women in Baptist History and Historiography," *Baptist Quarterly* 34, no. 2 (July 1991): 79.

[8] Ian M. Randall, *Spirituality and Social Change: The Contribution of F B Meyer (1847–1929)* (Carlisle, UK: Paternoster Press, 2003).

[9] See Morris, *Sisters of the People.*

[10] In July 2021 the Baptist Union of Great Britain launched "Project Violet" to explore issues around women in ministry. The year marked a century since the Rev. Violet Hedger was ordained as the first British Baptist minister in the classically understood sense as a "minister of the word and sacrament." For a short overview of the century

It was this world Jarman entered. In 1953 she began training as a deaconess at the Baptist Union College for Deaconesses, Struan, where she gained the London University Certificate in Religious Knowledge. After completing her course, she settled in the Pontesbury group of rural churches in Shropshire, ministering to these small churches. She was recognized as an accredited deaconess of the Baptist Union at the annual assembly in 1959. So far, so typical of the vocational route of women in full-time service to Baptist churches in the isles post-Second World War.

Jarman's eyes were opened to wider opportunities when she attended the European Baptist Federation Congress in Berlin in 1958 and afterwards stayed with the Order of German Baptist Deaconesses in Berlin and Hamburg.

Jarman was dissatisfied with the level of theological formation she had received at Struan. She enrolled for the external London University Bachelor of Divinity degree. In 1961 she entered Spurgeon's College in London to complete the degree. Though still on the list of deaconesses, she was the first woman to study for a theology degree at Spurgeon's (even though the school didn't count her as a "ministerial student").

National Denominational Staff

Having gained her degree, Jarman now served as a deaconess. She was asked by Ernest Payne, the General Secretary of the Baptist Union, to join the union staff as Organising Secretary in the Deaconess Department, and she accepted this position. This was a critical phase in the life of the order as a debate took place within the Baptist Union Council about the order and whether, in fact, most deaconesses were really exercising the classic ministry of word and sacrament and the key leadership of local churches.[11]

Because of her national role, Jarman attended the 1968 WCC Assembly in Uppsala, Sweden, representing the Diakonia network. This was followed by a world trip representing Diakonia to the USA and Australia, returning home via Bangkok and Bombay. In 1969 she attended a Diakonia conference in Finland and in 1969 an EBF conference in Vienna.

There is an ongoing debate amongst Baptists in the isles as to whether there has ever been an adequate discussion about gender and leadership, but in the late 1960s the Baptist Union Council decided to close the Order of Deaconesses and to invite them to be ordained. Jarman, now without a job because her post was

---

1918–2018, see *A Short History of Baptist Women in Ministry*.

[11] Ian M. Randall, *The English Baptists of the 20th Century* (Didcot: Baptist Historical Society, 2005), 347ff.

redundant, was ordained in 1967. Her ordination service at Holmesdale Baptist Church, South Norwood, London, was a distinguished event. The act of ordination was conducted by the Rev. Dr. Ernest A. Payne CH, perhaps the most important European Baptist of the twentieth century. The sermon was preached by the Rev. Dr. George Beasley-Murray, then Principal of Spurgeon's College in London and a leading Baptist New Testament scholar.[12]

In 1969 Jarman became minister at Dalston and Salters Hall, London. In 1977 she moved pastorates to the West Coventry Baptist Fellowship, where she served in a team until 1985.

Pioneering Moves

In 1982, Jarman was appointed chair of the Baptist Union Ministerial Recognition Committee, the first woman minister to occupy that post, and became a representative of the Baptist Union on the British Council of Churches and Free Church Federal Council.

Jarman felt a particular vocation to the life of prayer. In 1983 she became an oblate of the Community of St. Mary the Virgin at Wantage (an Anglican religious order) where Sister Margaret Magdalen (Margaret Evening), a former BMS missionary, was a community member. She later reflected:

> In retrospect I see that this enrichment of my Baptist tradition began in January 1983. I was due for a sabbatical and after the closing of a number of doors I had pushed, I finished up at the Convent of the Community of St Mary the Virgin, Wantage. I regarded this as somewhere to be housed and fed while I studied, but I received more than I had bargained for. I had never visited a Religious community before, indeed had not even met a Sister or a Brother. I knew nothing about the life and it seemed very strange to me. And yet I soon found myself caught up in the rhythm and atmosphere there....I was drawn into the ethos in which prayer was the priority and the journey in God central.[13]

---

[12] "The Ordination to the Christian Ministry of Margaret F Jarman BD, Holmesdale Baptist Church, South Norwood, London, Wednesday 6th September 1967 at 8.00pm," M. F. Jarman papers, in possession of the author and awaiting deposit in the Angus Library, Regent's Park College, Oxford.

[13] "The Route to Final Profession as a Baptist Religious (Nun) by Sister Margaret Jarman CPP," private document in the archive of the Rev. Sister Margaret Jarman CPP BD, M. F. Jarman papers.

After several weeks in the community Jarman wrote:

On reading through my review of that Sabbatical I can see how the seeds of future developments—my spiritual journey, the theme of my Baptist Union Presidency, Profession as a Religious, my hermit life—had all been sown and taken root in that Sabbatical.[14]

After this six-week sabbatical Jarman wrote:

On my last day there in a simple Service in the Chapel during an "Office" I became a Novice Oblate. An Oblate is one who, while not a member of the Community, offers her/his life to God in association with a religious Community and lives in that spirit. I was the only Baptist Oblate CSMV. In my case the Oblate rule was adapted for my Baptist Tradition....Throughout the following years...Wantage (CSMV) was a great resource for me....I looked through my diaries at the Wantage visits thus far and they totalled 365 days of support.[15]

In 1985 Jarman suffered a severe viral attack which grew worse and was later diagnosed as myalgic encephalomyelitis (ME). This restricted her physical activities though not her ministry and prayer ministry. She concluded her ministry in West Coventry but continued with her work for the British Council of Churches and Free Church Federal Council.

Presidency of the Baptist Union

Another first for Jarman was becoming the first female Baptist minister to assume the vice presidency (1986) and then the presidency of the Baptist Union of Great Britain. Her presidential address and theme (Bradford, 1987)[16] on "Prayer and Action" was a stimulus for forming the Baptist Union Retreat Group. It was rare for any lasting initiative to come out of a British Baptist Union presidential year—another first, we can assume. Jarman was the first chair of the retreat group, serving until 1993.[17] Jarman noted on the evening of her presidential address:

---

[14] "The Route to Final Profession."

[15] "The Route to Final Profession."

[16] "Prayer and Action," Presidential Address to the Baptist Assembly, Bradford, May 1987 (Didcot: Baptist Union of Great Britain, May 1987).

[17] The Baptist Union Retreat Group is still in existence, has a journal, and holds regular retreats throughout the year. See https://burg.org.uk, accessed September 28, 2021.

My special guests were my mother, my closest friend and Sister Anne Francis of Wantage. The sight of a Religious habit was pretty unusual at a (Baptist) assembly but her presence expressed both the support of the Community and the Oblates (she was Oblate Guardian as well as my Spiritual Director) and my recognition of the place of Wantage in my life.[18]

Jarman was to continue that association with Wantage. At the conclusion of her presidential year, she and the incoming President, the Rev. Colin Marchant, of east London, went to Wantage for a retreat led by the Rev. Michael Walker.[19]

Spiritual Direction

In 1988, after her presidential year, Jarman accepted the call to King's Stanley Baptist Church in Gloucestershire (part-time) and developed her ministry of leading retreats and of spiritual direction, in which she had developed an interest. For the academic year 1988–89 Jarman took an ecumenical course in Spiritual Direction held at the National Retreat Centre in London. Her training as a deaconess and her theological education at Spurgeon's College had been of a classic conservative evangelical form, but through the course in Spiritual Direction she was introduced to other traditions of spirituality, broadening her understanding of prayer and of styles and forms of prayer within other traditions. A few British Baptist ministers had explored wider spiritual traditions, but Jarman paved the way for others to do so by seeking to enhance her competences both in forms of prayer and in directing others in their prayer life and ministry. Since she had been president of the union, this seemed to give legitimacy to others in Baptist ministry to explore different traditions of Christian spirituality. Jarman's expertise in this field continued to be strengthened through her link with the community of St. Mary the Virgin at Wantage in Oxfordshire. By 1990 her diagnosis of ME was confirmed, and Jarman was advised to retire from pastoral ministry early. A retreat at Wantage gave her opportunity to face the situation in view of her physical limitations and the advice of her doctors. As she notes,

It was a time of hollowing out, a facing of the limitations of illness, a choosing of the poverty of powerlessness, a desire to be with Jesus in his earthly experience of limitation and powerlessness, a stripping

---

[18] "The Route to Final Profession."

[19] Michael Walker was a Baptist minister interested in worship who ultimately served on the staff of South Wales Baptist College.

down to the desire for God himself, an embracing of my situation as a way to be closer to Christ—all of which I can see, in retrospect, as being a preparation for the Religious life.[20]

Jarman, a lifelong Baptist, did consider whether her future lay with the Anglican community at Wantage, but her spiritual director thought it was not so—though former BMS missionary Margaret Evening had joined the community, accepting Anglican orders.[21] Jarman moved into a property of the Retired Baptist Minister's Housing Society.

Meanwhile, the Baptist Union Retreat Group, which Jarman had founded in her Presidential year, began to explore what a Baptist Rule of Life might look like. In 1992 it produced a document which is now known as the Burford Covenant.[22]

A Vocation in Community

Jarman was approached in 1994 by Evelyn Pritty, a member of a Baptist church in London, who felt a call to live in community. Jarman did not, by now, see this for herself, but met regularly with Pritty to encourage her in exploring this vocation. In 1996 whilst on annual retreat at Wantage she had another experience, writing in her journal

> I felt Christ inviting me to join in a dance with him, and then to walk and rest with him. It was a time of close fellowship with him....His closeness was cleansing a cavity in me, burning off the mess, then filling the space with himself...giving me a gift, a seed which I was to receive without knowing into what the seed would grow.[23]

Through 1996 Jarman continued to reflect on the persistent call to be a hermit, alongside discussing with Pritty and others about whether there was a place for an intentional, residential Baptist community with distinctives,

---

[20] "The Route to Final Profession."

[21] Margaret Evening became Sister Margaret Magdalen CSMV and wrote several books on spirituality, including *Jesus, Man of Prayer*; *Furnace of the Heart: Rekindling Our Longing for God*; and *A Spiritual Check-Up – Avoiding Mediocrity in the Christian Life*.

[22] The Burford covenant is so called because the Baptist Union Retreat Group Committee regularly met at the Anglican Benedictine Community based at Burford Priory in Oxfordshire. The story of the Baptist Union Retreat Group is available at https://burg.org.uk/wp-content/uploads/2017/02/occ-paper-10-the-journey.pdf, accessed June 29, 2021.

[23] "The Route to Final Profession."

nevertheless drawing insights from other Christian intentional communities, in the way Jarman had benefitted from Wantage and Burford. On February 9, 1999 Jarman spoke to the London Baptist Ministers on "A Baptist Religious Community." This was the first time she had gone public on the details of the Community of the Prince of Peace, which Pritty and Jarman had felt drawn to establish.

After much prayer, the Community of the Prince of Peace had been established at Carterton, in Oxfordshire, with Jarman and Pritty received as postulants at a service in the Anglican Burford Priory in April 1997, presided over by the prior and with myself as preacher. Their first profession was on March 15, 1999. Brother Stuart, prior at Burford, had served as novice guardian and I, as former Deputy General Secretary of the Baptist Union, served as visitor.[24] The community, having received another postulant, moved to a property in Derbyshire in May 1999.

The small community never grew beyond three members. Though there were many good aspects to it—the first Baptist community in England engaged in communal living—Jarman still felt the call to a hermit life. In April 2001 Prior Stuart and myself reviewed the community and it began to become clear that the community either needed to grow or change.[25] Sister Evelyn visited the Community of the Transfiguration in Australia, the only other known Baptist intentional residential community, which she found stimulating. However, as the Community of the Prince of Peace had not grown, she did not feel able to renew her profession. With the withdrawal of Pritty, the Community was no longer viable. On March 15, 2002 Jarman renewed her vows. The trustees of the community buildings at Riddings put the property on the market and agreed to repay Pritty her loan to the community.

---

[24] I was appointed rector of the International Baptist Theological Seminary of the EBF in the summer of 1998. I moved to Prague, Czech Republic, but continued as visitor to the Community of the Prince of Peace through the time of its existence and as visitor to the Rev. Sister Margaret CPP until her death in 2018.

[25] "Review of the Community of the Prince of Peace," April 3–4, 2001 by the Rev. Dr. Keith G. Jones (visitor) and Brother Stuart of Burford Priory, archival papers of Keith Jones.

A Baptist Hermit

In December 2001 Sister Jarman was consecrated as a hermit—another English Baptist first—and her hermitage dedicated.[26] By August 2002 the monastery at Riddings was sold, and Pritty withdrew from the community. In March 2003 Jarman made her final profession as a religious at Burford Priory and immersed herself in the life of a hermit, seeking guidance from other hermits in Wales. Sister Margaret continued her vocation undaunted by her ill health, though moving from Derbyshire to Devon and eventually to Yatton in Somerset. During a retreat on the Lyn peninsula in Wales (a place noted for the number of hermits who reside there) she commented:

> As I approach my three score years and ten next month there's a host of things to offer to you Lord: rich wine, plain water, polluted water, opportunities missed, selfish actions, unkind thoughts, thoughtless words and deeds which have harmed others.…Lord, take this mixed life, touch it with your transforming spirit, change the significance and meaning of it.[27]

Jarman drafted her rule of life as a hermit, and in March 2003 a service of final profession was held in the Prayer room at the Hermitage led by myself (BUGB visitor) and assisted by Abbott Stuart OSB (consultant) and Sister Pauline Margaret CHN (spiritual director). Jarman's Prayer of commitment was

> I, Sister Margaret, in the presence of the whole company of heaven and of those here present, do vow to you almighty God, Father, Son and Holy Spirit to live the rest of my life as a Religious sister according to my Rule of life and I promise, in obedience to your call, to serve you in stability, conversion of life, poverty, celibacy and obedience by the help of your grace and the bestowal of your gifts, all the days of my life.[28]

The journey from cowherd to deaconess, minister, then community member and hermit—in which a sense of calling and vocation was always at the

---

[26] An earlier former Baptist, Brother Ramon, lived as a hermit, but he had moved out of Baptist church membership to follow his calling. Sister Margaret remained a member of a Baptist church throughout her life; this was important to her.

[27] "The Route to Final Profession."

[28] "The Route to Final Profession."

forefront of Jarman's mind—was a powerful one, which affected and inspired others along the way. Jarman set out her journey for others to reflect on.[29]

Reflections on a Pioneering Life

For the present, we know that many in our Baptist family across Europe, in her former pastorates, in the ecumenical community, and especially in the religious communities and the family of hermits in the isles will have cause to give thanks for Sister Margaret and to recall her spirit of determination, especially against the many health challenges she had in life.

Jarman's commitment to remain firmly within the Baptist tradition, illustrated by her insistence of having a Baptist visitor both to the community and later to her life as a hermit, was persistent and unbreakable. Her work in founding the Baptist Union Retreat Group along with her dedicated role as chair and then later consultant ensured that the group flourished and grew as part of the British Baptist scene. Her work as a spiritual director drew many Baptist leaders into her orbit—both lay and ministerial. However, because there was no resource available of baptistic models of community life or of life as a hermit, she had to rely on the Anglo-Catholic communities in the Church of England to advise and shape the rule of life and the lifestyle of a hermit.

A review and analysis of Jarman's papers awaits future scholarly work. They describe the Community of the Prince of Peace and interaction with those who were members of the community, along with those who sampled the community but chose not to join it. Whatever future reflection and research show, we are presented with a woman with an absolute commitment to Christ and a desire to serve the wider church and the Baptist denomination, through a life focused on prayer. She seized opportunities that others did not take and left an indelible imprint on the people with whom she came into contact as a deaconess, local church minister, spiritual director, community member, and in her life of prayer as a hermit.

---

[29] "The Route to Final Profession."

THE ESTABLISHMENT OF WOMEN'S LEADERSHIP AMONG THE BAPTISTS OF GEORGIA

Malkhaz Songulashvili

On June 15, 2008, within the context of Pentecost liturgy, the first female bishop was consecrated by the Evangelical Baptist Church of Georgia at the Peace Cathedral. With the consecration of Rusundan Gotziridze, the church completed the formal way of recognizing and establishing women's leadership for the first time in Eastern Europe, not only among Baptists but among other Christian groups in the area as well. Because the autocephalous Evangelical Baptist Church of Georgia has affirmed the threefold ministry of deacons, presbyters, and bishops, this consecration was decisive for the role of women.[1] Why has it happened in Georgia, but it has not happened in Russia or Ukraine, which are equally Orthodox countries? Why has it not happened yet in Baltic, Central Asian, or even other Caucasian countries of Armenia and Azerbaijan? Three major factors have played a key part.

St. Nino's Legacy

It is pertinent to say that Georgian culture owes more to the conversion of Georgia to Christianity than to any other single event in its centuries-long history. According to a medieval legend, Mary the God-birther and the Apostles divided up the countries of the world among them for the preaching of the Gospel.[2] But Mary was too frail to carry out the mission. Centuries later, another woman, Nino, decided to carry out Mary's mission to Georgia. Nino arrived to Mtskheta, then the capital of Georgia, in 318. Because of her tireless efforts, first Queen Nana and then King Miriam accepted Christianity and Georgia became one of the earliest Christian nations in the fourth century.

---

[1] *Draft for the Restructuring of the Baptist Communities in Transcaucasia,* Appendix 4, in Malkhaz Songulashvili, *Evangelical Christian Baptists of Georgia, The History and Transformation of a Free Church Tradition* (Baylor University Press: Waco, 2015), 361–66.

[2] Platon Ioseliani, *A History of the Georgian Church,* trans. & comments S. C. Malan (London: Sanders, Otley, 1866), 1–2.

The authors or later editors of the *Life of St. Nino* included these stories that would strengthen her position as an apostle to the Georgians. They underline that Nino came from an evangelistic and clerical background. Her father was responsible for the conversion of Branjs (a Frankish tribe, perhaps) to Christianity and her mother had dedicated her life to serving the poor. The stories claimed (inaccurately) that her uncle had been a patriarch of Jerusalem.[3] The narrative also relates a very interesting story of her ordination and blessing in the church by the laying on of hands. In the words of Nino:

> My mother's brother called me and placed me on the steps of the altar
> and laid his hands upon my shoulders…and said: "O, Lord, God of
> fathers and ages, into your hands I place my sister's orphan child, and
> I send her to preach Your divinity, so that she may spread the good
> tidings of your resurrection, wherever it pleases you. May You be, O
> Christ, the guide and leader of your servant, on her course.[4]

The patriarch's prayer over Nino might be construed as an ordination prayer for an apostolic ministry, rather that ordination to one of the three offices of the historical church. Soon after her ordination Nino herself administered baptism to more than forty-one souls.[5] "I baptized under my hand," says Nino in the earliest manuscripts of the *Conversion* (N/Sin-50 and S-1141). A later manuscript that was obviously edited says: "I baptized by the hands of a priest under my hand."[6] This editing must have been done in order to deprive her of her liturgical authority. There is yet another extraordinary narrative recorded in the *Life of St. Nino*. When she arrived to Georgia, she dreamt that a man directed her on her mission to the king. She complained that she was an alien, a woman, unskilled, unable to speak the Georgian language and that she did not know what to tell these alien people. Then the man opened a book and she saw there sayings written "as the former tablets of stone."[7] She read the charter of her mission, which, according to the Armenian version of the Life of St. Nino, possessed "the whole force of the gospel."[8] It stressed several texts, including: "Wherever this

---

[3] See C. B. Lerner, ed., *The Wellspring of Georgian Historiography: The Early Medieval Historical Chronicle "Conversion of K'artli" and "The Life of St Nino,"* (London: Bennet & Bloom, 2004), 142.

[4] Lerner, ed., *Wellspring of Georgian Historiography*, 161.

[5] Among the baptized was Ripsime, who eventually died as a martyr of the church.

[6] Compare the reading in Lerner, ed., *Wellspring of Georgian Historiography*, 161n55.

[7] Lerner, ed., 163.

[8] Robert W. Thomson, *Rewriting Caucasian History: The Medieval Armenian*

gospel is preached throughout the world, what she has done will also be told, in memory of her" (Matthew 26:13, NIV); "nor is there male and female, for you are all one in Christ Jesus" (Galatians 3:38, NIV); and "Jesus said to Mary Magdalene: 'Go instead to my brothers and tell them, "I am ascending to my Father and your Father, to my God and your God."'" (John 20:17, NIV). The "whole force of the gospel" was nothing less than a feminist mission statement based on Christian Scriptures and tradition.[9]

Despite all the efforts made by the writers and redactors of this text, it took centuries until Nino's legacy was fully recognized. It happened in the reign of Queen Tamar (1160–1213), when the role of St. Mary and St. Nino in the conversion of Georgia was made prominent out of ideological reasons.[10] Queen Tamara was undoubtedly the most prominent Georgian monarch not only in historical chronicles but also in Georgian folklore.[11] Eight centuries later, after the dissolution of the Soviet Union, the Baptists of Georgia were keen to draw on St. Nino's heritage for the legitimacy for women's ordination into the deaconate, the presbyterate, and the episcopacy.

Pre-Soviet and Soviet Egalitarian Legacy

After the Great Revolution of 1917 in Russia, Georgia gained its independenece. Social Democrats came to power. They were committed to the principles of egalitarianism from the very beginning. Georgia became the first country in the world to elect women in the assembly/parliament of the country. On February 21, 1921, the Constituent Assembly of Georgia adopted a constitution of the Democratic Republic of Georgia, the first modern fundamental law in its history. Within four days, on February 25, Georgia was occupied by Soviet troops, and there was no chance to have constitutional principles fully implemented in the country. This tragic development in Georgian history had a young heroine, Maro Makashvili (1901–1921), who was compared to Joan of

---

Adaptation of the Georgian Chronicles: The Original Georgian Texts and the Armenian Adaptation [Oxford Oriental Monographs], (Oxford: Oxford University Press, 1996), 96. For the Georgian and Armenian parallel texts see: I. Abuladze, *Old Armenian Translation of the "Kartlis Tskhovreba"* (Tbilisi: Tbilisi State University Press, 1966), 82.

[9] See Lerner, ed., *Wellspring of Georgian Historiography*, 163–64.

[10] N. Gurabanidze, "The reading of Svetitskhoveli, the Lord's Tunic and the Catholic Church" in *Georgia's Paradise: Complete Description of the Merits and Marytrdom of Saints of Georgia*, ed. G. Sabinin (Petersburgh, 1889), 70.

[11] Tina Shioshvili, *Queen Tamar in Georgian Folklore* (Tbilisi: Lampari, 2014).

Arc in a newspaper article. She volunteered as a nurse in the battle for Tbilisi and was killed during the 1921 Red Army invasion of Georgia.[12]

The new Soviet Georgia became one of fifteen Soviet Republics and was under Soviet control for the next seventy years. These were years of captivity, but there were some progressive principles that were promoted during this time. Among them there were priciples of gender equality and egalitarianism. For Soviet authorities, the affirmation of women was also a hefty argument in an ideological battle with the capitalist West. It has already been noted in academic literature that "Marxism was to implicate capitalism and patriarchy in the opression of women."[13] Special academic studies have been made in order to explore the implications of emancipation for Georgian women and the specific ways it unfolded in Georgia.[14] As a result of the ideological battle, women in Georgia were promoted into positions that previously had never been occupied by women. The Georgian women were given a chance to make their space in the patriarchal society. They became established in the world of arts, music, science, literature, sports.

The Soviet era contributed to the resurgence of feminist art when Georgian women artists started exploring their feminist identities. For instance, Natela Iankoshvili (1918–2007), a woman who has been referred to as "the rebel of Georgian art, in her own lifetime was able to break from gender stereotypes."[15] Georgian cinematography also made significant contributions towards the emancipation of women in Georgia. Later in the Soviet era, a woman film director, Lana Gogoberidze, produced "one of the most overtly feminist Soviet films."[16] A Georgian woman chess player had a special role in raising the respect towards women. The chess world became dominated by Georgian women when

---

[12] In 2015, she was the first woman to be granted posthumously the Georgian Order of National Hero. *Biographical Dictionary of Georgia*: http://www.nplg.gov.ge/bios/ka/00008033/, accessed February 7, 2021.

[13] Choj Chatterjee, "Ideology, Gender and Propaganda in the Soviet Union: a Historical Survey," in *Left History* 6, no. 1 (Spring 1999), 19.

[14] Maia Barkaia, "The Country of the Happiest Women?: Ideology and Gender in Soviet Georgia," in *Gender in Georgia: Feminist Perspectives on Culture, Nation, and History in the South Caucasus*, ed. M. Barkaia and A. Waterston, 33–46 (New York and Oxford: Berghahn Books, 2018).

[15] See Nina Mdivani, "Woman's Identity in the Georgian Visual Art: Pagava, Iankoshvili, Kvesitadze, Khizanishvili," *Feminism and Gender Equality*, Heinrich Böl Stiftung South Caucasus, February 26, 2019, https://feminism-boell.org/en/2019/02/26/womans-identity-georgian-visual-art-pagava-iankoshvili-kvesitadze-khizanishvili.

[16] Lana Gogoberidze's film, *Some Interviews on Personal Matters* (1979).

four of the finals at the World Women's Championships between 1962 and 1991 were Georgians against Georgians (1975, 1978, 1981, and 1988).[17] By the end of the Soviet era, women were seen in all areas of social, political, and cultural life. The only exception was in religious life. The Baptists of Georgia were first in the former Soviet Union to start ordaining women into the deaconate and the presbyterate of the church by which they completed the circle of women's leadership in Georgian culture.

Denominational Legacy

When Soviets invaded Georgia in 1921, the first target of the atheist regime became the Georgian Orthodox church. Once they completed suppression of the Orthodox, in a few years they moved to other religious groups. They started persecuting the Baptists by dealing with their male leadership. In August 1927, the founding father of the Georgian Baptist movement was assassinated by Bolsheviks on his mission trip to East Georgia. Kandelaki's martyrdom and his martyrology, written by Areshin, have played decisive roles in the formation of Georgian Baptist identity.[18] His death was just the beginning of the Soviet persecution of Baptists. A few years after the martyr's death, other male leaders of the community, including Zakaria Patsiashvili and the Brothers Chakhvashvili, were also tried and exiled.[19]

The leadership of the church was naturally passed on to women. The authorities did not suspect that they were far more dangerous for Soviet ideology than men. The women became preachers, evangelists, counselors, and confessors of the church. Throughout the 1930s and early 1940s, women kept the underground church alive.[20]

In the early 1940s, Soviet policy towards religion started to change due to World War II. In 1944–45, the Baptist and Evangelical Christian churches were merged in Georgia and were legally allowed to resume their religious life. But even after the formal reestablishment of the church, women continued playing key roles in the life of the church. Ekaterine Kutateladze (1894–1965), for instance, became a spiritual leader for an entire community in the postwar

---

[17] See Fatima Hudoon, "The Real-life Queen's Gambit: How Georgia's Nona Gaprindashvili Conquered the Chess World," *The Calvert Journal*, November 27, 2020.

[18] I. F. Areshin, "The Death of Brother I. M. Kandelaki," in *Baptist* 9 (1927), 13.

[19] Giorgi Chachvashvili Files, The Ministry of Internal Affairs Archives, Tbilisi.

[20] They visited each other's families on a regular basis, read Scriptures, sang Baptist hymns, instructed their children with religious principles, and shared their faith with their relatives in rural villages.

period. She translated the New Testament and Psalms from ancient Georgian into the modern Georgian language. She composed and translated hymns in Georgian. She became the spiritual mentor for the young generation of clergy who joined the community after the reestablishment of the church. She was never formally ordained or recognized as the spiritual guide, but no one questioned her authority.[21]

The first step into formal recognition of the women in ministry was taken by establishing a theological seminary in the East Georgian town of Gurjaani in 1993, where sixty percent of the students were young women. The first female graduate of the Gurjaani Theological Seminary was ordained on January 31, 2001 into the deaconate and into the presbyterate on the Pentecost of 2007. That was Mrs. Tinatin Mevlupishvili, from the town of Lagodekhi, who has been serving the local congregation first as an ordained deacon and then as an ordained presbyter.

By 2008, several women were ordained into the deaconate (for social and liturgical ministry) and the presbyterate (for pastoral, liturgical, and preaching ministy), but there was no woman bishop (for teaching, spiritual guidance, and sociopolitical leadership) consecrated as yet. That year, the Synod of the Evangelical Baptist church unanimously endorsed Mrs. Rusudan Gotziridze together with two male candidates for episcopal consecration. Baptists have been known globally for endless debates on contested matters, but there were no debates about the legitimacy or pertinence of the consecration of a female bishop, neither in the Synod nor in the wider church community.

With the consecration of the female bishop, there were several risks to be taken into consideration. There was a danger that it would ruin the church's ecumenical and interfaith relations. It could posibly cause further sidelining of the church by the Orthodox majority culture. It could also tarnish the reputation of the church as a respectful religious community. It could upset relations with Eastern European and former Soviet Union correligionists, who in 2005 had already declared the Georgian Baptists in apostacy for ordaining women and for their ecumenical commitment.[22] Yet because of the strength of the threefold legacy, these risks were boldly taken.

---

[21] Malkhaz Songulashvili, *Evangelical Christian Baptists of Georgia, The History and Transformation of a Free Church Tradition* (Baylor University Press: Waco, 2015), 129, 224.

[22] "Letter to the Union Leadership and the Ministers of the Evangelical Christian-Baptist Churches of Georgia," Appendix 13, in Malkhaz Songulashvili, *Evangelical Christian Baptists of Georgia: The History and Transformation of a Free Church Tradition*

Female Episcopacy in a Patriarchal Society

The first woman bishop was well prepared for the job. She came from a traditional Baptist family; her great-grandmother was Melania Kandelaki, a lay preacher in the 1930s and 1940s. Her maternal grandfather, Lado Songuahvili, was the Superintendant of Tbilisi. Her mother, Mzia Gotziridze, was an immensely active lay minister in the church. She was married to Micheil Saralishvili and already had two children. She was a graduate of Tbilisi State University and had a degree in English literature. She was also a graduate of the Gurjaani Theological Seminary and soon after the consecration, she earned an MA in Theology from Ilia State University.[23]

Bishop Rusudan, in her own words, "never thought that it was possible for a woman to become a bishop."[24] The first woman she saw preaching in her church was Mrs. Hilde Sayers, the President of the European Baptist Women's Union from 1992 to 1998, and she thought that it was a Westerrn phenomenon. She was already a university graduate when someone first suggested she might enter ordained life, and she thought it was just "a great compliment and encouragement."[25] But when she realized that it was not just a compliment, she consulted with her family, which was very supportive of her, and accepted the offer.

Initially Bishop Rusudan thought that the main task for an ordained minister was the preaching, but after her ordination into the deaconate and then into the presbyterate, she realized that there was more to it than just preaching. She said that "the provision of spiritual leadership, counseling, and advocacy work became part of my ministry only later."[26] Gradually, she became more and more engaged both in the life of her own community and in wider Georgian society. However, accepting her as the bishop was not easy, even for her closest associates in the church.[27] Some people thought that she was consecrated not because of her leadership skills and qualities but because of her family

---

(Baylor University Press: Waco, 2015), 409. The letter was privately explained as referring to the ordination of women and participation in ecumenical prayers.

[23] I have interviewed Bishop Rusudan herself, and I have also sent some questions about her ministry to some representatives of Orthodox, Catholic, Protestant, and nondenominational members of the Georgian society.

[24] Interview with Bishop Rusudan Gotziridze, August 20, 2021, unpublished interview, Archives of the Evangelical Baptist Church of Georgia, 1.

[25] Interview with Bishop Rusudan Gotziridze, 4.

[26] Interview with Bishop Rusudan Gotziridze, 2.

[27] Interview with Bishop Rusudan Gotziridze, 2.

background. Later on, they had to admit that they were mistaken—she was a spiritual leader in her own right.

Recognition of her leadership by the ecumenical and interfaith partners came some years after the consecration. According to the bishop, it happened in the year 2011, the third year of her consecration. That year has been known in Georgia's recent religious history as the year of struggle over the rights of religious minorities to be formally registered. The Orthodox church received its registration and recognition by the state in 2001 by the constitutional agreement that was signed between the head of the state, Eduard Shevardnadze, and the head of the Georgian Orthodox Church, Ilia II.[28] The Orthodox church was against granting similar registration rights for minority religions. In order to avoid confrontation with the Orthodox church, the state came up with a proposal to recognize only a few (specifically, five) religions as being entititled to be registered with the same status as the Georgian Orthodox church. Even though her church was in the list of favored religions, Bishop Rusudan mobilized other religions not to accept the principle of the privileged few and supported the principle of equality for all religions.[29] That summer, Bishop Rusudan became the voice for all the minorities in opposition to the majority Orthodox voice. She fought for them as a lioness, courageously and fearlessly, and eventually won the argument with support of all other religions of Georgia. The state legally recognized the rights of minority religions.

As Bishop Rusudan remembers her experience with Georgia's Council of Religions:

> After those events…I felt for the first time that the members of the Council of Religions became interested to know what I thought and what I had to say. One of the Church leaders took me aside and told me that when I was consecrated he thought that when her church consecrated her it was an inappropriate action, but now he undestood that she was a worthy spiritual leader.[30]

---

[28] Constitutional Agreement between the Georgian State and Apostolic Autocephalous Orthodox Church of Georgia, 2002 in *The Legislative Messenger of Georgia*, https://matsne.gov.ge/ka/document/view/41626?publication=0, accessed August 9, 2021.

[29] Letter of Bishop Rusudan Gotzirigze to the Religious Leaders of Georgia and the Religious Leaders to the Georgian Parliament, July 4, 2011; in Songulashvili, *Evangelical Christian Baptists of Georgia*, 422–24.

[30] Interview with Bishop Rusudan Gotziridze, 6.

That summer was a breakthrough in her episcopal ministry, and not only in the church but the culture as well. Soon after that she found herself defending the rights of religious minorities throughout the country, protecting Muslim communities from Islamophobic attacks and humiliation, calling for international attention to the suffering of marginalized minorities, which included persecuted members of the LGBTQIA+ community, and others. She became a religious leader with great national recognition.

In 2014, Michelle Obama awarded Bishop Rusudan with the International Woman of Courage Award, which has significantly strengthened her episcopal ministry both in Georgia and internationally. On this occasion, the US Department of State issued a statement recognizing her special role and ministry in Georgia, where she as "a minority of a minority" was affirmed as an agent of tolerance and change "working in a predominantly male religous field."[31] Two years later, in 2016, the President of Georgia, Giorgi Margvelashvili, awarded Bishop Rusudan with a prestigious Medal of Honour for her "efforts to promote tolerance, charity work and enhancing dialogue."[32]

Basil Kobakhidze, the most prominent Georgian Orthodox theologian, thinks that the consecration of Bishop Rusudan was a very important decision, not only for her own church, but for Christianity in Georgia. He admits that her consecration was "indeed a challenge for the Orthodox Church and culture, but only such a positive challenge could bring this [Orthodox] church and culture out of the Medieval smelly swamp and show them the way of development."[33] In the opinion of Kobakhidze, consecration of a woman bishop was "snatching of religious legitimacy from the hands of patriarchy," and therefore there is no suprise that at the first stage of Bishop Rusudan's ministry there was an irritation about her among the Orthodox majority. Eventtually, however, the Georgian society "has accepted the existence of a woman bishop as reality and now considers her as an inseparable part of our life." As to the irritation that was caused by her consecration, he thinks that it was positive, because "it has given

---

[31] See *US State Department—Diplomacy in Action, Office of Global Women's Issues,* March 3, 2014; https://web.archive.org/web/20140307105823/http:/www.state.gov/s/gwi/programs/iwoc/2014/bio/index.htm "Michelle Obama Honours Georgian Woman with US Bravery Award," Agenda.ge, March 5, 2014, https://agenda.ge/en/news/2014/613.

[32] "Georgia's President awards Medal of Honour," Agenda.ge, November 16, 2016, https://agenda.ge/en/news/2016/2809.

[33] Basil Kobakhidze, "On the Consecration of the First Woman Bishop in Georgia," July 2, 2021, in *Marking the 13th Anniversary of Consecration of the First Woman Bishop in Georgia* (unpublished collection of reflections, 2021), 3.

stimulus to the thinking and discussing about this and other relevant ecclesial matters."[34]

Levan Sutidze, a Roman Catholic religious commentator and analytical thinker, agrees with Basil Kobakidze in his evaluation of the consecration of the woman bishop in Georgia. In his view, "the decision was of revolutionary sigificance" because it undermined "rigid and dominating theological beliefs which were, and remain, radically reactionary." In his evaluation of the acceptance of the female bishop by the patriarchal society, he also agrees with Kobakhidze by saying that "initally it was a great challange and courageous decision equally with heroism, but later her tireless work and courage and numerous stories [of her bravery] and her consistency [in her efforts] paved the way to positive change." He goes further in his theological reflections on the consecration and insists that her consecration "created a totally new dimension of the Gospel and religious vision, where social, political, and cultural aspects of the Gospel became equally reasonable for all social groups, for the most vulnerable and sidelined people, who used to consider Christianity as the oppressor and the enemy."[35]

Women respondents to my query were even more enthusiastic about Bishop Rusudan's consecration than men. Take, for example, Mako Gavtadze, a human rights lawyer and religious liberty activist. In her view, consecration of the woman bishop made the church more "down to earth and humane." She believes that the bishop's personal qualities have also played a significant role in establishing her leadership position in the wider Georgian society. In her view, "it is Rusudan's episcopacy that smashes prejudices and stereotypes." She also enthusiastically believes that Bishop Rusudan "has caused positive changes in the society and she is going to change things even more." [36] Another female respondent, Eka Chitanava, a scholar, social anthropologist, and human rights acivist, thinks that Bishop Rusudan's phenomenon will have an impact not only on Georgian society or Christian churches but on other religions as well. She thinks that the religious and ecclesial ministry of Bishop Rusudan "can be a stimulus for other religious organizations." She suggests that the religious

---

[34] Kobakhidze, "On the Consecration of the first Woman Bishop in Georgia," 2–3.

[35] Levan Sutitdze, "On the Consecration of the First Woman Bushop in Georgia," in *Marking the 13th Anniversary*, 4–5.

[36] Mako Gavtadze, "On the Consecration of the First Woman Bishop in Georgia," in *Marking the 13th Anniversary*, 7.

organizations may eventually be influenced by her in rethinking their doctrines and views on the position of women in religion."[37]

The only negative response I received on the consecration of the woman bishop came from an Italian-born Roman Catholic priest, Gabriel Bragantini. In his view, the consecration of a woman bishop distances the church from common tradition, and the decision to consecrate a woman was influenced by the culture. He also reminds Christians that "we should be in the world but should not be of the world," by which he implicitly maintains that the consecration of the woman bishop is a sign of the church's attempt to be seen more amenable to 'the world.'[38] It took years before the consecration of the first woman bishop in Eastern Europe was accepted and endorsed by the culture.

Conclusion

The establishment of female leadership among the Baptists of Georgia is chiefly due to three historical factors that have paved the way for the women's participation in the threefold ministry of deacons, presbyters, and bishops. With the consecration of Bishop Rusudan Gotziridze, the circle was completed and women became an integral part of Georgian Baptist life. But it did not stop there. Its impact and influence over the Georgian religious and cultural life has gradually become both visible and tangible. It happened in a small minority group of people, and eventually the idea was accepted by the entire nation.

Social psychology has shown remarkable studies of the power of the minority. In accordance with Serge Moscovici's theory, the key factor in minority influence is consistency.[39] His theory was taken up and developed by Gabriel Mugny.[40] The consistency of the Georgian Baptists in their vision to shape their culture has eventually started to produce results. The lay, ordained, and consecrated women have been playing a key role in implementing their vision: to bring positive changes to the patriarchal culture. With the establishment of women in religious leadership, the Georgian patriarchal culture finally accepted women into the domain that had usually been closed to them.

---

[37] Eka Chitanava, "On the Consecration of the First Woman Bishop in Georgia," in *Marking the 13th Anniversary*, 9.

[38] Gabriel Bragantini, "On the Consecration of the First Woman Bishop in Georgia." in *Marking the 13th Anniversary*, 12.

[39] S. Moscovici, *Social Influence and Social Change*, trans. C. Sherrard and G. Heinz (London: Academic Press, 1976), 109.

[40] G. Mugny, *The Power of Minorities,* trans. C. Sherrard (London: Academic Press, 1982).

Owing to the episcopal ministry of the first woman bishop, Rusudan Gotziridze, many forward-looking representatives of Georgian culture recognize the right of women to be a part of the sacred liturgical space and in religious leadership.

"IDEAL MANHOOD":
THE EARLY TWENTIETH-CENTURY
PERSPECTIVE OF WALTER MURSELL
OF PAISLEY, SCOTLAND

Brian Talbot

In 1902, Walter Mursell[1] published his first book, *Ideal Manhood and Other Addresses*.[2] This Baptist minister from Paisley, Scotland, with broad theological sympathies had no interest in the formal study of Christian doctrine or academic theology. His focus in this volume, and in other later published books of his sermons, was exclusively on a practical Christianity that engaged with the ever-changing world in which it was lived out. This brief study of a selection of his messages from the first two decades of the twentieth century will primarily focus on masculinity, while also referencing other topics that Mursell considered essential to address in guiding his hearers toward a healthy view of manhood. He was committed to addressing the young men in his congregation on topics that he viewed as relating directly to their daily lives.

Ideal Manhood

Walter Mursell addressed issues of manliness, or how a Christian man should conduct himself, with relative frequency in his published sermons. His 1902 volume *Ideal Manhood*, for example, consisted of seven messages on manhood delivered from the pulpit. In the sermon from which the book derives its title, for example, Mursell wrote: "The Christian religion comes forward with a magnificent proposal, it aims to supply mankind with the ideal character; it proposes to enable each human being to reach the highest point of ethical and spiritual

---

[1] Information on the life and ministry of Walter Mursell is given in Brian R. Talbot, *The "Fellowship of Trial": Religious Rhetoric in World War One: The Sermons and Poetry of Revd Walter Mursell* (John Howard Shakespeare Memorial Paper 2017; Helensburgh: United Board History Project, 2017).

[2] Walter A. Mursell, *Ideal Manhood and Other Addresses* (Paisley: Houlston and Sons, 1902).

development that he or she is capable of reaching."[3] This Paisley minister continued to affirm the importance of faith in God and of living by faith. However, in his sermon based on the text of Acts 3:16, the healing of the paralyzed man by Peter and John, he contrasted the passive medieval image of Christ who was gentle and submissive with a manly perspective in the present day. "Ideal Manhood is a positive, affirmative, aggressive power. Faith in the name of Christ had made this man 'strong': it had given him 'perfect soundness': Strength; soundness:"[4] Although he acknowledged the difficulties that may be faced in daily life, he repeatedly highlighted that "Ideal Manhood is a positive virtue, an aggressive activity; it goes forth in the wholeness of its strength conquering and to conquer."[5] A Christian man needs more than resignation and gentleness to handle uncongenial duties and to stand firm upon principle, and "to go through your Gethsemane and to carry your cross with the step of a conqueror. For these things we must have the spiritual power that imparts strength and soundness to the whole nature.…It is a supremely manly faith."[6] Walter Mursell conveyed clearly that though life could be difficult at times, Christian men could be resolute and determined and with God's empowering overcome their trials.

The Waggon and the Star

The second series of published sermons to those "on the threshold of Manhood"[7] was Mursell's 1903 volume entitled *The Waggon and the Star*. The purpose of this publication was "to seek to encourage and strengthen them in the daily strife of thought and temptation…to speak a word of hope and cheer…and to bring the subjects dealt with from the cloudland of mere theory into contact with everyday life."[8] A modern reader may conclude that the topics Mursell selected might be equally applicable to women as well as men; however, he chose them at that time to help guide young men in his congregation in their spiritual growth as Christians. These messages were a call to action. "The Soul of the Sluggard," for example, was a challenge to avoid procrastination and indecision: "Nothing but action can create character and give it due weight and significance in the scale

---

[3] Mursell, "Ideal Manhood," undated, in Mursell, *Ideal Manhood*, 13.

[4] Mursell, 20.

[5] Mursell, 22.

[6] Mursell, 23.

[7] Walter A. Mursell, "Prefatory Note," *The Waggon and the Star* (Paisley: Alexander Gardner, 1903).

[8] Mursell, "Prefatory Note."

of experience. By repeated decision we are building up our manhood."[9] This message challenged young men to take responsibility as they entered adulthood. Mursell assumed that they had the power and resources to make something significant of their lives through hard work and dedication. However, his message "The Irony of Sin" was a warning to learn from male biblical characters who made bad choices that had long-term impacts on their lives. These included King David, the monarch whose moral failure with Bathsheba had catastrophic consequences for her family; together with Achan and Gehazi, two lesser figures from the time of Joshua and the prophet Elisha respectively, whom the desire for money and possessions led astray. The most serious of all was Judas Iscariot, who betrayed Jesus to the Jewish religious authorities. Mursell repeatedly warned his hearers to "keep your heart with all diligence, for out of it are the issues of life" (Proverbs 4:23, KJV).[10] This Paisley minister was quite open in challenging the young men in his congregation about avoiding the perils of sexual sin and the dangers of materialism. He spoke plainly that overcoming the temptations we face to stray from God's pathway is one of our biggest challenges. However, each of us is able to overcome temptations, he explained in his sermon "Ways of Escape," based on 1 Corinthians 10:13.[11] A Christian man, Mursell believed, is able to resist the temptation to fall into sin by being watchful over his life and has to take responsibility for making good choices.

Another theme that featured in this call for Christian manliness related to physical health and wellbeing. Mursell spoke about the "creed of hygiene" and the "religion of sanitation," together with the "morality of diet," in his message "The Religion of the Body." "The maintaining of health is an aspect of Christianity, for the aim of Jesus Christ is to impart fullness of life....It is a part of a man's business as a Christian, and not only as a human being, to maintain himself as far as possible in a state of physical robustness."[12] This was a stirring call to these men to take care of their physical health, as their bodies were a temple of the Holy Spirit. "Such common things as eating and drinking, sleeping and waking, clothing, housing and drainage, exercise and cleanliness are not to be set outside the influence of our religion....Our physical condition will indeed determine largely the very scope and tone of our prayers."[13] Mursell highlighted the fact that he was a cricket enthusiast. He liked watching football although he had

---

[9] "The Soul of the Sluggard," undated, in Mursell, *The Waggon and the Star*, 25.

[10] "The Irony of Sin," in Mursell, *The Waggon and the Star*, 38–43.

[11] "Ways of Escape," in Mursell, *The Waggon and the Star*, 50–52.

[12] "The Religion of the Body," in Mursell, *The Waggon and the Star*, 74.

[13] Mursell, 74–75.

never played it. However, he declared: "I have covered hundreds of miles on my cycle; I believe in all manly outdoor sports; I think there is a great deal in the saying that Waterloo was won on the playing fields of Eton."[14]

Mursell reminded the congregation, though, of some words of the apostle Paul that "bodily exercise profiteth a little" (1 Timothy 4:8, KJV). He was concerned that some people were too obsessed with physical exercise. He declared, "if man's chief end is to glorify the physical and break records for ever, then the sporting view of life is the right one and athletics are the supreme concern. But…if life has a spiritual meaning and purpose, then the playground, the gymnasium, and the field of sport must be used to contribute to our mental, moral and spiritual power."[15] A concern that sport was taking people away from involvement in church and mission-related activities was a growing challenge across the United Kingdom at the beginning of the twentieth century.[16] Mursell was especially unenthusiastic about bodybuilding in the gym. He stated, "a mere Samson is one of the curiosities in life's portrait-gallery; he is a monstrosity of muscle."[17] Mursell was a Baptist pastor who knew his congregation and took a keen interest in their interests outside of work and family life. This address was given at a time of a growing interest in sports and physical recreation in the United Kingdom. Christian churches and especially the Young Men's Christian Association (YMCA) had been prominent in highlighting the need for physical health and exercise alongside care for a person's spiritual wellbeing.[18] It is likely that Mursell's perspective on this topic was representative of that of many church leaders in Scotland.

---

[14] Mursell, 77.

[15] Mursell, 79.

[16] For example, The Huddersfield YMCA committee in England reported these concerns regarding younger members in 1904. See W. E. Waterworth, *The Story of the Huddersfield YMCA* (Huddersfield, 1975), 6, 12, 16, 19–20, 24, cited in Dominic Erdozain, *The Problem of Pleasure: Sport, Recreation and the Crisis of Victorian Religion* (Woodbridge: The Boydell Press, 2010), 223–29. There were some exceptions to this trend: the 1905 annual report from the secretary of Newport YMCA in Wales, for example, highlighted the strength of their mainly religious work. Ernest J. Bakewell, *The History and Diary of the Newport Y.M.C.A. 1869–1990* (Newport: For the YMCA, 1996), 8.

[17] Mursell, "The Religion of the Body," 79.

[18] An introduction to the vast literature on this topic can be found in Erdozain, *Problem of Pleasure* and Hugh McLeod, "'Thews and Sinews': Nonconformity and Sport," in *Modern Christianity and Cultural Aspirations*, ed. David Bebbington and Timothy Larsen, 28–46 (London: Sheffield Academic Press, 2003).

Mursell displayed real confidence in the advance of God's kingdom on earth and modelled a positive outlook on life that was seen in his sermon "The Religion of an Optimist." It was not, though, a commendation of the power of positive thinking to these young men, because Mursell was well aware of the pressures and difficulties his audience faced in their daily lives. Instead, he grounded his belief on a surer foundation alongside that of the author of Psalm 119:50 (KJV), who wrote: "This is my comfort in my affliction: for thy word hath quickened me." After citing this verse, Mursell affirmed, "my hope in God, my belief in God's word, my love for God's truth, my confidence in God's law."[19] The Paisley minster was also aware that some men in his congregation and the wider community suffered from depressive illness. He addressed this subject in his "Spiritual Diagnosis" message based on Psalm 43:5a (KJV): "Why art thou cast down, O my soul? and why art thou disquieted within me?" He declared that "Religious melancholy is the saddest and most dangerous of all forms of mental gloom. Let the depressed and disquieted mind rouse itself to a sense of its peril. Let it ask the why of its condition; and let it not be satisfied with any superficial answer, but find a reason that corresponds adequately and vitally with the perilous symptoms."[20]

Unfortunately, for a person suffering from a severe form of depressive illness, a challenge to take action may not have been the wisest course of action, but understanding of this health issue was less advanced at that time. Later in life when Mursell himself suffered severely with mental health problems, he became aware of the real difficulties he and others had to endure. This led in time to his resignation from the pastorate of Thomas Coats Memorial Church in Paisley.[21]

The final sermon in this second volume from Mursell was entitled "Something Wanting." It was a challenge to men not to settle for a second-rate Christianity. He said, "We ought not to be satisfied with our Christianity if it leaves our hearts cold. If our study and experience of Christian truth does not kindle enthusiasm in the soul, if it does not inspire us with an unselfish and sacrificial passion, if it does not put down all rivalries and usurpers of the heart's affection, we may be sure we have not yet risen to the heights of Christian privilege."[22]

Mursell held to a robust and manly understanding of what it meant to be a follower of Jesus. He urged his hearers to take responsibility for their spiritual

---

[19] "The Religion of an Optimist," in Mursell, *The Waggon and the Star*, 93.
[20] "Spiritual Diagnosis," in Mursell, *The Waggon and the Star*, 106.
[21] *The Thomas Coats Memorial Church, Paisley, Jubilee Book 1944* (Paisley: James Paton Limited, 1945), 99.
[22] "Something Wanting," in Mursell, *The Waggon and the Star*, 171.

growth and not to settle for anything less than they could be as Christian men for God. In the prewar years his congregation prospered under his ministry. His sermons attracted a larger number of both men and women than was typical in Scottish Baptist churches in the early twentieth century. However, like every other congregation, his church faced new challenges when the First World War began.

Wartime Sermons

The sermons this Scottish Baptist pastor delivered in the first few weeks of the conflict contained no stirring rhetoric about the glories of war. On the contrary, he articulated to his congregation a solemn and sober recognition of what lay ahead.[23] Mursell was acutely aware that the challenges ahead to Christian men were much greater than many had imagined on the threshold of World War One. In his October 18, 1914 sermon "The Courage of Duty," the author highlighted the sacrifice of a young soldier of the Royal Irish Regiment who gave his life to save his colleagues. He emphasized that the cost of standing for principles would be high. "Such a time of heart-searching is with us now; and if we use such a time humbly and wisely, waiting upon God for light and strength, good will come out of this evil and blessing out of the curse of war; and the lessons learned in the stern school of suffering are not likely to be thrown away."[24] The issue in question was not whether "God is on our side" but whether "we are on God's." Here was an appeal to stand on higher moral ground. Mursell had no doubts that evil must be resisted, but in his view how we go about this monumental task was as important as the determination to stand firm and fight what he believed was a just war.

Mursell maintained this tone in his sermons. On September 20, 1914 he preached a sermon entitled "The Red Cross," in which he lauded the dedicated service of doctors and nurses in wartime: "It is a glorious work. It is the work of Christ."[25] By contrast, although declaring that "we have a right to hope for

---

[23] Some church leaders were enthusiastic about the war in August 1914 (A. J. Hoover, *God, Germany, and Britain in the Great War: A Study in Clerical Nationalism* [New York: Praeger, 1989], 115–16), but others, like Mursell, had a perception that this war, though just, would exact a heavy price before it was concluded.

[24] Walter A. Mursell, "The Courage of Duty," October 18, 1914, in *The Bruising of Belgium and Other Sermons During War Time* (Paisley: Alexander Gardner, 1915), 91–92, 94.

[25] "The Red Cross," September 20, 1914, in Mursell, *Bruising of Belgium and Other Sermons*, 104.

success, a right to pray for victory, because of the spiritual element in our motives and aims," with respect to military service his vocabulary was more restrained. He told the men present: "We can fight better, do our duty more faithfully, wait more patiently, suffer less complainingly, when we have the inspiration of a just cause."[26] He regarded the book of Psalms as a useful resource to help his hearers identify with the struggles of people of faith in earlier generations. Mursell drew on those insights to prepare these men for the difficult days that would lie ahead of them.[27] Remarkably, although Mursell drew attention in his 1915 "Love of Country" sermon to examples of inappropriate conduct by German men during the war, and referred to their misdirected patriotism, he also mentioned exemplary conduct by a German soldier towards British soldiers in need.[28] He wanted to remind his audience that "there are generous impulses in every kind of character, and 'God is not unrighteous to forget any labour of love.'"[29] In his view, ideal manhood could be demonstrated equally by German men as well as British men in this brutal war.

Mursell's volume of sermons *Ports in a Storm*, preached in 1918 but published in 1919, contains his considered reflections in the later stages of the war and its immediate aftermath. It was dedicated "To The Boys of the Congregation…who have laid down their lives, leaving us the task of helping to build a better world."[30] On February 10, 1918 he preached "The Heart of the Gospel" sermon, based on 1 Peter 1:21 (KJV): "So that your faith and hope might be in God." This was an exhortatory message urging his hearers to gain or retain a right view of the loving Father and his Son in the midst of their own trials. Once more he mentioned the agonies of Jesus in Gethsemane as the demonstration of costliness of obedience to the Father, allowing Christian men to connect their struggles and trials with the greater ones of the one who would lay down his life for them.[31] His thoughts in 1918 also turned to the possibilities of the future. In his "The Maker of Men" sermon, based on Matthew 4:19, Mursell highlighted

---

[26] Mursell, "The Courage of Duty," 93.

[27] "The Skylight," Psalms 40:12–13, October 4, 1914, in Mursell, *Bruising of Belgium and Other Sermons*, 243.

[28] "Love of Country," January 3, 1915, in Mursell, *Bruising of Belgium and Other Sermons*, 186–87.

[29] "The Inspiration of History," January 10, 1915, in Mursell, *Bruising of Belgium and Other Sermons*, 215.

[30] Walter A. Mursell, "Dedication," in *Ports in the Storm* (Paisley: Alexander Gardner, 1919).

[31] "The Heart of the Gospel," February 10, 1918, in Mursell, *Ports in the Storm*, 224.

the transformation possible in a man who dedicated his life to God. His examples included outstanding Christian men: missionaries James Chalmers and John G. Paton, together with social reformers Thomas Barnardo and William Quarrier. He saw in them models of hope to inspire his congregation to make a difference in their generation.[32]

Mursell constantly urged his hearers to grasp opportunities presented to them. His sermon "False Pretexts" in April 1918 was a good example. He believed that the future path before a man may be difficult, but this was no excuse for not embracing it. Once more he gave Jesus' example in Gethsemane of accepting the Father's plan as a model for Christian manliness. Christian men were left with this challenge: "You who have to make up your mind to stern decisions and to face up to situations that strain the sinews of the soul—dwell much in the garden of Gethsemane."[33] Mursell avowed that a fool was hesitant, unwilling to get on with the tasks before him. The message to be heeded was this: "Thought-Decision-Action: these are the watchwords of genuine manhood....Do *something*. Decide one way or another; but don't go on drifting, dreaming, postponing."[34] The Christian man who would play a useful role in the postwar years, according to Mursell, needed to have "something big about him," something "rugged" and something "solid" but also something "sweet and gracious." A wholehearted dedication to Christian service—along with a masculine character—was required.[35] The tone of Mursell's sermons was clear: the circumstances Christian men face are undoubtedly difficult, but they must rise to the challenge and not shrink from it. God's pathway for them, like that of Jesus in Gethsemane, may be difficult, but Christian men must accept their calling to play their part in overcoming the challenges before them.

Conclusion

How did Mursell view the future for the Christian church? He stated that the church needed to be "a Hospitable Church—a Church receptive to new ideas, fresh plans and purposes, fresh adaptations and applications."[36] He looked forward to a day when more generous and open-minded theological convictions were proclaimed. He declared: "Narrower views of the Christian idea of God are to be avoided. They are harmful to the mind that cherishes them, not only

---

[32] "The Maker of Men," March 10, 1918, in Mursell, *Ports in the Storm*, 259–60.

[33] "False Pretexts," April 28, 1918, in Mursell, *Ports in the Storm*, 145.

[34] "Mistaken Perspective," May 19, 1918, in Mursell, *Ports in the Storm*, 129–30.

[35] "A Man's Character," June 30, 1918, in Mursell, *Ports in the Storm*, 21.

[36] "More Stately Mansions," November 3, 1918, in Mursell, *Ports in the Storm*, 72.

because they are unworthy and untrue, but because they have a cramping and biasing effect upon the moral nature."[37] The church needed men of the caliber of Robertson Smith, A. B. Davidson, George Macdonald, and Henry Drummond, he claimed, to guide us "to the mountains of vision….The future must gratefully welcome the builders of the soul's more stately mansions."[38] Although the sacrifices of the war years had weighed heavily upon him, Mursell was still optimistic that a better future was in sight for Christian churches in the postwar years. Walter Mursell retained his vision for Christian manhood throughout his long pastorate in his Paisley church. The postwar world in which Christians would practice their faith was a more complex and challenging environment. But Mursell had no doubt that, in dependence on God, Christian men would rise to the challenge of addressing the issues of the day.

---

[37] "The Breadth of God's Interest," September 29, 1918, in Mursell, *Ports in the Storm,* 278.

[38] "More Stately Mansions," November 3, 1918, in Mursell, *Ports in the Storm,* 73.

BAPTISTS IN NORTH AMERICA

A BRUTAL FAITH: COLLEGE FOOTBALL AND MANHOOD AT AMOS ALONZO STAGG'S UNIVERSITY

Seth Dowland

In the late 1880s, a pair of Baptists, John D. Rockefeller and William Rainey Harper, planned to build a grand university of the south side of Chicago. The men shared a denominational identity but not a temperament. Where the oil baron Rockefeller was reserved and utilitarian, the scholar Harper was experimental and ebullient. A visionary biblical scholar and administrator, Harper sold Rockefeller on his vision of a practical and innovative university that could push the nation into the modern world. The oilman lavished funds on Harper's university, charging Harper with establishing the foremost research university in the nation.[1]

One of Harper's first hires—football coach, athletic director, and tenured faculty member Amos Alonzo Stagg—seemed difficult to square with this vision. Stagg had made a name for himself at Yale, but not as a scholar. Rather, he had starred for the Yale "nine" (the baseball team) in the mid-1880s and, later, for the Elis' "eleven" (the football team). Yale football coach Walter Camp selected Stagg to the first all-American team. Stagg's playing record dwarfed his academic credentials. After earning his bachelor's degree in 1887, Stagg completed just a single year of post-graduate studies at Yale Divinity School before accepting a teaching position at the newly formed YMCA International Training School in Springfield, Massachusetts, where he worked for three years. Stagg's thin academic record confounded both his fellow faculty members and reporters covering the new university, who wondered why hiring a thirty-year-old football coach was such a priority for Harper. One Midwest paper introduced Stagg to its readers by describing his rugged physicality. "His nose is billowy as if it might have been broken once or twice," the unsigned piece surmised, "and there is a look of pain, or at least tension, in his face that he would never have got behind a dry goods counter. He was also very much sunburned." Damning Stagg with faint

---

[1] Robin Lester, *Stagg's University: The Rise, Decline, and Fall of Big-Time Football at Chicago* (Urbana: University of Illinois Press, 1999), 2–6.

praise, the reporter conceded that Stagg spoke "in a perfectly composed manner."[2]

But Stagg's hiring aligned with dominant strains of thinking among a group of "muscular Christians" who were ascendant at many elite institutions. In an 1887 speech that Stagg likely attended, Yale president Timothy Dwight described what a "Yale man should be." Dwight argued that a "manly sense of duty" was "the primary object of a true education." The ideal Yale student, then, "should be a man whose prime quality and foundation of character is manliness…that manly sense of obligation to God and man which puts work before pleasure and inspires the soul to meet what is hard or distasteful with the spirit of a conqueror."[3] Connections of manliness to Christian virtue were ubiquitous by the late 1880s, and a growing number of elites believed their sons could develop their manhood best on the playing fields being built on campuses around the nation.

Sports—particularly football—seemed to offer Victorian men a space where they could develop manly character. Where earlier generations of white American men had settled the west and abolished slavery, fighting Native Americans and Confederates, the new industrialists of the late nineteenth century faced a crisis of masculinity. As muscular Christian (and Stagg's one-time boss) Luther Gulick put it, "we are built for activity and we live sitting-down lives."[4] The solution for the sedentary set was found on the gridiron. Coaches like Stagg argued that physical activity would arrest the feminization of American men, and that universities ought to put athletics at the center of college life.

Yet football in the 1890s and early 1900s was vicious. Debilitating injuries and even deaths occurred with some regularity. How could Baptists square such a violent game with the call to Christian manhood? That question loomed large over Stagg's first two decades at Chicago. "Football has been denounced by many as brutal," he conceded, "but its moral values to the contestants far outweigh its faults." Stagg prided himself on the relatively low injury rate for Chicago players, which he credited to superior training and smarter players. The injuries Chicago

---

[2] "Athletics and Prayer: Trainer Stagg Says They Can Be Used Together at the Chicago University," *Chicago Journal*, July 6, 1892, Amos Alonzo Stagg Papers, Box 274, Folder 5, Special Collections Research Center, University of Chicago.

[3] Timothy Dwight, "What a Yale Man Should Be" (Speech, Yale University, 1887), Amos Alonzo Stagg Papers, Box 266, Folder 5, Special Collections Research Center, University of Chicago.

[4] Luther Gulick, "The Making of a Life: Dangers of a Sedentary Life," (February 24, 1904), 9, Luther Halsey Gulick Papers, Series 4, Box 10, Folder 4, Springfield College Archives and Special Collections.

football players inflicted on other teams were not Stagg's problem. Good conditioning and preparation, he believed, not only minimized injury risks but also enhanced players' ability to think quickly and act decisively. This was the essence of manhood, according to Stagg. "What greater thing is there than to be masters of ourselves? If we were our complete masters, we would be supermen."[5]

The language of supermen echoed eugenic theories that were gaining ground among liberal Protestants in the early twentieth century. Stagg's colleague at Chicago, biologist John Coulter, argued for the complementary nature of (eugenic) science and religion. "Both seek to produce better men physically and morally."[6] Perhaps football simply weeded out the weak. Though Stagg never voiced full-throated support for eugenics, his views on manhood and the character-building elements of football found plenty of parallels with this burgeoning science. Careful consideration of Stagg's career at Chicago (where football was eliminated shortly after Stagg's retirement) can help us see the unholy merger of faith, sports, and racial purity.

A particular vision of masculinity took shape at Chicago around the turn of the twentieth century, one that fused Christian faith with a racialized depiction of manly duty. Harper's hiring of Stagg reflected the urgency university administrators felt to cultivate muscular Christianity among their students. These rising elites could not learn all they needed in the classroom and the chapel. The football field provided a proving ground where they could demonstrate quick thinking, physical strength, and racial superiority. This fusion positioned sports at the center of university life, where football stars became the personification of Christian manhood.

Muscular Christianity Personified

In 1887, Amos Alonzo Stagg was the most famous college athlete in the country. A dominant pitcher for the Yale University "nine"—as baseball teams were then called—Stagg's was a household name throughout the Northeast. As he approached graduation, Stagg began fielding offers from professional teams that would pay him as much as $5,000 annually (at least $135,000 in 2021 dollars). Such a sum surely tempted Stagg. It also brought him unwanted attention. Edgar Williams, the editor of Stagg's hometown newspaper, the *Orange (NJ) Journal*,

---

[5] Amos Alonzo Stagg, "Moral Value of Athletics," August 8, 1922, Amos Alonzo Stagg Papers, Box 109, Folder 7, Special Collections Research Center, University of Chicago.

[6] Christine Rosen, *Preaching Eugenics: Religious Leaders and the American Eugenics Movement* (New York: Oxford University Press, 2004), 52.

wrote, "I think your friends would not blame you if you decided to make two or three thousand dollars out of your strong right arm by playing professionally."[7] A lawyer in New York took a dimmer view. "While it is perhaps none of my business what you determine upon," wrote H. B. Jarrett, "I feel it my duty as a man somewhat your senior in years...to kindly enter my protest against your accepting any" offers from pro baseball teams.[8] Like a lot of elite Victorians, Jarrett felt that professionalism sullied sports and worried that Stagg would imperil his future prospects with a pro baseball career.

In the end, Stagg agreed. He turned down the pro baseball teams and enrolled at Yale Divinity School, convinced that the pursuit of ministry could go hand in hand with excellence in athletics. Stagg kept his spot as ace pitcher for Yale and caught the attention of high-minded defenders of amateur athletics around the country. Journalist Joseph Dennison praised Stagg's "illustrious" example of "early manhood," commending his countrymen to show such selflessness. "If more young men were to emulate the example of Yale's famous pitcher," Dennison wrote, "this country would overflow with that kind of man that makes a nation strong and respected among the nations of the earth."[9] Dennison captured the connections between sports, Christianity, masculinity, and national success that an increasing number of "muscular Christians" were making by the late 1880s.

Muscular Christianity had emerged a few decades earlier in England, where the Young Men's Christian Association (YMCA) was founded in 1844. Though the earliest YMCAs focused on traditional evangelism in English and American cities, the YMCAs of the 1870s and 1880s were devoting more and more space to gymnasia and swimming pools. They saw these amenities as both a lure to attract young men and a component of healthy spirituality. Concerns about the enervating effects of city life had reached epic proportions by the 1870s, and vigorous physical activity seemed an important antidote to flabbiness and effeminacy.

In Stagg, muscular Christians found a shining example of the salutary linkages between athletic and spiritual excellence. A star pitcher who forsook riches

---

[7] Edgar Williams, "Letter to Amos Alonzo Stagg," May 17, 1887, Amos Alonzo Stagg Papers, Box 1a, Folder 2, Special Collections Research Center, University of Chicago.

[8] H. B. Jarrett, "Letter to Amos Alonzo Stagg," May 19, 1887, Amos Alonzo Stagg Papers, Box 1a, Folder 2, Special Collections Research Center, University of Chicago.

[9] Joseph Dennison, "Newspaper Clippings," (1888) Amos Alonzo Stagg Papers, Box 267, Folder 7, Special Collections Research Center, University of Chicago.

for ministry: what could be more appealing? Stagg was earnest and devout—not to mention handsome. An 1891 article noted that Stagg used a "Bible and dumbbells" to instruct his students, while "pretty women send him their pictures."[10] So long as he maintained a chaste appearance, Stagg's desirability communicated a virility that muscular Christians prized. In an industrializing society concerned about the "enervation" of young men, Stagg embodied an appealing counterexample. He was strong and serious, worthy of emulation.

The leading theorist of muscular Christianity, Luther Gulick, saw a chance to enlist Stagg in his crusade for Christian manhood. He wrote Stagg in 1888, inviting the Yale star to join Gulick at the newly formed YMCA International Training School in Springfield, Massachusetts. Stagg joined three other men in Gulick's first class of instructors for the YMCA school in Springfield. One of these men, Canadian James Naismith, devised the game of basketball as a way to keep young men active in the winter months. Stagg, meanwhile, was shifting his attention to the sport that would come to define him: football.

In his first and only year at Yale Divinity School, Stagg joined Coach Walter Camp's star-studded "eleven" on the gridiron. At this point, Stagg was twenty-seven years old—he had enrolled as an undergraduate at Yale somewhat later than normal, as a twenty-one-year-old—and some opponents grumbled that he was a ringer. But Camp (just three years older than Stagg) loved his star's clean living and exemplary backstory. Having turned down professional baseball teams, Stagg accepted his classmates' election to the post of YMCA secretary at Yale, probably the most influential college Y in the nation. Camp was so impressed with Stagg, both on and off the field, that he added Stagg to the first "all-American" football team. Camp helped create the very concept of an all-American team, rightly seeing it as an excellent way to market football. The selection was also a boon to "Lonnie" Stagg. Stagg soon found himself fielding a new set of offers, these from universities interested in hiring Stagg as a physical instructor or perhaps even as a coach, following the pioneering model of Camp.[11]

The most intriguing of these offers came from William Rainey Harper. A Baptist minister and accomplished Semiticist, Harper had taught Stagg at Yale Divinity School before Rockefeller lured Harper to the Midwest. The oil magnate lavished his fortune on the newly established University of Chicago, where

---

[10] A. C. Merritt, "Gospel of Muscle: Bible and Dumbbells the Instruments," *Boston Daily Globe*, January 25, 1892, Amos Alonzo Stagg Papers, Box 275, Folder 5, Special Collections Research Center, University of Chicago.

[11] Julie Des Jardins, *Walter Camp: Football and the Modern Man* (New York: Oxford University Press, 2015), 71–74.

Harper was installed as the first president in 1891. Rockefeller's riches enabled Harper to fund a number of innovations at Chicago. Stagg's hiring ranked among the most notable of those innovations, a "double precedent" in American higher education. Stagg became the first tenured academic to head a university-wide physical education department, as well as the first athletic coach with academic tenure.[12] With such security, Stagg would eventually surpass his mentor Camp and become the face of a new ideal in the world of American athletics: the professional coach.

Camp had promoted the new profession of coaching through a series of articles in the late 1880s and early 1890s. Harper & Brothers published his influential book, *American Football*, in 1891. Throughout the volume, Camp harped on the discipline and organization required to succeed in the game. This approach called for a strong manager, one who would instruct the team and develop strategy in much the same way that a new managerial class was reshaping the American economy. Camp's approach nudged football away from the prevailing custom of playing captains who led their teams into (simulated) battle. While Camp did not worry too much about the physical violence of football, he saw the sport as ripe for scientific management. "Coachers" could help their teams thrive by giving each player a discrete, repetitive task that would facilitate their team's success.

Camp's approach succeeded. From 1890 to 1893, Yale's football team not only went undefeated; they also did not concede a single point, outscoring their opponents 1,265 to 0. The Elis' success on the gridiron made his players into stars and turned Camp into one of the most sought-after speakers in colleges across the nation. Camp's rigorous practices became the standard for football instruction. Players left class at two o'clock and rode horse-drawn shuttles to Yale Field, where they drilled in "routinized, disciplined work," with crowds for practices numbering in the hundreds. The undeniable success of Camp's approach spelled doom for the days of the playing captain dictating substitutions and strategy. Amongst amateur athletes, the professional coach was becoming the most notable figure on the field.[13]

Stagg modeled his coaching on Camp, but he had an even freer hand to shape the athletic culture at Chicago than his mentor enjoyed at Yale. Eager to prove Chicago's merits, Harper gave Stagg wide latitude (and plenty of money) to build a championship program. Only twelve men showed up for tryouts in

---

[12] Robin Lester, *Stagg's University: The Rise, Decline, and Fall of Big-Time Football at Chicago* (Urbana: University of Illinois Press, 1999), 17.

[13] Des Jardins, *Walter Camp*, 73–97, quote on 83.

1892, and Stagg played alongside his first charges as a means of steadying the team. But beginning in 1893, Stagg moved to the sidelines full time and started to field better and better teams. Unencumbered by East Coast prohibitions on recruiting, Stagg sent letters to Midwestern feeder schools, soliciting strong athletes for Chicago's football team. Like his mentor Camp, Stagg published a book, *A Scientific and Practical Treatise on American Football: For Schools and Colleges*, in 1894. This publication—alongside Chicago's victories over the formerly dominant University of Michigan—established Stagg as the preeminent coach in the Midwest.

Stagg's prominence and job security allowed him to skirt many of Harper's directives. In letters to Stagg, Harper chided the coach for a series of transgressions, from scheduling an early afternoon game that kept fifteen men "away from Mr. Smith's Chemistry" to playing students whose demerits should have kept them sidelined. In one letter, Harper complained about "a series of games with negroes etc. which has brought disgrace upon us."[14] Stagg's responses were curt and evasive, and the coach frequently needled Harper about funds that the president had promised the athletics program. If Camp invented the idea of a professional coach for college athletic teams, Stagg perfected the imperiousness that came to characterize the profession.

Yet Harper did not seem to think this was an example of the tail wagging the dog. Quite the contrary: Harper saw Stagg's football teams as essential ambassadors for the fledgling university. "I want you to develop teams which we can send around the country and knock out all the colleges," wrote Harper. "The University of Chicago believes in football."[15] Professors—both at Chicago and elsewhere—saw Harper's support for the game as an embarrassment. Chicago economist J. Laurence Laughlin called his university president the "P. T. Barnum of education."[16] But like Barnum, Harper got the last laugh. Intercollegiate sports were booming. Hiring Stagg gave Chicago the first great college football dynasty of the twentieth century. Faculty complaints would not stop the greatest show on turf.

---

[14] William R. Harper, "Letter to Amos Alonzo Stagg," May 10, 1895, Amos Alonzo Stagg Papers, Box 9, Folder 1, Special Collections Research Center, University of Chicago.

[15] Lester, *Stagg's University*, 19, 18.

[16] Lester, 18.

Football and Brutality

The growing popularity of football in the 1890s ran headlong into a more serious challenge: concerns about player safety. Rule changes over the preceding two decades had lessened the number of players on the field and increased the physical contact in the sport. Football games in the early 1870s had taken place with as many as twenty-five players per side. As that number shrank to eleven, the game grew increasingly brutal. Violent collisions were leading to paralysis and death. Among high school and college teams, the *New York Times* reported twenty-three football fatalities in 1890 and twenty-six in 1892. Several colleges banned the sport, and President Grover Cleveland canceled the 1893 Army-Navy game in response to concerns about football's dangers. An infamous Harvard-Yale game in 1894 ended with nine of the twenty-two players sidelined by injuries or ejection. Concussed players staggered across the field; one suffered a coma. A reporter described the game as "more bloody than some battles." Calls to abolish football reached fever pitch after the Harvard-Yale melee.[17]

Muscular Christians were undeterred in their conviction that football forged men's characters, even if it occasionally destroyed their bodies. "Football is a noble sport," Stagg said in 1892, "and tends to develop all the qualities usually found in the successful man."[18] After the 1894 Harvard-Yale debacle, Walter Camp surveyed hundreds of former college football players and delivered the sport a positive bill of health. Crucially, Camp's survey focused on the "Big Three" schools—Harvard, Yale, and Princeton—whose graduates occupied seats of power across law, business, and politics. A whopping fifty percent of Yale football alumni in business had risen to the position of chief executive officer. Many attributed their business success to the character-building skills they learned on the gridiron. In reality, Yale men in the late nineteenth century came to college with family connections that smoothed their paths to the top of industry. But it served Camp's cause to name football as the source of these men's success. In 1894, he published the results of his survey as *Football Facts & Figures* in *Harper's* magazine. The piece gave football's defenders crucial ammunition to support the sport.[19]

Football survived the calls for its abolition thanks to its powerful defenders and changes to the rules. New York police commissioner and future President

---

[17] Des Jardins, *Walter Camp*, 112–14.

[18] "Stagg on Athletics: What the Famous Collegian Thinks of the Modern Craze in Sports," *Buffalo Courier*, January 3, 1892, Amos Alonzo Stagg Papers, Box 275, Folder 1, Special Collections Research Center, University of Chicago.

[19] Des Jardins, *Walter Camp*, 116–22.

Theodore Roosevelt wrote Camp in the midst of the mid-1890s controversy. Roosevelt lamented the "leisure and sedentary classes" that were producing "a type of man not much above the Bengali baboon." Fortunately, according to Teddy, "the athletic spirit has saved us. Of all games I personally like foot ball best....I have no patience with the people who declaim against it because it necessitates rough play and occasional injuries."[20] Roosevelt brokered a truce between Yale and Harvard that allowed the schools to begin playing one another after a two-year hiatus. Another spate of football deaths after the turn of the century led to watershed rules changes, most notably the legalization of the forward pass in 1906. At a 1910 dinner for University of Chicago football lettermen, Stagg invited his former players to weigh in on the sport's brutality. Several disparaged the "open play" created by the new rules as more dangerous than the "mass play" of the 1890s. All agreed that the real problem was conditioning. Though Stagg listed nine Chicago men "knocked insensible" over the years, their opponents fared worse. "We were very much stronger than the other teams," declared Stagg. "It was like a steam roller going over them. They were constantly filling up the ranks."[21]

Why did Christians like Stagg see such a brutal game as a beneficent molder of men? For starters, Stagg thought boys were naturally inclined to the rough and tumble nature of football. They wanted physical play, and football gave them a healthy outlet for that desire. Glossing over the deaths and debilitating injuries that could result from the game, Stagg contended, "the training undergone in athletics has <u>saved</u> hundreds of young men unto purity and right living and it has given to a great number such a physical foundation that it has been possible for them to successfully fight the manifold temptations which beset them."[22] Like Gulick, Stagg saw a connection between physical and spiritual strength. The flabby bodies produced by cities and sedentary jobs demanded that men build physical and moral fiber through athletics. In Stagg's view, no sport better served those ends than football.

While baseball remained the most popular sport across the nation, a growing number of players and fans saw football as the sport that best forged character

---

[20] Des Jardins, 124.

[21] "Comments of Football Men at 'C' Dinner," January 22, 1910, Amos Alonzo Stagg Papers, Box 23, Folder 3, Special Collections Research Center, University of Chicago.

[22] Amos Alonzo Stagg, "Lecture on Sports and Christianity," 1895, Amos Alonzo Stagg Papers, Box 109, Folder 3, Special Collections Research Center, University of Chicago.

in young men. "All hail to football," read an 1899 editorial in *Physical Culture*. "It takes retiring, undeveloped, mediocre boys and develops all the traits of character that accompany increased confidence and the superior physique of superb health." Critics who censured football's brutality were missing the point. The injuries and occasional deaths resulted from neglect to "properly prepare." Violence was endemic to the game—and that was a good thing. Boys wanted the rough play, and good training would prepare them to weather both the brutality of the gridiron and the subsequent temptations of modern life. "If you want your boys to be men," the essay concluded, "encourage them to play football."[23]

Masculinity for Elites

Concerns about men's physical decline led to this promotion of college football. They also underscored the elitism of the game. Plenty of American men weren't leading "sitting-down lives" in 1900. Deckhands, dockworkers, coal miners, and carpenters hardly needed to worry about flabbiness and effeminacy. But these men—many of them recent immigrants—were not the audience that Camp, Gulick, and Stagg had in mind. Muscular Christians spoke to an ascendant elite, comprised mainly of native-born white Protestants. The movement's focus on college campuses ensured its elitism: only about two percent of eighteen-to-twenty-four-year-old Americans were enrolled in postsecondary institutions at the turn of the twentieth century.[24]

Only a fraction of that fraction could enroll at Chicago. Rockefeller's largesse inspired grand ambitions on the neo-Gothic quads of Hyde Park, where scholars and administrators fashioned a research university modeled on German institutions. Graduate students vastly outnumbered undergraduates. Generous salaries attracted scholars from well-established universities to Chicago, which counted "several college presidents" among its faculty when the university opened in 1892.[25] Rockefeller charged Harper with creating an innovative institution that would outpace all other American research universities. Chicago was to be the purest of ivory towers.

---

[23] Bernarr Macfadden, "The Advantages of Football," *Physical Culture*, November 1899, William Blaikie Papers, Series 1A, Box 1, Folder 29, Springfield College Archives and Special Collections.

[24] "120 Years of American Education: A Statistical Portrait" (National Center for Education Statistics, 1993), accessed December 17, 2021, http://nces.ed.gov/pubs93/93442.pdf.

[25] "Our History & Culture," The University of Chicago website, accessed September 29, 2021, https://college.uchicago.edu/about/our-history-culture.

Yet intellectual elitism for its own sake struck a discordant note in a nation awash in populism, especially in the "city of the broad shoulders." Though research was the coin of the realm in faculty hiring and promotion, Chicago took pains to emphasize its meritocratic approach to student admission. The university was coeducational from the beginning, and it emphasized liberal education for a democratic citizenry. The American Baptist Education Society (ABES), formed by the Home Mission Society in 1888, oversaw the formation of the university, connecting it to one of the largest Protestant bodies in the nation. Though Chicago was nonsectarian, both its Baptist benefactor (Rockefeller) and its Baptist president (Harper) saw the scholarly study of religion and the cultivation of Christian leaders as essential elements of the university's curriculum. Harper acquired Morgan Park seminary and rechristened it the University of Chicago Divinity School, the first professional school at the university.

Harper's concern for the cultivation of Christian faith at Chicago has been overlooked. The university's rigorous curriculum and highly specialized research connotes rationality and secularity. But like Timothy Dwight at Yale, Harper put faith at the forefront of Chicago's mission. "There has been a peculiar and a fatal lack of proper religious instruction for the young during the past twenty years," Harper told one of the earliest classes of students at Chicago. He promised them that Chicago would be a place where "infidelity, so far from increasing, is rapidly decreasing."[26]

Stagg's Christianity—along with his sense that education ought to instill faith in students—resonated with Harper's vision for Chicago. When Harper hired Stagg, the president emphasized Stagg's role as the director of the Physical Culture department. Stagg's remit was to build a great football program, to be sure, but he was also charged with integrating physical education into the curriculum. Stagg and Harper shared the YMCA's view that a sound mind, body, and spirituality were interconnected legs of a triangle. As a result, Chicago required more physical education classes than any other American university. For at least the first decade of Chicago's existence, the Physical Culture requirement for undergraduates was the largest of any department at the university: four and a half hours per week for the entirety of students' first two years, and most of the final two years, as well.[27]

But this democratic model of physical education hardly lined up with Stagg's interests. He cared most about the football team and spent little time tending to the duties of the Physical Culture department. This was a different

---

[26] Lester, *Stagg's University*, 6.
[27] Lester, 17.

type of elitism than that displayed by the rest of the faculty, who viewed Chicago as the pinnacle of American higher education. Stagg was among the first coaches—but not the last—to view the superiority of the football team an essential part of reaching this pinnacle. Just as a world-class faculty required recruiting the best researchers, Stagg knew he needed to funnel the best high school athletes to Chicago. In 1900, Stagg had denounced recruiting as "contrary to the 'spirit of amateurism.'" Shortly thereafter he implemented a massive recruiting system. President Harper fully supported his coach. In a 1904 speech to Chicago graduates, Harper asked, "Why do not these alumni see that the university gets its fair share of the athletic material?" He didn't have to ask twice. Within days, Chicago alumni had organized the first college football recruiting organization in the country.[28]

Recruiting is such a massive industry today that it's hard to remember how radical such a concept sounded in the first decade of the twentieth century. Even for professors willing to grant a place for physical education, the notion that a university would admit students solely because of their playing potential was absurd. Nearly everyone affiliated with higher education understood scholarship as the central occupation of the university. Stagg never directly challenged that belief, but his insistence that elite football players belonged at Chicago, even if they didn't quite make the grade, was novel. Football, according to Stagg, would unite the campus and bring prestige to the university.

A 1905 Thanksgiving Day victory over the University of Michigan proved Stagg partially correct. Twenty-seven thousand spectators—including Stagg's mentor, Walter Camp—turned out on a bitterly cold afternoon to watch the Maroons hand Michigan its first loss in five years. 2500 students staged an impromptu parade to President Harper's house after the game, where they sang the alma mater and called for the president to give a speech. Harper was too ill to make an appearance (he would pass away six weeks later), but he understood the importance of the game for Chicago. He rallied corporate supporters and Chicago alumni for a Monday celebration of the win over Michigan, where they reaffirmed their commitment to the university.[29]

Even more, football had emerged as a kind of unifying ritual for the university. Though Harper had launched the divinity school and saw faith as integral to university, Chicago was nonsectarian from its outset. Mandatory chapel had disappeared among elite universities before Chicago's founding. Football, then, had a quasi-religious role to play in uniting the campus around a common

---

[28] Lester, 47–48.
[29] Lester, 67–71.

purpose. One football player made this religious function of football explicit when he penned a paean to the team's victory over Michigan, sung to the tune of the Baptist standard, "Beulah Land":

We have reached the day of turkey and wine
And we have been winners every time,
Here stand undimmed one happy day.
For all our foes have passed away.[30]

But if football were to play a religious role at Chicago, it was never quite as unifying as Stagg hoped. The critics deploring football's brutality got louder in 1905. A couple of years after the Michigan triumph—with Chicago entrenched as the football power of the Midwest—the president of the city's board of education, Otto C. Schneider, said, "If I had my way, I would abolish [football] entirely."[31] The faculty at the university attempted to do just that. On February 2, 1906, less than a month after Harper's death, the faculty senate unanimously passed a resolution calling for the "abolition of the game for a period of two years."[32] They expressed concern about both the violence of the game and the underground economy of recruitment. Schools were shopping for players with their alumni's money, and the whole business threatened the premise of amateurism. Stagg rallied supporters from within the university and outside it, ultimately promising to standardize the awarding of scholarships and to comply with rule changes aimed at lessening the violence of the game. These maneuvers— along with the pressure of student protests and alumni donors—saved football at Chicago for the time being.

Intercollegiate football at Chicago and elsewhere emerged from the crisis of 1905–1906 on a firmer footing than anyone at the time had reason to suspect. National reforms to the rules of the game and regarding the awarding of scholarships legitimated football as a normal part of university life. The forward pass reduced the number of brutal collisions, but the rules created for athletic scholarships might have been even more important for football's survival. Stagg's recruiting program had scandalized the faculty and even some of his fellow muscular Christians, who believed amateurism to be essential for football's purity. The widespread suspicion that schools were buying the best players had to be

---

[30] Lester, 71.
[31] "FOOTBALL BRUTAL GAME: President of Chicago's Board of Education Condemns the Sport," *New York Times*, November 7, 1907.
[32] "Vote to Suspend Football," *New York Times*, February 2, 1906.

allayed. With the 1906 reforms, athletic scholarships became part of the university's budget.

Stagg used the new rules expertly, and Chicago emerged as the nation's foremost football power from 1905 to 1924. Legendary Notre Dame coach Knute Rockne, who took the reins in South Bend in 1918, credited Stagg with perfecting the modern game, which was based more on speed than on strength. "All football comes from Stagg," Rockne said.[33] Stagg's teams pioneered formations that would become a hallmark of modern football, and they won at a remarkable clip. The undefeated Chicago teams of 1905 and 1913 won (unofficial) national championships, and Stagg racked up seven Big Ten titles, as well. Harper's intuition that football would become a rallying point for the university proved true. Stagg won more attention from the press than any other Chicago faculty member, and football games brought together students, (some) faculty, and donors. The game seemed well entrenched at Chicago. And Stagg had a platform as big as anyone at the university.

Manliness in an Age of Racial Purity

Stagg's success on the gridiron led to countless speaking invitations. Some came from smaller colleges attempting to launch football programs; others came from civic organizations looking for lessons from the famous coach. Stagg selectively accepted a small portion of these requests, seeing them as a chance to reach new audiences, to recruit players and supporters for Chicago, and to shape the national discourse around physical development and athletics. Some of his most interesting speeches concerned his fear about a nation going soft—concerns that one could trace back to his days with Gulick at Springfield.

A 1913 address called "Physical Development and Its Problems" illuminated Stagg's thinking about the connections between sports and character. He saw unencumbered play as the most salutary way of developing healthy bodies. Since the wealthiest children had the fewest responsibilities, there were "no finer physical specimens," even among children "who do general manual labor." Stagg extended this thought by considering the disparate characteristics of "different races and tribes." These included anatomical differences in "proportion of limbs, pelvic structure, and in conformation of the skull." Stagg was reflecting widely accepted racial science of the early twentieth century in this speech. Like other muscular Christians, he connected these physical differences to character traits.

---

[33] John R. Schmidt, "Amos Alonzo Stagg, Football Legend," WBEZ Chicago, December 14, 2012, accessed December 17, 2021, https://www.wbez.org/stories/amos-alonzo-stagg-football-legend/5b09a4be-737a-48ae-9523-bd3664583f6d.

Properly proportioned, well-trained bodies produced "beauty...self possession, and physical courage."[34] They were, in a word Stagg used often, pure.

The discourse of purity among progressive era muscular Christians showed the intertwined nature of race, sex, and gender. Psychologist G. Stanley Hall, president of Clark University and a frequent contributor to middlebrow magazines, depicted boys as racially primitive savages, most famously in an 1899 address to national kindergarten teachers. This depiction of young white boys as savages scandalized Hall's "civilized" audiences, even though he was at pains to emphasize that he did not view savagery as a desirable state. Rather, he thought that allowing boys to indulge their savagery through physical contests would channel their innate virility away from the dirtier aspect of their nature, sexual desire. Put simply, Hall thought violence was better for boys than sex. Self-control was at the heart of middle-class masculinity, but it was self-control of a particular sort. Men could turn themselves over fully to the wildness within when they were playing football. The aggression unleashed on the field would translate to restraint where it counted: in one's sexual life.[35]

Cultivating purity in one's sexual life distinguished middle-class white men from the "savages" that gave free rein to their natural impulses. Here muscular Christians drew on the language of eugenics, the then-fashionable science of improving human genetics. In his 1917 book *Jesus, the Christ, in the Light of Psychology*, Hall described Jesus as "the best unipersonal exemplar of the race idea, the true superman."[36] The "superman" represented the highest evolutionary state humanity could reach. Jesus had set the ideal. According to early twentieth-century eugenicists, the Anglo-Saxon race had come closest to attaining that ideal. To reach even closer, this most highly civilized race would need to maintain self-control and strength at the same time.

Physical activity during adolescence helped white men reach their highest potential. Hall's contention that boys were "little savages" was part of his theory of evolutionary progress. Since over-civilization could sap men's virility, they needed physical outlets during adolescence to stave off neurasthenia and masturbation in adulthood, both of which depleted men's energy and power. Playing

---

[34] Amos Alonzo Stagg, "Physical Development and Its Problems," 1913, Amos Alonzo Stagg Papers, Box 109, Folder 7, Special Collections Research Center, University of Chicago.

[35] Gail Bederman, *Manliness & Civilization: A Cultural History of Gender and Race in the United States, 1880–1917* (Chicago: University of Chicago Press, 1995), 77–120.

[36] Granville Stanley Hall, *Jesus, the Christ, in the Light of Psychology* (New York: Doubleday, Page, 1917), 260.

sports would help boys grow into strong, balanced young men. These young men would help the Anglo-Saxon race reach its destiny as the most powerful race in human history. Historian Gail Bederman has described this eugenic theory of racial progress as a "secularized version of Protestant millennialism."[37] White men fulfilled their destiny by unleashing aggression in their youth in order to develop the strength and restraint that would enable their race to reach its fullest potential. Hall wrote that eugenics was "simply a legitimate new interpretation of our Christianity."[38]

The prevailing racial teachings of the era insisted that only white men could reach the highest plane of civilization. Hall described African Americans and Native Americans as the "adolescent races" of the nation.[39] He taught that their educational window was shorter than that of white men, and their full development limited. Likely through the influence of such teachings, Stagg's 1913 address on physical development imagined Adam and Eve as "fully developed by God's own hand." Because of that divine design, "they must have had perfect proportions and were beautiful to behold." He wondered about the resemblance they might show to "the most perfect types of men and women found in these days."[40] Given the racial climate of the era—and the lily-white depictions of biblical figures that prevailed in popular art—Stagg's audience almost certainly imagined Adam and Eve as Anglo-Saxon. The pervasiveness of racial science in the 1910s allowed for an easy assumption of white racial superiority that had deep Christian roots. Stagg's colleague at Chicago, divinity school dean Shailer Mathews, wrote, "It is hard not to see how sympathetic Augustine might have been with our modern knowledge of evolution and eugenics."[41]

Mathews and Stagg were not particularly close—Mathews had been one of the leading voices calling for football's abolition in 1906—but the influence of racial science on Stagg's ideas about making men was undeniable. As early as 1887 at Yale, Stagg was reading the blockbuster book by Josiah Strong, *Our Country*, which tasked the "Anglo-Saxon race" with colonizing the continent. In a series of lectures at Yale that year, Strong warned the students about the perils of immigration, Catholicism, intemperance, and socialism. The famous Congregationalist minister called students to head west and ensure the perseverance of

---

[37] Bederman, *Manliness & Civilization*, 96.

[38] Christine Rosen, *Preaching Eugenics: Religious Leaders and the American Eugenics Movement* (New York: Oxford University Press, 2004), 38.

[39] Bederman, *Manliness & Civilization*, 114.

[40] Stagg, "Physical Development and Its Problems."

[41] Rosen, *Preaching Eugenics*, 134.

"American" (that is to say, white Protestant) values. Stagg himself likely understood his move to Chicago as a response to Strong's charge.[42]

Throughout his career, Stagg echoed the themes of racial science and eugenics. He never expressed hardline support for racial segregation, and one of his most famous athletes—track star and Olympic gold medalist Henry Dismond—was black. But Dismond was the exception. Stagg's Chicago teams usually played one intersectional game each year during the 1920s. In games against southern universities—Georgia in 1922, Kentucky in 1925, Florida in 1926—Chicago abided by the "gentlemen's agreement" that forbid northern teams from playing their black athletes against racially segregated southern squads. Newspapers almost never commented on this *de facto* segregation of the sport, though the careful work of historian Charles H. Martin has demonstrated that the growing popularity of college football in the 1920s depended on these intersectional contests. Southern universities would only play these games if the northern schools accepted the racial strictures of Jim Crow.[43]

Stagg dedicated his career to molding men, and the men in his charge were overwhelmingly white and elite. He talked frequently of how football developed self-control and discipline. It tempered the passions and "washed" the brain with "rich, pure blood." Even the earliest Christians, in Stagg's estimation, would have commended football. "No priest or church father," he suggested, "could have prescribed a course of dieting and regularity of living which could do more for the body" than football did.[44] Four years under Stagg's tutelage undoubtedly trained men's bodies and minds, but it also marked them as part of an select cadre. "C Men" graduated into a network of professional connections that made them some of Chicago's leading lights.

The assumptions underlying Stagg's project of making men reflected the racial and class biases of the era. Stagg's understanding of masculinity blended racial science with the physical and mental discipline required to excel on the gridiron, leading him to hold up his overwhelmingly white alumni as the pinnacle of modern manhood. The racial lines that governed football at Chicago created a vicious circle: because people of color were mostly excluded from the

---

[42] Erin A. McCarthy, "Making Men: The Life and Career of Amos Alonzo Stagg, 1862–1933," (PhD diss., Loyola University Chicago, 1994), 54–55, https://ecommons.luc.edu/luc_diss/3463.

[43] Charles H. Martin, *Benching Jim Crow: The Rise and Fall of the Color Line in Southern College Sports, 1890–1980* (Urbana: University of Illinois Press, 2010), 1–26.

[44] Amos Alonzo Stagg, "American Football," 1920, Amos Alonzo Stagg Papers, Box 109, Folder 9, Special Collections Research Center, University of Chicago.

Maroons, so too were they excluded from the ideal of masculinity that Stagg preached. Stagg almost never addressed race explicitly—but race was never absent.

Postscript: The Grand Old Man of Football

Stagg's career at Chicago came to an abrupt end in 1932, when the new university president Robert Maynard Hutchins forced the "Grand Old Man" to step down at the mandatory retirement age of seventy. Stagg protested the move and vowed to keep coaching, which he did for another twenty-six years! Stagg served as the head coach at the University of the Pacific for thirteen years, then served in assistant coaching roles at Susquehanna and Stockton College. Seven years after his second, voluntary retirement, Stagg died in 1965, at the age of 103.

During the last ten years of his life, Stagg received a series of badgering missives from Don McLanen, a headstrong young football coach in Oklahoma who saw Stagg as a model for his fledgling organization, the Fellowship of Christian Athletes. McLanen was convinced that Stagg's presence at one of the early FCA conferences would lend the new organization instant credibility. Health concerns led Stagg to decline McClanen's repeated entreaties, though he encouraged the young coach to continue the mission of developing Christian men through sports.

Football was the preeminent sport in the early years of FCA. Chapters at Baylor (a Baptist school) and Duke (a Methodist one) were among the strongest early FCA chapters, and nearly all of the membership at those schools were football players.[45] FCA was racially integrated, reflecting the growing concern over civil rights, though its leadership was overwhelmingly white. Stagg's legacy of connecting football and faith was, by the early 1960s, secure. His arguments about the positive, character-building aspects of football had won the day among a majority of American Christians. His relative lack of concern about the brutality, racism, and corruption of big-time college football had, too.

---

[45] Paul Emory Putz, *The Spirit of the Game: American Protestants, Big-Time Sports, and the Contest for National Identity* (New York: Oxford University Press, forthcoming).

NEITHER SHALL THEY LEARN WAR ANY MORE: WILLIAM BISHOP JOHNSON AND THE PERILS OF BLACK BAPTIST MANHOOD

Malcolm Foley

On April 23, 1899, eleven days after the death of Alfred Cranford and the alleged rape of his wife, a mob found Sam Hose, born Sam Wilkes. Ida B. Wells described what followed as a deed "of unspeakable barbarism…for it is conceded universally that no other nation on earth, civilized or savage, has put to death any human being with such atrocious cruelty as that inflicted upon Samuel Hose by the Christian white people of Georgia."[1] Hose, accused of murder when it had likely been self-defense, evaded capture for a week and a half before he was found and a mob of two thousand people attached him to a tree, stripped him naked, cut his ears off, and burned him alive. When he fell from the stake to which he was fastened, the mob stoked the flames and kicked him back in. After his eventual death, the mob rushed the site and, according to Wells-Barnett's report, "almost fought over the ashes of the dead criminal."[2] They grabbed bones and body parts, even the stake itself. The narrative of this particular lynching would be repeated time and time again in contemporary newspapers, in later anti-lynching activism and in scholarship. The brutality of this particular lynching was even what incited sociologist and activist W. E. B. Du Bois to devote his time to activism rather than armchair scholarship.[3] While the spectacle lynching of Hose was the main attraction, he was not the only victim of this white mob. Elijah Strickland also met a torturous end the following day at the hands of the mob. An elderly preacher, Elijah had apparently been implicated by Hose as having paid Hose to murder Cranford, but these claims were never substantiated.

---

[1] Ida B. Wells-Barnett, *Lynch Law in Georgia* (Chicago: Chicago Colored Citizens, 1899), 7.

[2] Wells-Barnett, *Lynch Law in Georgia*, 10.

[3] Philip Dray, *At the Hands of Persons Unknown: The Lynching of Black America* (New York: Modern Library, 2003), 15. Philip Dray, among others, draws attention to Du Bois' skipping a meeting with Joel Chandler Harris because he saw Hose's knuckles for sale in a grocer's window. This incident told Du Bois that he could no longer sit idly by while "Negroes were lynched, murdered and starved."

Unfortunately, substantiated claims were not necessary to snuff out a Black man's life; allegations would do.

The *Atlanta Constitution* would report on April 24 that the body of Lige Strickland was found on a persimmon tree with his ears and the little finger of his left hand severed. On his chest was a piece of paper that summarized the gendered, sexual, and racialized nature of spectacle lynching. On one side, it read, "N.Y. Journal. We must protect our Ladies. 23–99," and on the other side, it read, "Beware all darkies. You will be treated the same way."[4] On one piece of paper, the pathology of racialized lynching was disturbingly displayed on the body of an innocent Black man, making the display even more terroristic. The phrase, "we must protect our Ladies" at once communicated the racial solidarity of the white mob, the necessity of violent reinforcement of gender norms, and a perception of masculine possession of and ultimately idolization of white female bodies. This manifested itself in the violent subjugation and ultimately extermination of Black male life. The narrative that lynching occurred because Black men raped white women was the most common justification of spectacle lynching and that very explanation intricately wove race, gender, and sexuality into a toxic quilt. It is remarkably easy, however, to leave the analysis at that level. Much of the conversation about gender and lynching focuses on the perpetuation of white male hegemony through its violent protection of white women. As an example, Gail Bederman's excellent monograph, *Manliness and Civilization*, discusses the terminology of civilization "as a discourse that worked, albeit unevenly, to establish (or to challenge) white male hegemony."[5] In this chapter, however, I seek to investigate the work of a prominent Black Baptist pastor, William Bishop Johnson, to determine how he understood masculinity in the lynching era. White male hegemony then is ancillary to this consideration; instead, Black masculinity is sought on its own terms. I pose the following question to this pastor: what did it mean to be a Black man in a society that sought to define Black manhood not only from outside of Black communities but particularly with an eye toward the destruction of Black male life?

---

[4] Wells-Barnett, *Lynch Law In Georgia*, 11.
[5] Gail Bederman, *Manliness and Civilization: A Cultural History of Gender and Race in the United States, 1880–1917* (Chicago: University of Chicago Press, 1995), 23.

Race, Gender and their Interaction

At the outset, it is important to understand the particular relationship concerning race, gender, and social construction. First, concerning race, I adopt the framework developed by social scientist Joe Feagin in his definition of what he calls the "white racial frame." By this, he means that particularly in the US, race is a "perspectival frame that gets imbedded in individual minds (brains), as well as in collective memories and histories, and helps people make sense out of everyday situations." He argues for a particular "white racial frame" with various elements: beliefs; cognitive, visual, and auditory elements; a "feelings" aspect; an inclination to action; strong positive orientation toward white people and whiteness; and a strong negative orientation toward racial "others."[6] Such a frame in US society is hegemonic, according to Feagin. Yet this chapter, though it will interact with the assumptions of that frame, is explicitly not an articulation of it. Instead, I attempt to operate out of one of what Feagin calls the counter-frames, particularly those frames created by Black people to resist systemic racial oppression. Feagin names two: the anti-oppression counter frames and the home-culture frames. These frames were initially developed for survival in the midst of catastrophic, existential violence, but over the course of American history, they developed into constitutive racial narratives. I ask of William Bishop Johnson: what ought it mean to be Black in the United States?

More particularly, however, the question is: what ought it mean to be a Black *man* in the United States? Asking the question this way requires an understanding of the way that gender functions/ed in Black communities. The European framing of the great chain of being placed men above women in the human hierarchy, and in European colonial efforts, that view was not found in colonized peoples; rather, it was imposed. As Feagin also notes, "European male conquerors were 'superior,' 'powerful,' and 'manly,' while the subordinated peoples, *male and female*, were 'inferior,' 'weak,' and 'childlike.'"[7] It is especially notable that those characteristics applied regardless of gender. In the history of the construction of race, people's bodies were gendered in some cases *after* races were gendered. Anne McClintock argues as much, saying:

> The rhetoric of *race* was used to invent distinctions between what we would now call classes. At the same time, the rhetoric of *gender* was used to make increasingly refined distinctions among the different

---

[6] Joe R. Feagin, *The White Racial Frame: Centuries of Racial Framing and Counter-Framing* (New York: Routledge, 2013), 9–10.

[7] Feagin, *The White Racial Frame*, 41. Emphasis added.

races. The white race was figured as the male of the species and the [B]lack race as the female. Similarly, the rhetoric of *class* was used to inscribe minute and subtle distinctions between other races. The Zulu male was regarded as the 'gentleman' of the [B]lack race, but was seen to display features typical of females of the white race.[8]

McClintock's quote reminds the reader that for Black men and women, a perception of race and gender was imposed along with assumptions of inferiority. In light of that framework, both Black men and Black women had considerable reason to resist much of what was said about them in regard to both race and gender. Fighting for self-determination required self-definition first, and that would not take place without ideological struggle and careful definition. The crisis of racialized lynching sharpened this need.

Racialized lynching and its social normalization proclaimed that especially Black male life was expendable. Tommy Curry expressed a fear of that particular impulse in scholarship on race and gender as he investigated the erasure of Black masculinity from the scholarly landscape, arguing that the "erasure that accepts the normalcy of Black male death simultaneously accepts the racist disposability of Black male life....Dehumanization finds its extremity in making the lives of the oppressed inconsequential; it is not being able to think of the Black male beyond his corpse that is the real result of racism's dehumanization."[9] In investigating the sermons of William Bishop Johnson, I intend to center the Black man as a normative subject of thinking, entirely capable of constructing understandings of humanity and manhood for himself even if influenced by colonial constructs. In fact, Black ministers in particular were uniquely tasked with such an endeavor as spiritual leaders of their communities. In a society in which lynching was an existential threat, maleness paired with Blackness created a unique position of vulnerability. By centering Johnson's thought and writing, one can begin to answer the question of how Black men combatted an almost ever-present risk to their lives.

William Bishop Johnson: The Scourging of a Race

On April 12, 1904, the *New York Times* ran a special, short article on its sixth page. The title was sharp and accusatory: "Negro Minister Heavily Scores The

---

[8] Anne McClintock, *Imperial Leather: Race, Gender and Sexuality in the Colonial Contest* (New York: Routledge, 1995), 54–55.

[9] Tommy J. Curry, *The Man-Not: Race, Class, Genre, and the Dilemmas of Black Manhood* (Philadelphia: Temple University Press, 2017), 145.

Negro Race: Says Scourging of Colored Men is Necessary and Deserved." The writer continued to apparently describe a sermon from Baptist preacher, William Bishop Johnson, which they noted was "unusual." Quoting from the sermon, the *Times* drew attention to Johnson's references to the "notable loss of manhood among us," the lack of chivalry toward women, and general laziness. The article ended with a seemingly damning quote from Johnson: "The disfranchisement of the negro, by which he is reduced to a political nonentity, is one scourge with which God is whipping the negro to acquire property and education." The sum of this, according to the *Times*, was that disfranchisement and, by extension, oppression, were deserved and necessary divine judgments, a claim that, as mentioned before, the writer assumed that the congregation would understand to be "unusual talk."[10] But that statement raised a question: was this truly unusual talk? Contrary to the *New York Times*, Johnson's sermon was more than excoriation and, as is inferred from the article, justification of injustice. In this case, the *New York Times* reporter misrepresented the DC minister's sermon, highlighting the affirmation of the moral failures of Black people without the necessary context of Black dignity. To affirm the former without the latter is to mischaracterize Johnson as well as to ignore the fact that even the category of moral suasion was not an unequivocal affirmation of Black inferiority. In Johnson's case, it was an act of pastoral care for his congregation: an affirmation of Black dignity that framed moral reform as an act of anti-lynching resistance. In addition, this particular sermon along with the sermons that Johnson would gather together into a volume would give an account of Black manhood rooted not in a pursuit of hegemony, but in a liberative picture of humanity.

William Bishop Johnson was born in Toronto, Ontario, Canada, on December 11, 1858. A man of many pursuits, he was valedictorian of his class at Wayland Seminary in Richmond, Virginia, and he won a prize as best orator. He was ordained in 1879 to pastor the First Baptist Church, Frederick, Maryland, and in 1881, he was appointed by the American Baptist Home Mission Society as a general missionary to Maryland, Virginia, West Virginia, and Washington, DC. In 1882, he became a Professor of Mathematics and Political Science at Wayland, a position he maintained for twelve years before moving back to full-time pastoral ministry. Johnson's greatest accomplishments, however, were

---

[10] Special to The New York Times. "NEGRO MINISTER HEAVILY SCORES THE NEGRO RACE: SAYS SCOURGING OF COLORED MEN IS NECESSARY AND DESERVED. LACK OF RACE COHESION. WASHINGTON PREACHER ASSERTS NEGROES ARE NOT CAREFUL ENOUGH ABOUT MORAL ATMOSPHERE OF THEIR HOMES," *New York Times*, April 12, 1904.

educational: he organized the National Baptist Educational Convention and through that organization, federated all of the schools owned, controlled, and managed by Black Baptists. In addition to those institutional roles, he also edited multiple influential Black Baptist magazines and journals including the *National Baptist Magazine, Baptist Companion*, and the *Wayland Alumni Journal.* As Evelyn Brooks Higginbotham noted, the *National Baptist Magazine* was one of the ways in which Black Baptists formed a counterpublic: associating a press with the convention gave Black Baptists a platform to produce literature that would enhance racial pride while a beleaguered minority. In the three years preceding the release of Johnson's book of sermons, the magazine reported a circulation of more than thirteen million issues of various materials.[11] If one is looking for an influential Black Baptist minister, Johnson fits that mold. As a pastor, educator, and race man, he also provides an excellent example of thoughtful work on race and masculinity during the lynching era. The first helpful case study is his apparently controversial sermon, *The Scourging of a Race.*

Obviously, the sermon itself is a more faithful interpretation of Johnson's thought than its editorial framing in the *New York Times.* Johnson began his sermon by drawing attention to the apparent incongruity between Black achievement and the current state of Black communities under a regime of white supremacy. Preaching from Proverbs 16:7 and Exodus 19:3–8, he recounted the events of the forty years that had passed since emancipation, in which "the American Negro has contributed his part to the world's civilization, and to the peace and progress of the American people."[12] Here, as was the case for many Black writers of this period, Johnson undermined hegemonic discourses of civilization by positing Black people as contributors rather than threats to it. Yet this was not the full extent of Johnson's analysis. There was no indication from his writing that he was comparing Black achievement to white achievement or any such metric. Rather, Johnson presented Black progress on a continuum all its own, an important detail to consider when interpreting the sermon. The outsider (likely white) reading this sermon could be tempted to see excoriation where Johnson meant internal exhortation. Any observer would be deeply surprised about the amount of progress that Black people had made, given the conditions foisted upon them. Johnson continued, vigorously affirming that "the Negro has made

---

[11] Evelyn Brooks Higginbotham, *Righteous Discontent: The Women's Movement in the Black Baptist Church, 1880–1920*, rev. ed. (Cambridge, MA: Harvard University Press, 1994), 11–12.

[12] William Bishop Johnson, *The Scourging of a Race: And Other Sermons and Addresses* (Washington, D.C.: Beresford, 1904), 1.

unparalleled strides toward the meridian of the highest and best achieve-ments.…The mighty achievements of the Negro stand like the granite walls of a Gibraltar" even while "crying in the wilderness of American prejudice and Cau-casian hatred."[13] Notably, Johnson also summarized what Black people in Amer-ica wanted, and the answer was not hegemony. Rather, the Black man cried "for the right to live and move and have his being, not as a slave nor pauper, not as a criminal nor moral leper; but as a man, a citizen, a brother."[14] The gendered inflection of this description is intentional: while one could make the argument that "man" and "he" can sometimes be used to signify the universal human in texts of this type, in this case, Johnson has men in mind. It is particularly the Black man glossed as "criminal and a moral leper."[15] Thus, recognition as a man and as a brother has a twofold meaning: Johnson desired to be treated as a human being and as a "masculine" man, the particulars of which require further reading to explicate. After these affirmations, Johnson then asked the question that would shape the sermon: if we have achieved so much and made so much pro-gress, why are we still suffering so bitterly? His conclusion was that God's inten-tion was to teach Black people a lesson "of love and endurance."

The sermon itself was a rhetorical dance if one sought to discern the audi-ence. One can parse two distinct addressees: Black men in particular and Black people in general. The commands and exhortations to the former, however, flowed out of the general outline of the condition of the latter. Drawing an anal-ogy between Israel and Black people, particularly through emancipation from slavery, Johnson argued that God was allowing enemies to scourge Black com-munities just as God allowed foreign nations to punish Israel. This distinction was entirely lost on outside interpreters like the *Times*: God was the ultimate providential driver of human action, but the proximate cause was white people, the "enemies" in view. White people served as the enemies of God's people in Johnson's formulation, used by God as instruments for Black uplift. The discus-sion of primary and secondary causes was a theological conversation that Johnson was more than willing to discuss with his congregants, chastising them that "we

---

[13] Johnson, *The Scouring of a Race*, 2–3.

[14] Johnson, 2.

[15] Perhaps the best work on the history of the narratives surrounding Black criminality is Khalil Gibran Muhammad's *The Condemnation of Blackness*. While the narrative was explicitly racial in tagging Black people as a race of criminals, the ones who suffered most of the carceral violence were the males. In an important way, such narratives were not only examples of racism but also examples of racist misandry. See Khalil Gibran Muhammad, *The Condemnation of Blackness: Race, Crime, and the Making of Modern Urban America* (Cambridge, MA: Harvard University Press, 2010).

make the mistake of attributing *all our prosperity* to secondary causes."[16] To Johnson, if Black people attributed their success to human skill rather than divine grace, they were preparing for disaster. In a cascade of literary and historical references, Johnson rattled off a pantheon of pride including Caesar, Diocletian, Godfrey of Bouillon, Charles V, Galileo, Napoleon, the Count of Mirabeau, and others. To Johnson, lynching, segregating legislation, and disenfranchisement were ways in which God scourged Black people broadly in order to create racial solidarity.

In Johnson's delineation of the particular scourges that Black people as a whole suffered under, his gendered exhortations became more specific. Johnson's manuscript emphasizes in all capital letters that "there is a notable loss of manhood among us."[17] Here, manhood is not humanity; it is masculinity. Johnson lamented the lack of chivalry toward women and the lack of willingness to defend women from insult. This manifested itself in "[ignoring] hard labor, and [scorning] the man whose hand is hard and horny, and whose sinewy arm is the bread winner for the home."[18] While this may appear to be a framing of masculinity as exemplified primarily in those engaged in work with their hands, that was not the primary point of Johnson's statement. He would go on to clarify: "I mean by manly men, those who are swayed by noble principles, honesty, industry, purity of morals, thrift, courteous, friends of truth and righteousness." One will note that these characteristics of masculinity are entirely moral rather than alluding to class or other social categories of division. With this as his model, Johnson's lament was that the classes within the race were divided, particularly the intelligentsia and the illiterate.

For Johnson, this was the primary racial scourge: that Black people were divided, and publicly so. He noted that Black communities were disposed "to underrate [the character and ability of prominent Black leaders] to white people, when they have no concern in the matter," diluting a coherent witness to the world. It is almost humorous to consider that this very concern of Johnson is immediately manifested in the *New York Times* as a misunderstanding of his message as a whole. Johnson referred to the phenomenon of white onlookers taking advantage of whatever opportunity they could to affirm Black inferiority and their own superiority, and a supreme opportunity was the degradation of Black leadership. Johnson lamented that "Negroes are the only people who murder their leaders, with slander and misrepresentation, and then permit them to

---

[16] Johnson, *The Scourging of a Race*, 12. Emphasis original.
[17] Johnson, 10.
[18] Johnson, 10.

lead as though they were paragons of perfection."[19] To those who did so, Johnson sought to reorient their eyes toward the home and toward the Lord, as that turn would lead to racial uplift rather than internal bickering.

The *Times'* attempt to frame this sermon as an uncharacteristic scolding of Black people and, notably, Black masculinity was first and foremost sensationalizing, signaling to a white audience that even Black people said that what they were undergoing was deserved and justified. Close attention to the sermon, however, reveals a much more complex story and one that does not neatly fit into a narrative of deserved and undeserved suffering. The *New York Times* writer glossed over the importance of their final quote, in addition to the fact that the final quote of the editorial occurred well before the conclusion of the sermon. Johnson had indeed preached that "the disfranchisement of the Negro, by which he is reduced to a political nonentity, is another scourge with which God is whipping the Negro to acquire property and education."[20] The suggestion, left open by the editorial writer but clearly present in the framing of the editorial, was that Johnson was not preaching that disfranchisement is a profound injustice meant to be resisted as evil. Rather, disfranchisement was a tool of God not to be resisted but to be submitted to. This could not be farther from Johnson's actual point. As he continued, he explained that the purpose of this scourge was not primarily to punish and to judge, but rather to goad and to strengthen. This "disfranchisement" was to be the means by which Black communities grew stronger, in that they were forced to band together to amass what political and social power they could. Disfranchisement was, by definition, theft, but it was theft that the Lord would use in order to build the characters of Black communities and galvanize public opinion on their behalf. Far from acquiescing to political injustice, Johnson argued that this particular injustice and its publicizing would actually be its downfall, as Black people would eventually acquire so much property and education that they would be impossible to ignore.

Yet even more painful of a scourge than legal oppression was that of lynching, which Johnson noticed as a profoundly American evil. It especially posed a threat to Black manhood by being a check on self-expression: "The fact that *the Negro is not secure in his life and property*, but is ruthlessly lynched under any pretext or exiled from home because he has an opinion and expressed it, is another scourge."[21] Having witnessed the rise of racialized lynching in the 1890s, Johnson gave a clearheaded indictment of the nation: "Our fame as a nation of

---

[19] Johnson, 11.
[20] Johnson, 14.
[21] Johnson, 14.

lynchers, who does not believe in the courts we, ourselves, have established, but resorts to lawlessness and murder, is international—universal."[22] He spared no ammunition against naïve American exceptionalism, classifying the United States with "the Russian Massacre, Chinese Boxers and African Cannibals. Lynching is now an American pastime."[23] Even more depressing was the fact, as Johnson would go on to affirm, that the unpredictability of said pastime meant that "representative [Negroes]" were most at risk as victims of the rope and stake. Those in mind for Johnson were not women but men. While disenfranchisement and Jim Crow legislation were bad, burning Black men alive was the worst. Johnson placed this state of affairs before his congregation as a reasoning for their discontent.

Yet, to Johnson, even these scourges served a providential purpose: God allowed the lawlessness and injustice perpetrated by white men and women in order to make people "perfect through suffering," deftly appropriating the language of Hebrews 2:10 to apply not to Christ, but to His Black brothers and sisters.[24] Ultimately, Johnson's solution was spiritual and moral: repent and turn to the Lord and the enemies of God's people would turn away. Even more than that, white people would realize that they had much to learn from Black people. In a fascinating conclusion, Johnson reversed assumptions about criminality and progress in Black and white communities. While lynching and its attendant violence was predicated on the belief that Black men were violent criminals and threats to white femininity and while Black people clearly had ways in which they could grow, education supported and entrenched Black humanity and masculinity. One will remember that Johnson's definition of masculinity was fundamentally a moral one. Education's effect on Black communities was that it kept them out of prison and even though they faced social injustices, "yet we find them in possession of sterling character, church, school, and private property; their homes are models of refinement and their children clothed in neat and becoming apparel."[25] But Johnson also had a critique to lob: "Can the Anglo-Saxon say as much?" Johnson, in surveying the prison population, found a preponderance of educated whites in the system for crimes of theft and murder at a larger scale than anything present in Black communities, leading to the

---

[22] Johnson, 15.

[23] Johnson, 15.

[24] Hebrews 2:10: "For it became him, for whom are all things, and by whom are all things, in bringing many sons to glory, to make the captain of their salvation perfect through sufferings." (KJV)

[25] Johnson, 16.

accusation that while education builds up the Black person, it ruins the white man. This brilliant reversal of expectations undermines two ways in which William Bishop Johnson's message could have been pigeonholed. First, his framing of Black masculinity and humanity could be glossed as mimetic: seeking to imitate the norm set by white communities. Second, in a way that intertwines with the first but is separable from it, his framing of Black masculinity and humanity could be glossed as an instantiation of the politics of respectability so eloquently coined by Evelyn Brooks Higginbotham.[26] To the former, Johnson's message cannot be glossed as an acquiescence to hegemonic masculinity. He did not advocate for manhood in order to maintain a particular position of power or dominance; rather, his moral exhortations were aimed at racial uplift as a general project for men and women. Similarly, the politics of respectability, by the very definition of the term, are concerned with the understanding of outsiders. Said another way, what white people think is an important data point that shapes action. When Higginbotham argued that "while adherence to respectability enabled black women to counter racist images and structures, their discursive contestation was not directed solely at white Americans," she acknowledged that the discourse was still directed at white Americans. In this particular sermon, Johnson does not devote much attention to what white people may think. He spent much more time discerning how white people treat their Black neighbors and what God might require of Black people. In addition, choosing to title a collection of sermons *The Scourging of a Race* and beginning the collection with the sermon of the same name communicates that this sermon was meant to be seen as representative, both socially and theologically. Thus, as an act of just reading, one can see the claims in this sermon as normative for the volume itself and a picture of Johnson's mature thought. But this sermon gives only a piece of Johnson's gendered, racial, and theological framing. The particular gendered content of Johnson's message gained more data in a sermon that Johnson preached in 1887 to a fraternal order of women called the Household of Ruth. He preached on their namesake, titling his sermon: "Ruth—A Noble Type of True Womanhood."

Johnson and Womanhood

Oyèrónké Oyěwùmí summarized well the picture of gender as often theorized: "Differences and hierarchy...are enshrined on bodies; and bodies enshrine differences and hierarchy. Hence, dualisms like nature/culture, public/private, and

---

[26] Higginbotham, *Righteous Discontent*, 185–229.

visible/invisible are variations on the theme of male/female bodies hierarchically ordered, differentially placed in relation to power, and spatially distanced one from the other."[27] With this explicitly Western framing of gender, discussions of male and female necessarily become conversations about power where one is dominant and the other subservient. In most of those conversations, men occupy the dominant position and women the subservient, but when this Western framework is refracted through the prism of race or non-Western culture more broadly, the picture becomes more complicated. Assuming a Western account of gender, one would expect Johnson's sermon to find a definition of womanhood that places women below men in some way. Yet the text suggests something different.

Following a repetition of Ruth's story and relationship with Boaz, Johnson went on to name the characteristics of womanhood, some in isolation, others in relationship with manhood. When referring to the Odd Fellows fraternal lodge of which the Household of Ruth was a branch, Johnson emphasized the partnership of men and women, saying "the blending of woman's sweetness with man's service has crystalized the order into an Elysium" and "the conception which harmonizes the grace of woman with the strength of man in the performance of good works embodies a grand and irresistible power."[28] Emphasized here is the mutuality of man and woman with a healthy dose of gender essentialism, which pervades the sermon. This essentialism, however, serves a particular purpose: to give flesh to the mutuality of the male-female relationship and, explicitly in this sermon, to elevate women's status. Johnson argues as much when he quotes Gail Hamilton's words: "The perfect woman is as beautiful as she is strong; as tender as she is sensible. She is calm, deliberate, dignified, leisurely. She is gay, graceful, sprightly, sympathetic. She is severe upon occasions and upon occasions playful. She has fancies, dreams, romances, ideas."[29] What follows are a cascade of quotes clearly taken from various sources concerning womanhood. At one point, the Baptist pastor either draws from Catholic sources or exhibits Catholic sympathies by affirming Marian devotion. Beginning by affirming that the Son of God

---

[27] Oyèrónké Oyěwùmí, *The Invention of Women: Making an African Sense of Western Gender Discourses* (Minneapolis: University of Minnesota Press, 1997), 7.

[28] Johnson, *The Scourging of a Race*, 75.

[29] Johnson, 75. Fascinatingly, this is one of four consecutive quotes that Johnson lifts verbatim from an encyclopedia's entry on Woman. For that encyclopedia see James Henry Potts, *Our thrones and crowns and how to reach them, or, The golden way to the highest attainments in the life of time: and the true preparation for the glories of eternity* (Philadelphia: P. W. Zeigler, 1885), 230–31.

elevated woman by taking Mary's human nature, a perfectly ecumenical theological move, he took a second step: "Bearing the image and likeness of our Creator, matrixed and tutored by a mother's love, our reverence and veneration for her become an enduring part of our nature. In despair we appeal to heaven for relief, *and in distress we welcome the celestial intervention of woman.*"[30] Beyond this invocation of Mary possibly as mediatrix, Johnson's sermon is a paean to womanhood and its strengths, none of which foreground subordination to men. In fact, contrarily, when he noted "the obligation of Ruth," by which he meant the spiritual obligation placed upon women, he extended to women a call to "go forth into the highways and hedges and compel men to bow allegiance to Calvary's cross."[31] In a sermon devoted to womanhood, the recurring theme was not subjugation, but mutuality and exaltation rooted in a liberative view of humanity.

William Bishop Johnson's Egalitarian Masculinity

Johnson would refer to manhood and womanhood throughout the collection of sermons in various isolated ways. Between rousing sermons outlining the intricacies of the Christian Gospel, he gathered sermons on citizenship, suffrage, the role of the church in American society and the principles of racial uplift. Yet the egalitarian bent of his masculinity is notable. In his sermon on citizenship and suffrage, he lamented the absurdity of restricting Black men and women from the vote, interestingly basing such a claim on Aristotle's definition of citizen: "one to whom belongs the right of part in both the deliberative and judicial proceedings of the community of which he is a member."[32] To Aristotle, the masculine pronoun was intentional.[33] Women, as deformed men, were technically citizens, but they needed to be ruled by men in public and in the home. Johnson, if he knew this context, ignored it, operating from his own assumption of the equality of men and women. It would be "absurd" to deny women citizenship,

---

[30] Johnson, 76. Paying special attention to Mary was not anomalous in Johnson's preaching. In a 1900 sermon titled "The Divine-Humanity," he made the same point about God honoring womanhood through Christ's birth.

[31] Johnson, 78.

[32] Johnson, 60–61.

[33] Dorothea Frede, "Equal But Not Equal: Plato and Aristotle on Women as Citizens," in *Democracy, Justice, and Equality in Ancient Greece*, ed. Georgios Anagnostopoulos and Gerasimos Santas, Philosophical Studies Series, vol. 132, 287–306 (Cham, Switzerland: Springer, 2018).

and if the masculine pronoun in Aristotle's definition were, in fact, meant generically,

> We then have the naked assumption that every citizen, regardless of age, sex, condition, degree of intelligence, or personal responsibility, has the "right of participation" in both the legislative and judicial proceedings of the community—a proposition that would have horrified even the extremest radical democrat in the convention.[34]

This, for Johnson, was a commonsense argument for Black male and female suffrage, a fascinating appropriation of Aristotle as well as a complete overturning of the Greek philosopher's conceptions of gender difference. He repeated his gendered egalitarianism in an 1888 sermon titled *The Religious Status of the Negro*, claiming that at that point in American history, there were now "possibilities of development into a perfect and symmetrical manhood and womanhood."[35] Here, as throughout Johnson's sermons, racial solidarity took precedence over gendered distinctions. Where both categories were frequently used to divide, Johnson intentionally used both to unite Black men and women. Through the positive influences of the church, home, and schools, Johnson was confident that Black men and women would achieve the freedom promised to them and would be bearers of a civilization the likes of which had not yet been witnessed on American soil. While willing to ascribe particular traits to masculinity and femininity, Johnson had no place for a strict hierarchy between men and women. Instead, Black men were necessary to Black female success and vice versa.

Resist Like a Man:
William Bishop Johnson's Forms of Lynching Resistance

Fifteen years before *The Scourging of a Race*, Johnson preached a sermon to his church on the day set apart by the American Baptist National Convention to pray against "southern outrages," a common euphemism for racialized lynchings. In 1889, lynching was on the rise, and it was more explicitly racialized. The mid to late 1880s saw the number of white-on-Black lynchings rise dramatically and the number of white victims of vigilantism drop sharply. Paired with that statistical change, the narratives surrounding lynching also shifted: there were now explicitly anti-Black narratives used to justify spectacularly brutal executions.[36]

---

[34] Johnson, *The Scourging of a Race*, 61.

[35] Johnson, 124.

[36] For more on the racialization of lynching, see Karlos K. Hill, *Beyond the Rope: The Impact of Lynching on Black Culture and Memory* (New York: Cambridge University

This decade witnessed the rise of the "Black beast rapist" narrative, the most prominent racial, gendered, and sexual depiction of Black men and the most convenient for a society that wanted to maintain white dominance.[37] The hero of these narratives was the white woman, a victim of the rapacious Black beast. As a defense against the "brute passion of the Negro," the *Daily Commercial*, a Memphis newspaper, suggested this explanation of the actions of white men who lynched:

> The crime of rape is always horrible, but [for] the Southern man there is nothing which so fills the soul with horror, loathing and fury as the outraging of a white woman by a Negro. It is the race question in the ugliest, vilest, most dangerous aspect. The Negro as a political factor can be controlled. But neither laws nor lynchings can subdue his lusts. Sooner or later it will force a crisis. We do not know in what form it will come.[38]

These words were chilling but they clearly defined the role of the white man: righteous defender against the brutish Negro. The anger and brutality present in lynching were by no means excessive in this construct; rather, they were the natural outworking of the outrage suffered not merely by white womanhood but by white manhood.

These salacious narratives culminated in framings of the Black man, the very formulation that William Bishop Johnson was trying to construct and defend. In his cultural milieu, he had to reckon with claims like that made in Memphis' *Evening Scimitar* which drew a sickening portrait:

> In the state of slavery he learned politeness from association with white people, who took pains to teach him. Since the emancipation came and the tie of mutual interest and regard between master and servant was broken, the Negro has drifted away into a state which is neither freedom nor bondage. Lacking the proper inspiration of the one and the restraining force of the other he has taken up the idea that boorish

---

Press, 2016), 28–39.

[37] For more on the development of these narratives, see Crystal N. Feimster, *Southern Horrors: Women and the Politics of Rape and Lynching* (Cambridge, MA: Harvard University Press, 2011); Jacqueline Dowd Hall, *Revolt against Chivalry: Jessie Daniel Ames and the Women's Campaign against Lynching* (New York: Columbia University Press, 1993).

[38] Quoted in Ida B. Wells, "Southern Horrors: Lynch Law in All Its Phases," *The New York Age Print*, 1892, 17.

insolence is independence, and the exercise of a decent degree of breeding toward white people is identical with servile submission....They have got just enough of learning to make them realize how hopelessly their race is behind the other in everything that makes a great people, and they attempt to "get even" by insolence, which is ever the resentment of inferiors. *There are well-bred Negroes among us, and it is truly unfortunate that they should have to pay, even in part, the penalty of the offenses committed by the baser sort, but this is the way of the world. The innocent must suffer for the guilty.*[39]

Such a depiction is telling and was not uncommon. The narrative of Black male identity began in slavery, which, according to the author of the piece and according to many proslavery apologists, played a civilizing role in the life of the African. It was within this institution that the slave "learned politeness." Emancipation, however, created a challenge for the poor, undeveloped mind of the Black man. Unable to deal with the new pressures of freedom without the comforting presence of the overseeing white authority, he grew insolent and thus worthy of repression by any means necessary. The reference to "well-bred Negroes" makes the consistent affirmation of Black inferiority seem more benign, as it suggests that the author did not find all Black people necessarily savage. But what the author gave with one hand, he took back with the other, continuing to affirm that even innocent Black men must suffer. Here, justice is explicitly and disturbingly not the ideal. Rather, one must merely accept "the way of the world." Unfortunately, the way of the world happened to involve the indiscriminate violation of black, overwhelmingly male bodies.[40]

William Bishop Johnson offered a counternarrative. After emancipation, Black men and women had developed themselves rather than being dependent

---

[39] Wells, "Southern Horrors," 17–18. Emphasis mine.

[40] For more on this particular phenomenon across US history, see Curry, *The Man-Not*. As noted above, Curry's text significantly shapes the gendered discussion in this chapter. Curry argues aptly for the distinction of Black male victimization in a way that is neither reducible to complicity in patriarchy, often invoked in these treatments, nor solely racism. Controversially and brilliantly, Curry argues that blackness either negates or transforms what is commonly thought of as gender or sexuality; those categories are recontextualized under racial constructions. Black male sexuality is often glossed as pathological, which is precisely what one witnesses in the lynching era. Black men are generalized as sexual predators, a menace to be dealt with by any means necessary. Curry's brilliant book highlights the ways in which understandings of Black masculinity traffic more in stereotypes than evidence.

on slavery for civilization. The threats they faced now were multiple: lynching was one prominent threat, but others challenged their full integration into American life. Johnson named socialism, illiteracy of the masses, and intemperance as threats to the nation, though, interestingly not the most prominent threats to Black life, save illiteracy. After naming the national threats, he focused his attention on a characterization of Black life, framing Black men particularly as "industrious, good-natured, honest—for his honesty has been tested both as a slave and freeman—when he stayed at home while his master went forth to fight to keep him a slave, he watched with a sleepless eye, and protected with a strong arm his wife and daughters."[41] Suppressing narratives of Black men fighting for their own freedom, one of the primary reasons for the liberation that came with the Civil War, Johnson found it more useful to narrate the Black man as a faithful servant. This cannot be glossed, however, as an acquiescence to terror: other activists like Ida B. Wells would repeat this same language.[42] Its primary purpose was to explicitly refute the public perception of the Black man as a threat. But presenting Black men as harmless was not Johnson's goal; after all, he was not preaching to a white audience. Instead, Johnson wanted to focus on Black male dignity and progress.

His narration of "national perils" was punctuated by claims of innocence: "There are perils surrounding us. But does the Negro make them? Is he responsible for them? He is improving intellectually; he has acquired over $2,000,000 in property…when he organizes, it is either for moral, material, religious or intellectual purposes." That emphasis on innocence, however, also hid a veiled threat to white society. As other Black pastors would emphasize in the lynching era, there were many ways to resist lynching. Patience was only one of them, and that patience would not last long.[43] Johnson, in encouraging his Black congregants, expressed that Black people had learned from socialists and the Irish: "[the Negro] is taking notes, and what will be the result, the future alone must reveal."

---

[41] Johnson, *The Scourging of a Race*, 137.

[42] For Wells, see Ida B. Wells, "A Red Record: Tabulated Statistics and Alleged Causes of Lynchings in the United States, 1892-1893-1894, Respectfully Submitted to the Nineteenth Century Civilization in 'The Land of the Free and the Home of the Brave,'" in *The Light of Truth: Writings of an Anti-Lynching Crusader* (New York: Penguin, 2014).

[43] For another example, see Malcolm Foley, "'The Only Way to Stop a Mob': Francis Grimké's Biblical Case for Lynching Resistance," in *Every Leaf, Line, and Letter: Evangelicals and the Bible from the 1730s to the Present* (Downers Grove, IL: Intervarsity Press, 2021).

What followed was a veiled promise of self-defense: the once patient Black man would be forced to fight for his dignity. Prejudice would be weakened ultimately only by resistance. Johnson explained the resistance that he had in mind: property purchase that, if necessary, would be defended even if it required "every inch [to] be converted into a fort with Winchester and Gatling guns to keep off the wildcats and crows."[44] His audience would have received the message, even alongside Johnson's clarifications that he was not seeking to incite violence. The first priority was Black dignity, not white comfort, and in order to reach that goal, he affirmed Black manliness in the form of self-defense. Centuries had been spent investing in white people's lives but the time for self-determination had come. His conclusion was bracing:

> We are in their blood, their homes, their schools, their courts; with them, waking or sleeping, in their downsitting and uprising; we are irrepressible – almost omnipresent – they cannot kill us out, for the more they hang the more numerous the army becomes. Extermination won't do; lynching won't do; intimidation won't do. Nothing but giving him what is justly his as a citizen.

Johnson's affirmation of Black humanity and Black manhood was first and foremost contextual. It was not a reaction to a loss of hegemony but rather an establishing of the ideological infrastructure that would sustain a life of self-determination. For William Bishop Johnson, to be a Black man was to be an intelligent man of Christian virtue willing to do what it takes to defend himself and his family. Distinct from the white colonial framing of hegemonic masculinity, Johnson's affirmation required no subordination.

Conclusion: Masculinity as Liberation

William Bishop Johnson's milieu was fraught and riddled with crisis. In the midst of an era in which Black life was constantly threatened, he had the responsibility to guide a church and, in some ways, a denomination through his educational efforts. In the midst of those difficulties, he, like many of his Black ministerial colleagues, had to offer his people hope in the midst of circumstances that could easily lead to despair. He did so through his sermons. This particular collection titled *The Scourging of a Race and Other Sermons and Addresses* drew special attention to the pains of Black life, but the laments were each tinged with hope. If Black men and women would turn to the Lord and grow in

---

[44] Johnson, *The Scourging of a Race*, 138.

Christlikeness, racial uplift would soon follow. Only the Gospel offered true salvation, yet within that framework, men and women had equal parts to play, because spiritual development fed into the advancement of the race. Absent from Johnson's sermons was a desire for domination. Rather, affirmations of Black humanity, Black manhood, and Black womanhood were driven by an unqualified desire for dignity. Such a drive would lead to eschatological peace: a time when, as Johnson would conclude a sermon quoting Isaiah 2:4, "men shall learn war no more, but beat their swords into plowshares and their spears into pruning hooks."[45]

---

[45] Johnson, 139.

"WE BECAME A FAMILY":
ORDAINED ATLANTIC BAPTIST WOMEN
AND RELATIONSHIPS, 1976–1987

Melody Maxwell

The women's movement that began in the 1960s affected churches across North America. Congregations and individuals began to reconsider what they had been taught about gender roles and who could be ordained. Scholars reexamined biblical passages about women's leadership and posited that the bent of scripture was toward women's equality.[1] Women enrolled in theological education in increasing numbers, and some sought ordination. This was often true among evangelical groups as well as those of a more liberal theological persuasion. Yet studies of such women, especially using their own words, are scarce.[2] In this essay, I seek to remedy this gap in scholarship by examining the experiences of eight women ordained as ministers by Baptists in Atlantic Canada between 1976 and 1987, based on oral history interviews. I thus provide a case study of some of the first women ordained within an evangelical Canadian denomination. The paper focuses on the women's relationships with both their nuclear families and the congregations to whom they ministered, recognizing that female ministers face unique relational challenges.[3] I argue that as the women experienced the joys and

---

[1] Debated biblical passages included 1 Corinthians 14:34–35, Galatians 3:28, and 1 Timothy 2:11–15.

[2] For such a study within the Canadian context, see Kathleen Steeves, "The Lived Experiences of Women in Christian Ministry in Canada," (PhD diss., McMaster University, 2017). For scholarship about Canadian Christian women, see Sharon S. Bowler, ed., *Canadian Baptist Women* (Eugene, OR: Wipf & Stock, 2016); and Elizabeth G. Muir and Marilyn F. Whiteley, eds., *Changing Roles of Women within the Christian Church in Canada* (Toronto: University of Toronto Press, 1995). For research into earlier women ministers in Atlantic Canada, see D. G. Bell, "Allowed Irregularities: Women Preachers in the Early 19th-Century Maritimes," *Acadiensis* 30, no. 2 (Spring 2001): 3–39; and Linda Merlene Eaton, "The Issue of Female Ordination in the Maritime Baptist Convention, 1929–1954," (Bachelor's thesis, Mount Allison University, 1989). For oral histories of the Canadian women's movement, see Judy Rebick, *Ten Thousand Roses: The Making of a Feminist Revolution* (Toronto: Penguin Canada, 2005).

[3] For more on interpersonal relationships among female ministers, see Jackson W.

hardships of their own family situations related to ministry, they also came to regard their congregations as "family."

Among Baptists in Atlantic Canada, most of whom were part of the United Baptist Convention of the Atlantic Provinces (UBCAP), Josephine Kinley was the first woman ordained, in 1954. Her ordination was a harbinger of future events but an outlier at the time. The next two ordinations of women did not take place until 1964 and 1970. Of these three women, two are now deceased and the third has dementia. Atlantic Baptist churches ordained ten women (eight of whom are still living) in the years that followed, between 1976 and 1987, when the UBCAP voted to affirm women's ordination.[4] That churches ordained ten women during these years demonstrates a growing interest among women in ministering. It also shows an increased desire among the churches and denomination to recognize that ministry formally. To better understand this history, I—along with my research assistant—conducted oral history interviews of the eight living women who were ordained by churches within the UBCAP between 1976 and 1987.[5] This essay analyzes these interviews as they relate to women's family relationships and role models, marriage and singleness, and congregational relationships.

Relationships and Role Models

Family relationships were important to the interviewees, from their childhood to their older adult years. These relationships provided both encouragement and challenges related to the women serving in ministry roles. Seven of the eight women grew up in families that were active in Baptist churches, absorbing the faith tradition in which they would later lead. They had generally positive relationships with their family members and felt affirmed by their parents as they

---

Carroll, Barbara Hargrove, and Adair T. Lummis, *Women of the Cloth: A New Opportunity for the Churches* (San Francisco: Harper & Row, 1983), 160–202. See also Barbara Brown Zikmund, Adair T. Lummis, and Patricia M. Y. Chang, *Clergy Women: An Uphill Calling* (Louisville: Westminster John Knox Press, 1998). I am writing a separate paper on my interviewees' experiences of calling, ordination, and ministry.

[4] See Melody Maxwell, "'Proceed with Care': Atlantic Baptists and Women's Ordination in the 1980s." *Baptist History and Heritage* 55, no. 1 (Spring 2020): 52–69.

[5] UCBAP is today known as Canadian Baptists of Atlantic Canada. I am grateful to my research assistant Samantha Diotte, along with my teaching assistant Tracey Wooden, for their hard work on these interviews. We interviewed the following women: Ida Armstrong-Whitehouse, Sharon Budd, Joyce Hancock, Elizabeth Legassie, Chris MacDormand, Kathy Neily, Sara Palmater, and Miriam Uhrstrom.

sought to understand their vocational callings. Miriam Uhrstrom explained that her father, a Baptist minister, "didn't know what he thought about women in ministry, but he always told me, 'Do whatever God calls you to do.'"[6] Parents of interviewees like Uhrstrom had not usually seen women serving as ministers, but they affirmed what they considered to be God's work in their daughters' lives. Their supportive, faith-filled homes gave the women a secure environment from which to work out their vocations within their denominational context.

Like their parents and most Atlantic Baptists at the time, most of these women did not know any female ministers. In fact, when asked about role models in ministry, several responded as did Sara Palmater: "I really can't say I had female role models."[7] One interviewee named a female seminary professor; several mentioned female missionaries, who served in a more common role for Baptist women during this time. One woman did describe an unordained female Baptist minister as helping pave the way for her future pastorate, demonstrating that though such women were few, they influenced other women to serve as ministers. Most interviewees, however, did not know any female ministers. Elizabeth Legassie noted some practical implications of this lack of female role models:

> Without knowing it, I guess you, you model yourself on male pastors, you know, that you knew. You sort of felt maybe a bit like you, you had to, to do the same things that they did just because that's your only role model, without even thinking about it, you know….I do remember, I guess kind of having the question, well, how are you supposed to dress?…I don't want to necessarily wear a suit all the time, you know, or that sort of thing.[8]

Women like Legassie did not have mentors to model women's pulpit attire, among other things. This lack of a relational connection with female role models was a challenge for the first generation of women in ordained ministry. While they experienced positive support from their own families, they usually had to imagine for themselves what a woman in ministry looked like.

---

[6] Miriam Uhrstrom, interview by Melody Maxwell and Samantha Diotte, April 28, 2020, Wolfville, NS, and Belleville, ON, transcript, 6.

[7] Sara Palmater, interview by Melody Maxwell and Samantha Diotte, December 3, 2019, Wolfville, NS, and Fredericton, NB, transcript, 12.

[8] Elizabeth Legassie, interview by Melody Maxwell and Samantha Diotte, January 30, 2020, Wolfville, NS and Annapolis Royal, NS, transcript, 16–17.

Marriage and Singleness

Marital and family status play an important role in the career path of women in ministry. Most women in Atlantic Canada in the late twentieth century were expected to assume the primary responsibility for the care of their families, whether they worked outside the home or not. Of the eight women I interviewed, five were married during at least part of their working years. This introduced both the closeness of family relationships and the challenges of family responsibilities to their lives. As the interviewees had children, some stepped down from full-time ministry to care for their families. Sara Palmater commented, "I think it's still a really hard struggle for women with young children in ministry, because all the expectations are still there. They're expected to do all the pastoral duties, but they also have young families."[9] Congregations without prior experience with mothers in ministry often assumed that their ministers would be available at any time and would attend evening meetings, as most male ministers had done while their wives cared for their families at home.

Women's "second shift" at home often proved difficult for those who were in full-time ministry. Kathy Neily understood this challenge, as she gave birth to three children in four years. Rather than attempting to juggle numerous responsibilities of work and family, she chose to resign from her ministry role and take ten years to raise her children.[10] Later she resumed work on a part-time basis.[11] Elizabeth Legassie found that serving part-time with the governmental agency Family and Children's Services provided flexibility for her young family; she and her husband did not both serve in pastoral ministry roles until their children were older.[12] Her husband also cooked most meals for their family, demonstrating how non-traditional family roles allowed her to balance work and home.[13] Ida Armstrong-Whitehouse's husband went further, staying home to care for their two children while she worked.[14] When her children were infants, she explained, "my husband would bring them at 10 o'clock for a feeding for 10 minutes and then he'd go on his way and I'd go back to ministry."[15] In this way,

---

[9] Palmater, interview, 10.

[10] Kathy Neily, interview by Melody Maxwell and Samantha Diotte, Wolfville, NS and Charlottetown, PEI, December 11, 2019, transcript, 6.

[11] Neily, interview, 8.

[12] Legassie, interview, 17.

[13] Legassie, 17.

[14] Ida Armstrong-Whitehouse, interview by Melody Maxwell and Samantha Diotte, Wolfville, NS, December 4, 2019, transcript, 22.

[15] Armstrong-Whitehouse, interview, 22.

Armstrong-Whitehouse and her husband negotiated the roles and requirements of parenting while allowing her to minister full-time. Married women whom I interviewed sometimes found creative ways to balance the demands of family and ministry.

Three of the eight interviewees remained single throughout their careers, as had some of the female missionary role models they admired.[16] This presented them with both opportunities and challenges, especially as related to relationships. Single women were "freer to do things as they opened up for me," as Joyce Hancock recounted.[17] They did not have responsibilities toward a spouse and children. But they also reported feeling lonely, especially those who served in remote locations. Sara Palmater was single during her first pastorate, and she became depressed because she had few friends her age that lived within an hour's drive.[18] Chris MacDormand reported: "Being in ministry was very lonely, because if you didn't have a family, and didn't have a husband, it's like you're, kind of, outside of…Like what do people do with a single woman, right?"[19] Single women in ministry were in the minority both because of their vocation and their marital status. Especially in ministry roles, churches typically assumed that their pastors would be married. They also often assumed that women serving on church staff were supplementing their family's income, rather than serving as the main provider. Chris MacDormand recalled that she did not go to the dentist for twenty-five years because of a lack of adequate health coverage.[20] Interviewees related both benefits and drawbacks to being single, especially connected to relationships.

Whether they were single or married, interviewees also expressed a commitment to care for family members, especially aging parents. Three of the eight women resigned from their ministry roles to care for ailing family members. Because women have typically been seen as nurturers, they have assumed such caretaking roles more frequently than men. It is unlikely that a similar percentage of male ministers among Atlantic Baptists resigned from their ministries to care for family members in need. Joyce Hancock, who was serving as a missionary in

---

[16] Single female missionaries have been common in missions work over the past 150 years as a result of the woman's missionary movement as well as women's exclusion from other ministerial roles in some traditions.

[17] Joyce Hancock, interview by Melody Maxwell and Samantha Diotte, Wolfville, NS, and Thunder Bay, ON, January 30, 2020, transcript, 25.

[18] Palmater, interview, 8.

[19] Christine MacDormand, interview by Melody Maxwell and Samantha Diotte, Wolfville, NS, and Halifax, NS, February 14, 2020, transcript, 41.

[20] MacDormand, interview, 38.

Brazil, recounted that "the Lord said, 'You need to go home and take care of your mom.'"[21] Using similar language of divine calling, Miriam Uhrstrom stated, "now [God has] asked me to stay home, take care of my husband," although she acknowledged that "that was tough."[22] Both women believed it was their God-ordained duty to care for their sick family members. They did so with gratitude but also with some reluctance, as ministering to their family members required that they end their paid vocational ministries.

Congregational Relationships

However, the women interviewed in this project also noted some crossover between ministry among family members and congregants. More specifically, some explained that they regarded their congregations as a kind of family. After Ida Armstrong-Whitehouse left her first pastoral charge for her husband to become a minister elsewhere, she reported feeling a deep sense of loss, as if she had lost a family member. "I just was so grieving over the loss of this congregation," she related.[23] When she assumed pastoral responsibilities at another location, she explained that "we became, again, a family."[24] Armstrong-Whitehouse used a metaphor of family, familiar from her personal experience, to describe her relationship with her congregation. Sharon Budd similarly used familial language, this time detailing the way her congregation behaved toward her: "They also treated me like a family, like, you know—and whether that's because of my gender or just because I was there so long, I was almost family."[25] Budd wondered whether her congregation was more likely to regard a female minister than a male minister as a family member, perhaps because of popular conceptions of women as mothers and carers. Miriam Uhrstrom demonstrated a compassionate, familial approach to ministry with her congregation, remembering, "I could stand in the pulpit and look my whole congregation in the eye, and I would say, 'Good morning church, I love you so much. Let's worship God who loves us.' What man could say that?"[26] Uhrstrom understood that cultural gender expectations would have made it harder for a male minister to profess their love to their congregation.

---

[21] Hancock, interview, 19.

[22] Uhrstrom, interview, 19.

[23] Armstrong-Whitehouse, interview, 9–10.

[24] Armstrong-Whitehouse, 12.

[25] Sharon Budd, interview by Melody Maxwell and Samantha Diotte, Wolfville, NS, and Digby, NS, December 12, 2019, transcript, 13.

[26] Uhrstrom, interview, 20.

Not only Uhrstrom but multiple interviewees used emotions associated with family relationships to describe their ministry connections.

Several interviewees elaborated on what they considered to be women's unique approach to ministry. Sharon Budd explained, "I think sometimes women have…more sensitivity."[27] "Women are made to be nurturers," Sara Palmater affirmed.[28] While acknowledging that she was making generalizations, Miriam Uhrstrom avowed, "I think it is far easier for women to be a pastor than men….They [women] love to lead people to healing, wholeness, and health."[29] All of these comments reflected a belief that on the whole, women were innately more sensitive and caring than were men. While others at this time would likely have noted the challenges that female ministers faced, Miriam Uhrstrom emphasized women's natural fitness for ministry. Similarly, Ida Armstrong-Whitehouse noted that her gender gave her leeway to serve pastorally. She stated, "Being a woman…It was easy for them [the congregation] to allow me to be creative, compassionate, or show the softer side."[30] Rather than regarding their nurturing tendencies as complicating their work, these women felt that these traits were advantageous to ministry. Scholars such as Steeves have demonstrated that other female ministers in Canada held similar convictions.[31]

These women, then, felt uniquely equipped for pastoral ministry as they served compassionately among their congregations, which often had become like family to them. Interviewees worked to balance responsibilities among their congregations with those of their immediate and extended families, sometimes leaving full-time ministry to attend to family concerns. Their roles as daughters, mothers, and wives claimed priority, although their church families were a close second. Single women experienced both fulfillment and loneliness as they defied stereotypes of traditional ministers. Both single and married women expressed gratitude for their family's support but noted that they had few female pastoral mentors. The relationships that these women cultivated, along with those that they lacked, yield insight into women serving in ordained ministry among Canadian evangelicals in the late twentieth century, supplementing studies by scholars such as Steeves. They demonstrate that for these women, and many others like them, family mattered.

---

[27] Budd, interview, 12.

[28] Palmater, interview, 11.

[29] Uhrstrom, interview, 20.

[30] Armstrong-Whitehouse, interview, 23.

[31] Steeves, "Lived Experiences of Women," 127–29, 135–38.

FUNDAMENTALIST AND FEMALE: THE FOUNDING OF THE WOMEN'S MISSIONARY SOCIETY OF THE REGULAR BAPTISTS OF CANADA, 1926–1927

Taylor Murray

To date, the prevailing historiography of Baptist fundamentalism in Canada is decidedly male-focused.[1] If women are mentioned at all, it is usually only for posterity. While women generally had fewer opportunities to engage at a denominational level during the early twentieth century, another likely reason for this omission comes from the fact that fundamentalism has a reputation for oppressing women. Recently, however, several historical studies have challenged this latter stereotype by arguing that some fundamentalist women were, in fact, the creators and drivers of various public ministries in the early twentieth century.[2] This chapter explores this theme in the Canadian context by examining the formation of the Women's Missionary Society of the Regular Baptists of Canada (WMS), which came into being almost a full year before the fundamentalist-modernist controversy solidified into schism within the Baptist Convention of Ontario and Quebec (BCOQ) in 1927.

The chapter shows that Baptist fundamentalist women in central Canada during this period did not believe there was a contradiction between their

---

[1] Unfortunately, there are several places throughout this study where I have been unable to locate the first name of a particular woman. In these instances, I retained the traditional usage of "Mrs."

[2] E.g., Michael S. Hamilton, "Women, Public Ministry, and American Fundamentalism, 1920–1950," *Religion and American Culture* 3, no. 2 (1993): 171–96; Janette Hassey, *No Time For Silence: Evangelical Women in Public Ministry Around the Turn of the Century* (Grand Rapids, MI: Zondervan Academic, 1986); Timothy Larsen, *Christabel Pankhurst: Fundamentalism and Feminism in Coalition* (Woodbridge, UK: Boydell, 2002); Margaret Bendroth, *Fundamentalism and Gender: 1875 to the Present* (New Haven: Yale University Press, 1993); and Mark A. Noll, *American Evangelical Christianity* (Malden, MA: Blackwell, 2001), 87–91. Even among Baptist fundamentalists, this appears to have been the case. See Kevin Bauder and Robert Delnay, *One in Hope and Doctrine: Origins of Baptist Fundamentalism, 1870–1950* (Schaumburg: Regular Baptist Books, 2014), 200–205.

fundamentalist perspective and their calling to serve in lay ministry. Their new missionary society provided fundamentalist women with significant opportunities to contribute to church life and ministry, both at home and abroad. The chapter begins with a brief overview of the schism as it affected women in the BCOQ, before exploring the WMS's organizational meeting, the contents of their constitution, and their early perspectives.

Background and Schism

The creation of the WMS was a direct response to the perceived drift toward liberalism within the BCOQ, especially at McMaster University in Toronto. The university's apparent adoption of a modernist curriculum had been an issue for fundamentalists since the first decade of the twentieth century. By the early 1920s, occasional critical comments from fundamentalists had turned into a chorus of unrelenting public protests. Fundamentalist disapproval reached its zenith in the wake of the university's appointment of L. H. Marshall, a purported modernist, to the Chair of Practical Theology in 1925. Marshall represented everything against which the fundamentalists protested: he had reportedly denied the Mosaic authorship of the Pentateuch, challenged the historicity of the Old Testament book of Jonah, expressed doubts related to other supernatural elements of the Bible, and affirmed modern science. Leading the fundamentalist charge was T. T. Shields, longtime pastor of Jarvis Street Baptist Church, also in Toronto, who relentlessly criticized the university both in the press and from his pulpit.[3]

As the controversy reverberated throughout the convention, the Women's Baptist Home Missionary Society of Ontario West (formed 1889; WBHMS) felt the effects keenly. The WBHMS was one of four women's missionary auxiliaries that operated within the BCOQ at the time of the schism.[4] Of the four, it was most affected by the controversy. Not only was it based out of Toronto and thus had close contact with many of the key players and events, but also, its leadership was comprised of a cross section the convention that almost equally

---

[3] For a few examples, see T. T. Shields, "A Religious Devil," *The Gospel Witness*, April 10, 1924, 4; T. T. Shields, "Professor L. H. Marshall's Position Summarized to Date," *The Gospel Witness*, September 23, 1926, 11–20; and T. T. Shields, "An Analysis of Prof. Marshall's Confession of Faith," *The Gospel Witness*, November 4, 1926, 43–50.

[4] The other three were the Women's Baptist Foreign Mission Society of Eastern Ontario and Quebec (formed 1876); the Women's Baptist Foreign Missionary Society of Ontario West (formed 1876); and the Women's Baptist Home Missionary Society of Eastern Ontario and Quebec (formed 1884).

represented those who were critical of McMaster and those who supported McMaster.[5] As Pamela Cullen has noted, this division exacerbated existing disagreements over financial policies, leadership, and commitment to interdenominational ministries, and effectively slowed the WBHMS's work to a crawl.[6] Perhaps the most obvious display of the division within the WBHMS occurred at the November 1925 meeting, when their long-time president, Caroline "Carrie" Holman (née Haigh), lost reelection for the first time since 1893.[7]

Holman was an articulate, persuasive, and theologically astute woman with a zeal for mission work. A survey of the Baptists' *Canadian Missionary Link* in the years leading up to the schism reveals that she was a frequent and prodigious speaker in various women's missionary circles throughout southern Ontario.[8] That Holman had established herself as a significant figure in the BCOQ during this period is demonstrated in the words of one woman in early 1925, who asked: "Who would ever think of asking a mere man to take…Mrs. Chas. J. Holman's place in the chair?"[9]

Despite Holman's deep commitment to mission work and her influence, tensions caused by the emerging fundamentalist-modernist schism in the BCOQ had led many of her contemporaries to the conclusion that a changing of the guard was necessary. Fanning the flames for a change in leadership were two obvious factors: first, Holman was a member of Jarvis Street Baptist Church, where Shields, the outspoken leader of the fundamentalist forces, was pastor; and second, she was also married to Charles J. Holman, a well-known Toronto attorney and one of Shields's closest allies in the battle against modernism at McMaster. At the November 1925 WBHMS meeting, Holman lost the presidency by thirty-six votes to Jessie E. Zavitz (née Dryden), a McMaster graduate and the first woman to serve on the university's Senate. As a long-time active

---

[5] Pamela Cullen, "Debating and Dividing: The Women's Baptist Home Missionary Society of Ontario West, 1925–1927," *McMaster Journal of Theology and Ministry* 4 (2001).

[6] Cullen, "Debating and Dividing."

[7] Cullen documents this turbulence in "Debating and Dividing." For Shields's commentary, see T. T. Shields, "Even the Women are not Immune," *The Gospel Witness*, January 28, 1926, 11.

[8] E.g., "The Mission Circles," *Canadian Missionary Link*, May 1918, 155.

[9] This quotation was from Mrs. John Lillie's address on the fortieth anniversary celebrations of the WBHMS in January 1925, as quoted in Esther Barnes, *Our Heritage Becomes Our Challenge: A Scrapbook History of the Baptist Women's Movement in Ontario and Quebec* (Etobicoke, ON: Canadian Baptist Women of Ontario and Quebec, 2013), 31.

member of the WBHMS's sister organization, the Women's Baptist Foreign Missionary Society of Ontario West, Zavitz promised closer relations between the women's societies and redoubled the WBHMS's commitment to "[a] very close cooperation with, and accession to, the desires of all the General Boards [of the BCOQ] in whose territory we do any work."[10] In early 1926, Shields criticized Zavitz's election as "a conspiracy" to put the WBHMS "into the hands of women who would be subject to McMaster's direction,"[11] but the reality was different: the vote could be interpreted as a referendum not only on Holman's leadership, but also, more importantly, on the fundamentalism to which she subscribed.

The Birth of the Women's Missionary Society

On November 16, 1926, one year after her election loss, Holman held a meeting at her home to discuss whether or not it would be feasible to separate entirely from the WBHMS and instead form a new women's missionary organization that operated from a fundamentalist perspective. The meeting was triggered by a particularly contentious annual gathering of the BCOQ, during which the assembled delegates voted by a margin of 708 to 256 to express their confidence in McMaster University, including an affirmation of Marshall.[12] To Holman and her allies, this was akin to "officially endorsing Modernism and Modernistic tendencies."[13] Thirty-seven women attended the meeting at Holman's house, among whom twelve were members of the WBHMS and the remaining represented nine churches, primarily from the Toronto area.[14] At the meeting, the women determined that the McMaster issue, which they viewed as a matter of doctrinal integrity, was of primary importance and that God had called them to leave the WBHMS behind and create a new women's missionary organization.

---

[10] As quoted in Barnes, *Our Heritage Becomes our Challenge*, 81.

[11] "Even the Women are Not Immune," *The Gospel Witness*, January 28, 1926, 11.

[12] "Educational Day," *Canadian Baptist*, October 28, 1926, 1.

[13] "A Call to Baptist Women to Form a New Women's Missionary Society of Canada," 1926, in Canadian Baptist Archives, J. B. Rowell Fonds (hereafter CBA JBR) 10/9.

[14] Minnie L. Whitelock, "Initial Committee Meeting," *The Regular Baptist Call*, January-February 1927, 12. The churches included Annette Street Baptist Church, Bedford Park Baptist Church, Christie Street Baptist Church, Grace Baptist Church, Oakwood Baptist Church, Mount Pleasant Baptist Church, Jarvis Street Baptist Church, Runnymede Baptist Church, and Parkdale Baptist Church.

Following the meeting, Holman and her allies issued a pamphlet entitled, "A Call to Baptist Women to Form a New Women's Missionary Society of Regular Baptists of Canada," which gave their rationale for separating and forming a new body. They offered the BCOQ's affirmation of the modernism of McMaster University as the primary justification for their actions. In particular, they reflected the general fundamentalist criticism of the university's appointment of Marshall and the convention's subsequent refusal to seek his termination. Such tolerance of modernism, even if only tacit, the women reasoned, had allowed that perspective to flourish throughout the convention and had set a dangerous precedent.[15]

They argued that this tendency toward modernism had "become dominant in all our [BCOQ] Boards," which was of significant consequence because "the Women's Home and Foreign Mission Boards are auxiliary to, and linked with, the General Home and Foreign Mission Boards."[16] Across the denominational spectrum, it was common during this period for women's missionary organizations to function as auxiliaries to their respective denomination's general mission board. For their part, each of the four Baptist women's groups had individually and variously pledged that their decisions would be subject to "the approval of the general Board."[17] Such a close connection meant that the WBHMS could not escape the controversy. Holman believed that standing by and doing nothing was akin to endorsing those theological ideals with which she and others so strongly disagreed. Furthermore, Zavitz's commitment to "cooperate with" and "assent to" the "desires" of the BCOQ's Home Mission Board confirmed Holman's suspicions of future complicity.[18]

Holman and her allies also claimed that the formation of a new women's missionary organization would fill a practical need. Because an increasing number of churches within the BCOQ had come to believe that McMaster (and possibly the convention itself) had been infected with modernism, they were now reluctant to support its missionary efforts. A new women's missionary organization, the women reasoned, could fill this emerging gap. Theirs would be "a society to which [the dissenting churches'] funds can be sent, and administered in mission work, based upon the Word of God, and controlled by the Holy Spirit, where freedom to seek the will of God is permitted, and Scriptural Baptist

---

[15] "A Call to Baptist Women," CBA JBR 10/9.
[16] "A Call to Baptist Women," CBA JBR 10/9.
[17] Mrs. W. S. Porteous, "Montreal," *Canadian Missionary Link*, October 1878, 7.
[18] As quoted in Barnes, *Our Heritage Becomes our Challenge*, 81.

principles upheld."[19] The pamphlet closed by announcing a meeting to be held on Thursday morning, November 25, 1926, at Jarvis Street Baptist Church.

Responses to the announcement were mixed. Shields happily reprinted it in his weekly periodical, *The Gospel Witness*, with the heading in all capital and bold lettering: "WOMEN—ATTENTION!" Ahead of the article, he included an editorial comment, noting that he was glad to give the announcement space in his newspaper and that "it is a critical hour in our Denomination's history when every Baptist man and woman should heed the call of privilege and duty."[20] Shields's statement should be read as an endorsement. He was seeking to wage war on the BCOQ on all fronts, which included encouraging women to do their part. For the convention's response, Zavitz used *The Canadian Baptist* to offer a rebuttal. Perhaps because she did not sense the severity of the situation, her article was surprisingly light on substance. Throughout, she dismissed the charges variously as "a creature of the imagination with no foundation in fact," "so utterly ridiculous," and "so foreign to the ideals and aspirations of all our Baptist women." She closed: "Women of our churches! *Think* before you divide yourselves from the work established under God's guidance by your mother and your grandmothers."[21]

Despite Zavitz's appeal, on November 25, 1926—nine days after their initial meeting—the fundamentalist women went ahead with their meeting at Jarvis Street Baptist Church. The women's decision to hold their meeting in the middle of a weekday provides some insight into those whom they wished to attract to their new society. Rather than the working class, they clearly appealed to middle-class women with few or no work or home obligations, or who otherwise had the means to hire someone to help in the home.[22] The report from the meeting noted that approximately three hundred women were present for the morning session, which swelled to approximately four hundred for the afternoon session. While the majority of these women attended from various locations in southern Ontario, others had travelled a significant distance for the meeting, coming from as far as Sault Ste. Marie. During the afternoon session, Mrs. Nathaniel Mills from

---

[19] "A Call to Baptist Women," CBA JBR 10/9.

[20] "Women—Attention!," *The Gospel Witness*, November 18, 1926, 1.

[21] Jessie E. Zavitz, "Women, Attention!" *Canadian Baptist*, December 9, 1926, 6. Emphasis in original.

[22] This was common for women's missionary organizations in Canada during this period. See Brian Clarke, "English-Speaking Canada from 1854," in *A Concise History of Christianity in Canada*, ed. Terrence Murphy and Roberto Perin (Oxford: Oxford University Press, 1996), 290.

London (Ontario) moved that "this assembly proceed to organize a new Women's Missionary Society." Mrs. D. N. Cameron from Toronto seconded the motion, which passed by a nearly unanimous standing vote.[23] Immediately after the vote, the women summoned Shields, who was present at the meeting, to the platform, where he again voiced his approval of "the movement to form the new Society." Before leaving the stage, he "promised the prayers and co-operation" of Jarvis Street Baptist Church.[24]

Forming a Constitution

At the afternoon session of the November 1926 meeting, the assembled women adopted a constitution and officially became the Women's Missionary Society of the Regular Baptists of Canada (WMS). With unanimous support, those women named Holman to the position of president of the WMS. It was "her devotion to the Lord Jesus Christ, her long history of successful missionary efforts in the past, and her own personal qualities," that made her the obvious choice. Other officers included Mary R. Kingdon as first vice president and Elizabeth Brown as second vice president.[25]

The WMS's membership was open to "any Baptist woman belonging to a Regular Baptist Church" who could affirm the "fundamentals of the Faith."[26] They defined "Regular Baptist" using the same phrasing of the Regular Baptist Missionary Convention of Canada (formed in Hamilton, Ontario in 1851) as "Churches which restrict their Communion to baptized believers and administer the ordinances generally through ordained elders, should be considered REGULAR."[27] Among those theological principles they enshrined as "fundamentals" were the deity and lordship of Christ; the divine inspiration, authority, and infallibility of the Bible; the atonement through faith, accomplished through the propitiatory sacrifice of Christ; the ordinances of believer's baptism by immersion and closed communion; voluntary and systematic giving; total human depravity and spiritual regeneration by the Holy Spirit; and the necessity of sharing

---

[23] Minnie L. Whitelock, "Organization Meeting," *The Regular Baptist Call*, January-February 1927, 5. Once the newly-formed WMS approved the constitution, 243 women signed it as charter members.

[24] Whitelock, "Organization Meeting," 5.

[25] Whitelock, "Organization Meeting," 6.

[26] "Constitution of the Women's Missionary Society of Regular Baptists of Canada, As Adopted on Day of Organization, November 25th, 1926," Jarvis Street Baptist Church Archives (hereafter JSBCA).

[27] As quoted in "Constitution," JSBCA.

the gospel "throughout the world."[28] The constitution added that this statement of faith "shall never be changed" because it was "fundamental and essential to the maintenance and purity of the Regular Baptist position."[29] If one's views on any of these matters were to shift, that person would be required to resign her membership immediately.[30] Significantly, rather than have mandatory dues for members, the primary basis for membership was to be strict adherence to their doctrinal statement.[31] The message in this decision was clear: this society would place doctrinal orthodoxy above all else.[32]

Within the WMS's constitution were two significant features of the new organization. First, aside from generally affirming the Regular Baptist position, it contained no specific denominational affiliation. The women who formulated the constitution envisioned it as a purely independent organization that was "not to be an auxiliary to any other Societies, but co-operating with such *if advisable.*"[33] During this period, such independence was uncommon among Canadian women's missionary organizations, most of which maintained some form of compliant connection to the larger denominational boards. Even the language in this statement is significant. The notion of *cooperation* implied a certain level of partnership, rather than subservience; and the emphasis on *advisability* clearly underscored that the decision was theirs, not that of a domineering board. Holman was not interested in forming an auxiliary to a denominational mission agency, as had been the case with the BCOQ women's societies, but instead desired to be "independent of other such Boards."[34] As a result, when Shields formed the Union of Regular Baptist Churches of Ontario and Quebec the following year, the WMS remained fully independent, albeit aligned with the new denominational body as long as it was "advisable." Second, and related to the first point, the WMS was to be comprised entirely of women. The WBHMS's leadership was likewise made up of only women; however, at its core, it had functioned as an auxiliary to the BCOQ's Home Mission Board, and thus operated ultimately under the larger group governed by men. Holman would later claim that the WMS's arrangement had been necessary to ensure that the female

---

[28] "Constitution," JSBCA.

[29] "Constitution," JSBCA.

[30] "Constitution," JSBCA.

[31] Minnie L. Whitelock, "Initial Committee Meeting," *The Regular Baptist Call*, January-February 1927, 13.

[32] "Questions and Answers," *The Regular Baptist Call*, January-February 1927, 16.

[33] Whitelock, "Initial Committee Meeting," 13. Emphasis added.

[34] Caroline Holman to T. T. Shields, November 22, 1930, JSBCA.

voices were not overpowered or silenced by male voices, and that, in fact, "the union of women and men has everywhere been a failure."[35] The result of these two features taken together was that Holman and her allies had created a female-led fundamentalist missionary organization with more freedom and authority than had been accorded to women in the more modern and open-minded BCOQ.

Early Perspectives

With their newfound independence, the WMS initiated various ministries in order "to spread the gospel of God's grace in the Dominion of Canada and throughout the world."[36] Although Holman was a fundamentalist and believed that there were certain limitations to what women could and could not do in the church (such as fill the office of pastor), she appears to have had few reservations about women serving in ministry. On at least one occasion, for example, she hosted an event featuring Christabel Pankhurst, the transatlantic suffragette-turned-evangelist whom Timothy Larsen has identified as both a fundamentalist and a feminist.[37] Years after the schism, when pressed on her own position, she explained that she believed women "may be witnesses and may give the Gospel to others, even to men," both in foreign and domestic settings. As for biblical precedent, she noted, women were the first to witness to the resurrection and they were variously identified as deacons and apostles. Not only that, she maintained that women had just as much of a calling to fulfill the Great Commission as men; indeed, "in many places in heathen lands and even in our own land men would not receive the Gospel at all or be instructed as necessary, did they not receive such at the mouths of women."[38]

Holman's views on this matter appear also to have undergirded the WMS's approach to missions. Among their stated goals were "the preaching of the Word, the teaching of believers, the building of churches, and the establishment of

---

[35] "Annual Convention of the Union of Regular Baptist Churches, London, 1930," *Sunday Morning*, October 22, 1930, Minutes, JSBCA.

[36] "Constitution," JSBCA. This dual emphasis on fields domestic and abroad was in keeping with Holman's belief that the division between foreign missions and home missions was an artificial one, as she routinely taught "the two are really one Mission." See "The Mission Circles," *Canadian Missionary Link*, May 1918, 155.

[37] "Miss Pankhurst to Speak," *Canadian Baptist*, September 13, 1923, 2. On Larsen's assessment, see Larsen, *Christabel Pankhurst*.

[38] Caroline Holman, "Are Women Chosen of God to Serve Him?" *The Regular Baptist Call*, March 1931, 12–13.

schools whose teachings shall be in accord with the principles set forth in this Constitution, both in Canada and in other lands."[39] Worth noting is that many of the tasks listed here—preaching, teaching, and otherwise leading churches—were ones typically reserved for men, at least on the domestic front. The WMS planned to support men as well as women and did not directly state that women alone would carry out these tasks; however, significantly, nor did it close the door on the possibility that women would be involved in the "preaching of the Word…both in Canada and in other lands." Indeed, as they reflected on their founding years later, "the women of our churches were called together…to make Christ known to those at home and to the farthest ends of the earth."[40]

Conclusion

The formation of the Women's Missionary Society of the Regular Baptists of Canada was among the first tangible actions taken by the fundamentalists during the schism within the Baptist Convention of Ontario and Quebec. Holman and her allies were determined to create a fundamentalist mission society that was independent of denominational control and comprised solely of women. As a result, they created a context in which women actually received wider authority than in the BCOQ counterpart from which they had departed. Put another way, their fundamentalist context did not oppress them; rather, it provided them with a platform to speak into church life and ministry. That the WMS had created such a significant space for women is reflected in the fact that early in the next decade, one of its members felt comfortable writing (albeit anonymously) that she was "convinced that Jesus taught the essential equality of men and women in spiritual service."[41]

Paired with the fact that the WMS had limited membership to women and remained wholly independent of denominational structures, they had managed to carve out a significant place for women in the burgeoning Baptist fundamentalist movement in Canada. The WMS's independence would eventually put them at odds with Shields and his autocratic leadership style in the following decade; however, even after that later controversy, the WMS retained its independent status and the support of a large portion of the Baptist fundamentalist community in Canada. Despite future setbacks, they continued to function on the same principles established in 1926 and remained operational until 1987.

---

[39] "Constitution," JSBCA.

[40] Minnie L. Whitelock, "Our Day of Prayer for Revival," *The Regular Baptist Call*, August 1932, 2.

[41] "The Service of Christian Women," *The Regular Baptist Call*, February 1931, 8.

"THE IMMIGRANTS OF TODAY WILL BE THE CITIZENS OF TOMORROW": WOMAN'S AMERICAN BAPTIST HOME MISSION SOCIETY'S SOCIAL SERVICES AND EVANGELISM, 1908–1918[1]

T. Laine Scales

In the first decades of the twentieth century, the forces of urbanization, industrialization, and immigration coalesced to change the American landscape. As immigration increased, Baptist women and men agreed that immigrants were an open field for soul-winning. Northern Baptist Convention (NBC) leader A. B. Coats reported in 1915 that a little more than fifty-one percent of the population in New England were foreign born or born to foreign parents.[2] Coats made the case for converting immigrants to Baptist life since they were future citizens and leaders. He called on his fellow Northern Baptists to offer tolerance, patience, and help:

> The converted New Americans are excellent Christians. They are not like us in every respect. They have a genius for religion all their own. Some of the things they do shock us. Some of the things we do shock them. They need our patient watchcare and our sympathetic and generous help. They will prove neither ungrateful nor unworthy. The time is coming, and sooner, possibly, than some of us think, when here in New England the high interest of the kingdom will be in the hands of the New Americans.[3]

---

[1] The title of this chapter draws from the title of a magazine article by Northern Baptist Mary Clark Barnes, in *Missions* 8 (1917), 838.

[2] The term Northern Baptists will be used throughout to indicate members of the Northern Baptist Convention in the United States. Other Baptist groups, such as the Southern Baptist Convention, also invested resources in evangelizing immigrants.

[3] A. B. Coats, New Americans in New England, *Watchman-Examiner,* September 2, 1915, 1135–36.

While Northern Baptists had been sending American missionaries overseas since the early nineteenth century, a well-developed domestic missionary program drew evangelistic energy at the turn of the twentieth century. African Americans and Native Americans were initially the focus of domestic missions within the Northern Baptist Convention, but rapidly increasing numbers of immigrants brought a new urgency for mission work among "new Americans," especially in urban centers. As Leon McBeth noted, "no denomination in America made a more valiant effort to evangelize the new Americans than did Northern Baptists."[4]

Northern Baptist "home missionaries," both men and women, learned new languages in order to reach potential converts, as their foreign missionary counterparts had done. In this way, home missionaries could share the gospel message in a familiar tongue and with cultural meanings immigrants understood. The ultimate goal was for the convert to profess faith in Jesus Christ, to be baptized, and to join a Baptist church.

Northern Baptists and Gendered Methods of Sharing the Gospel

Although the common goal was to gain as many baptisms as possible, men and women used different pathways to win converts. First, Baptist men were free to use public spaces, preaching to gathered immigrants on a street corner or in a church pulpit, often in the native language of the neighborhood. Women's activities took place in private spaces such as a home, a settlement house, or a schoolroom. Second, when a man preached to attract converts, he cast a wide net to win souls of any age or gender. In contrast, women drew upon the "separate spheres" formula of their mothers and grandmothers to design programs primarily for immigrant women and children. Third, male preachers emphasized spiritual salvation and conversion in their efforts, with a focus on saving the soul, while Baptist women addressed corporeal needs by adding social services to their message of salvation. NBC women created a vast array of programs in which immigrants received Bible lessons and Christian teachings along with health care, hygiene, and English lessons.[5]

---

[4] Leon McBeth, *A Sourcebook for Baptist Heritage* (Nashville, Broadman Press, 1990), 408.

[5] Some men did participate in promoting social services and Walter Rauschenbusch, a Northern Baptist pastor, presented a notable exception to the usual gender pattern. Among male preachers, he was rare in his emphasis on social services as an important part of holistic ministry in the Hell's Kitchen area of New York City where

Through their Woman's American Baptist Home Mission Society (WABHMS), women of the NBC developed three specific methods of social service that provided a platform for their evangelistic message: industrial schools, home visiting, and settlement houses or centers. This chapter analyzes a cross section of annual reports, magazines, and mission study materials from the WABHMS for the decade 1908 to 1918. Concrete examples provide a glimpse of how women home missionaries used social services to establish methods of evangelizing immigrants that were different from their male counterparts in the NBC.

Women Organize for Mission

To contextualize the WABHMS home mission materials from 1908 to 1918, we must examine the roots of the organization. Organizing their mission work on American soil in the late nineteenth century, Baptist women braided together several existing strands of mission organizations. Combining groups in Michigan, Chicago, and Boston, the WABHMS emerged in 1877. The new group proposed to "extend the kingdom of God among the women and children of America."[6] Through their missionary societies, Northern Baptist women responded to the perceived needs of immigrant populations, particularly women and children. They believed that the most important gift they could give to immigrants was the gospel message, and they set up a vast network of urban missionaries to share the good news.

Women home missionaries were supported financially by Northern Baptist women as they established three primary methods of social services to win converts among America's newcomers: industrial schools, home visitation, and settlement houses (also called centers). To document their success, women counted baptisms that resulted from their mission work and published these numbers in their annual reports. The earliest home missionaries developed each of the three methods through trial and error and the practical experiences of daily mission work. Women had two ways of sharing the practical wisdom from their on-the-job training. First, they wrote detailed reports published yearly and distributed

---

he served. While he made this a part of his preaching message, many women volunteers and home missionaries helped to carry out the daily services. For a full treatment of Rauschenbusch's thought on social thought, see Donavon Smucker, *The Origins of Walter Rauschenbusch's Social Ethics* (Montreal: McGill-Queen's University Press, 1994).

[6] Mary L. Mild, "From Ocean to Ocean," *American Baptist Quarterly* 14, 311–22; quoted in Bertha Grimmell Judd, *Fifty Golden Years* (New York: Woman's American Baptist Home Mission Society, 1927), i.

widely. In this way, each mission worker (as well as church women supporting the cause) could read about methods of women in other cities. Second, the Baptist Missionary Training School opened in 1881 in Chicago to formally train women for both foreign and home missionary careers.[7] By publishing reports of their activities and training the next generation of missionaries in a women-only context, Northern Baptist women ensured the continuation of their work while at the same time reinforcing gendered expectations.

Ellis Island Welcome

Evangelism to immigrants often began at Ellis Island, where missionaries from a variety of denominations met the boats, spoke with people during immigration processing, and comforted those facing deportation. Women of the WABHMS stood ready to speak a welcoming word and to share the gospel message in a newcomer's native language. Baptist women drew immigrants in, not by preaching, but by wrapping their message in social services and educational opportunities. For children, the missionaries took "toys, dolls, sweetmeats and picture cards," and for adults, fresh clothing and evangelistic tracts in many languages.[8] Baptist women visited ill immigrants who had been detained and sometimes advocated for those facing deportation. Marie Coltorti Conversano reported on an extended encounter with an Italian woman with sick children:

> It is four months now since I saw Paolina sitting at the end of the big detention room. She was waiting for two children who are in the hospital—they first had measles, then scarlet fever and then diphtheria, so it has taken a long time. Her face is a little bit thinner every day, as she anxiously waits for the children. Every morning when I see her, my heart just goes out to her in love, and I am glad to see the smile that comes into her face.[9]

After processing, immigrants often settled into neighborhoods in urban centers like New York, Boston, or Chicago. Brochures offered at Ellis Island sometimes led them to a network of social services from the NBC in churches, industrial schools, and settlement houses.

---

[7] Faith Coxe Bailey, *Two Directions* (Rochester, NY: Baptist Missionary Training School, 1964).

[8] Frances Schuyler, *From Ocean to Ocean: A Record of the Work of the Woman's American Baptist Missionary Society, 1912–1913* (Chicago: Woman's American Baptist Missionary Society, 1913), 84.

[9] Schuyler, *Ocean to Ocean*, 85.

Industrial Schools and New Americans

One of the earliest strategies Northern Baptist women developed to evangelize immigrants was industrial education. Establishing schools was a key part of women's missionary efforts, both overseas and in the United States. Industrial schools for immigrants were designed to prepare women and children with marketable skills so that they could earn wages and enter American society as useful citizens.[10] At the same time, the immigrants would learn about the Baptist faith and perhaps join a church. While some industrial schools were operating in English, others conducted classes in the native languages of the immigrants to prepare them for employment soon after arrival.[11] Multilingual missionaries taught sewing, sang songs, and prayed in the native tongue of the neighborhood. For example, Maime Davio used her Italian language skills to pray and tell Bible stories to over one hundred Italian children and mothers each week in Bowdoin Square Baptist Church, where she and a colleague operated an industrial school in the heart of Boston.[12]

The 1910 home mission study of the WABHMS, written by Mary Burdette, provided a concrete description of the goals and methods of industrial schools as a feeder for the church. As Burdette explained, the industrial school attracted children to practical, skill-based lessons, but then they would stay to attend religious programming. A manual skill such as sewing was taught and followed by Bible study and lessons in character formation. The curriculum emphasized "habits of personal cleanliness, truthfulness, industry, honesty, politeness, and purity, as the outgrowth of true religion."[13]

In some cases, the Baptist missionaries arranged for the sale of goods that women and children made. This small profit would pay for materials and

---

[10] Progressive-Era Americans used the term "industrial school" in a variety of ways. The term originated in nineteenth-century England to indicate schools training homeless and delinquent boys to learn a trade. Americans adopted the term and used it widely for schools teaching practical skills to impoverished populations. The well-known Carlisle Indian Industrial School in Pennsylvania exemplified the full-time residential model, while the Montgomery Industrial School for Girls in Alabama was a day school. In the reports examined for this article, Baptist women used the term "industrial school" to indicate a part-time training, primarily for children. Sewing for both boys and girls was a popular subject.

[11] Bailey, *Two Directions*, 20–21.

[12] Schuyler, *Ocean to Ocean*, 98.

[13] Mary G. Burdette, *Home Study Lesson* (Chicago: Woman's American Baptist Home Mission Society, 1910), 9–10.

promote pride in the work. Florence Randolph was particularly pleased with her students, whom she believed were learning values and attitudes in addition to skills. She taught "cooking, laundering, sewing, serving, and household economics" and paid for the enterprise by selling "the little dainties" that her students prepared. In her report, Randolph emphasized the positive attitudes toward manual work students learned in addition to the skills: "During my years of teaching, I have never come in contact with a group of young girls more anxious and willing to take the industrial work than these pupils. They seem to understand that manual labor goes hand in hand with the higher education and instead of looking at it in the light of drudgery, see the useful, helpful side of it."[14]

From 1908 to 1918, increasing numbers of immigrant children attended public schools during the day. Therefore, Baptist women offered afternoon and night classes. The most active industrial schools met daily, while others met weekly. Baptist women used their settlement houses as a location for the classes, or when a house was not available, they used church buildings that were empty on weekdays. When children became engaged in industrial schools, Baptist women often found an opening to visit their parents in the home, leading to a second strategy for social services and evangelism: home visits.

The WABHMS and Home Visits

For immigrants who settled into urban neighborhoods, the practice of "friendly visiting" was a mainstay of missionary work among Protestant women of this era. As women's historian Lori Ginzberg explains, the visitor entered the homes of poor and immigrant families to determine their needs and instruct them in self-help, and in the case of Baptist women, share the Gospel message. While not directly distributing money to the poor, friendly visitors coordinated various charitable resources available in the city and kept careful records in order to prevent the poor from "duplicity and duplication."[15]

Using typical methods of visitation, Northern Baptist women documented their visits to immigrant homes and summarized them in annual reports, often recounting colorful stories of immigrant families. These records provide insight into the patterns of visitation. Home visits served several purposes: to communicate interest in the family and invite them to attend a Baptist church, to examine the circumstances in which the immigrant was living, and to share the gospel

---

[14] Schuyler, *Ocean to Ocean*, 16.

[15] Lori Ginzberg, *Women and the Work of Benevolence: Morality, Politics, and Class in the Nineteenth Century United States* (New Haven, CT: Yale University Press, 1990), 196–97.

message in a private setting. Minnie Schoeffel, serving in Chicago among Hungarians and Germans, described the connection between home visitation, conversion, and church involvement in her report of 1912: "In their homes we are always received with friendliness and even courtesy, and quite a few have been converted and become members of the church. In our church are representatives of all the German speaking populations of the globe, a very interesting and inspiring congregation."[16]

Elise Hueni also worked with German populations, but in West Hoboken, New Jersey. She was disappointed that her mission recorded only four baptisms in 1912, and she speculated about reasons why conversions were not easily won. "In my visitation from house to house I come into contact with all classes of German people....Some are infidels, some are socialists, some are too busy to think about their soul's welfare....Many calls, many conversations and invitations ofttimes are needed to bring one to church."[17]

In Pittsburgh, that same year, Lilla Sawyer made a remarkable number of visits: 1,375 visits, "to give the gospel to the parents" of her Italian neighborhood.[18] Visiting in homes created an intimate setting for sharing the good news of the gospel, but gathering groups of women and children for activities served as a third strategy for evangelism: settlement houses or centers.

Settlement Houses and Centers

In addition to industrial schools and home visits, Northern Baptist women missionaries created community hubs in which immigrants could gather. In our period of examination, settlement houses were a popular method of social service, particularly for making contact with urban immigrants. Social welfare historian Allen Davis reports that at the Progressive-Era peak of the settlement movement, over four hundred settlement houses were in operation, primarily in urban areas of the United States.[19] The idea had been imported from England, where Toynbee Hall, the first settlement house, was founded in 1884. Toynbee Hall set in motion the pattern of volunteers, primarily students or recent graduates from Oxford or Cambridge, moving into impoverished neighborhoods to learn about

---

[16] Schuyler, *Ocean to Ocean*, 87.
[17] Schuyler, 88.
[18] Schuyler, 110.
[19] Allen F. Davis, "Settlements: History," ed. John B. Turner, *Encyclopedia of Social Work* (Washington, D.C.: National Association of Social Workers, 1977), 1266–71.

poverty and attempt to find solutions. Toynbee was founded by a clergyman, Samuel Barnett, and engaged clergy as volunteers.[20]

As the movement spread to the United States in the 1880s, women leaders became involved as well, with Jane Addams becoming the most famous head resident through the flagship settlement, Hull House in Chicago. Hull House worked primarily with immigrants and involved women volunteers moving into the settlement house to build egalitarian relationships with poor and working-class neighbors.[21] As Addams expressed it, settlements were based "on the theory that the dependence of classes on each other is reciprocal."[22] The usual social and educational activities included English language classes, industrial training, kindergartens, and playgrounds. Settlement workers carried out the first systematic attempts to study immigrant communities and used their research to advocate for reforms in child labor, sanitation, and women's working conditions.[23]

While Hull House itself was not affiliated with a church, women and men established religiously affiliated settlement houses. Baptists joined Methodists, Presbyterians, Catholics, and others in using this method of social service.[24] New York City, for example, supported eighty-two settlement houses in 1911, with two of these listing Baptist affiliations.[25]

---

[20] Emily K. Abel, "Toynbee Hall: 1884–1914," *Social Service Review* 53, no. 4 (December 1979): 606–32.

[21] Many biographical accounts of Jane Addams have been written; two describing her democratic vision are Jean Bethke Elshtain, *Jane Addams and the Dream of American Democracy: A Life* (New York: Basic Books, 2002); and Louise W. Knight, *Citizen: Jane Addams and the Struggle for Democracy* (Chicago: University of Chicago Press, 2005).

[22] A classic resource on settlements in the United States is Allen F. Davis, *Spearheads for Reform: The Social Settlements and the Progressive Movement, 1890–1914* (New Brunswick, NJ: Rutgers University Press, 1984). The quote is from page 99.

[23] Davis, *Spearheads of Reform*. See especially 96–97 and 170–73.

[24] Davis, "Settlements: History." For a comparison of Southern Baptist and Catholic settlement houses, see T. Laine Scales and Michael Kelly, "'To Give Christ to the Neighborhood': A Corrective Look at the Settlement Movement and Early Christian Social Workers," *Social Work and Christianity* 38, no. 3 (2011): 356–76.

[25] Robert A. Woods and Albert J. Kennedy, eds., *Handbook of Settlements* (New York: Charity Publication Committee, 1911), 234, 239. Two settlements in New York City listed Baptist affiliations, although there are no clear ties to the WABHMS. The Children's Home Settlement was organized in 1902 "to demonstrate the merits of a religious social settlement," and the Amity Baptist Church and Settlement House, organized in 1896, provided "a union of the religious and industrial forces in the salvation of mankind."

Northern Baptist women found settlement house methods well-suited for missionary purposes and founded houses in cities such as New York, Philadelphia, and Chicago.[26] Living in crowded tenements and working in loud and polluted factories, many immigrants found a pleasant, welcoming environment when they visited a settlement house for recreation, clubs, English classes, and Bible study lessons.

The Rankin Christian Center was not located in a large urban area, but nevertheless served large numbers of immigrants working on the outskirts of Pittsburgh. With a population of about nine thousand, Rankin was known for its steel mills, which employed immigrants, primarily those from Eastern Europe. The settlement house work began in 1916 when the WABHMS appointed Luella Adams, a recent graduate of the Baptist Missionary Training School in Chicago, to establish a new work with the citizens of Rankin.[27]

At first, Adams began her work in a donated church building, but with 250 children and adults attending Bible classes, English classes, and Sunday school, the activities soon outgrew the small space. Adams described her constraints as she campaigned for funds to build a center:

> I shall conduct the clubs as best I can in the chapel. The Rankin children will have free access to our small library of donated books. When the Sunday school is packed and some are standing I shall refrain from the desire to burst the walls asunder until there is sufficient room. I shall do my best with what we have, but I shall not cease to pray that our vision may be realized until the day when the air-castle comes to Rankin in the form of a Christian Center.[28]

Adams was able to interest enough Baptist donors to build the Rankin Christian Center, which opened in 1923.

In their reports, Baptist women referred to centers like the one at Rankin with three interchangeable terms: settlement house, mission, or community center. Although the names varied, the methods were the same. A large building was used as a gathering place for education and recreation for people of all ages.

---

[26] W. Coleman Bitting, ed., *A Manual of the Northern Baptist Convention* (Philadelphia: American Baptist Publication Society, 1918), 53.

[27] William E. Brammer, "Luella E. Adams: Builder of Air-Castles in Mission," *American Baptist Quarterly* 14, no. 4 (December 1995): 372–80.

[28] Luella Adams, "When the Air-Castle Comes to Rankin," *Missions*, September 1919, 662, quoted in Brammer, "Adams: Builder of Air-Castles," 376.

Baptist women added Bible study and prayer as means of evangelism to the new Americans.

Baptist centers differed from other settlements, however, in that the workers typically did not live in the house where services were offered. Settlement pioneers like Jane Addams insisted that volunteers must take up residence within the settlement house (or at least in the same neighborhood) as a key component for settlement work.[29] By living daily life alongside immigrants and other settlement visitors, the volunteer residents would communicate an egalitarian spirit and grow in their understanding of their immigrant neighbors. Without a team of resident "settlers," like those at Hull House, many Baptist centers did not fit the parameters for inclusion in settlement directories.[30]

Yet Northern Baptist missionary women often lived in modest housing among their immigrant neighbors and found that the arrangement enhanced their work. Ida Belle Davis lived and worked in a "very thickly settled Italian section of Buffalo" and assisted with sewing classes for girls ages seven to ten at the Trenton Avenue Mission. The mission was "conducted along settlement house plans" and directed by a graduate of the Baptist Missionary Training School at Chicago. Although Davis did not live inside the mission building, as settlement workers typically did, she lived in the neighborhood, allowing her to reverse the usual practice of home visiting, and invite the Italian girls to visit her:

> My little attic room is very dear to me, for it brings me closer to my people. From here I can see many of the homes, and I find that they watch my windows and know when I am at home or away. I notice that the girls talk more freely to me in my room than they do in their own homes. I want to get just as close to them as possible and make them feel that every act of their lives is of importance to me."[31]

Neighborhood hubs, whether called settlements, missions, or community centers, provided spaces for Baptist women to offer education, recreation, and evangelism.

Conclusion

At the height of immigration to the United States, Northern Baptists invested a great deal of energy in evangelizing new Americans. While men of the NBC

---

[29] Davis, "Settlements: History."

[30] *The Handbook of Settlements* was perhaps the most authoritative listing of contemporary settlements with contact information.

[31] Schuyler, *Ocean to Ocean*, 104.

focused on preaching and establishing churches, women organized the WABHMS to create their own methods of evangelism that included social services. They modified methods of charitable work modeled by their contemporaries and used those methods to meet evangelistic goals. Industrial schools, home visits, and settlement houses (community centers) comprised the three primary methods of sharing the gospel message and bringing immigrants to baptism and church membership. In the decades following this period, professional social work would emerge and change the volunteer and professional landscape for missionaries and charity workers. As men and women earned social work degrees, a professional workforce, serving in both public and private agencies, would take over many of the social services for immigrants that missionary women had begun.

BAPTISTS IN AUSTRALIA

"SWAYED BY LIFE'S STORMS": MARION DOWNES, AUSTRALIAN BAPTIST POET AND NOVELIST

Ken R. Manley

Marion Downes (1864–1926) was one of a small group of female Australian Baptists who made a mark in the history of Australian literature. Although her literary fame was relatively short-lived, her story deserves to be recalled. Her stories and poems illuminate aspects of women's life in her denomination, although her interests and insights ranged far beyond evangelical circles. Downes may also possibly be claimed as an early Australian Baptist feminist writer; certainly she celebrated the place of women in Australian society.

Downes was born in 1864 in Melbourne into a large family of Irish descent. Her father John Patrick Downes and his wife Mary had arrived in Australia aboard the *Vanguard* in November 1863. They had twelve children, and Marion was the eldest of their eight daughters. Marion joined the Collins Street Baptist Church after her baptism on August 27, 1883. Significantly, her mother and father had been baptized in the previous year, and her sisters Emily, Ada, Adelaide, and Maud were baptized in the following years.[1]

Collins Street was the leading Baptist church in the colony of Victoria and indeed in Australia. The pastor since 1877 had been Samuel Chapman (1831–1899), long regarded as the leading preacher across all denominations in Melbourne.[2] Downes was attached to Chapman and became his voluntary personal secretary. This experience was vividly recalled in her first novel, *Swayed by the Storm* (1911), where the character of Rev. Stephen Moore is based on Chapman. He was described as

> a tall, noble-looking man, scarcely past his prime. A commanding figure, although his shoulders drooped slightly; rugged features, a massive brow, from which the hair was brushed back, deep-set blue eyes that

---

[1] Details of baptisms from the church's membership book were kindly supplied by Dr. Roslyn Otzen. See Roslyn Otzen, "Calling the Roll: What We Can Learn from the Membership Roll of the Collins Street Baptist Church," *Our Yesterdays* 27 (2019): 39–57.

[2] For details of Chapman and the Collins Street Church, see Ken R. Manley, *From Woolloomooloo to "Eternity": A History of Australian Baptists* (Milton Keynes: Paternoster, 2006), 120–23.

gleamed like fire from beneath bushy eyebrows; eyes that seemed to pierce you through with their keen, clear glance, yet, at the same time were full of mother-tenderness.…You seemed to feel with the congregation as though this man standing before you had come straight from the presence of God.[3]

Downes's attachment to Chapman was revealed in a lengthy "In Memoriam" poem she composed for him, which was read at the unveiling of a monument to his memory at Kew cemetery on September 8, 1900.[4]

Downes's church affiliation could well have stimulated her literary interests and ambitions. Chapman's successor at Collins Street from 1900 to 1908 was Samuel Pearce Carey (1862–1953), great-grandson of William Carey, who established a literary society in the church where he gave lectures on Dante, George Eliot, and the Romantic poets.[5] Among the young people influenced by Carey was Edmund Morris Miller (1881–1964), whom Carey had introduced to "the wonder of books." Miller in later life became Vice-Chancellor of the University of Tasmania, and his authoritative work on Australian literature included an account of Downes's work.[6]

When Carey's successor at Collins Street, T. E. Ruth (1875–1956), was leaving the church in 1923, an anonymous poem praised him in extravagant lines, particularly his stand against the Catholic Archbishop Daniel Mannix.[7] Downes was almost certainly the author of the poem, which began:

TO T.E.R.
A NEW YEAR'S WISH. January 1, 1923.
Strong son of Empire,
Soldier of Jesus Christ,
Thy flashing zeal has purified
The atmosphere of city and of State;
For thou did'st make us see the enemy—

---

[3] Marion Downes, *Swayed by the Storm* (Melbourne: Thomas C Lothian,1911), 8–9.

[4] *Weekly Times* (Melbourne), September 15, 1900, 7.

[5] Ken R. Manley, *"An Honoured Name": Samuel Pearce Carey (1862–1953)* (Oxford: Regent's Park College, 2016), 74–76.

[6] Edmond Morris Miller, *Australian Literature 1795–1938*, 2 vols. (Sydney: Sydney University Press, 1938), 328, 716.

[7] See Ken R. Manley, *T. E. Ruth (1875–1956): Preacher and Controversialist* (Eugene, OR: Wipf & Stock, 2021), 131.

The heartless enemy within our midst—
Emissary of the invisible fiend,
Masquerading in a garb divine.

Downes's Stories and Novels

Downes's short stories and novels for a period were extremely popular among young women. Miller summarized her novels as "simple love stories, more descriptive than imaginative, with religious applications."[8] Kerry M. White suggested that her novels "gave girl readers an opportunity to enjoy some over-the-top passion packaged as religious fervour."[9] In fact, the dominant literary genre of this post-federation period was novel-length family stories written by women for girl readers:

> These fat cloth-bound books with their thick creamy pages and gilt decorations are today instantly recognisable sitting on library shelves next to more austere tomes. Inscriptions show they were often given as school and scripture prizes or as gifts from aunts but however girls obtained these relatively expensive books it is apparent they were widely read.[10]

Downes, it has been suggested, wavers between realism and romanticism in her writings.[11] There are vivid descriptions of an Australian bush fire and the celebration of Wattle Day in Melbourne. Romanticism is evident in her pro-bush stories and her poems about flowers and other colonial scenery. At the same time, melodramatic plots stretch any reader's credibility.

Religious periodicals of the nineteenth and early twentieth centuries regularly featured stories, sometimes serialized, as a way of teaching the faith and reinforcing the values of their traditions, especially for young people.[12] Some, like Downes, attempted this in the secular market as well, although her religious

---

[8] Miller, *Australian Literature*, 716.

[9] Kerry M. White, "The Real Australian Girl? Some Post-Federation Writers for Girls," in *The Time to Write: Australian Women Writers 1890–1930*, ed. Kay Ferres (Ringwood, VIC: Penguin, 1993), 82.

[10] White, "The Real Australian Girl," 73.

[11] Maurice Saxby, *Offered to Children: A History of Australian Children's Literature, 1841–1941* (Sydney: Scholastic Australia, 1998), 265.

[12] See Ken R. Manley, "'When Harry Met Molly': Story and Baptist Identity" in *Our Yesterdays* 5 (1997): 5–20.

elements are integral to her tales. No one pretends this is great literature, but it is a valuable resource for the religious and social historian. Jane Tompkins concluded that such stories offer insights into the way a culture thinks about itself or the problems that shape a particular historical moment; they wish "to win the belief and influence the behavior of the widest possible audience." Moreover, "the presence of stereotyped characters, rather than constituting a defect in these novels, was what allowed them to operate as instruments of cultural self-definition."[13]

Downes's earliest published works were poems and several short stories, some serialized in various regional newspapers. The short story has a long tradition of being a powerful mode of literary expression among Australian women writers, and these have been characterized by great versatility.[14] Possibly the first of Downes's stories was "Monica: A Seashore Idyll," an absurdly melodramatic tale which appeared in the Warragul weekly paper *West Gippsland Gazette* over two issues in October 1899.[15]

There is no doubt, however, that in their day Downes's four novels were her best-known works, widely read and valued. First was *Swayed by the Storm* (1911), which was clearly of most interest to Baptist readers because of the portrayal of Chapman and his city ministry as well as details of the way in which the hero Donald Cameron became a bush missionary.[16] The plot is rather complicated, with Donald first falling in love with Kathleen, "an Irish girl, not long out from Dublin," who asks him to give up his missionary calling. When he refuses, she leaves him, even though she loves him.

At one stage Kathleen laments what she feels would have been her role as a minister's wife and reflects a common stereotype:

> She has to be at the beck and call of everyone. She has to please a lot of Church people who each want something different, and each sets up an ideal of his or her own. That would never suit me. I would be shocking them all the time, and I would just take pleasure in shocking them.[17]

---

[13] Jane Marjorie Tompkins, *Sensational Designs: The Cultural Work of American Fiction, 1790–1860* (New York: Oxford University Press, 1985), xi.

[14] Ewa Gajer, ed., *Australian Women Short Story Writers* (Armidale: Centre for Australian Language and Literature Studies, 1995), v.

[15] *West Gippsland Gazette* (Warragul), October 3 and 10, 1899.

[16] See the comments by Dr. Stuart McColl in *Southern Baptist*, November 16, 1911, 757, and the review on 766.

[17] Downes, *Swayed*, 174.

Another insight into contemporary Baptist mission ethos is offered when Rev. Stephen Moore declares to Donald that the work of the home missionary is "one that requires the highest courage and the noblest intellect in conjunction with a heart that is wholly yielded to God":

> We are a young Commonwealth, but the Australian nation has a magnificent future. We are at the beginning of things. On the pioneers of the ministry in the Australian bush much depends. We want a man who is intensely passionate for souls, who longs for the conversion of men and women, who would lay down his life if need were, in the service of the Lord Jesus Christ.[18]

One significant theme of the story is a question of importance to many Christian women and to which Downes often returned: "Do you think God meant every woman to be married?" Moore responds:

> By no means. Why some of the most beautiful, some of the noblest and the best women the world has ever seen, have never married....Think of Florence Nightingale and Frances Ridley Havergal, and a host of others....Not that I for one moment admire what is called the "new" woman. The greatest charm of a woman is her womanliness. Take that away, and she becomes—I was going to say a monstrosity.[19]

This observation suggests that Downes, or at least her character Moore, espoused a mix of feminist and traditional sentiments about women's roles.

The title of the novel, *Swayed by the Storm*, is a poem which Downes had previously published,[20] which likens life to a storm and concludes:

Out on life's mountains God's sunlight is shining
Back of the storm and the conflict and night
God is enthroned, then take courage, my brother,
Crown Him your King and your path will have light,
And your life dreary,
Shall become cheery
For men and women

---

[18] Downes, 84.

[19] Downes, 127. Havergal (1836–1879) was an Anglican author of many hymns, poems, and devotional books.

[20] *The Australasian* (Melbourne), February 18, 1905, 51.

Swayed by life's storm.
If by God guided.
If looking upward
Godward and heavenward,
Grow stronger, purer,
Nobler and brighter
Strong through the Storm.[21]

Anxious readers must have found comfort that, at the end, Donald rescues Kathleen from a fire at the hospital and (at last!) they declare their love for each other, with Kathleen recalling the poem and saying, "You and I have been swayed by the storm, haven't we?...but like the trees you wrote about, we are all the stronger and better for the storm."[22]

The second novel by Downes was *Brave Bush Girl* (London: Bateman, 1912), but I have not been able to find a copy of this work, nor any reviews.

Flower o' the Bush (1914), written in what one modern critic has called "passionate purple prose," is the story of Dora Swayle.[23] "Dreamy and idealistic" Dora is motherless and keeps house for her rather dour father in their bush cottage. She is much loved by her neighbour Hugh MacNeil, "a splendid specimen of Australian manhood."[24] Dora eventually moves to Melbourne, where she meets and marries a mediocre specimen of Australian manhood, Robert Patrick. A daughter is born, Robert conveniently dies, and Hugh reappears: "And the man who had waited so patiently, who had so nobly endured and so heroically struggled throughout the years, took the woman he loved into his long-empty arms and held her close to his hungry, lonely heart, pouring into her willing ears the story of his hope."[25]

Included in this novel are fine descriptions of Collins Street in Melbourne, "the Queen City of the South." Downes described the city on Wattle Day, held on the first day of September, when many acacia species are in flower. At this time, people wore a sprig of the flowers and celebrated the arrival of spring. At its foundation the day was also intended to promote patriotism for the new

---

[21] Downes, *Swayed*, 139–40.

[22] Downes, 264.

[23] Saxby, *Offered to Children*, 265.

[24] Saxby, 265.

[25] Marion Downes, *Flower o' the Bush* (London & Melbourne: Ward, Lock, 1914), 320.

nation; the golden wattle was incorporated in the design of the Coat of Arms of Australia in 1912. Downes's description included the following:

> [I]n and out among its busy traffic one caught glimpses of motors as they flashed past, handsomely decorated with large yellow sprays while the broad, clean pavements were thronged with thousands of smiling people, all, with few exceptions, wearing a spray of the fluffy, downy, yellow ball. Everyone wore it, from the navvies, the porters, the small boys, up to the ultra-fashionable English "Johnny" who "did the block."[26]

The last novel of Downes was *In the Track of the Sunset: An Australian Story for Girls* (1919). Located in one of "Sydney's prettiest suburbs," this had "the scent of mignonette through its prose."[27] The passionate and artistic Evelyn Carlingford, after a quarrel with her fiancé, the worthy Esmond, marries Ralph Dyster, a man she does not love. Ralph, it emerges, is "a charming snake in the grass" and heads off overseas, leaving Evelyn with her infant Nancy. Eventually Evelyn is reunited with Esmond, who has forgiven Ralph on his deathbed; the two now-elderly lovers walk off into "God's Sunset."

Downes's stories, it has been noted, are also quite different from those of other authors writing for girls at this time in that "they address sexuality, euphemistic as this might be."[28] Nancy and character John Sterne's sister both fend off unwanted advances; Nancy indeed had to leave her job as a typist because of harassment from her boss. Downes was clearly sympathetic with these feminist concerns.

At the rear of *In the Track* are six pages crammed with "press opinions" which advertise the two earlier titles. These reviews are taken from both British and Australasian sources and emphasize both their value for girls and their religious value. Religious journals were ecstatic in praising her novels. *The Presbyterian Messenger* praised this "good, wholesome reading" and suggested that it should be in every Sunday School library.

Flower o' the Bush also provoked warm praise. Significantly, *The Woman* (the official organ of the Australian Women's National League) declared this was "a welcome addition to the clean, healthy books our Australian women are giving our young people to read." The *Adelaide Register* reassured its readers that this novel was "of the wholesome Melbourne rather than of the brilliant Sydney type"

---

[26] Downes, 162.
[27] Saxby, *Offered to Children*, 265.
[28] White, "The Real Australian Girl," 82.

and has "a healthy religious tone." A rather prosaic report appeared in the *Victorian Education Gazette and Teachers' Aid:* "The plot is skilfully constructed and holds the reader's interest throughout."[29]

The novels and stories of Marion Downes were popular and widely read. These, however, formed only one dimension of her literary work. To many, she was best remembered for her poems.

Downes's Poems

Downes had some of her early work published by the Victorian Education Department in *The School Paper.* One of these was her poem "The First March Past," which celebrated the march by seventeen thousand senior military cadets in Melbourne on November 16, 1912. Her friend Charlotte Boesser wrote a musical accompaniment to the rhythmic line, "Tramp, tramp, on they come."[30]

Downes published many poems in the local press in both Australia and Britain, and most of these were included in her two volumes of collected poems.[31] All the poems published in *Wayside Songs for Women* (1921) were reprinted in the posthumous *Wayside Songs* (1927) so that the second volume provides a comprehensive collection of her poetry. The first volume was dedicated "To my loved and leal comrade Charlotte"; Charlotte Boesser, a music teacher and composer, was a close friend of Downes. It was Charlotte who prepared the second volume, which included a striking studio portrait of Downes. Charlotte grouped the 123 poems into four sections: Nature Songs (thirty-one poems), Wayside Songs for Women (twenty-nine poems, unchanged from the 1921 volume), Battle Songs (twenty poems), and Sacred Songs (forty-three poems).

What at first surprises the reader are the twenty poems called "Battle Songs," which reveal an imperialist and militaristic tone. The first in this section, "His Last Commission," is an "In Memoriam" for Lord Kitchener (1850–1916), who after his famous exploits in the Sudan, the Boer War, and the early years of World War I, was killed when his ship was torpedoed on June 5, 1916. "This Moses on the mount of duty stern" was lamented:

---

[29] These quotations from reviews are in unnumbered pages in the rear of *In the Track of the Sunset.*

[30] *The School Paper Grades V and VI,* January 1913, 2f (first published in the Melbourne *Herald*); her poem "A Cluster of Flowers" was included with floral illustrations in November 1913, 168f. For the patent of her music by Charlotte Boesser, see *Commonwealth Gazette,* no. 91, November 7, 1914, 2476.

[31] A note in *Wayside Songs* thanks several publishers for permission to publish: *Chambers' Journal, Glasgow Herald, Weekly Times,* and *The Herald* (Melbourne).

No human hands for him
Should turn the sod;
Fitting that he should be
Buried by God…[32]

Some earlier poems reach back to the time of the Boer War, with long son-
nets to mark the Relief of Ladysmith and that of Mafeking in May 1900: "Look!
The British flag is flying. Hark! The British Nation prays."[33]

However, the world war evoked several poems of a type that F. W. Norwood, who wrote the foreword to *Wayside Songs*, recalled. Whilst serving as a
YMCA officer he had witnessed that many of Downes's poems were "greatly
esteemed by Australian soldiers." These rugged men "responded to her deep spirituality."[34] Many of these sentimental pieces sound rather maudlin to the modern
ear, but this kind of poetry was effective during those anxious years. Typical was
"My Soldier Lad":

My lad is brave and tall,
A hero he,
Who rose at country's call
Obediently.[35]

Similarly, "The Horrors of the War" is a striking demonstration of a sensitive soul. It concludes:

Oh! Carnal fiend! All blood-stained is thy track.
Art not yet satiate? War horse! Stand back!
Dark rider! Sheathe thy sword, thy sword so red,
Thou ridest through a "City of the Dead."
God of armies through the ages.
God of hosts! When battle rages
Be Thou near, and save.[36]

---

[32] Marion Downes, *Wayside Songs* (London: Simpkin, Marshall, Kent & Co.,
1927), 127–30.

[33] Downes, 152,157–59.

[34] Downes, vii.

[35] Downes, 131–32.

[36] Downes, 135–36.

There are poems dedicated to the Australian Light Horse Contingent; a moving depiction of the farewell to Australian soldiers; and laments for orphaned French children and for the destruction of Rheims Cathedral. "The British Flag" dramatically reveals the prime Australian sentiment regarding Empire at this time:

> Though wife and child be dying
> The Flag must still be flying.
> The nation still must pray.[37]

In addition, Downes wrote poems about some individuals who were significant in her life. They were an intriguing mix, including not only Samuel Chapman but also Robert Louis Stevenson, Australian poet Henry Kendall, and British evangelist and writer Henry Drummond. A more intimate poem is "Marjorie," a portrait of her young niece Marjorie Pater.[38]

In the spirit of the Romantic poets whom Downes loved, there is a deep love for nature throughout her works, including in her "Nature Songs," with some specific places, such as Mount Buffalo in the Australian Alps, receiving reverent treatment.[39] At the same time, her compassion was evident in her poem prompted by a major mining disaster at Mount Mulligan, Queensland, when seventy-five workers were killed on September 19, 1921.[40]

The "Australian-Briton" sentiment so dominant at that time pervades her poems. Queen Victoria was given a final tribute after her death:

> Sleep on, OUR QUEEN, and take thy rest, so nobly earned and won....
> Greatest of earthly monarchs thou, strong in God's faithfulness.[41]

This brief survey must finally focus on two intertwining central themes in Downes's poetry that have also been traced in her prose: her understanding of the place of women and her spirituality. Her poem "Woman's Work" rehearses familiar roles:

---

[37] Downes, 150–51.
[38] Downes, 69–71.
[39] Downes, 41–42.
[40] Downes, 40.
[41] Downes, 95–96.

Her work—to sweeten human life,
And make it glad;
To bring back Hope to those who fail:
To cheer the sad.…

To be to Man his guiding star,
When dark his skies;
His helpmeet in his hour of need,
Strong, patient, wise.[42]

One long poem of thirty-seven stanzas, "What is Motherhood?" again raised the question: how did a childless, unmarried woman, like herself, feel when motherhood was so highly and consistently lauded as *the* Christian vocation for women? Her answer to this key question also demonstrates central dimensions of her spirituality. Downes begins the poem with her basic question:

Oh! Tell me what is Motherhood,
That poets, preachers, singers praise
In rapturous language, choicest lays,
As something wholly sweet and good?…

Tell me what is true motherhood,
That word so oft on lips of men,
From pulpit uttered, flung from pen,
This sacred thing, the gift of God…

But she is "Mother" in God's sight,
Who loves, with empty arms that ache,
And heart that loneliness may break—
Yet keeps unsullied virtue bright…

We care not what her state in life—
Who sacred holds her womanhood,
Whose heart throbs with deep sympathy,
Who loves— and loves unselfishly—
To her belongs true "Motherhood."[43]

---

[42] Downes, 97–98.
[43] Downes, 77–82. This was published in *The Kyneton Observer*, July 1, 1899, 5.

Whilst not a radical feminist, both Downes and her mother were among the thirty thousand who signed the 1891 Women's Petition for Women's Franchise to the Victorian Parliament. As seen in her poem above, Downes also expressed strong convictions about the role that single women played in church and society.

Downes was not afraid to be different, and she demonstrated this through her literary achievements. Her spirituality included a deep devotion to God and to Christ as her personal Savior. The clearest literary expression of this faith and spirituality is found in the forty-three poems within the "Sacred Songs" section of *Wayside Songs*. Her personal faith is embodied in a poem in which Christ is honored as "My Royal Guest":

No longer stand'st Thou at my heart's barred door
In patient, weary quest;
But, dwelling in the throne-room of my life,
Thou art my Royal Guest!
And, bathing with my tears Thy nail-pierced feet,
My soul finds perfect rest.[44]

Downes died on February 20, 1926 and was buried in Brighton cemetery, not far from the grave of the famous Australian poet, Adam Lindsay Gordon. Eva Hurst, a friend in literary circles, suggested that there "'the pathway of the loving heart' will be worn by the feet of those who, in their different ways, love both Australian poets." She described Downes as "a great and noble soul, teller of charming tales and maker of beautiful verse, one of the chosen who, by writing of Australia and its people, helped to make it better known and loved on the other side of the world. She was a fine, splendid woman, an ideal friend, and one of Australia's sweetest writers."[45] Hurst also made special mention of Charlotte Boesser, "whose name will always be linked with Downes's and whose untiring devotion smoothed her path to the end."[46]

Marion Downes's faith was unambiguous and deeply personal—she may not have been a strident feminist, but she was clearly an evangelical poet. This evangelical perspective is shown in the last poem in her book. In "Going on Further with Jesus" (based on the text in Luke 24:28, KJV, where Jesus "made as though he would have gone further"), she explores this possibility and concludes:

---

[44] Downes, 183–84.
[45] *Australian Baptist*, March 1926, 3.
[46] *Australian Baptist*, March 1926, 3.

We would not stay at Emmaus, sweet though its mem'ries be;
We would rise up and go further, further, dear Christ with Thee,
In the white light of Thy presence, though penitent, we bow,
Saviour, we still would go with Thee, Prince of Companions,
Thou![47]

---

[47] Downes, *Wayside Songs*, 249.

BAPTISTS IN THE MAJORITY WORLD

THE FOUNDING OF THE JAPAN BAPTIST WOMEN'S UNION: AKIKO MATSUMURA'S PASSION FOR EQUAL STATUS IN GOD'S MISSION

Eiko Kanamaru

Akiko Matsumura is a forgotten Japanese Baptist leader in spite of her contributions, not only to the national Baptists, but also the global Baptist family. She was active in the Baptist World Alliance (BWA) in the late 1970s as a vice president for its Women's Department. She was President of the Japan Baptist Women's Union and of the Asian Baptist Women's Union as well. Upon accepting these responsibilities, she expressed her strong desire to be part of Baptist life as a woman as well as an Asian claiming an equal status in God's mission. She was also the pioneer Japanese Baptist woman who developed many fields of work for church women who received God's call as their Christian vocations. The intention of this essay is to share the story of her Christian life as she worked hard to be faithful to God's calling in the culture of Japan.

Yearning for Equality and Independence: Akiko's Life-Long Struggle

Akiko Endo, who was later Akiko Matsumura, was born on March 14, 1917, in Tokyo, Japan, as the youngest in a traditional Buddhist family that had a higher social status at that time. When she reached school age, her father sent her to a private elementary school rather than a public one. This was a rather unusual custom of the older generation of her parents. The school she attended was founded by a successful international trading merchant whose major business was producing porcelain tableware for export. His business eventually brought him great success and enormous wealth. As a successful international businessman, the founder of this school was painfully aware of the importance of language skills for promising Japanese youth. At the opening of the new school, he insisted on offering English language as one of the major subjects, even to the elementary schoolers.

The language education of this school brought Akiko her unexpected life in her later years. It was a solid base for her being sent to the Southern Baptist Woman's Missionary Union Training School in the United States as a preparation for future leadership for the Japanese Baptists as well as the global Baptist community.

Akiko was a brilliant little girl, no less brilliant than her two older brothers. She loved to study and made good grades. Naturally, this achievement made her wish for higher education. Unfortunately, this was the beginning of her lifelong struggle to be her own person by challenging the given status and role of traditional Japanese womanhood. If boys wished to pursue higher education, they had no trouble in getting the greatest support from the whole family, but this was not true in her case. Most of the women of her time were subordinated to their male family members in the strict parental discipline that perpetuated Japanese patriarchal social structure. This was the culture in which she was born and grew up.

The parent-daughter relationship became rough and full of tension. Her parents couldn't handle well Akiko's rebellious attitude. Then they finally gave up and gave her permission to go to high school. This school was famous for training young girls to be independent and smart in the assigned areas for women, such as housekeeping and raising children. She did well in that school too—not in the class of home economics but in that of foreign language. Even in school, she still kept her strong desire for a college education. However, such an ambition was squelched because of her gender and the social status of her family. Her parents asserted that, since she was the youngest, she did not need a college education, but asked her to be sweet and obedient, saying "education is a grave obstacle for girls to be a sweet house wife. Education makes girls argumentative which most men dislike for their future wife, you know that."[1]

Akiko later interpreted these words in this way: "My parents thought that higher education would make me too independent and stubborn to be a sweet and obedient wife. Instead of buying textbooks and providing tuition fees for me, they bought me pretty clothes. But I refuse to dress as a doll, a doll with a sign hanging out in front, 'For sale to the highest bidder.'"[2]

Akiko's Independent Will and Natural "Stubbornness" for Her New Life

Akiko thoroughly resented her parents' attitude and became rebellious, as noted earlier. She later described herself: "It seems I had an independent will with

---

[1] Akiko Matsumura, unpublished manuscript, "Global Discipleship," Foreign Mission Conference, Ridgecrest, NC, June 22, 1980, 1.

[2] Matsumura, "Global Discipleship," 1.

stubborn streaks."[3] This stubbornness knew no way to give up on her dream. This was the same stubbornness, however, that eventually won her parents' reluctant permission for her to take a six-month English conversation course at the nearby Young Men's Christian Association (YMCA). There Akiko met a Southern Baptist female missionary from the United States named Dorothy Carver, and they became good friends, even through World War II.

Dorothy Carver was a daughter of William Owen Carver, a Southern Baptist missiologist legend and long-time professor at the Southern Baptist Theological Seminary. She later married William Maxfield Garrott, who also served in Japan for years as a Southern Baptist missionary. It was this missionary couple who gave Akiko undeniable influence in assisting her spiritual growth. Akiko and Dorothy started getting together regularly for study—Dorothy teaching Akiko English, and Akiko helping Dorothy with Japanese. Dorothy chose the English New Testament as a textbook to teach Akiko.

Growing up in a traditional Buddhist family, Akiko had only a vague idea of what the New Testament would be and was at first not very excited about the choice of her textbook. In addition, one of her older brothers, who openly confessed himself to be a communist, preached to her that religion is opium to the people and Christianity is its worst sort. However, her burning interest in the language study and great excitement for free English lessons won over her caution and suspicion toward the Bible. Her parents' disdain for Christianity was no problem until she became interested more in Dorothy's teaching of the Bible.

Two years later, Akiko accepted Jesus as her savior. She later recalled her conversion experience as a thrilling revelation and the beginning of her new life. Her conversion made her father furious, and he confronted her with his alternative, "You have become a believer of a foreign religion. This is a disgrace to the family tradition and to my social standing. You give up your faith and enjoy my love and protection, or you must leave home."[4]

Her choice was to leave home and go to Dorothy, who lived nearly seven hundred miles away from where Akiko was. Dorothy welcomed her and offered her a place to stay. Of this specific moment, Akiko clearly remembered what Dorothy told her, "You are gifted in language study. It is our responsibility to develop your talent for the cause of the Kingdom."[5] As described in another

---

[3] Matsumura, *The Book I Treasure*, unpublished monograph in the author's possession, 1982, 2.

[4] Matsumura, *The Book I Treasure*, 4.

[5] Matsumura, 5.

article, Akiko heard Dorothy say that she saw Akiko's language ability as God's investment in her.[6]

It was a very surprising discovery to Akiko that she was someone in whom God had invested something. It was also a surprise that someone like Dorothy saw value and talent in her. Looking back on her early family life, she was always placed at a lower status and looked down on because of her gender and age. The culture and environment in which Akiko grew up set her on a long and winding road to fight against those negative circumstances and to win independence and equality from them. Dorothy Carver also believed that her missionary responsibility was to help Akiko be a good Christian worker. Taking Dorothy's recommendation, Akiko went to a Methodist women's college in Nagasaki to study English.

After finishing school, Akiko was offered a three-year contract to teach English at her alma mater. At this time, anti-American feelings were beginning to grow throughout the country, and the US bombers began to destroy Japanese cities. Akiko later moved back to her hometown in Tokyo. This relocation eventually helped her to escape the dropping of the second atomic bomb on the city of Nagasaki.

World War II was over in August 1945 with Japan's unconditional surrender to the Allied forces. Seven months later, Akiko received a letter from W. O. Carver expressing his desire to provide all possible help with regard to her wish to study in the States. Carver had heard of Akiko from his missionary daughter and her husband as well. Carver seemed determined to bring this Japanese young Christian woman to the Woman's Missionary Union Training School in Louisville, Kentucky as part of his postwar missionary commitment. In 1947, Akiko was given permission from General McArthur's headquarters to go to the United States as one of the first four students permitted to leave occupied Japan.

In the United States, she fully enjoyed breathing the air of liberty and fell in love with the Greek language and biblical study. Women students attended classes with male professors from the Southern Baptist Theological Seminary. Akiko's academic performance in Greek especially impressed New Testament professor Edward McDowell. He encouraged her to extend her stay to study a higher level of Greek because Greek was essential for a deep study of the Bible. He even promised to provide a special tutor for her.

---

[6] Nancy Carter, "Japanese Women Discovering Self-Worth, says BWA Officer." *Foreign Mission News*, Foreign Mission Board, Southern Baptist Convention, Richmond, VA, July 30, 1975, 1.

However, unexpected discouragement came from the woman principal at the Training School. One day, she called Akiko to her office and reprimanded her. Akiko later wrote about this disheartening experience, "With much dignity, she said 'My dear, I thought that a Japanese girl is obedient. I have protected you from overwork and outside engagements because you get sick rather often. It was a surprise to me that I heard you are studying Greek with a private teacher.'"[7]

These comments were a double blow to her—first because her gender was called into question and then her nationality. What made it even more severe was that it came from someone of her own gender. During the second half of Akiko's professional life, these two aspects—being female and being Asian—were paired in the assignments that constantly forced her to work out a complex leadership role both in national and international settings.

In spite of this discouraging incident, she kept pushing herself to study Greek, fed with the encouragement and spiritual support of Carver. Her personal encounter with Carver enormously helped her spiritual maturity grow as she wrote, "When he talked about the plan of God, he let me see a glimpse of the eternal plan of God. He accepted me as I was, treated me as a fellow worker in the Kingdom. He saw in me potentialities and expected me to live true to the high calling of God of my own."[8]

Reflecting upon the course of her life, Akiko occasionally mentioned that she was disgusted with the criticism of her stubbornness which her family said was her bad luck. It was "bad luck" in the sense that she was doomed to be an "old maid," never to be someone's preferable, sweet, and loving wife. But her Christian faith shed a different light on it. She learned that God could change such a disfavored nature into an indispensable divine tool for God's work.

In 1950, Akiko graduated from the WMU Training School with a bachelor's degree in religious education. As she continued private Greek study with a tutor for the next academic degree, she came to stand at a crossroads. The longer she stayed in the United States, the more she felt isolated from her peers in Japan. It was not because of her homesickness but because of her concern with the danger of alienating herself from her fellow workers in Japan with whom she should identify in the first place.[9]

Then she went to seek Carver's advice. Instead of comforting her, he said, "Whatever you decide should be your decision. If my opinion prevails, you would not assume full responsibility for the result of your decision. You must

---

[7] Matsumura, *The Book I Treasure*, 16.

[8] Matsumura, 16.

[9] Matsumura, 16.

find the Lord's will for yourself."[10] He even showed her step by step how to do it. She faithfully followed each step of that direction that finally brought her to reach a decision—the decision to go back home.

Struggle in Her Own Land

After returning to Japan, she was offered the full secretary position of the Japan Baptist Convention's (JBC) youth ministry in 1952. This hiring was the first in the newly organized JBC. Her boss was Rev. Shuichi Matsumura, who later proposed to her to become his second wife after he lost his first wife due to illness. Together with a Southern Baptist missionary, she organized the youth movement on a national scale. Then she moved to the Sunday School Department as a writer and editor to publish teaching materials for the local church Sunday Schools. For this project, she translated the Southern Baptist Sunday School materials that were recommended by the missionary specialist of that field. Through this experience, she came to realize that the local church had to train its members through education in order to carry out the missions and evangelism task of the church. Indeed, she was very successful in this project. Because of her achievement as a project leader, the Baptist World Alliance Youth Department authorized her to supervise the organization of the first Asian youth conference.

It was such a high time when Rev. Matsumura asked her to marry him. At that time, he was struggling to raise three little children after his first wife had passed away the previous year. He was a senior pastor of a local Baptist church and was working as Chair of the Youth Division of the JBC as well. Akiko found herself at the crossroads again—giving up her promising career or becoming a stepmother of three little children and a busy pastor's wife. This was another difficult decision to make after that of her giving up study for her dedication to her fellow Japanese. However, by this time, she had mastered how to seek God's will for her with what Carver taught her years before.

Her decision for this time was to leave the full-time position which would promise her many respectable titles in the future. She chose the local church as her place to serve God rather than the JBC office or other related official institutions. On this decision, Carver's book on Ephesians was the inspiration to her, as she confessed:

> The church is an incarnation of the Risen Lord. The Holy Spirit who dwells in the church continues to carry out Christ's redemptive plan for the whole world. To participate in the ministry of a local church is

---

[10] Matsumura, 20–21.

a great privilege and honor to me. To find a place of service in the plan of God as a pastor's wife would fulfill my destiny as woman called by grace of God.[11]

Even after she married, however, she never quit her old custom of studying the New Testament intensively and an hour-long morning meditation and prayer. This custom was her lifelong daily routine—waking up at four o'clock every morning, hours before she was swamped with her busy schedule as a wife, mother, and student of the Scriptures. She studied the New Testament both in Greek and English, followed by meditation and prayer. This routine was the time of her spiritual discipline as she prepared to manage various engagements including church evangelism, Bible teaching, and work for the JBC and the similar international offices.

For such an active individual, spiritual discipline was always her top priority. She wrote:

If we want to grow spiritually, we must set apart a definite time and a place for our devotional period. This is a matter of spiritual discipline. Take time to know God through intensive study of his word. Are not we so busy with housework, church work, meetings, and entertainment that we neglect the most important things? Do not we sometimes justify our neglect by saying, "After all, we are busy in the Lord's work?"[12]

To serve others well, Akiko acknowledged the value of seeking to be alone, as Dietrich Bonhoeffer suggested: that one who cannot be alone cannot thrive in fellowship with others.[13]

It seems that marriage did not block Akiko's way to serve God. From her point of view, being a pastor's wife was the work for which God had prepared her. In this place, she thought she could use the gifts from God and take part in the divine work that God had planned for her. This interpretation made Akiko work hard to do housekeeping matters as perfectly as possible, with little laziness, as if working for God and for the family were essentially the same thing. In this way, she challenged the stereotypical image of a Japanese housewife and that of a Christian woman in the church.

If this view is correct, the reason Akiko favored Martha instead of Mary in the Gospel of Luke is understandable. She also highly praised Lydia, a dealer of

---

[11] Matsumura, 26.

[12] Matsumura, 8.

[13] See Dietrich Bonhoeffer, *Life Together* (New York: Harper & Row, 1954), 77

purple cloth in Philippi in the Book of Acts, for a similar reason. To Akiko, the commonality of these two women was their swiftness to respond to Jesus with their practicality in the areas for which they had responsibility. In a Bible study in New Orleans in 1982, as Akiko taught a lesson on Lydia, she fully disclosed her view on ideal Christian womanhood:

> She was a saleswoman. To be successful, a saleswoman must have certain qualities: Thorough knowledge about the goods with which she deals; an ability to distinguish good and genuine ones from cheap imitations; an attractive personality to make new customers and hold old ones; sensitivity to see the needs and tastes of her customers; good judgement and speedy actions to meet the specific needs and make profit out of them. Lydia certainly had these qualities, which became apparent when she was touched by the gospel. Or rather, the Lord used these characteristics of hers to advance His cause.[14]

Surpassing Male Leadership: The Birth of the Baptist Women's Work

In the late 1960s, Akiko's devotion to serving God as a vocation faced the real test: the JBC's drastic policy change that aimed at eliminating the women's division from the organization due to the lack of Convention funds. This massive structural reorganization was mainly discussed by the male leadership. Women were extremely uncomfortable with this plan and strongly opposed to the JBC's resolution. Women fought to keep their women's division in the JBC, but they failed. As a consequence, the women decided to leave the JBC structure and form their own missionary society, Japan Baptist Women's Union, as the convention auxiliary. With this establishment, Akiko was the engine and spirit of opening the new era of Japanese Baptist women.

Historically, the Baptist women's work in Japan started in 1915 with five missionary wives. They first got together to organize a group of local church women for missions. But this attempt failed as premature. Five years later, in 1920, the first Baptist women's group was officially organized with the purpose of encouraging female members of all local churches for foreign missions. They promoted activities such as prayer meetings for foreign missions, Bible study, training for evangelism and soul-winning, and raising money for missionary activities. The slogan of this new body was "the whole world for Christ" based on

---

[14] Matsumura, "Lydia," in unpublished monograph of the Bible study session, 1982.

1 Corinthian 3:9, which was also the watchword of the Southern Baptist Woman's Missionary Union.

The working relationship between the missionary wives and native Baptist women was desirable for both. They also invented a systematic method for stabilizing income for the work. As they controlled their own funding, their independent spirit pushed them to expand more effective mission activities, mainly for women.

Educating boys, girls, and young adults, including women, for mission work was another important task. Specifically, the women raised scholarships for young women who felt God's calling to evangelism. For those women, this was an act of investing in the future generation of churches. They were also interested in social betterment and organized a welfare center called "Lighthouse for the Neighbors" in one of the most neglected parts of the designated area. The women did Christian missions in their own way and became quite successful, even surpassing the male JBC leadership in their activities.

In the meantime, the JBC's male leadership did not hesitate to ask the women to give money for the Convention's own activities, including both home and foreign missions. In 1933, the JBC's annual meeting unanimously adopted a motion that the independent women's group should be merged with the Convention organization under the new name Women's Department of the Baptist Convention. Some female leaders innocently viewed this decision as the beginning of male-female equality in mission work. They were even pleased with this result as the answer to their diligent prayer for years requesting God to "make women humbler to men."[15]

At the same time, however, this was the beginning of the JBC's attempt to absorb the women's group and its work under the organization's umbrella and to control politically. Though it was not a smooth transition, the women finally accepted the JBC's decision and moved into the Convention's structure. The President of the newly established Women's Department wrote on this organizational relocation as follows:

> We should never forget our independent spirit even after this reorganization is done. However, now we are the one of the JBC's organizational branches. We ought to devote ourselves to work for the Convention and throw behind our self-centered spirit just like the female

---

[15] Japan Baptist Missionary Union, ed., *Baptist Women: Forty-year History of Japan Baptist Missionary Union* (Tokyo: Japan, 1962), 58.

members of the Philippian church who willingly helped St. Paul and his missions.[16]

The JBC leadership never stopped asking for the money women raised. Besides the Convention's own activities, it even requested financial assistance for local church pastors, which should be the Convention's initial responsibility. When the JBC suggested that the Women's Department could request that local church women raise a special offering, the women declined the idea. Instead, they chose to do it in "the womanly way" by encouraging women to make their family dish simpler than usual at least once a week and save the extra money for the Convention.

By the end of the 1930s, the Women's Department was no longer able to spend its own Christmas Offering for itself. The whole amount of the money automatically went to the JBC's budget. The Convention's control over the women in this way continued before, during, and even after World War II. The Convention decided to cut the women's work from the organization from the late 1960s to the mid-1970s in order to achieve financial independence from the Southern Baptist Convention.

The Independent Spirit of the Women: Leaving the Establishment and Making Their Own

Though the Southern Baptist mission in Japan began in 1889 with two missionary couples and enjoyed its growth, the missionary work was suspended for some years during World War II. The current Japan Baptist Convention was organized in 1947 along the lines of the Southern Baptist Post-War Policy on foreign missions. Under the circumstances, JBC was privileged to receive abundant support of both economic and human resources from the Southern Baptist Convention. Since this time, the relationship between the two became almost a customized system that resulted in the national Baptists' heavy financial dependence in many ways for quite a long time. This was one of the major contributing factors to the Japanese Baptists' delay in their independence. Their financial independence would not be realized until the mid-1970s.

Throughout the entire decade of the 1970s, the momentum toward independence from foreign support gradually grew among the native Baptists. In 1969, while celebrating the eightieth anniversary of the Southern Baptist missions in Japan, the JBC decided to accomplish its financial independence as soon as possible under the watchword "Independence and Cooperation." At the same

---

[16] Japan Baptist Missionary Union, ed., *Baptist Women*, 58.

time, they were aiming at drastic organizational change, consolidating the numbers of existing departments to achieve this goal. Those sections included the departments of youth, men, and women under the Convention's expectation to make them independent bodies of operation.

Among the three departments, the women's department was the most impregnable fortress and refused absolutely to accept the policy change. In order to settle the clash between the two, a special conference was called by the JBC leadership at the end of 1970 with the Convention's vice president, the Chair of the Organizational Reconstruction Committee, along with fifteen female representatives of the local Baptist associations. The last group was led by Akiko Matsumura. In spite of many discussions, the group failed to reach an agreement.

The JBC leadership recognized that Japanese Baptists would never be able to stand on their own feet as long as they kept receiving foreign money, as was the custom. Though the SBC showed its willingness to give them money for direct evangelism and mission, they were unwilling to pay the Convention's running expenses. This position resulted in a shortage in the budget of the JBC. Responding to this difficult situation, the Convention chose a policy to minimize mission programs and reduce the existing departments through a drastic budget cut. This policy change was reasonable and a practical way to deal with the issue.

Since the Women's Department was the largest one among them, the JBC leadership told the women that sufficient financial resources for the women's work were no longer available. Therefore, the best possible option for the women to resolve the problem was to get out of the Convention's organization and to become their own organization again. Akiko Matsumura, who occupied a leadership role in the Women's Department at the time, felt less satisfaction with this reasoning:

> They gave us oh, nice talks, all kinds of talk, and when the men have their own way, having their will really so they talked to us: The real way you can develop the lay movement, the women's movement. And as long as you are depending on men's leadership and the Convention money, you cannot really develop as a lay movement. But the Convention voted on that new organization. But I did not really like it.[17]

The fact was that the women were independent from the beginning, budgeting by themselves and carrying out their mission work by themselves. They

---

[17] Akiko Matsumra, interviewed by Johnni Johnson, Louis McCullough, Elen Libis, Charlie Warren, Bob Shoemake, Ken Lawson, and Floyd North, July 16, 1975, Tokyo, Japan, transcript, 4.

were willing to decide to support the JBC financially. JBC male leaders may have misinterpreted such goodwill and a spirit of cooperation. Perhaps they perceived this as the women depending on men's leadership and JBC money.

A year later the JBC passed a resolution on a new agreement aiming at the Convention's independence from the Southern Baptist Convention in the USA. Based on the resolution, all lay departments of the JBC, including the Women's Department, had to leave and separate from the JBC structure. This decision was made without substantial consent from the women, who expressed their strong request to have their voices reflected in the process.

Hearing the report of the resolution, in disappointment and frustration, the women again got together to discuss for hours how to respond to it. The agreement they finally reached was to separate and start a new organization on their own. Akiko was the major one who led these women to this conclusion and an exciting new adventure.

Interestingly, Akiko had refused earlier to separate the women's work from the JBC. Her basic idea was to develop mutual cooperation between men and women for God's mission on the same ground and with equal status within the same working environment. However, even in the midst of irritations and frustrations caused by the Convention's resolution, she finally came to find a few good things in this new set-up based on her practicality and objectivity. She thought if the organizational separation of the women could be a necessary step for the JBC to have equal status with the missionaries as a team, the women had to welcome their separation.[18]

As stated earlier, equality and independence of women were her lifetime goals. In the first case, it was the issue between men and women, but equality was also needed between the Japanese and the missionaries. Even though situations differed, the point of the matter was the same to Akiko. She renewed her view on the theme of equality and independence, not as a matter of gender difference but a universal matter for the fellow human beings created by God regardless of gender and nationality.

---

[18] Matsumura, interview.

Akiko as a Leader for National and
International Baptist Women

Based on this new recognition, Akiko started tirelessly and vigorously to travel all over Japan and visited local church women's groups to explain the value of the JBC's resolution for the women and encouraged them to separate willingly in order to organize a new women's body outside the Convention structure. In 1973, the Japan Baptist Women's Union was organized as an independent body supported exclusively by membership fees.

Akiko's remarkable and energetic activities, nationally and internationally, started from this time as if she finally found her real place. She was in her late fifties at that time. Though she may have seemed to be a rather slow bloomer for top leadership, her career was colorful, including vice president of the BWA Women's Department, president of the Asian Baptist Women's Union, and the founding president of the Japan Baptist Women's Union.

Nationally, she spared no time or energy in raising the issue of the excellence of Japanese Baptist women in their faith and mission activities. She provided major leadership to develop mission programs, launching the publication of the Japan Baptist Women's Union's monthly journal as a writer and editor, organizing conferences and retreats for leadership training, and carrying out the popular promotion of the Christmas Offering for foreign missions, which originated from the Southern Baptist Lottie Moon Christmas Offering.

The Japan Baptist Women's Union's monthly publication was the ideal opportunity for Akiko to teach the Bible to church women. For nearly ten years after the publication started, Akiko always wrote excellent Bible study lessons for the readers. Since the major task of the Japan Baptist Women's Union was world mission, this publication made a deep impact on interests by providing knowledge not only of related subjects, but also information on current world affairs and human rights issues. This publication was truly the church school for the Baptist women who had difficulties taking time for themselves because of their responsibilities in the church and family. It was through this publication that Baptist women received opportunities to nurture their faith and inspiration for their mission activities. All this could not have been done without Akiko's passion for and dedication to missions, backed by her faithful daily Bible study followed by meditative prayer. The realism and practicality in her leadership style and its strength were actually nurtured by her spiritual discipline through her daily custom.

In 1975, she was elected as one of twelve BWA vice presidents. Even in this great honor, she was quite calm with her presence of mind. She believed this election was not based on her actual capacity as a leader but a recognition of her husband's success in the 1970 Tokyo BWA congress. Rev. Matsumura did not speak English, and Akiko as his wife translated for him when he served as the chairman of the local arrangement committee. Since translation was difficult for both of them and for others, she felt she was chosen for the vice presidency as a tribute to her husband.[19]

Even if this could be true, she was neither discouraged nor disappointed with this election. Instead, she was determined to be a part of the BWA Executive Committee and speak out as a woman and an Asian. Further, she expressed her eagerness to contribute to the global Baptist family as she said, "not as the wife of Shuichi Matsumura, but as Akiko Matsumura."[20] She wanted neither to content herself with the given title of vice president nor to make it just an honor. She wanted to be present as her own self: the one who received the call from God for building the Kingdom of God.

Conclusions

Akiko Matsumura provides an excellent example of a woman who dedicated her life to Christian mission. Yet, she is surely not the only one. There must be some other undiscovered female leadership like her in the history of Japanese Baptists. We as Japanese Baptists, especially Japanese Baptist women, should pay more attention to her life and let posterity know of her contributions as a role model.

It is true that compared to our current point of view she remained relatively conservative and traditional in her theology and her view of womanhood. For instance, she did not seek to make a drastic change in the structure of the church. This can be seen in her criticism of the 1960s women's liberation movement both in the church and in larger society. She thought marriage was the divinely prepared place for her to fulfill her Christian calling, in spite of the risk of losing her privacy and time for herself. However, marriage did not mean that she completely lost her liberty as a woman who was determined to serve the Lord as her own vocation. To her, the assignment was how to be creative in being her own person as she served God under the surrounding limitations. She might have not been a submissive wife, but she was a great partner to her pastor-husband for the sake of missions.

Her way of life resembles the Japanese fringed pink flower called *Nadeshiko*, which we take to express the ideal Japanese womanhood. To us, this little flower

---

[19] Matsumura, 8–9.
[20] Matsumura, 9.

gives the image of women who wear simplicity and dignity and are not easily beaten down, even in a harsh environment, but bloom beautifully in their own ways.

Akiko attempted neither to shake the foundation of the church establishment nor to throw a stone to crack it, although she did not fully accept it as an ideal environment for women. Akiko, however, might have been imagining something more radical and surprisingly unexpected. From the limitation of her place, she might have been looking at the highest peak of mutual and cooperative relationships between male and female, Japanese and non-Japanese as God's co-workers. As the Apostle Paul says, "For we are God's fellow workers." (1 Cor. 3:19; ESV).

When founding the Japan Baptist Women's Union, Baptist women such as Akiko might have been convinced that they were fellow workers with all others, with equal status in the eyes of God regardless of their many differences. Akiko expressed this view in 1978 at an international gathering of Asian Christian women: "We cannot and should not say that some parts of the world are mission fields of particular mission boards. The whole world is the mission field where all Christians, regardless of nationalities and cultural backgrounds, must work together in evangelism."[21]

---

[21] Matsumura, unpublished manuscript of the Keynote Address, "Called to Change: Committed to Serve Along with the Spirit from 12:11," Sixth Asian Christian Women's Conference Assembly, Gotemba, Japan, October 10–15, 1978.

FROM PAGAN PRIESTESSES TO PROTESTANT PASTORS: ROLES OF WOMEN IN EARLY BAPTIST MISSIONS IN WESTERN VISAYAS, PHILIPPINES, 1900–1925[1]

Francis Jr. S. Samdao

For centuries, Filipino women have struggled to find their role in society, but they have found an opportunity to shine through the early Baptist missions. In this essay, I will argue that women in Western Visayas were able to regain something that they lost through Baptist ministry. I contend that women (American Baptist missionaries and Filipinas[2]) contributed major roles in the early Baptist missions in Western Visayas of the Philippines. The main contribution of the Baptist female missionaries was through the methodology of education, which empowered many Visayan women to propagate the Gospel in their homeland.

This essay will reveal the roles of women in the early Baptist missions in Western Visayas between 1900 and 1925. Embedded in this research is the purpose of elucidating a cultural and spiritual "evolution" of Visayan women from pagan priestesses to Protestant pastors. First, I will briefly present the status of women in the Philippines before and during the Spanish domination; then, I will explore the methodology employed by the Baptist women missionaries in reaching Filipinas in Western Visayas as a case study. Lastly, I will present the result of that methodology to the Visayan women.

Filipinas before and during the Spanish Colonization

Western Visayas is comprised of the province of Negros Occidental on Negros Island and the provinces of Aklan, Antique, Capiz, Iloilo, and Guimaras on Panay Island. The land area is about 8,028 square miles.

---

[1] I am grateful to Dr. Stephen Blair Waddell of Providence Baptist Church for his valuable comments and edits on this manuscript.

[2] The term "Filipinas" refers to Filipino women. I will use Filipinas and Filipino women interchangeably.

Babaylan: The Antecedent of Religious Leaders. Women in the Philippines were highly esteemed compared to other Asian women. For example, the Mangyan people in Mindoro perceived women as equal to men. In the Cordillera region of Luzon Island, it was not unusual for women to provide spiritual leadership or direction for the tribe.[3] The lone exceptions were those from the Moro and the Negrito tribes.[4] Nonetheless, author Juana Jimenez Pelmoka argues, "An authentic and unimpeachable culture that foreshadowed a Christian principle is the Filipino man's high view of woman."[5] Before the Spanish ascendancy, Filipinas had the right to take part in businesses and even govern as the chief of a barangay or a village.[6] In the area of religion and culture, priests were mainly women; they were called *katalonan* (in *Tagalog*) and *babaylan* (in *Visayan*).[7]

The *babaylan* was knowledgeable in astrology and agricultural matters. Therefore, she led the rituals within a village and determined the sacred time such as the perfect season to plant, to harvest, and to rest.[8] The *babaylan's* role in the areas of medicine, religion, and culture made her one of the significant specialists in the ancient Philippine civilization.[9]

The invasion of the Spanish jettisoned the cultures of the Filipino people. The colonizers' imposition of their culture and religion demeaned women from their roles in society.[10] Filipinas were stripped of their status, abased, and became

---

[3] Lilia Quindoza Santiago, *Sexuality and the Filipina* (Quezon City, Philippines: The University of the Philippines Press, 2007), 8–13.

[4] Hamilton Wright, *A Handbook of the Philippines*, 3rd ed. (Chicago: McClurg, 1909), 53–54.

[5] Juana Jimenez Pelmoka, *Pre-Spanish Philippines* (Caloocan City, Philippines: J. J. de Pelmoka, E.P. Ujano, 1996), 122.

[6] Gregorio F. Zaide, *Philippine Political and Cultural History*, vol. 1, *The Philippines Since Pre-Spanish Times* (Manila: Philippine Education Company, 1949), 54.

[7] Arthur Leonard Tuggy and Ralph Toliver, *Seeing the Church in the Philippines* (Manila: OMF Publishers, 1972), 7.

[8] Mylene D. Hega, Veronica C. Alporha, and Meggan S. Evangelista, *Feminism and the Women's Movement in the Philippines: Struggles, Advances, and Challenges* (Manila: Friedrich Ebert Stiftung, 2017), 1.

[9] Proserpina Tapales, "The Babaylan in Philippine History," in *Women's Role in the Philippine History: Selected Essays*, 2nd ed. (Quezon City, Philippines: University Center for Women's Studies, 1996), 213.

[10] Myrna S. Feliciano, "The Filipina: A Historical Legal Perspective," in *Women's Role in the Philippine History: Selected Essays*, 2nd ed. (Quezon City, Philippines: University Center for Women's Studies, 1996), 24.

completely subservient to men. As a result, many of these women priests withdrew from the community and led some revolutions.[11]

The Birth of Baptists in the Philippines

On May 1, 1898, Commodore George Dewey defeated Admiral Patricio Montojo by sinking the Spanish vessels in Manila Bay, which subsequently started to end the control Spain had over the Philippines.[12] Months later, Protestants from America came to evangelize the country.[13] At that time, a native from the province of Aklan in Western Visayas, Braulio Manikan,[14] considered to be the first Visayan Baptist, was converted in Spain under the supervision of Rev. Eric Lund,[15] a Swedish Baptist of the American Baptist Missionary Union (ABMU).[16] The latter worked with this Filipino convert in translating the Gospels, other New Testament books, and a few Christian tracts into the Visayan language.[17]

Charles W. Briggs, one of the earliest Baptist missionaries in Panay and Negros from 1900 to 1910,[18] stated in his letters that the mission work in Visayas

---

[11] Zeus Salazar, "Ang Babaylan sa Kasaysayan ng Pilipinas," in *Women's Role in the Philippine History: Selected Essays*, 2nd ed. (Quezon City, Philippines: University Center for Women's Studies, 1996), 62.

[12] Daniel Trowbridge Mallett, *What Dewey Did: A Brief History of the Hero of Manila* (New York: D. T. Mallett, 1899), 36.

[13] Arthur Judson Brown, *The New Era in the Philippines* (New York: Fleming H. Revell Company, 1903), 173.

[14] Francis Neil G. Jalando-on, *A History of Philippine Baptist Pastors 1898–2002* (Iloilo City, Philippines: REMS, 2003), 77.

[15] Jean Uy Uayan, *A Study of the Emergence and Early Development of Selected Protestant Churches in the Philippines* (UK: Langham Monographs, 2017), 241. The ABMU stated that Lund was in America during the Spanish-American War and that Manikan was converted when he met a Baptist anthropologist, Mr. Armstrong, who taught him the Bible comprehensively. American Baptist Missionary Union, *Missions in the Philippines* (Boston: American Baptist Missionary Union, between 1906 and 1911), 13.

[16] In 1910, the ABMU changed its name to American Baptist Foreign Mission Society (ABFMS). Nestor Distor Bunda, *A Mission History of the Philippine Baptist Churches 1898–1998 from a Philippine Perspective* (Aachen: Verlag an der Lottbek im Besitz des Verlags Mainz, 1999), 88.

[17] Edmund F. Merriam, *A History of American Baptist Missions* (Philadelphia: American Baptist Publication Society, 1900), 180–81.

[18] Charles W. Briggs, *The Progressing Philippines* (Philadelphia: The Griffith and Rowland Press, 1913), 1.

was like a repetition of the book of Acts where the downtrodden welcomed the Gospel. Further, many of them were potential preachers.[19] The challenge was a lack of workers,[20] for there were more than one million people in Western Visayas, particularly in Iloilo, Capiz, and Bacolod.[21] During the annual meeting of the Northern Baptist Convention in 1919, it was noted in the convention minutes that there were only seventy-one Baptist missionaries in the Philippines.[22]

Women in the Early Baptist Missions in Western Visayas

Missionary wives were paramount in the success of missions because they could model for the people the Christian family—not to mention that in many Filipino societies, only females can work with children and women at home.[23] There were also exemplary single females. The ABMU noted some single women missionaries from 1900 to 1906: Miss A. V. Johnson, Miss L. B. Kuhlen, and Miss Celia Sainz. These women were good models in doing ministry outside the home. Although few in numbers, married and single women missionaries had an enormous impact in reaching the natives.[24]

In the early years of Baptist missions, women were foundational in establishing institutions that served as vehicles in reaching Filipinas and children in Western Visayas. The missiological strategy was to implement a "women ministering with women" paradigm. The American women ministered to Filipinas in a way that men could not achieve.[25] They were even more successful than men in evangelizing in villages. Mrs. Briggs, for example, laboriously cared for women

---

[19] American Baptist Missionary Union, "The Philippine Opportunity," *The Baptist Missionary Magazine*, vol. 87, June 1902, 164.

[20] Charles W. Briggs, *Harvest Time among the Filipino Peasants* (Boston: American Baptist Missionary Union, 1905), 4.

[21] Homer C. Stuntz, *The Philippines and the Far East* (Cincinnati: Jennings and Pye, 1904), 462–63.

[22] American Baptist Convention, *Annual of the Northern Baptist Convention 1919* (Philadelphia: American Baptist Publication Society, 1919), 78.

[23] Ann Kay Windus, "The Roles and Identity of Missionary Women: A Pilot Study," (PhD diss., The Southern Baptist Theological Seminary, 1999), 19.

[24] See American Baptist Missionary Union, *Missions in the Philippines*, 42.

[25] Laura R. Prieto "'New Women,' American Imperialism, and Filipina Nationalism: The Politics of Dress in Philippine Mission Stations, 1898–1940," in *Women in Transnational History: Connecting the Local and the Global*, ed. Clare Midgley, Alison Twells, and Julie Carlier (New York: Routledge, 2016), 78.

and children in Iloilo.[26] Miss Caroline M. Bissinger, after her successful teaching career as a graduate of the Chicago Training School, was particularly sent to the Philippines because she was a convert from Roman Catholicism.[27] With that, she was very effective in ministering to the Filipinas of the upper classes.[28]

Miss Anna V. Johnson was also aware that women were vital in the accomplishment of missionary endeavors in Western Visayas. She asserted that the key to successful missions in the country was to minister to Filipinas since when they were converted they could become faithful propagators of the Gospel.[29] During the annual convention in 1914, the Woman's Baptist Foreign Missionary Society of the West put to record the argument of Johnson: "If we get the women, we get the Philippine Islands."[30] Melba Maggay, a Filipina writer and anthropologist, confirms that the American missionaries saw the potential of women in the proliferation of the Gospel since they labored to share their newfound faith with their family, neighbors, and to remote places.[31]

Education for Women

A mistake of the Spanish friars was neglecting education.[32] When the early Baptist missionaries arrived in Western Visayas, they emphasized the vitality of education because they believed that it was for the good of the church and of the people to whom they were ministering.[33] There were at least three important places in Western Visayas that women ministered fruitfully using that strategy: Iloilo, Capiz, and Bacolod.

---

[26] American Baptist Missionary Union, *Ninety-Second Annual Report* (Boston: The Fort Hill Press, 1906), 371.

[27] American Baptist Missionary Union, "Our Newly-Appointed Workers," *The Baptist Missionary Magazine*, vol. 88, November 1907, 450.

[28] Helen Barrett Montgomery, *Following the Sunrise: A Century of Baptist Missions, 1813–1913* (Philadelphia: American Baptist Publication Society, 1913), 267.

[29] American Baptist Convention, *Annual of the Northern Baptist Convention 1915* (Los Angeles: Annual of the Northern Baptist Convention, 1915), 952.

[30] American Baptist Convention, *Annual of the Northern Baptist Convention 1914* (Boston: Annual of the Northern Baptist Convention, 1914), 597.

[31] Melba Padilla Maggay, *A Clash of Cultures: Early American Protestant Missions and Filipino Religious Consciousness* (Manila: Anvil, 2011), 55.

[32] George Waldo Browne, *Pearl of the Orient: The Philippine Islands* (Boston: Dana Estes & Company, 1900), 112.

[33] Arthur Tuggy, *The Philippine Church: Growth in a Changing Society* (Grand Rapids, MI: William B. Eerdmans Publishing Company, 1971), 112–13.

The earliest college started by Baptist missionaries was the Jaro Industrial School in Iloilo in 1905; within seven years, they admitted female students.[34] The name of the school was changed to Central Philippine College in 1922,[35] which is known today as Central Philippine University (CPU). It continues to train evangelists, pastors, and church leaders under its school of theology.[36] The Philippine Mission Conference at Jaro, held December 9–18, 1908, recorded that establishing schools for girls in Iloilo was the most important priority.[37] Caroline M. Bissinger served as Principal, and Miss Alice M. Stanard worked as an associate in the Academy for Girls in Iloilo.[38]

Dr. and Mrs. Lerrigo started the mission work in Capiz in 1903. They founded a school in their home in 1906 and, four years later, the charge was given to Miss Margaret Suman, who took care of seventy-five children.[39] The ministry in Capiz continued because of women like Anna Johnson and Celia Sainz.[40]

In Bacolod, the early missionaries were Rev. and Mrs. A. Archibald Forshee, Rev. and Mrs. C. L. Maxfield, and Miss L. B. Kuhlen. They realized that Bacolod was a very strategic urban place because it was a center of provincial high school for the whole of Western Negros. Therefore, Forshee started a dormitory for students to whom they could teach the Scripture.[41] Soon, the ABMU built a dormitory designated for young women, which was headed by Miss Kuhlen. Because of the good result of the dormitory ministry in Bacolod, particularly in reaching high school students, the ABMU labored to see the completion of a training school for young women at Jaro, which led to Visayan women doing ministry.[42]

---

[34] Central Philippine University, "Brief History," https://cpu.edu.ph/about-us/history/, accessed November 29, 2020.

[35] Robert G. Torbet, *Venture of Faith: The Story of the American Baptist Foreign Mission Society and the Woman's American Baptist Foreign Mission Society 1814–1954* (Philadelphia: The Judson Press, 1955), 556.

[36] Catalino P. Pamplona, *Baptist History for Church Leaders* (Manila: Church Strengthening Ministry, 1992), 302.

[37] Thomas Seymour Barbour, *A Visit to Mission Conferences in Japan, China and the Philippine Islands* (Boston: American Baptist Missionary Union, 1908), 89, 92. Jaro is located in Iloilo City in Panay Island.

[38] Torbet, *Venture of Faith*, 356.

[39] Torbet, 356.

[40] American Baptist Missionary Union, *Missions in the Philippines*, 27.

[41] American Baptist Missionary Union, 31.

[42] American Baptist Missionary Union, "Our War in the Philippines," *The Baptist*

Education by Women

Celia Sainz helped in organizing a school in her home to minister to children. This ministry was pivotal since it brought more opportunities to reach the relatives of these kids. Later, Sainz and others taught women home industry like domestic skills in caring for the home. This school at home became the Filamer Christian College known today as Filamer Christian University.[43] In 1906, Miss Margaret Suman took charge of this school for children, and the girls under her care who became Christians helped in the mission work.[44] Some of the women educated under Suman went to Jaro to be trained as Bible women.[45]

Miss Johnson, one of the very significant female missionaries who helped with the evangelization effort in Western Visayas, championed the Bible women in her twenty-five-year career. She spent most of her life ministering to women and girls at Jaro and other surrounding districts.[46] As early as 1904, she started to teach women about the Scripture in her home. The success of the ministry developed an initial plan to start a school for young women.[47] A year later, on October 20, she founded the Baptist Missionary Training School for women (BMTS).[48] To be prepared for evangelistic work, Filipinas at Jaro learned specific courses like church history, exegesis, and theology. While engaging in rigorous studies, these Bible women also took pride in evangelizing the neighboring villages.[49]

Missionary Magazine, vol. 88, July 1908, 288.

[43] Bunda, *A Mission History*, 130, 133.

[44] American Baptist Missionary Union, *Missions in the Philippines*, 29. See American Baptist Convention, *Annual of the Northern Baptist Convention 1923* (Philadelphia: The American Baptist Publication Society, 1923), 654.

[45] American Baptist Convention, *Annual of the Northern Baptist Convention 1915*, 953. A Bible woman refers to a woman minister who leads a Bible study, teaches, and does evangelistic work. Today, the Convention of Philippine Baptist Churches recognizes women pastors. Most Southern Baptist churches today in the Philippines are still using that nomenclature.

[46] American Baptist Missionary Union, *Missions in the Philippines*, 23.

[47] American Baptist Missionary Union, *Ninety-First Annual Report* (Boston: American Baptist Missionary Union, 1905), 323.

[48] Francis Neil G. Jalando-on, "Anna V. Johnson and the 'Bible Women,'" *Central Philippine University* website, April 12, 2019, https://cpu.edu.ph/news/anna-v-johnson-and-the-bible-women/?fbclid=.

[49] American Baptist Convention, *Annual of Northern Baptist Convention 1916* (Philadelphia: American Baptist Publication Society, 1916), 603.

Johnson loved her students, so she learned to adapt to some of the Filipino women's culture; during their graduation in 1916, she was seen wearing the same native gown along with the seven Filipina graduates.[50] It was a strategy to reach the Visayan women. Nine years after she died in 1930, Johnson Hall was constructed, and then restored in 1950 after the war, to honor her passion for educating women ministers theologically. Johnson Hall was specifically used to teach the course Bible 101, which was later changed to Religion and Ethics. The BMTS was then merged to CPU and became Women's Division of the College of Theology in line with her vision of theological education for women pastors.[51]

By 1921, there were schools for children and churches established in Capiz. There were also dormitories for young women in Bacolod. In Iloilo, the Bible Mission Training School at Jaro was established. Also, the Woman's Society was founded, which later became the Baptist Student Center.[52] Hence, success came from educating the Visayan women. Education by women and education for women would then lead to the rise of the women "pastors."

The Rise of the Bible Women

The American Baptists[53] not only educated the Filipinas, but also allowed them to preach, to distribute Christian literature, to conduct home visitation, to lead Bible study, and to teach Sunday school classes. Further, Maggay claims, "they worked as hard as male Filipino preachers in bringing the Gospel to the people, particularly in far-flung places, where they labored with hardly any remuneration. Known as 'Bible women,' they were often products of Bible training schools set up by women missionaries."[54]

There were also women who taught at BMTS other than Anna Johnson and her group; most were early converts like Miss Gregoria Jaime, the first Filipina "Bible woman."[55] Another important Visayan woman was Miss Simprosa Sobremisana. She was noted as being a "courageous Bible woman" because she fearlessly preached in front of a crowd of outlaws who were suspected of killing people and pillaging. Accordingly, her death in 1910 was described as "a serious

---

[50] Prieto, "New Women," 92.

[51] Jalando-on, "Anna V. Johnson."

[52] Jesse Earl Posey, Jr., "A Historical Study of Baptist Missions in the Philippines 1900–1967" (ThD diss., New Orleans Baptist Theological Seminary, 1968), 52.

[53] This refers to Northern Baptists.

[54] Maggay, *A Clash of Cultures,* 55.

[55] Jalando-on, "Anna V. Johnson."

loss," for she was "a valued helper in the school and one of the earliest converts in the mission."[56]

At BMTS, women were trained for six months, and the rest of the year was spent in the field with other missionaries. These Bible women at BMTS were in demand as evangelists in Western Visayas.[57] In 1917, a Filipina in Capiz named Listina Alabi founded a kindergarten that became a springboard to reach not only children but also their relatives.[58] She planted a church after graduating from BMTS and is therefore remembered as a "woman church planter."[59]

These Bible women graduates of BMTS gained valuable experience by visiting hundreds of homes, ministering to children in the market, and leading eleven Sunday schools with approximately 512 enrollees.[60] During the annual meeting of the Northern Baptist Convention in 1916, the American Baptist Foreign Mission Society recognized the usefulness of these Bible women.[61]

As early as 1901, thirty to fifty women who attended Sunday and midweek services engaged themselves in the ministry in Bacolod.[62] It became, therefore, a paradigm for American missionaries to start a women's class and then pass it on to the Filipinas. These Bible women, single or married, took the vital roles as teachers, deaconesses, and evangelists.[63] From 1908 to 1914, BMTS trained 229 Filipino Bible women.[64] Helen Barrett Montgomery (1861–1934) claims: "One of these trained women, a widow of forty-five (a great-grandmother, by the way), has a Bible class of sixty men in a church of five hundred members."[65] The assiduous works of these Filipino Bible women contributed to the expansion of the Gospel in Western Visayas, and they were trained earlier than men in 1904.[66]

During the twenty-fifth anniversary of Baptist missions in the Philippines in 1925, three Baptist headquarters were strongly established in Western Visayas:

---

[56] Jalando-on, "Anna V. Johnson."

[57] American Baptist Convention, *Annual of the Northern Baptist Convention 1915*, 952.

[58] Bunda, *A Mission History*, 131.

[59] Nestor D. Bunda, Francis Neil G. Jalando-on, and Jerson B. Narciso, eds., *Revisiting Faith Resources* (Iloilo City, Philippines: Halad Prints Collective, 2002), 24.

[60] American Baptist Convention, *Annual of the Northern Baptist Convention 1915*, 952.

[61] American Baptist Convention, *Annual of Northern Baptist Convention 1916*, 603.

[62] Bunda, *A Mission History*, 128.

[63] Laura Prieto, "Bibles, Baseball and Butterfly Sleeves: Filipina Women and American Protestant Missions, 1900–1930," in *Divine Domesticities: Christian Paradoxes in Asia and Pacific*, ed. Hyaeweol Choi and Margaret Jolly (Australia: ANU Press, 2014), 378.

[64] Bunda, Jalando-on, and Narciso, *Revisiting Faith Resources*, 23.

[65] Montgomery, *Following the Sunrise*, 267.

[66] Jalando-on, *A History of Philippine Baptist Pastors*, 61.

Bacolod City in Negros Occidental, the province of Capiz, and Iloilo City in Panay Island. There were about 232 Filipino and Filipina workers. The mission work produced eighty-six churches having 5,581 members. The missionaries established twenty-three schools having 1,875 pupils, four dormitories for students, and two hospitals. At Central Philippine College, there were more than four hundred students. In Bacolod, there were 1,200 baptisms in just a single year.[67] Indeed, the first quarter of a century of mission work was very fruitful, and the Gospel had been preached to most of the towns in Western Visayas.[68] In honor of the ministry efforts of the women Baptist missionaries and the Filipinas in Western Visayas, the Woman's American Baptist Foreign Mission Society ended its report during the annual meeting of the Northern Baptist Convention in 1915 with these words, "Blessed are the women who fill the gaps!"[69]

In 1980, the Convention of Philippine Baptist Churches ordained its first Filipino woman, Rev. Angelina Belluga Buensuceso, who ministered in the Visayas. She served as a pastor in five Baptist churches and a professor at Central Philippine University in Iloilo.[70] Today, it is common for the Convention of Philippine Baptist Churches to ordain women ministers.

Conclusion

In general, women were not considered to hold inferior status to men during the pre-colonial era of the Philippines, but they were suppressed during the Spanish settlement. The coming of the Baptist missionaries in Western Visayas marked a very critical period for Filipinas in that region. They were able to slowly regain the status they lost during the Spanish colonization. The roles of women in the early Baptist missions in Western Visayas from 1900 to 1925 were linked to education that included studying the Scripture, preaching, visitation, establishing dormitories for high school classes, teaching young Filipinas, etc. Education for women and education by women were inextricably vital in propagating Baptist beliefs. From the viewpoint of the Filipinas, the opportunity to become Bible

---

[67] Torbet, *Venture of Faith*, 556.

[68] Domingo J. Diel, Jr., "Perspectives on Baptist Church History," in *Chapters in Philippine Church History*, ed. Anne C. Kwantes (Manila: OMF, 2001), 231.

[69] American Baptist Convention, *Annual of the Northern Baptist Convention 1915*, 953.

[70] Michael E. Williams, Sr. and Walter B. Shurden, eds., *Turning Points in Baptist History: A Festschrift in Honor of Harry Leon McBeth* (Macon: Mercer University Press, 2008), 282.

women signified an advantageous change from being merely subservient to men into being catalysts for the Gospel.[71]

Today, in the Philippines, it is increasingly ubiquitous that Baptist women carry major responsibilities and important roles in the Christian community through teaching in seminaries or Bible schools, participating in mission work, leading small groups, speaking in seminars, witnessing, etc.[72] The metamorphosis that transpired from pagan priestesses to Protestant pastors presents a strong message that Filipino women make important contributions to the body of Christ.

---

[71] Prieto, "Bibles, Baseball and Butterfly Sleeves," 370.

[72] Woman's Missionary Union of the Philippines, *Philippine Baptist Women's Manual* (Makati, Philippines: Woman's Missionary Union of the Philippines, 1980), 22–23.

MARY CRAWFORD AND THE GENDERED LEGACY OF THE SHANTUNG REVIVAL, 1927–1937

C. Douglas Weaver

On January 28, 1922, thirty-four-year-old Mary Katherine Crawford (1888–1979) of Atlanta, Georgia, applied to be a student volunteer with the Foreign Mission Board (FMB) of the Southern Baptist Convention (SBC). At the time she was a student at the Woman's Missionary Union (WMU) Training School in Louisville, expecting to graduate in May 1922. She had completed her junior year at Bessie Tift College in Forsyth, Georgia, and one summer term at Columbia University. Crawford was a Georgia native and a member of Druid Hills Baptist Church in Atlanta. Having done "practical field work" in Louisville, she hoped to do evangelistic or pioneer educational work in Argentina or some other South American country. She had nine years of experience teaching in the Atlanta public schools and two years in rural Georgia schools.

Mary Crawford: Becoming a Missionary

The application form to be a female missionary in the SBC was a fascinating example of gender expectations. The woman was asked if she was in debt, whether she slept well, and if she could follow the decision of a majority. If she was not married, was she contemplating marriage? Crawford said no, and she remained single her whole life. Crawford exercised regularly, she told the FMB, since she had taught physical training. To the question, do you acquire languages readily, the spunky candidate responded, "I cannot tell you until I make the effort." Crawford was asked if she played the piano or organ. She said "not well." Asked if she could teach them, she said, "if forced to, yes." Crawford had taught sight-singing in public schools but did not want to do that anywhere else. In terms of her spirituality, she said she had taught Sunday School and her evangelistic efforts led to the conversion of four intermediate boys, but her prayer life and devotional reading of the Bible was "not as good as it ought to be." The FMB asked if she smoked or drank, and she easily said no. They also asked if she had a Christian family background where the family said grace at meals; here she said yes, noting that she had been calmly converted at age eleven. She desired to be a missionary because she considered it to be the "greatest investment for a human life." An elderly Sunday School teacher and an agnostic professor at

Columbia University who pushed her to defend her faith had been the most influential in her call to missions. In words that many contemporary Southern Baptists consider doctrinally askew regarding the role of women in the church, Crawford testified that her primary goal in being a missionary was to "preach the gospel." Such is a picture of a missionary candidate for Southern Baptist missions.[1]

Mary Crawford, not to be confused with the more well-known missionary couple Martha and T. P. Crawford, served as part of the North China Southern Baptist Mission from 1922 to 1941. Because of World War II, Crawford was on furlough stateside until 1947 and then left China in 1949. Begging for another place to serve, Crawford taught at a Baptist academy for children from 1951 to 1954 in Hawaii before retiring.[2] Her life as a missionary would most likely be lost, and given the absence of her name in accounts of Baptist history, is lost, except for those who are aware of her account of the Shantung Revival of the late 1920s and 1930s. Crawford's primary source account of the revival is indispensable for understanding the revival's role in the story of Baptist missions[3] as well as indigenous Christian work in North China.[4] Studying the revival through the lens of Crawford's legacy points to larger concerns: how Baptists ultimately

---

[1] Mary Crawford, Student Volunteer for Work under Foreign Mission Board, SBC (1922). Mary Crawford, Application for Appointment as Missionary, Foreign Mission Board, SBC (1922).

[2] Mary Crawford, "The Call to Foreign Missions" form (1961).

[3] For a discussion of Baptist involvement in the Shantung Revival, see Wesley L. Handy, "An Historical Analysis of the North China Mission (SBC) and Keswick Sanctification in the Shandong Revival, 1927–1937" (PhD diss., Southeastern Baptist Theological Seminary, 2012). Participants in the revival referred to it as the Shantung Revival, and I have kept that language. The region of Shantung is known as Shandong and most current literature reflects that terminology. Hardy has good coverage of several Baptist participants in the revival (e.g., C. L. Culpepper, John Abernathy, and Bonnie Ray). He used Crawford's 1932 account as a source but did not focus on her role in the revival nor deal with her legacy. Non-Baptist sources like Marie Monsen, *The Awakening: Revival in China, A Work of the Holy Spirit* (China Inland Mission, 1959), briefly cite Crawford's *The Shantung Revival*.

[4] Baptists acknowledged the indigenous component of the Shantung Revival but highlighted the role of missionaries. Hardy's study better acknowledges the role of indigenous leadership while focusing on the Baptist contribution. Lian Xi strongly argues that the revival was an indigenous Chinese revival. See Lian Xi, *Redeemed by Fire: The Rise of Popular Christianity in Modern China* (New Haven: Yale University Press, 2010). See also "Indigenous Revivals in Shantung," *The Chinese Recorder* 52, no. 12 (December 1931): 767–72.

diminished the role of pentecostal practices that emphasized the miraculous in Baptist missions history and how they gendered the revival's narrative, which distorted the role of women in missionary ministry.

Shantung Revival: Beginnings

In 1927, political unrest from the Nationalist Revolution led by Chiang Kai-shek wracked the Shantung Province (now Shandong) in eastern China. Two dozen Baptist missionaries were stationed there as part of the North China Mission. They were temporarily evacuated to the port city of Chefoo. The holiness teaching of a Norwegian Lutheran missionary from Norway, Marie Monsen, augmented the group's prayer sessions. When Charles Culpepper, president of the North China Baptist Theological Seminary, asked Monsen about prayer for his wife Ola's eye condition, the missionary replied, "Brother Culpepper, have you been filled with the Holy Spirit?" That evening the Culpeppers read James 5 on prayer and healing, and the next morning, Monsen prayed for Ola's healing. Not only was Ola healed, Culpepper testified, Chinese cooks that were present were saved. Southern Baptists consider Ola Culpepper's healing to be the trigger event of a miraculous revival that occurred soon afterward when the missionaries were able to return to Shantung. According to reports, missionaries received the baptism of the Holy Spirit and hundreds of Chinese natives were converted, filled with the Holy Spirit, and miraculously healed of illnesses.[5]

In 1933, Mary Crawford published an account of the Shantung Revival.[6] While the revival was ongoing and lasted until 1937, Crawford became the editor and compiler of unsigned missionary letters describing events both missionaries and Chinese converts considered a miracle. Crawford's editorial comments as a revival participant, though often brief, testified to the letters' value and authenticity and how she made the revival narrative her own. In private correspondence to Charles Maddry, the executive-secretary of the FMB, she enthusiastically affirmed the revival as a "great work of the Holy Spirit" and asked if the Sunday School Board of the SBC would publish her book because it described a Southern Baptist revival. Crawford thought her account would help produce revival in America and help overcome the crushing debt of the Great Depression. When Maddry said financial concerns were too pressing to publish, Crawford found a

---

[5] C. L. Culpepper, *The Shantung Revival* (Dallas: Crescendo Publications, 1971), 7, 12–13.

[6] Mary K. Crawford, *The Shantung Revival* (Shanghai: China Baptist Publication Society, 1934).

different publisher, the China Baptist Publication Society, and a second printing by an individual in Louisiana spread the story among Southern Baptists.[7]

Shantung Revival: Keswick Holiness

While she never used the identifier, Crawford was a Keswick-influenced holiness Baptist. Keswick advocates—named after the phase of the Holiness Movement which began in Keswick, England in 1875—affirmed a need of a distinct, post-conversion religious experience to receive the empowerment of the Holy Spirit for witnessing and service. The empowering experience, usually called the baptism or filling of the Holy Spirit, enabled believers to experience the "deeper life" or the "victorious life" through full surrender to Christ.

Crawford emphasized the necessity of personal conversion—a typical Baptist identity marker—but in Keswick terms, desired the power of the Holy Spirit for evangelism and the salvation of Chinese souls. She highlighted the primary influence of the Keswick teaching of Marie Monsen, the Norwegian Lutheran missionary with a reputation of being soft-spoken but who preached confrontational, direct messages that required each person who already claimed to be Christian to ask him or herself if they were really born again. In Keswick fashion, a genuine believer had to confess each and every sin to be confident of salvation. According to Crawford, some gatherings of public confession lasted five or six hours with such widespread Spirit-led questioning. Unsurprisingly, many Christians decided they had previously been converted, in the missionaries' words, to Christianity rather than Christ. In the revival, believers were urged to demonstrate full surrender to Christ to secure the victorious life—the goal of full salvation for Keswick holiness theology.[8]

The best contemporary descriptor of Mary Crawford is bapticostal, someone who practices pentecostal experiences of faith. The less anachronistic accurate identifier is that of radical holiness evangelical. In the late nineteenth century and early twentieth century, radical holiness evangelicals, which included

---

[7] Mary Crawford, letter to Charles Maddry (March 15, 1932). Mary Crawford, letter to Charles Maddry (December 10, 1932). Charles Maddry, letter to Mary Crawford (April 10, 1933). All letters and missionary biographical forms of Mary Crawford are from the archives of the International Mission Board of the Southern Baptist Convention.

[8] Crawford, *Shantung Revival*, 27, 41, 66. For more on Baptists and Keswick holiness, see C. Douglas Weaver, *Baptists and the Holy Spirit: The Contested History with the Holiness-Pentecostal-Charismatic Traditions* (Waco: Baylor University Press, 2019), 4–5, 25–29, 259–79.

Baptists like A. J. Gordon and John Q. Adams, affirmed a fourfold gospel of personal conversion, a second experience of grace after conversion called the baptism of the Holy Spirit, the affirmation that miraculous divine healings were not confined to biblical times but were still available today, and an expectation of an imminent second coming of Jesus Christ. In radical holiness terms, this fourfold gospel was called full salvation, a phrase that is found in Crawford's letters. The ups and downs of sin which holiness believers and Crawford called a "Romans chapter 7" lifestyle had finally been defeated and replaced with a victorious life.[9]

Shantung Revival: Pentecostal Practices

Baptists had long spoken in restorationist terms, meaning they thought they embodied primitive New Testament faith with their insistence on believer's baptism by immersion and focus on the church as a local body with congregational polity led by pastors rather than bishops.[10] Radical holiness evangelicals anchored their restoration of full salvation with a Holy Spirit baptism signaled by an enduement of power to evangelize. When Pentecostals were born at the turn of the twentieth century, they asserted that they were the most developed and thus only authentic restorationists with their full gospel which practiced the miraculous gifts found in the book of Acts like divine healing and experiencing visions. As Pentecostals, they received the baptism of the Holy Spirit via speaking in tongues as they interpreted the book of Acts, especially Acts chapter two. These competing Baptist, radical holiness evangelical, and Pentecostal visions of restorationism intersected and took on another level with the Crawford reporting of the Shantung Revival.

Crawford's account included numerous references to the baptism in the Holy Spirit as a second experience of grace. One letter said the revival was "like the story in the book of Acts."[11] One school had over one hundred students and teachers experience the Spirit baptism. At least twenty-four missionaries from 1930 to 1932, including Crawford, claimed the experience of the Spirit's indwelling for abiding peace and power to evangelize.[12] All the faculty of the North

---

[9] Crawford, *Shantung Revival*, 43. For more on the holiness theology of John Q. Adams and A. J. Gordon, see Weaver, *Baptists and the Holy Spirit*, 9–13, 21–29. Radical holiness advocates often described the lack of holiness in the language of Romans 7:19, NIV, "I do not do the good I want to do, but the evil I do not want to do—this I keep on doing."

[10] For Baptists and restorationism, see C. Douglas Weaver, *In Search of the New Testament Church: The Baptist Story* (Macon: Mercer University Press, 2008).

[11] Crawford, *Shantung Revival*, 39–40, 45, 66. Quotation on p. 66.

[12] Crawford, 23.

China Baptist Theological Seminary and Bible School claimed the experience of Holy Spirit baptism. Just as radical holiness evangelicals and Pentecostals utilized the language of Pentecost to describe this post-conversion experience, Crawford did the same. At the conclusion of her book, Crawford blurted out a final plea, "O friends, let us turn back to Pentecost." She told her readers there was no fear in the word Pentecost; the baptism of the Holy Spirit was biblical and needed to be experienced. If there was doubt, she shared her experience of receiving the Spirit baptism, "O the peace and joy that filled my soul. My heart was filled with joy and ecstasy for weeks. Not that ecstasy is the thing we plead for; it is the power from on high, the Holy Spirit who is power, even the Baptism with the Holy Spirit."[13]

Beyond experiences of Spirit baptism, the Shantung Revival was filled with stories of healings, despite the claim that healing was not the focus of the revival. Revival participants affirmed Hebrews 13:8 (NIV) "Jesus Christ the same yesterday, today and forever," the go-to verse for holiness and Pentecostal advocates of the restoration of belief in healing, along with James 5, healing via the practice of the prayer of faith and anointed oil.[14] Readers who had concerns about divine healing, Crawford exhorted, needed to read Baptist holiness advocate A. J. Gordon on the reality of miraculous healings in the modern age to calm their anxiety.[15] Many testimonies included accounts of demon exorcisms and tied them to miracles of healing. Conservative Baptists of the twentieth century had no hesitation in speaking of the reality of Satan but rarely, if ever, actually performed demon exorcisms.[16] In the Shantung Revival, missionaries testified to witnessing demon exorcisms, another restoration of apostolic practice.[17]

Crawford's affirmation of a pentecostalization of the faith found expression in other elements of full salvation. Letters affirmed that the experience of the Spirit could feel like electric currents, a well-worn image in radical evangelical and pentecostal literature.[18] Accounts of believers falling to the ground in ecstatic

---

[13] Crawford, 54, 55, 105.

[14] Crawford, *Shantung Revival,* 36, 42, 56, 86, 100.

[15] See A. J. Gordon, *The Ministry of Healing or Miracles of Cure in All Ages* (New York: Fleming H. Revell Company, 1882).

[16] See for example, how conservative Baptists spoke of Pentecostal evangelist, Aimee Semple McPherson. They described "McPhersonism" as a code word for Pentecostalism as a Satanic religion. Weaver, *Baptists and the Holy Spirit,* 172–82.

[17] Crawford, *Shantung Revival,* 27, 48, 87–88.

[18] Crawford, 47. For one popular example of the language of electricity, Martin Wells Knapp, *Lightning Bolts from Pentecostal Skies* (Cincinnati, OH: The Revivalist, c. 1898).

obedience to the Spirit (known as being "slain in the Spirit") were common. This phenomenon, perhaps the most demonstrable Spirit-led experience in the holiness-pentecostal tradition and later the charismatic story of the latter twentieth century, astounded Crawford and friends, but they never denied its validity.[19] Revival participants even testified to holy laughter, an extraordinary manifestation—described as a laughter unlike any kind of human laughter—that sometimes accompanies being slain in the Spirit.[20]

Crawford included letters that attempted to soothe Baptist readers back in the States that missionaries and Chinese believers had not become full-fledged Pentecostals in China.[21] Since Marie Monsen was so quiet and calm, surely the revival was divinely inspired rather than a human-initiated, manufactured experience. One letter assured readers excessive emotion had not been artificially created since there were no special altar calls and singing was of such poor quality in worship services. While services included experiences of being slain in the Spirit, the letters insisted that they were not characterized by ecstatic frenzy. Rather, worship had "the least taint of sensationalism."[22] In one case, the Holy Spirit baptism was experienced when a believer was alone just reading the Bible.[23] Crawford's letters included experiences that no doubt referenced speaking in tongues, but they were never identified as such even though private correspondence confirmed the practice.[24] Crawford herself was accused of speaking in tongues, but denied doing so.[25] To calm fear, Crawford affirmed that while Pentecostals tarried for the Holy Spirit, Shantung Baptists just received the Spirit.[26]

Missionary letters also affirmed the experience of visions and dreams but attempted to soften their impact. Visions sometimes predicted an imminent return of Christ, a marker of the pentecostal full gospel, or focused on salvation,

---

[19] Crawford, *Shantung Revival*, 30, 41, 62–63.

[20] Crawford, 43, 48.

[21] Crawford, 54–55.

[22] Crawford, 8, 22. Quotation on p. 8.

[23] Crawford, 49.

[24] Crawford, 47. Charles Maddry, letter to Mary Crawford (January 3, 1934).

[25] One letter describing the revival to Southern Baptists mentioned Crawford having an experience that could have been speaking in tongues, but it was not described as such. Missionary W. B. Glass said in one of his revival services that Crawford "stood up, stretching out her arms toward heaven and seemed to be transfigured. Her lips were moving, but her voice was not audible to me, for everyone was praying, some in a very loud voice." W. B. Gloss (Glass), "A Remarkable Revival in Shantung," *Home and Foreign Fields* (May 1932): 15–16.

[26] Crawford, *Shantung Revival*, 54–55.

including one where a child saw a vision of Christ on the cross for her sins. The missionaries emphasized, in a rather colonialist fashion, however, that the phenomenon of dreams and visions was confined to Chinese believers and was acceptable because they were compatible with oriental practices.[27] Moreover, the revival's orthodoxy was secure, the letters affirmed, since the core was "born again revival work" rather than the compromised social gospel missions of the Presbyterians.[28]

Shantung Revival: Women in Ministry

Crawford's account of the Shantung Revival also sheds light on the role of women in ministry. Southern Baptists had a conflicted and mostly negative understanding of women's roles in ministry. In 1880, influential Southern Baptist Theological Seminary educator John Broadus, in his infamous broadside "Should Women Speak in Mixed Assemblies?" offered up a patriarchal rebuke to women who found any equality or liberation in the Scriptures. He said that women could speak to other women about the gospel, but not even a male newspaper editor could visit women's meetings to write up a report. Women should never speak, and surely never preach, to men. At the same time, Baptists did have women on the mission field like Lottie Moon who spoke and even preached as needed. When the Woman's Missionary Union, founded in 1888, finally began giving reports at the annual meeting of the SBC in 1913, men initially gave the report. The first report delivered by a woman did not occur until 1929.[29]

Crawford's account of women's participation in the Shantung Revival reveals the openness of missionaries to the pentecostalization of the faith on the Baptist mission field. Her account reads more like restorationist, radical holiness evangelicals and Pentecostals. These groups had no qualms with women preaching and teaching because their non-cessationist reading of Acts 2 as a fulfillment of Joel's prophecy affirmed that in the end times young women would prophesy. Crawford included frequent references to "girls" preaching and serving as evangelists in the revival. For example, young women organized preaching bands to share the gospel with the natives.

---

[27] Crawford, 66, 71–72, 80–81.

[28] Crawford, 12.

[29] John Broadus, "Shall a Woman Speak in Mixed Assemblies?" in *Feminism: Woman and Her Work*, ed. J. W. Porter (Louisville: Baptist Book Concern, 1923). Broadus's 1880 article was reprinted in Porter's compilation of articles by Southern Baptists opposed to women's public speaking.

Crawford's story about a female Chinese preacher whose church invited her to be the pastor of their flock illustrates the affirmation of women not just preaching, but pastoring.[30] The theologically conservative Crawford did not go out of her way to emphasize women's contributions in contrast to men's. Her account sees the restoring work of the Spirit as gender-neutral or in the language of Acts cited in one letter, God is no respecter of persons. The Spirit fell on both women and men, both testified, both preached, and both affirmed miracles of healing and baptisms of the Spirit. Still, it is noteworthy that Crawford not only emphasized the ministry of Lutheran Marie Monsen, as other revival participants did, but she introduced her story by noting that five years before the revival actually erupted in 1930, a women's prayer group had been praying for and seeking a revival from God. Crawford no doubt agreed with one missionary colleague who wrote that the Shantung Revival was "perhaps the greatest revival in the history of Southern Baptists in North China."[31]

During the Shantung Revival, FMB leader Charles Maddry was often flustered with the reports of Pentecostalism coming from Southern Baptist missionaries in North China. He made several missionaries demonstrate that they had not departed from historic Baptist doctrine. He told Crawford that her book on the revival had fanned the flames of controversy and he scolded her for her involvement. He strongly opposed her and other missionaries' willingness to use non-Baptist teachers in their mission work.[32] In turn, Crawford stiffened her back and defended her Baptist family legacy and her own Baptist identity. What did it mean to be a Baptist anyway, she retorted, if Baptist bookstores were selling the works of liberal Harry Emerson Fosdick? Crawford said that after two years on the mission field she knew she had to have more of the Spirit or her ministry would not have survived the conditions. She concluded being "revived…does not mean we are any less Baptist." Crawford kept her missionary position—her commitment to child evangelism was not lost on her employers—and once the revival was over, Maddry actually reached out to apologize and to reconcile with his missionary evangelist.[33]

---

[30] Crawford, *Shantung Revival*, 33, 36, 85.

[31] Crawford, 7, 26. Quotation on p. 26.

[32] Charles Maddry, letter to Mary Crawford (October 18, 1933). Charles Maddry, letter to Mary Crawford (October 27, 1935). Charles Maddry, letter to Mary Crawford (March 13, 1936).

[33] Mary Crawford, letter to Charles Maddry (December 6, 1933). Charles Maddry, letter to Mary Crawford (January 3, 1934). Mary Crawford letter to Charles Maddry (February 10, 1936). Charles Maddry letter to Mary Crawford (February 18, 1939).

The Legacy of Crawford's Narrative

Mary Crawford's book, *The Shantung Revival*, was reproduced twice (1971, 2005). The most recent was by former Baptist Randy Clark, one of the key leaders of the "Toronto Blessing," part of the most recent phase of the charismatic movement called the "third wave" or "power evangelism,"[34] which is a form of revivalism that centers on miraculous signs and wonders to produce conversions and experiences of the baptism of the Holy Spirit. In the 1980s, while attending Southern Baptist Theological Seminary, Clark became fascinated by Mary Crawford's book on the Shantung Revival and then in 2005 reprinted it as part of his current ministry, Global Awakening.[35] Clark, like some participants of the Shantung Revival, called it the greatest revival in Baptist history. He strongly lamented, however, that Southern Baptists had abandoned the signs and wonders evident in the Shantung narrative. Clark highlighted that Texas Baptists published an edition of the Shantung Revival to promote evangelism, but badly distorted the story by cutting out all the signs and wonders of the Spirit.[36]

Clark's claim that all signs and wonders were extracted from the Shantung narrative is an exaggeration, but descriptions of the miraculous were de-emphasized and recast in the 1971 edition of *The Shantung Revival*, published by C. L. Culpepper, who was also a leading participant in the Shantung experience. In his forward, Culpepper said he was writing "simply a revision of Miss Crawford's treatise, expanded by additions, reflections and comments."[37] He noted that

---

[34] Peter Wagner of Fuller Theological Seminary highlighted the term, Third Wave, to indicate a third manifestation of the Pentecostal story. The first was the emergence of Pentecostalism in the early twentieth century and the second was the Charismatic Movement of the 1960s. Wagner, along with John Wimber, promoted evangelism that relied on miraculous signs and wonders (power evangelism). The Toronto Blessing, which occurred in the 1990s, is part of the Third Wave, and featured holy laughter, being slain in the Spirit, and other demonstrable experiences. Ironically, Wimber broke with Randy Clark because of the Toronto Blessing's reliance on the strong emotionalism of holy laughter and other manifestations.

[35] While a Baptist, Randy Clark graduated from Southern Baptist Theological Seminary (SBTS) before joining the charismatic Vineyard movement founded by John Wimber. Clark attributes his interest in revivals to Louis Drummond, an evangelism professor and Keswick advocate at SBTS. For more on Randy Clark, the "Third Wave," and the Toronto Blessing, see Weaver, *Baptists and the Holy Spirit*, 321–27.

[36] Mary Crawford, *The Shantung Revival: The Greatest Revival in Baptist Church History* (Mechanicsburg, PA: Global Awakening, 2005). C. L. Culpepper, *The Shantung Revival* (Dallas: Crescendo Publications, 1971).

[37] Culpepper, *Shantung Revival*, 8.

Crawford had agreed that he could use her original material. Culpepper quoted Crawford only once, however, to confirm that the revival avoided sensationalism.[38] But he does not deny the existence of the miraculous in the Shantung Revival. While examples of healings and being slain in the Spirit are included, he emphasized that some healings led to conversions and he identified incidents of speaking in tongues as an unfortunate extreme.[39] Neither is Culpepper void of references to the fullness of the Spirit, though the language of being baptized in the Holy Spirit is missing and the occasions are not as plentiful as in Crawford's account. Even more than Crawford, Culpepper focuses on the evangelistic conversions experienced in the revival.[40]

Beyond his de-emphasis on the radical holiness and pentecostal characteristics, what is missing in Culpepper's narrative is any focus on women's roles that might be controversial in Southern Baptist circles. Culpepper never mentioned the bands of young Chinese women who spread the gospel as evangelists nor does he ever acknowledge missionary women preaching or Chinese women pastoring. He does not mention the prayer bands of missionary women that preceded the revival. While Crawford noted that God was "no respecter of persons," Culpepper deleted the women's voices, including Crawford's. Such is not a surprise, given that Culpepper had to know how the Crawford book was controversial in the Southern USA when it was published, except that Culpepper had said he was going to use Crawford's account. In essence, Culpepper told a safer story, one that sought to respect the male voices in the States in the early 1970s, a time when Texas Baptist fundamentalist patriarchs like W. A. Criswell were blaming women for the eruption of the charismatic movement in Southern Baptist churches.[41]

Concluding Reflections

---

[38] Culpepper, 19.

[39] Culpepper, 23, 33, 45, 50, 60, 66.

[40] Culpepper, 27, 36, 40.

[41] During the debate over charismatic practices among Southern Baptists in the 1970s, W. A. Criswell bellowed, "You stop the women from speaking in tongues, and the practice will absolutely disappear from the earth. The tongues movement is a woman movement. And when she's taken out of it, it perishes on the vine." "Charismatic Movement Draws Criticism of W.A. Criswell," *Baptist Standard* 87 (April 23, 1975), 3. For support of Criswell's comments, see "Weber Views 'Divisive' Move," *Baptist Standard* (June 18, 1975), 7.

Mary Crawford is missing in the pages of Baptist history books. She was not the only participant to write about the experiences of the Shantung Revival. The Lutheran Marie Monsen wrote about the revival and her involvement. Baptist participants who wrote included not only C. L. Culpepper but also Miss Bertha Smith, who became a missionary celebrity in her elder years among Southern Baptist conservatives. Smith wrote about the miraculous in the revival, but like Culpepper, her writings published in the 1970s condemned any association of the Shantung event with any pentecostalization of the faith. In private letters to officials from the FMB, Crawford had repeatedly defended herself from charges that she was Pentecostal. She defended her commitment to Baptist identity and faithfulness to the Bible. Yet, Crawford's account in 1933 is the most compelling primary account of the Shantung Revival that points not only to the revival's charismatic legacy but also the role of young women in the spread of the gospel through evangelistic testimony, preaching, and pastoring. Baptist missions did not simply feature the preaching of men. Women, even those whose primary responsibility was children's education, were teachers and preachers to men.

Southern Baptists, always interested in revival, still like to speak about the Shantung Revival, but their cessationist orientation toward the modern use of spiritual gifts leaves them in a quandary. As one former missionary declared, "God knocked down some key people (at Shantung). But they didn't expect anyone to repeat it."[42] The larger legacy of Crawford's account, however, is relevant in the current conflicted climate on women's voices in Southern Baptist life. She was theologically conservative, and she constantly warned against modernism and the social gospel.[43] At the same time, Crawford's story is a reminder that within the revival fires of Baptist history both women and men testified, both were filled with the baptism of the Spirit, and both preached the gospel to both men and women. If the Shantung Revival was one of the greatest, perhaps the greatest, revivals in Baptist history, the irony of the role of women like Mary Crawford and the bands of praying and preaching women is the irony of history that does not allow readers to forget it.

---

[42] Greg Warner and Bob Allen, "Most Missionaries Cautious About 'Signs and Wonders,'" *The Christian Index* (February 1, 1996), 1.

[43] Mary Crawford, letter to Charles Maddry (February 10, 1936). Mary Crawford, letter to M. Theron Rankin (December 31, 1948).